D0712194

Beloved Strangers

Beloved Strangers

∾ INTERFAITH FAMILIES IN
NINETEENTH-CENTURY AMERICA

ANNE C. ROSE

HARVARD UNIVERSITY PRESS

Cambridge, Massachusetts, and London, England   2001

Library of Congress Cataloging-in-Publication Data

Rose, Anne C., 1950–
    Beloved strangers : interfaith families in nineteenth-century America / Anne C. Rose.
        p. cm.
    Includes bibliographical references (p.) and index.
    ISBN 0-674-00640-2 (alk. paper)
    1. Interfaith marriage—United States—History—19th century.   2. Interfaith
families—United States—History—19th century.   I. Title.
HQ1031 .R648 2001
    306.84′3′0973—dc21   2001024102

*For Adam, Ellie, Jon, Lucy,
Wally, Katie, and George*

Acknowledgments

Interfaith families are so much a part of modern America that my personal observations and scholarship have been able to enrich one another. I thank my students, colleagues, friends, and acquaintances who have shared stories of intermarriages in their families with me.

My work has been generously supported by a Bernard and Audre Rapoport Fellowship in American Jewish Studies from the Jacob Rader Marcus Center of the American Jewish Archives, Hebrew Union College-Jewish Institute of Religion; a travel grant from the Cushwa Center for the Study of American Catholicism, University of Notre Dame; a Melvin and Rosalind Jacobs University Endowed Fellowship in the Humanities as well as a sabbatical leave from the College of the Liberal Arts, Pennsylvania State University. The staffs of archives and special collections libraries have facilitated my work with cordiality and efficiency. I thank those of the American Philosophical Society; the Archives of the University of Notre Dame; Department of Rare Books and Manuscripts, Boston Public Library; Department of Special Collections, Joseph Regenstein Library, University of Chicago; Henry E. Huntington Library; Historical Society of Pennsylvania; Houghton and Pusey Libraries, Harvard University; Jacob Rader Marcus Center of the American Jewish Archives and Klau Library, Hebrew Union College-Jewish Institute of Religion, Cincinnati; Manuscripts Department, Wilson Library, University of North Carolina at Chapel Hill; Manuscript Division, Library of Congress; Massachusetts Historical Society; North Carolina Department of Cultural Resources; Rare Book and Manuscript Library, University of Pennsylvania; Rare Book, Manuscript, and Special Collection Library, Duke University; and Special Collections, Robert W. Woodruff Library, Emory University. I am especially grateful for the expert assistance and kindness of Kevin Proffitt of the American Jewish Archives. The staffs of Pattee and Paterno Libraries, Pennsylvania State University, have supported my research at every stage.

Illustrations have been provided by the Archives of the University of Notre Dame; Jacob Rader Marcus Center of the American Jewish Archives; Mordecai Historic Park, Raleigh; Ohio Historical Society; and Ralph Barton Perry III. I thank Kevin Cawley of Notre Dame, Terri Jones of the Mordecai Historic Park, and Duryea Kemp of the Ohio Historical Society. Ralph Barton Perry III not only generously offered a photograph of his grandparents, but read what I wrote about them and shared his recollections. I am grateful for his interest in my work.

Time is the most valuable possession of scholars, and so it is with special appreciation that I acknowledge colleagues who read the manuscript, sent me information, and gave me opportunities to circulate my ideas. Amy Greenberg, Amanda Porterfield, and Johanna Shields read the entire manuscript with insight and offered excellent suggestions. I thank Rabbi Jonathan Brown and Gary Knoppers for their careful reading of parts of the text. Others who have given me indispensable assistance are Dianne Ashton, Barbara Cantalupo, Natalie Zemon Davis, Karla Goldman, Karen Halttunen, Paul Harvey, Christine Heyrman, Philip Jenkins, Alan Kraut, Chris Monaco, Lewis Perry, Jonathan Sarna, Leslie Woodcock Tentler, Beno Weiss, and Peter W. Williams. Three anonymous readers' reports provided profitable guidance for revisions. I thank former Penn State students, now pursuing their own careers, for their careful work as research assistants: Seth Bruggeman, Benjamin DeGrow, Sarah Lawrence, Mary Anne Lindskog, Susan E. Myers Shirk, and Melissa Westrate. Jan Moyer expertly created the genealogies.

My deepest intellectual debts are to my teachers, the late Sydney Ahlstrom and especially David Brion Davis, who has given me his personal as well as professional insights into interfaith families. From them I learned to see individual human lives as the groundwork of history and to try to write with respect for the answers Americans devised in the past.

Peg Fulton, my editor at Harvard University Press, was enthusiastic about this book from the beginning. I thank her warmly for her excellent advice and careful management of the publication process. I am grateful to Anita Safran for her guidance in editing the manuscript.

Friends and family are the essential foundation of my work. In all the good and bad moments that go into writing a book, I have been able to count on true friends: Dolores Dungee, Amy Golahny, Susan and Billy Harris, R. Scott Lenhart, Diane Lichtman, Mary Miles, and Judith Van Herik. My debt to my family is beyond measure, and I dedicate this book to all of them with love.

Contents

Appendix   *193*
*The Interfaith Couples Studied, Listed in Chronological Order by
Wedding Date   Genealogy of the Sherman Family   Genealogy of
the Mordecai Family*

Abbreviations Used in the Notes   *197*

Notes   *199*

Index   *279*

ILLUSTRATIONS

Beloved Strangers

In Search of Ancestors

This is a book about the American interfaith families begun by marriages celebrated between the War of 1812 and World War I. The families whose stories I tell were composed of either Protestants and Catholics, Protestants and Jews, or Catholics and Jews. These religious communities were not equal in America; Catholics and Jews could not mistake prejudices against themselves. But there was tolerance, too, enough to permit mixed marriages. Because interfaith families constituted a small proportion of American homes, they must sometimes have felt isolated, but not always. On frontiers and in cities, or any place where social and religious barriers were relaxed, substantial numbers of Catholics and Jews intermarried.[1] Nor did the households stand out by being religiously indifferent. Couples made their private peace and settled into routines of public practice. Besides neighborly ties, they could rely for support on extended kin. Only rarely do records show that family bonds ruptured in anger over a child's choice of a spouse; on the contrary, it was not unusual for one intermarriage to encourage others, creating sprawling, religiously diverse clans. Decisions about faith grew out of a couple's dialogues, first with parents and grandparents and later with children, sometimes with sharp turning points. These unexpected moments of reckoning remind us to look beyond wedding parties and investigate the histories of interfaith families.

One such episode occurred in 1878. On May 18, Tom Sherman

graduated from the law school of Washington University in St. Louis. Kept in Washington by his work as General of the Army, William Tecumseh Sherman did not attend his son's commencement. He was shaken, however, by a letter on May 22. Six months earlier, Tom had told his father that "your idea of putting me with an old lawyer is of course most agreeable to me, as nothing can be more trying for a young man than to be obliged to wait indefinitely for his first client." Now he confessed, "I do not intend to become a lawyer" because "I

1. William Tecumseh Sherman and his son Tom (1856–1933), at age nine, posed in front of maps representing his father's recent Civil War victories. Courtesy of the Ohio Historical Society.

have chosen another profession—in one word I desire to become a priest—a Catholic priest."[2] William, born a Protestant, adhered to a condensed faith in God who governs by "invariable laws" and requires "good works" of humankind.[3] His wife, Ellen, was Catholic, and she wrote from St. Louis in terms she hoped her husband would understand. "We would freely offer our son's life in battle for his country. In his belief he is offering his life in a higher holier cause & for the country which has no bounds." Ellen knew, though, that "you have not the faith which makes it to us such a solemn & holy duty to obey such a call."[4] In the context of Tom's vocation, Catholic conviction—and its absence—threatened to divide the family.

The Shermans' long-standing differences about religion had not led to conflict over their children's training. Ellen ran a Catholic household. Cump—short for Tecumseh—set the stage for this solution when he asked Lieutenant James Hardie, "a *Catholic's Catholic*" in Ellen's words, to be best man at their wedding in 1850. "The lady is a Catholic," Sherman told Hardie, "which makes me very anxious to have a friend near me who will appreciate the piety of her character and purity of motives."[5] The seven Sherman children who survived infancy attended a variety of Catholic schools. Their father worried that the boys—Willie, Tom, and Cumpy—might not get first-rate teaching in practical subjects or learn "that this world has claims as well as the next."[6] After Willie's death at age nine in 1863, Tom, "our only boy" until the birth of Cumpy in 1867, carried his father's charge to succeed as a man.[7] He met his parent's expectations. In "Science and Religion," Tom's commencement address at Georgetown Academy in 1874, he argued for the compatibility of natural and supernatural truths.[8] In 1876, he received a degree from the Sheffield Scientific School at Yale. Tom appeared to be a young man who wore his religion lightly, and in the son Sherman must gladly have found an image of himself. After all, a priest had baptized Cump when he became a foster child in the household of Thomas and Maria Ewing, Ellen's parents, in 1829. This made him a Catholic in the eyes of the priest who married the Shermans; but in his letters to Ellen he spoke of "your creed" and "your church."[9] Sherman pursued his ambitions with small reference to religion of any kind.

Although Ellen now coaxed him to lay aside his "terrible disappointment," she contested family patterns that reached back three generations.[10] Tom's decision to become a priest took place in a lineage of Protestant husbands wed to Catholic wives. Ellen's mother

Maria was raised by her Catholic aunt Susan, who had married Philemon Beecher in Lancaster, Ohio, in 1803. Maria in turn wed a Protestant, Thomas Ewing, a lawyer trained by Beecher. Ellen was born in 1824, and Cump soon came to live with the Ewings after his father's death. Even Sherman worried in the 1840s about the meager career prospects in the peacetime army and considered studying law. Pressed to choose secular employment, Tom was to follow in the footsteps of his male kin.[11]

The women became more fervently Catholic. When a priest visited Lancaster in 1810, Maria had to ask her aunt if they were Catholic. "Why yes child, we were in Brownsville [Pennsylvania]," Susan Beecher was said to reply.[12] Far less equivocally, "troubled for some time, that she had not been confirmed," Susan received the sacrament three months before her death in 1854. "Poor soul," Maria told Ellen, "she was affected to tears and sobs! and was a monument of God's mercy and goodness!"[13] Both Maria and Ellen prayed for their husbands' conversions. "Oh! my dear Ellen," Maria wrote typically in 1841, "that we may live to see your dear Father kneeling before the same altar with us!"[14] The husbands willingly did Catholic errands, inspecting a boarding school or carrying a wife's greetings to prelates. Neither woman lived to see her husband receive last rites on his deathbed, however, and, until their final hours, the men kept their distance from the Catholic Church.[15]

The crisis over Tom might have occurred in a family with two parents of the same religion. Tom's piety conflicted with a pragmatic standard of manliness widely held in nineteenth-century America. William resisted Tom's choice in part because he judged it effeminate. Nonetheless, Sherman saw his family's Catholicism as crucial as well. The events have "embittered me," he confided to one daughter, "against the cause of his action, the Catholic Church." "I realise that all I held most dear" in reality "belong to a power that heeds no claim but its own."[16] In his anger, Sherman marshaled the stereotyped image of a power-hungry church to explain the conflict in his family. More accurately, William's truce with Catholicism was upset by his son's rebellion against the family's settlement of questions of gender and faith.

Tom sailed for England to begin his novitiate on June 5. The Shermans continued to live apart, Cump nursing his sense of betrayal, Ellen wounded by his rejection of their son, and the children trying to avoid taking sides. In 1940, Cumpy recalled that his father was "embittered for some years" by Tom's change of plan.[17] Sherman was in Denver on the day of Tom's ordination in Philadelphia in 1889, seven months after Ellen's death. This enduring hurt was offset, however, by the Shermans' tough family loyalty. Relations between husband and wife remained strained, but they resided together during the 1880s. One by one, their daughters married Catholics. Cumpy graduated from Georgetown Academy, then Yale, and in 1891, the year of his father's death, he began to practice law.

The Shermans acted out this family drama against a backdrop even wider than their several generations of kin: Judeo-Christian teaching. Almost surely, Ellen, her mother, and "Ma Beecher," as Ellen's great-aunt Susan was called, heard of the American Catholic bishops' warning against mixed marriages in their Pastoral Letter of 1840. Passages from Exodus, Deuteronomy, and Corinthians supported the prelates' doctrine.[18] This was not just a Catholic lesson. For Americans born before World War I, the Bible was a common heritage. When they read it, they saw that interfaith marriage was not something new, but instead very old. If they studied history, they learned how much biblical pronouncements shaped interfaith families up to the present day.

Do not marry out of the people of Israel: this was the litany of the Hebrew Bible beginning with the lives of the patriarchs. Esau, seemingly cheated of his father's blessing by his brother Jacob, lost his parents' favor because he took Hittite wives, who "were a source of bitterness to Isaac and Rebekah."[19] Centuries later, Moses in Sinai clarified the danger of idolatry if the Jews married into the seven nations of Canaan: "For they will turn your children away from Me to worship other gods, and the Lord's anger will blaze forth against you and He will promptly wipe you out."[20] When the Jews returned to Israel once again from the Babylonian exile, Ezra called the "land unclean through the uncleanness of the peoples of the land, through their abhorrent practices with which they, in their impurity, have filled it from one end to the other." Not only did he forbid intermarriage, but he instructed Hebrew men to separate themselves from the "foreign women" they brought home from Babylon.[21]

On the surface, the passages reveal a simple logic: marriage to an unbeliever tempts the faithful to worship false gods. This cause-and-effect reasoning is part of Scripture. But it obscures the fact that issues of purity and orthodoxy are distinguishable and that these separate commitments support more or less strict marriage policies. Ezra's disgust at "uncleanness" links his militancy to elemental human anxieties about order. All cultures differentiate purity from pollution and create a guarded circle of safety and holiness by prescribing taboos. Because the body commonly serves as a symbol for the community, and sex—a breach of physical boundaries—carries the ambiguous potential for impurity along with renewal, marriage laws are an essential defense of society.[22] In ancient Israel, marriage bore the added symbolic weight of mirroring the Jews' covenant with God. The prophet Malachi mixed images of religious disloyalty and sexual dishonor: the tribe of Judah was guilty of "profaning the covenant of our ancestors" because husbands abandoned their "covenanted spouse[s]" and "espoused daughters of alien gods."[23] Unequivocally, to be a Jew required endogamous marriage. Once the Hebrew Bible equated the covenant of Abraham, preserved by marriage, with the sphere of purity, intermarriage signified pollution.

The fear of idolatry, though verbally folded into the language of purity, did, however, permit a more patient view of mixed marriage. Impurity imposed by foreign birth was irreversible. Worship of false gods, in contrast, was behavior within an individual's control and could be changed. The story of Ruth the Moabite carries the message that social boundaries can be crossed because character is malleable. There is a legalistic side to Ruth's history. As a childless widow, she is passed to Boaz, her dead husband's kinsman, as a levirate wife. More darkly, this settlement ignores the Mosaic commandment to bar Moabites for ten generations from the community of Israel.[24] Yet the sweet loyalty of Ruth's spirit overshadows these details. Of foreign birth, she nonetheless clung to her mother-in-law, Naomi, professing that "your people shall be my people, and your God my God."[25] The account provokes questions about biological determinism by humanizing the outsider and showing that she could leave, in all senses, her native land.

Ruth stands on the margin of Jewish tradition, however. Praising her faithfulness, the narrative obscures her family origins. This consigns her to an anomalous place in Hebrew writings, where the dominant note is that holy practice must be rooted in community purity.[26] Perhaps Judaism favored the logic of Ezra because of the unpredictable consequences of commitment alone. Although Ruth chose the Hebrew God, the men denounced by Ezra were as easily led to apostasy by foreign wives. Any religious change in marriage would be suspect. Early Christians inherited the Jewish mood, but personal transformation—conversion—was far closer to the heart of Christianity than Judaism. If marriage became a site of spiritual rebirth, then Ruth's experience might recur.

One set of teachings in Paul's letters to Christian communities reiterated ancient concerns about purity. "Do not be mismated with unbelievers," he instructed the Corinthians; "touch nothing unclean" and "let us cleanse ourselves from every defilement of body and spirit."[27] The dichotomies of Paul's prose make it clear that the distance between Christians and non-Christians is unbridgeable: "For what partnership have righteousness and iniquity? Or what fellowship has light with darkness? What accord has Christ with Be'lial? Or what has a believer in common with an unbeliever? What agreement has the temple of God with idols?"[28] Indeed, in contrast to the Hebrew prohibitions against marriages with idolatrous tribes, the oppositions of light and darkness and Christ against Be'lial have a metaphysical edge. Intermarriage, in these terms, violates the conditions of existence. So, too, marriage symbolizes and reenacts Christ's relation to his followers. The "husband is the head of the wife as Christ is the head of the church," Paul wrote to Christian wives at Ephesus, and he instructed their husbands to "love your wives, as Christ loved the church."[29] Because marriage to an unbeliever upset the symmetry between temporal and spiritual salvation, Christians could not mistake their duty to marry fellow believers.

Nonetheless, the evangelical setting of Paul's lessons competed with a simple rule of in-marriage. The first Christians entered churches through conversion, and this might create mixed marriages. Paul responded to families that had been divided by the convictions of the Christian spouse. If a "brother has a wife who is an unbeliever, and she consents to live with him, he should not divorce her," he wrote to Corinth; no less if a "woman has a husband who is an unbeliever, and he consents to live with her, she should not divorce him." Worried that divorces would destabilize Christian communities, Paul, counterintuitively, prescribed further change through family evangelism: "Wife, how do you know whether you will save your husband? Husband, how do you know whether you will save your wife?"[30] The Christian became the agent of salvation, and mixed marriage was a matter of mistaken convictions subject to correction by a change of heart.

These temperaments of biblical Jews and Christians persisted. Commitment to descent nearly defines Judaism; Christianity's more open borders can ease discussions of interfaith marriage. Yet the difference, in the end, is a matter of emphasis. Both traditions associate proscribed forms of intimacy with religious heterodoxy; both, more optimistically, imagine that acquired faith can restore family purity. Over time, Jewish and Christian positions repeatedly shifted within a range of basic principles, and, in Western culture, each side defined itself in relation to the other.[31] Two postbiblical trends laid the groundwork for events in America: the rise of Christian dominance and the entrenchment of ancient ideas about women.

Inequalities among religious communities much influenced mixed relationships. For centuries, interfaith families did not combine two traditions perceived as valid, but religions with uneven access to legitimacy and power. Both Jews and Christians in the Middle Ages denied the legality of mixed marriages. *Halakhah,* the body of Jewish law, did not recognize their existence; they were equated with adultery by the Christian Theodosian Code (C.E. 429–438).[32] In legal and social fact, Jews were subject to Christians, however, and Christians could exact punishment at will. Interfaith couples in Christian Europe were guilty of a capital crime, although they were less often executed than fined and forced to separate. Power also permitted Christians to look the other way when illicit acts served their interests. Intolerant of the affairs of Jewish men and Christian women, they were patient with Christian men because, as one historian explains, "Jewish mistresses were likely to adopt their lovers' faith."[33] In sum, the inflexible marriage policies of medieval Jews and Christians, ostensibly similar, will be misread if taken out of the context of inequality. The communities were divided by the difference between subjugation and control.

These configurations of religious power continued to change. Catholics in nineteenth-century America, for example, felt the weight of Protestant culture. With the supremacy of the medieval Catholic Church a thing of the past, American Catholics faced disdain from Protestants similar to the kind that early Christians reserved for Jews. Yet shifting religious patterns did not erase the effects of social superiority and inferiority on interfaith marriages. Even if mixed couples were free in America from threats of punishment, they could not escape issues of social ambition, prejudice, and self-hatred. Historically, intermarriage involved not only movement across boundaries, but up or down ladders of legitimacy and reward.[34]

Inequalities of gender shaped mixed marriages as well. Like all families in Judeo-Christian culture, interfaith couples united women and men loaded down with ideas about each one's weaknesses and strengths. Medieval thinking extended one key biblical habit of reasoning: judgments about women were entwined in intermarriage discussions. Anxieties about sexual mixing were expressed as doubts about women. The Book of Proverbs drew foreign wives in the image of temptresses. The "lips of a forbidden woman drip honey," but "in the end she is as bitter as wormwood."[35] Ruth, though praiseworthy, is also changeable. Here the malleability of women appears alongside their seductiveness, and, though nearly opposite traits, each endangers faithful worship. It was the assumption of women's passivity that drove one twelfth-century commentary on Paul. A female convert, married to an unbeliever, should leave him "lest he recall her to her former error," wrote Johannes Teutonicus; "not so if a man is converted, for women are more easily influenced by a man than the other way around."[36]

This literary emphasis on women may be read as a sign of their subordination. In fact, marriages were commonly arranged by prospective husbands and the fathers of brides. Warnings that women would either persuade or be persuaded to follow alien gods were sincere expressions of men's misgivings about both women and exogamy, but they bore little relation to social agency. The rhetoric's inaccuracy, however, did not deter its use. Jewish women who hosted salons for intellectuals in Berlin around 1800 and then converted to marry Christians were "decadent" in the eyes of more than one modern commentator. Although in truth more responsible for making their own marriages than wives of earlier times, the salon women were still judged by habits of thought rooted in antiquity: equating intermarriage with the behavior of women and censuring them for it.[37]

The wider prerogatives of these German-Jewish women belonged to the age of revolution. New ideals of liberty and equality challenged age-old taboos. "Can a Jewess marry a Christian," Napoleon asked French Jewish leaders in 1806, "or a Jew a Christian woman?"[38] Although republican theory said "yes," prejudice complicated the discussion. Napoleon had cornered the rabbis with an impossible question: if they agreed to intermarriage, they would stir anti-Semitism; if they resisted, they seemed unfit citizens. In the rabbis' response, tradition battled with eagerness for rights and recognition. They stumbled over negatives to appear tolerant: Jewish "law does not say that a Jewess cannot marry a Christian, nor a Jew a Christian woman." Only later did they confess, "we cannot deny that the opinion of the Rabbis is against these marriages."[39] Liberal rabbis meeting at Braunschweig (1844), Leipzig (1869), Philadelphia (1869), and elsewhere tried repeatedly to reconcile their loyalty to in-marriage with political freedom. But "the authority of these conferences is not generally acknowledged," one rabbi sadly noted, because "our conservative co-religionists regard all the norms of the rabbinical code as ever binding and unchangeable."[40] True for the orthodox, his analysis skimmed over the liberals' own conflicted thoughts about looser interpretations of Jewish law.[41] Although the logic of civil liberty favored interfaith marriage, liberalism did not cleanly upset Judeo-Christian teachings and instead opened hard questions.

Ideology tested religion only at an abstract level, however, compared with the opportunities of free society. As aspiration increasingly displaced inheritance as social capital, old boundaries were more easily crossed. If a state did not permit civil marriage, then a Jew became a Christian or a Catholic a Protestant in order to marry the person of choice. One German Catholic tract spoke harshly of "avaricious parents who persuade [a] daughter or son to marry a rich Protestant." Catholic men took Protestant wives to help them rise in government service; women made matches with military officers, magistrates, or professors for the sake of success. The polemic judged the importance of social climbing correctly, but its reduction of mixed marriage to status-seeking obscures other motives.[42] Freedom in nineteenth-century Europe meant everything from indulgence in romance to enjoyment of the arts. The intermarried Jewish women of the Berlin salons, one scholar observes, "were complex adults with intricate emotional and intellectual lives."[43] Interfaith marriage was a powerful expression of social liberty precisely because of the complicated desires behind it.

In the eyes of postrevolutionary Europeans, freedom threatened religion. But Judeo-Christian thinking on interfaith marriage is complex, and to say that modernity forced a reconfiguration of inherited values is closer to the truth. New messages applauding self-determination, transition, and growth amplified the muted lesson of the story of Ruth. Communal boundaries, strongly supported by historical precedent, were challenged and repaired, but did not collapse. Families continued to bear religious expectations with ancient roots.

In America, the encounter of religion and modernity was dramatic. Here, intensely held Judeo-Christian principles met nearly unrestrained liberalism. On an intimate scale, mixed marriages were scenes of interaction between belief and rising forces of individuality and diversity. They were both mirrors and instruments of religious transformation: limited options and tight-knit communities gave way to heterogeneity and openness. Rather than spell the end of religion, they hastened lay-centered and experimental forms of practice. Twenty-six interfaith couples in eighteen extended families are the focus of this study. A list of their names and the genealogies of two especially complicated families may be found in the Appendix.[44] Like most of us, they spent their time thinking about careers and childrearing, small pleasures and friends. But the world around them was changing in ways that had much to do with their private lives.

America became a religiously diverse nation in the century before World War I. New expressions of Protestantism flourished, and immigration turned tiny Catholic and Jewish populations into established communities.[45] One would expect to find interfaith families in a landscape characterized by religious variety and civil freedom. Institution-building and policy-making, especially among Catholics and Jews, affected households as well. The nineteenth and early twentieth centuries were the formative period for American interfaith families, not only because they grew along with pluralism but because they were so much discussed. Today mixed marriages seem a recent phenomenon, perhaps a product of the sixties. Yet they were news a hundred years ago too, when religions in America first tried to demarcate their borders and muster their troops from the family. By the 1920s, communal policies were in place and debate slowed, though the number of marriages continued to rise. I write about how interfaith families behaved and what they heard said about themselves during this foundational era.

Time must also be measured by the rhythms of families. Life cycles and generations are important here, as aging and relationships put their mark on individual lives. From this perspective, my time frame stretches. One father of intermarried children was born in 1760; the last surviving wife among my families died in 1967. Although I concentrate on a century, some stories extend beyond it. Small habits, too, may cause significant turning points. As intermarried wives became more offbeat around 1900, dabbling in the occult or Christian Science, their families drifted from the mainstream. History seen from the parlor and pulpit is not the same, and I ask readers to alternate between private and public viewpoints.

Sometimes these angles of vision seem scarcely to converge. Individual interfaith families, for example, are barely visible in religious and civil records. Marginal by nature, they fall between official cracks, and compiling a group of couples for study required as much luck as persistence, following two initial decisions. I wanted families whose religious differences were dramatic. Defining "intermarriage" is partly subjective: it is a family connection with anyone seen as different. A Lutheran may object to a daughter's marriage to a Methodist by the same logic as an Italian rejects a son's choice of an Irish wife. Such distinctions of doctrine and ethnicity are influential. Not only can they raise barriers but also lower them: one nineteenth-century Irish-American clan, Protestants and Catholics, took pride in their national heritage. This book is about religion, however, and so I chose the broad American religious communities of the pre-World War I era: Protestants, Catholics, and Jews. Cultural distances between them were imposing, and individuals who crossed the lines experienced the conflicts and rewards of interfaith marriage in bold terms. The distinctiveness of the traditions makes it clear that "interfaith" connotes more than dissimilar principles. Because faith gives rise to values and customs, an interfaith family consists not simply of a couple that disagrees, but of different kinds of people.[46]

I also wanted to write a cultural history. Rather than chart quantifiable trends, I describe thoughts and feelings, and this affected the families selected. My sources are literary—letters, journals, memoirs—and implicitly, families were sufficiently well-to-do to secure good educations for their members. This social status might affect my conclusions. If the children received liberal schooling, they might be more likely to intermarry with less family strife. Yet love can contest tradition anywhere, and there were mixed marriages among the poor as well. Although one historian claims that less than one percent of Jews wed gentiles on New York's Lower East Side at the turn of the century, a Columbia sociologist wrote in 1911 that this was "not so rare as generally supposed."[47] A rabbi he knew was called to circumcise mixed-faith couples' sons. Hearsay, newspaper fillers, dispensation certificates: scant records exist to explore the marriages of the less affluent. But nothing I have seen makes me doubt that well-placed families resembled interfaith homes overall.

At its heart, this is a study of religion in families. Stories evolved over many years, as did events for the Shermans, and Judeo-Christian culture shaped American choices. In the Bible, Abraham pledged his household to the service of God, and tradition imagines the family as the instrument for the transmission of faith.[48] Nineteenth-century Americans had a keen appreciation of romance and home life. Romanticism savored feeling and Victorianism honored the hearth, and it is not surprising that interfaith families of the era tried hard to manage disagreements for the sake of harmony. These families still acted as religion's agent, but with this difference: instead of preserving memory, they furthered change. Liberalism entered the family in the form of greater freedom of children from parents and wives from husbands. All could worship in their own ways, straining but rarely shattering good will. Families, in turn, claimed their rights by making decisions with modest attention to the opinions of clergy. Freedom expressed itself in small questions: which minister will consent to perform the marriage? should the boarding school be Catholic? who will recite the mourner's prayer for the Jewish father? Taken together, the answers transformed religion in interfaith homes from a set of precepts to a series of possibilities. My purpose is to explain how this happened.[49]

Children of the Religious Enlightenment

Early American clergymen preached many wedding sermons, and two homilies by Catholic prelates suggest the way the challenge of liberalism to traditional marriage began. Ambrose Marechal, appointed archbishop of Baltimore in 1817, gave no sign in an undated discourse that the couple he married faced unusual temptations. Marriage was "a sacrament," an avenue of "grace" to help men and women fulfill their duties in an uncertain world. "Death alone," he solemnly instructed, "can break asunder the sacred bonds which you are to impose on your individual freedom." Although sin was an "impediment to the infusion of [God's] grace," Marechal did not detect dangers to Christian marriage in historical circumstances.[1]

John Carroll, the first archbishop of Baltimore in 1808, was more apprehensive. He, too, believed God intended nature and spirit to meet in the family: marriage was "a representation of that indissoluble union, which subsists between Christ and his church." But in 1802 he admonished a wedding party that "companions thro life" should be "only such as are united in the profession of the same faith." Opposing views in parents "perplex" children: "they fall an easy prey to the artificial sophistry of Deists; & finally discard from their minds even the belief of Gods moral government." These hazards were not new. "I have spoken so often & so much against marriages thus contracted," Carroll reminded his listeners. Because disregard of authority was the root of the problem, the remedy ought to be clear. Children must "take direction from their parents"; no less, the "directions of the Church require your dutiful obedience."[2]

Archbishops Marechal and Carroll did not perceive the same social and moral world. Both views, however, were partly true. Marechal understood classic marital problems—infidelity, perhaps, or cruelty—provoked by sin. But for him, the Catholic community was intact. Carroll, in contrast, saw the church in America as rent and exposed. Self-seeking and free thinking diminished respect, produced intermarriages, and jeopardized the children's faith. Born in Maryland and for years a pastor, Carroll grasped the American temper in an instinctive way that eluded Marechal, who spent most of his life in France and, by vocation, taught seminarians.[3] Even so, Carroll's didactic intent exaggerated the frequency of interfaith marriages in the early republic. The traditional families of Marechal and the mixed households of Carroll could both be found. Carroll was right, however, that laypeople were thinking in new ways about deference and freedom that would bring diversity to family religion.

Interfaith marriage in America before 1830 was an issue between generations, though the dynamics of young and old were more subtle than Carroll believed. Rebelliousness did not simply upset authority; children acted out a subversive strain in their parents' values. Both intermarried couples and their parents were committed to religious traditionalism and Enlightenment liberalism. They were "traditional" because they adhered to Judeo-Christian beliefs and institutions; religion remained important and seemed to hold answers. This did not preclude embrace of the Enlightenment's "liberal" mood of openness, tolerance, and pragmatism. With amazing comfort, parents balanced faith and civility. Their children, still religious, read reasonableness and accommodation more broadly: not only did they treat strangers amicably, they married them. The distance between generations was a matter of differing interpretations of common convictions. Interfaith marriages in the 1810s and 1820s were children's practical commentaries on their parents' moral commitments.[4]

These dialogues with parents in the early republic were also part of another journey. Interfaith marriages permitted young people to leave religious minorities and join the Protestant majority. Perhaps sadly, parents, children, even grandchildren shared pious feelings and liberal principles, yet stood on opposite sides of religious fences. Moving toward Protestantism secured status and at times spiritual satisfaction, but tested the goodwill of kin. These families faced their culture's essential questions: the limits of freedom, the hazards of self-creation, the fragility of community. Only love of family itself sustained communication among relatives dispersed in other senses.

Parents

The fathers, mothers, and guardians of young Americans who intermarried had a remarkable ability to balance loyalty to sacred traditions with receptiveness to new ideas. Steadily observant, they also read widely, enjoyed varied acquaintances, and cultivated secular interests. This easy union of instinctive piety and expansive curiosity was a trait of the "religious Enlightenment." All the more striking, sturdy faith was widespread among older Catholics and Jews despite the scarcity of priests in America, absence of rabbis, and scattered congregations.[5] The children of this generation understood their parents' liberality, but could not duplicate their unquestioning traditionalism. Mixed marriages were the result; yet even then, the decisions of the young grew most deeply from the elders' complex personalities. Mathew Carey, Jacob Mordecai, and Rebecca Gratz unknowingly laid paths toward interfaith families.

"Difficulty about who shall marry Henry," Mathew Carey wrote in his journal in 1819 with characteristic terseness: "Stay[ed] up till 2:15." Sleepless, it seems, over who would perform the marriage of his oldest son to a Protestant, he was "low spirited" again the next week. "Went to bed before dinner." Two days later, however, "Henry married. Pleasant evening. Received $10,172 from Tiernan to pay for stock."[6] The events perfectly evoked Carey's temperament. A firm Catholic, he was no less a politic and practical man, just the kind to be distressed by his son's intermarriage and then let it go.

Mathew Carey (1760–1839) was born in Dublin, and his fiery Irish nationalism reinforced his Catholicism, faith based most deeply in his down-to-earth piety. He fled to Philadelphia in 1784 to avoid prosecution for pro-Irish republican journalism, but did not forget his countrymen. A founder of the Hibernian Society for the Relief of Emigrants from Ireland in the 1790s, he could not have missed the irony that he was elected its director two days before his son Henry took an Episcopal wife in 1819.[7] Yet for all his Irish pride, Carey's attachment to the Catholic religion transcended ethnicity. In 1791 he urged John

Carroll, then Bishop of Baltimore, to begin a church "printing fund" to produce Catholic books, lest American Catholics be "ignorant not only of their religious principles, but even of the moral duties."[8] From his earliest years as a bookseller he distributed Bibles; in 1801, he edited his own quarto edition priced at ten dollars. Behind his Catholic publishing efforts were private religious habits, ingrained but not perfunctory. He attended Mass "with Mrs. Carey" soon after their wedding in 1791. "Went to St. Mary's to church," he wrote typically in his journal in 1815; "went to church at St. Augustine's" in 1820. He listened to the sermons. "Mr. Hurley preached a political sermon" in 1812, "which gave uneasiness to some."[9] Nor did he slight obligations and rites. "Fast day," he noted periodically in his diary, and, in one letter to his wife, enclosed a communion wafer.[10] Carey's piety, though undemonstrative, was integrated into his weekly routine.

Faith that was secure but not dogmatic admitted compromise. Carey sometimes skipped church, as he did one Sunday in 1813: "Read about two pages of Tacitus."[11] Catholicism did not mark the bounds of his thinking; it shared his attention with a vast range of interests. A prolific pamphleteer, turning out fifty-nine titles between 1819 and 1833 alone, Carey wrote passionately about political economy. Comments on Adam Smith and Thomas Malthus appear in his journal. "Low spirited about public affairs" in 1813, he "sent for Tench Coxe," an advocate of manufactures: "Had a long talk."[12] He met other non-Catholics in voluntary associations, the Franklinian Society for one, and the Literary Society, where a subject in 1791 was "whether the colour of the negroes be the effect of climate & other external factors." Nor did his religion keep him from enjoying the arts. He saw *The Merchant of Venice* "performed wonderfully well" in 1821 and stayed up reading Scott's *Kenilworth* until one in the morning.[13] Carey had time for so much because he was disciplined. Sunday afternoons were devoted to writing, and he was fast. One pamphlet "took me about an hour and a half. Four octavo pages."[14] His efficiency drew more deeply on his eagerness to understand and improve human society.

The Carey children found the same qualities in their mother. Bridget Flavahan Carey (b. ca. 1770) practiced an unadorned Catholicism that stood easily beside temporal interests. She was as critical of a Catholic "Mass performed in State" at the Baltimore cathedral—much like "play house music"—as she was of a Protestant camp meeting in 1806, where "some [were] preaching, some singing, & others clapping their hands & laughing at the joy they experienced by the conversion of so many sinners." She preferred their own "solemn" Mass, she wrote home from Baltimore, but still appreciated new experiences. "I regret very much you had it not in your power to see" the revival, she told Mathew, "altho' to me it is an awful sight such as I w[oul]d never have any desire to witness again."[15] Curiosity about the world brought Bridget to the publishing business. Her husband away in 1806, she determined not borrow funds, "but I fear I shall have a dreadful day on Friday. However make yourself easy[;] I shall leave nothing undone."[16] Because her husband respected her good sense, he listened to her opinion on the finances of Isaac Lea, a Quaker who became her son-in-law in 1821. "Had some further conversation with I. L. on the state of his affairs," Mathew Carey recorded in 1820, "& with Mrs. C. on the same subject."[17] There was no sign that this second intermarriage among their children worried the parents on any except practical grounds. The Careys opened two doors into Philadelphia: one led to its Catholic community, the other to the city at large. Isaac Lea, his prospects scrutinized, came through the latter.

The Careys' Catholicism and liberalism met most eloquently in Mathew's vision of a republican church. When a fiery dispute about the rights of laymen, priests, and prelates shook St. Mary's in the early 1820s, he issued pamphlets as a "spectator," "ardently desirous of peace."[18] Carey in fact attended "tumultuous" meetings that preceded the priest's excommunication, and the furor occasioned his exposition of canon law as a guard against "arbitrary exercise of power."[19] Far from inimical, liberty and devotion were necessary partners, even if now "the comfort, the happiness, the harmony, and the unity of the largest congregation in Philadelphia" were sadly "offered up as a sacrifice to the passions and high temper of the one [the priest], and the obstinacy and despotic view of clerical authority of the other [the bishop]."[20] A masterful rhetorician, Carey designed his critique to evoke a counterimage of reasonable and peaceable religion. His family's spiritual commitments, less malleable than words, were more ragged. By the end of 1822, Henry and Frances had wed Protestants, and Elizabeth, a Catholic; three children never married.[21] Their choices exposed the disparate strands of values that their parents wove snugly together.

Jacob Mordecai (1762–1838) similarly joined cosmopolitanism and solid Jewish loyalty, though the fit was less comfortable. How precariously his keen pursuit of knowledge rested on inherited faith became clear in 1817. Because Jacob was master of an academy in Warrenton, North Carolina, and a well-read man, Rachel, his oldest daughter, expected him to respond tolerantly to his son Moses' desire to marry a Christian. "I have not seen our father since" hearing the news, she reflected, "but know he will not refuse."[22] Although Jacob acquiesced in the end, Rachel utterly misread his mood. He was "bowed down with anxiety & grief" even after three days; four days later, still "afflicted with one of those dreadful head aches."[23] Only as adults did Jacob's children understand the limits of his liberalism, so intimately did his own wide and cordial acquaintance with people and ideas mingle with his Judaism.

The thirteen children of Jacob Mordecai, born to two successive wives between 1785 and 1818, grew up in a household that was ritually observant yet intellectually free. Born in Philadelphia into one of the country's oldest Jewish communities, Jacob moved to Warrenton in 1792, where he stayed until he settled outside Richmond in 1819. The town's only Jewish family, the Mordecais adhered to religious law. One son worried in 1814 about where he would find matzoh when he set out on a journey during Passover. Rachel recorded her unwillingness to travel on the Sabbath and knew the Hebrew liturgy well enough to act as reader on Yom Kippur in 1821.[24] Yet respect for tradition did not set the tone of Jacob's Warrenton Female Academy (1809–1818). Subjects advertised to attract parents were a catalogue of Enlightenment knowledge: "the English language, grammatically; spelling; reading; writing; arithmetic; composition; history; geography, and the use of globes."[25] The younger Mordecais were pupils, while the older children taught, and the breadth of Rachel's reading led her to write to Maria Edgeworth, the Irish novelist, in 1815. Although she initially wrote to protest Edgeworth's portrayal of a Jewish villain, the women's correspondence turned generally to Anglo-American authors, Scott, for one, Byron, Sedgwick, and Cooper.[26] Assimilation into the world of Western letters placed Rachel in a strange position, though, with respect to Jews. One year she predicted that the Warrenton Academy would soon "be well stocked not only with South Carolinians, but with Yehooda."[27] Not quite derogatory, the term betrayed Rachel's sense of her distance from other Jews. Her disengagement was a reflection of Jacob's unrestrained intellectual travels.

The father, however, commanded a body of Jewish knowledge that his children did not possess. In 1832 Rebecca Gratz was "much delighted" with his "patriarchal manner and conversation" when he visited her in Philadelphia: "he has the advantage of understanding the language in which the scriptures were written—and has a large learned library, a liberal spirit—and leisure to devote to his favorite study."[28] Circulating closely written manuscripts to opponents and friends, Jacob defended "the fortress of Judaism."[29] "Visionary and destructive" were his words for Jewish reformers in Charleston in 1826. Their belief that America was the promised land of Jewish restoration was "fanciful conjecture"; equally, using English in the liturgy risked losing Jews in "the common mass."[30] Torah, Mishnah, Talmud, Maimonides, Abravenel, and Mendelssohn appeared in his text to contest the reformers' intent, which, as Mordecai saw it, was "to destroy the sacred fabric of Israelite worship."[31] Ten years later, he pitted his intelligence against Harriet Martineau, a Unitarian who called the Jews "a God-forsaken people, a people scattered among the nations for rejecting" Jesus.[32] Here, his dense citations from the Hebrew Bible built a case for the Jews' covenantal status, at the same time that he plumbed Christian writings by Irenaeus, Origen, and Tertullian to cast doubt on the redemptive mission of Jesus. Even more, because modern-day crucifixions of criminals in Surinam and Russia did not always kill the victims, Jesus might not have died on the cross or been miraculously resurrected.[33] Arguing with Christians, Jacob enlisted his encyclopedic studies. It was Judaism, however, that framed his information and defined his values.

Why, then, did Mordecai transmit his convictions to his children so ineffectively? Only three grew up to marry Jews, and at least five as adults were baptized. Delayed self-understanding was instrumental. The children's romances with gentiles were the first sign to Jacob that he had taken his Judaism for granted. Religiously safe himself as he surveyed Western culture, he taught his children erratically. Solomon, Jacob's third son, tried to improve his minimal Hebrew by studying in his twenties with a priest. Caroline, the third daughter, "was nominally brought up an Israelite," Rachel recalled in 1834, "because that was the faith of her parents"; but "no time was given to instruction in the religion of her fathers."[34] Jacob's second wife, named Rebecca, could offer little assistance beyond keeping a Jewish home. The stepmother of six children, she bore seven herself and supervised the care of the Academy's girls. Suffering by comparison with the older Mordecais' "sainted mother," Rebecca interceded with the angry father in extreme cases, but, as the unwanted stepmother, was often ignored.[35] She was no more able to help the children understand how their father's unquestioned Judaism coexisted with his panoramic curiosity than was Jacob himself.

Civility finally smoothed over Jacob's distress at Moses' wedding plans in 1817. Good manners, the bridge to gentile and Jew that had served Mordecai as schoolmaster, now carried the family through its religious trial. Moses repaired the breach of respect to his father, committed when he informed Jacob of the engagement by mail: traveling hastily from Raleigh to Warrenton to speak to Jacob, Moses promised to return after the ceremony with his wife.[36] His siblings debated who would attend the wedding, to be hosted by the aunt of the bride, and fretted that their brother Samuel, living in Virginia, was not formally invited. Samuel himself, professing "not [to] require the ceremony of an invitation," determined not to be "hurt by [Moses'] silence."[37] Rachel and Solomon represented the Mordecais at the event. Jacob, perhaps still pondering the unexpected conflict between liberality and faith, stayed home.

2. Mordecai House, Raleigh, North Carolina, where Moses Mordecai (1785–1824) moved in with his bride, Margaret Lane, in 1817. Built in 1785 by Margaret's father, the house was enlarged to its present size in 1826 with the financial assistance of Moses' estate. Courtesy of Mordecai Historic Park.

In the small world of early American Jewry, Rebecca Gratz was related to Jacob Mordecai. Alfred, Jacob's ninth child, married Sara
Ann Hays, Gratz's niece, in 1836. "The wedding is over and all went
on smoothly," Samuel Mordecai wrote home from Philadelphia; "the
company separated at 11—all pleased and happy."[38] Not all Gratz
weddings were so placid. When Benjamin, Rebecca's youngest
brother, chose a Christian bride in Kentucky in 1819, his sister confided to a friend that "in a family connection I have always thought
conformity of religious opinions essential and therefore could not ap-
prove my brothers selection."[39] Generous feelings, though, soon prevailed. "You must banish reserve now, My dear Maria, for we are Sisters," Rebecca wrote to Benjamin's wife, and "you have a claim to my
warmest affection."[40] Her instinct to guard tradition gave way to an
impulse to disregard boundaries. Piety and breadth contended as subtly in Gratz's character as they did in Mordecai and Carey's.

Rebecca Gratz (1781–1869), two decades younger than these fathers and unmarried, nonetheless acted as matriarch of an extended
clan. Her mother, Miriam, bore twelve children after her wedding to
Michael Gratz in Philadelphia in 1769. Of the ten who survived childhood, five never married and remained at home. Rebecca was nearly
thirty when her mother died in 1808; her father's death followed in
1811. She took charge of the household, adding the six children of her
sister Rachel when their mother died in 1823 to the stream of visiting nephews and nieces. The family was her element. Saddened by
"the division of hearts we so often witness when the members of the
same family live face to face," Rebecca prized her home, she wrote to
Benjamin in 1856, "among the numerous gifts the God of Israel has
vouchsafed unto us."[41]

Judaism structured her convictions. You "know my opinions and
have witnessed their influence on my conduct [thro'?] life," Rebecca
reminded a friend in 1819.[42] High standards brought criticism of current practice. "I have come home, from a large congregation," she
told her niece Miriam Cohen, "haunted by seeing the want of spirituality w[h]ere all profess religion."[43] The "spirit of innovation," she
complained to Miriam again, led their neighbors "to sing the songs of
Zion in a strange land," indifferent to whether "they would be restored to [their homeland] in the time God chose to appoint."[44] Even
among her kin, "I have no pleasure in the birth of sons in this generation of our family, for their parents no longer remember the duty of

Jewish parents to enter them into the covenant of Abrahams descendants" by circumcision.[45] These private laments, voiced when Gratz was near sixty, followed a lifetime of observance. In 1812, one of Rebecca's earliest surviving letters reminded Benjamin to perform the rites of "our day of Memorial" or *yahrzeit,* "the mournful anniversary of our Beloved Parents death."[46] Her letters to dispersed relatives regularly described Jewish holidays celebrated at home. In 1838, she made her lasting public mark as founder of the first Hebrew Sunday School Society in America. "Thank God I have the law & the prophets and am willing to hear them," Gratz exclaimed in a letter in 1834.[47] Her life gave substance to her words.

Yet Judaism was not the touchstone of all her social relations. It was to "my dearest friend" Maria Fenno Hoffman that Rebecca unburdened her disappointment at Benjamin's engagement. Mixed marriage seemed unbearable, she confessed to a Christian, though "my most cherished friends" have "generally been worshipers of a different faith from mine and I have not loved them less on that account."[48] Publicly, she worked for nonsectarian benevolence, first the Female Association for the Relief of Women and Children in Reduced Circumstances, beginning in 1801, and later the Philadelphia Orphan Society from 1815. Pleasant conversation normally kept prejudice from view. But when the "good Christians" at the Orphan Society refused to assign a child to Mrs. Furness, wife of a Unitarian minister, Gratz pressed the issue: "'Ladies, said I, there are many children under my special direction—you all know my creed—suppose I should want one to bring up in my family?'—'you may have one,' said a church woman—'because the Jews do not think it a duty to convert.'"[49] Still, bluntness of this kind was rare. "I got into a long discussion on the subject of religion, with a lady after the meeting, and though we have been more than twenty years acquainted—I expect she will look shy on me for the rest of our lives." "Ashamed by such an illiberal spirit" as she witnessed that day, Gratz wished for open-mindedness that was wide-ranging and honest.[50] Republican Philadelphia generally stopped short at cordial cooperation. But even civic friendliness suited her taste.

In a household looking inward to Judaism and outward on polite society, the interfaith marriage of "the very Benjamin of his father's house" stirred more consternation than surprise.[51] Nor did the alienation last: in 1865, the largest single gift in Rebecca's will went to her youngest brother.[52] Yet the subtle effect of the Gratz connection with Benjamin's bride was the entry of good-natured formality, a tone hitherto used with strangers, into the family. A good correspondent, Rebecca wrote steadily to Benjamin's successive wives, first Maria, and, after Maria's death in 1841, her niece Ann. Warm but not intimate, the letters worked to cross the space between Jew and Christian. Patient accounts of Jewish practices appeared as information. "A period of self examination," she explained to Maria in 1833, precedes the "day of Atonement." It "is not customary among pious Jews to name a child after a living parent," she told Ann after a son's birth in 1845, then stepped back from intrusion: "I have no *reasons* against it—only a prejudice."[53] Far differently, Rebecca filled letters to Miriam Cohen, the niece she had raised, with opinions. "Alas," she wrote mournfully about Miriam's brother in 1855, "that Gratz [Moses] should have been so heedless—so indifferent to the observance of his own belief" to marry a Catholic.[54] The varied ways Gratz spoke now with different members of her family reflected her personality's genteel and traditional sides.

Mathew Carey, Jacob Mordecai, and Rebecca Gratz all held together inherited convictions and expansive views with arresting ease. For them, faith and knowledge worked in tandem to guard tradition: piety inspired religious study, and rationality defended moral truth. Even so, parents and guardians of children who intermarried found themselves at a series of intellectual and social boundaries. This made the consequences of their mix of Enlightened liberalism and spiritual conservatism unpredictable, more so for their children than themselves.

How Children Reinterpreted Their Parents' Values

The children of Enlightened parents who later intermarried took their elders' broadmindedness so seriously that they risked crossing religious bounds when choosing a spouse. This subversive family encounter, however, was subtle. Parents situated on their society's progressive edge watched young people take small steps toward innovation. In their use of reason, choice of residence, understanding of emotion, and approach to power, the generations were similar in temperament, yet also different.

The religious Enlightenment expected rationality to serve inher-

ited faith. Mathew Carey and Jacob Mordecai excelled as polemicists. When Carey denounced the "mass of folly and error" in the St.
Mary's controversy, and Mordecai dismissed the Charleston reformers as "enthusiasts" of a "fanciful system," their rhetoric made reason
the handmaid of religion.[55] No culture imagines the mind limited to
one function, however, and the vitality of the American Enlightenment made it certain that reason served masters other than faith.
Mathew Carey invoked rationality as a kind of deliberation. "Want of
order in the arrangement of business" in 1791 led to "shameful" neglect of his diary: "I now determine to be regular and systematic
henceforward."[56] In 1833, he credited "care, indefatigable industry,
the most rigid punctuality, and frugality" as the means by which "I
gradually advanced in the world."[57] Carey's belief in system did not
displace religious devotion, but gave reason worldly applications in
addition to pious ones.

Among the younger generation, the uses of reason proliferated in
potentially explosive ways. Children who married outside their faith
were independent, critical, ambitious, detached: reasonable without
deference. Solomon Mordecai thought for himself. Jewish services in
Philadelphia, he complained in 1820, showed "no marked devotion"
and instead, represented "noise and confusion," enough to make Jews
"blush," at least "those of them who can blush, when they see a
stranger enter their place of worship."[58] It was easy for a sharp-witted
man to turn his back on flawed practices for more promising fields.
Solomon told his parents that he aimed at "attaining an independence."[59] In the long run, minds habituated to practical analysis
might simply put religion at arm's length. "Cathedral very old" was
the cryptic journal entry of Isaac Lea—Carey's son-in-law, a lapsed
Quaker and amateur scientist—in France in 1832.[60] Being indepen-
dent-minded did not lead invariably to interfaith marriage, nor did
mixed couples consistently display skeptical tempers. Reason, however, could take brash, self-serving directions and lay the groundwork
for unexpected religious decisions among the Enlightenment's descendants.

A similar transition occurred in a more tangible sphere: place of
residence. Parents chose open social environments; their offspring
preferred frontiers. It is not accidental that no early American interfaith families for this study could be found in New England. Catholics
and Jews did not fail to see the social walls maintained by latter-day

Puritans. Pennsylvania was one of the few colonies before the Revolution with no established church, and its mood of freedom attracted religious minorities. "I hesitated between New York, Philadelphia, and Baltimore," Mathew Carey reflected on his emigration from Ireland in 1784. Only the Philadelphia papers carried news of his prosecution by the House of Commons for anti-English agitation; he settled there.[61] Warrenton, North Carolina, Jacob Mordecai's home after 1792, was also open-minded. The town induced the state in 1786 to charter an academy "to hold forth every possibility, opportunity, and encouragement to liberal education."[62] Yet less than two months after Moses' engagement to a Christian in 1817, Jacob decided to move. He dispatched a son to find "a plantation" near Richmond; six years later, he had "a good many acquaintances in town," his daughter Ellen wrote, while "I have so few."[63] Many were Jewish, because Richmond had a synagogue. Perhaps Jacob saw the religious risk in Warrenton's friendliness after Moses married a gentile, and he learned to discriminate between borderlands. Virginia's constitution protected religious freedom, while its society offered Jewish company. Warrenton took liberality too far.

Caroline, however, Jacob's sixth child, returned to Warrenton in 1820, when she married Achilles Plunkett, a Christian who had taught in her father's school. She was as comfortable with vague social boundaries as her aging father felt anxious.[64] Even more, young men settled in rising places before they intermarried. Caroline's brothers, Moses and Solomon, chose Raleigh and Mobile respectively; Benjamin Gratz, Lexington, Kentucky. Social advantage was one attraction of communities still taking shape. Frank Blair, a Democratic politician, became Gratz's brother-in-law in Lexington, and Henry Clay was Benjamin's close friend.[65] But the deeper lure of transitional societies was subjective: the chance to make one's way socially matched the young men's state of mind. Rebecca Gratz and Rachel Mordecai, sisters at home, wrote fearfully to their brothers, as if they had crossed into a domain of indeterminate values. "You have had a delightful season for your travels," Rebecca told Benjamin before his wedding, but she disapproved of "a wandering life" in "the western wilds."[66] Rachel spoke of Moses' engagement as nearly a betrayal of civilization. His fiancée grew up among "common people, with every day understandings & no education."[67] The sisters' distress grew in part from anticipating long-term separation from their brothers. Yet their pleas for cultivation were equally confessions that the men were lost already to past standards of religious and family integrity. Where the brothers decided to live simply made their comfort with cultural mixing plain.[68]

Their adventurousness belonged to a new mood that accelerated mixed-faith weddings. Around 1820, there was a near rush to this altar, as three Mordecais, two Careys, two granddaughters of the Gillespies, and Benjamin Gratz intermarried between 1817 and 1824. Old and young alike felt a change in sensibility. The emotions of parents were entwined with their religion; for their children, feeling could contest faith.

Pious parents now became advocates. Their children's intermarriages sounded one alarm, but impassioned contention was also the rising public mood. Isaac Lea counted 2,322 pamphlet pages written by his father-in-law, Mathew Carey, in a little more than a decade after 1819. A "vigilant guard against public abuses," in Lea's words, "the friend of civil & religious liberty," Carey entered Catholic disputes to restore peace, yet never was deterred by "a furious storm."[69] Nor was Rebecca Gratz dispassionate in 1834 when a neighbor, believing "the time was *near at hand* when the Jews would be gathered to their own land," gave "me more books than I can read" to make her a Christian. Gratz dismissed the woman's wish "to canonize herself by my conversion."[70] Both religious feuding and evangelicalism accelerated around 1820, and Enlightened elders harnessed reason to their accented zeal.

This is not to say the older generation expended emotion only on religion. But they tended to be restrained in private and did not change with age. Mathew Carey, who loved his wife fully, expressed himself with economy. "Married to miss Bridget Flavahan," he noted in his diary in 1791; weeks later, "love & esteem Mrs. Carey more than before marriage." Ill the next week, his wife went "to bed in her clothes at seven. Go & lie with her for half an hour."[71] When she was "dangerously ill" in 1814, "the family [was] greatly alarmed."[72] Carey's feelings were intense yet compact, admitting neither self-indulgence nor display. So bounded, emotion was not likely to disrupt the continuity of religious tradition.

Far differently, the Mordecai children spoke a language of happiness and love. Anticipating Moses' wedding in 1817, Ellen wished "everything for the happiness of our excellent brother which is not incompatible with the tranquillity of our beloved father."[73] When Ellen herself painfully declined marriage to a Christian in 1823, Rachel consoled her sister that "the *present* sacrifice will have proved the means of ensuring on a solid basis your own happiness." The next year, Ellen advised her brother Solomon to "ensure your happiness" by marrying "a sweet girl to make you happy."[74] All the while, Ellen poured out affection for Solomon—"my beloved S"—in letter after letter. "Surely never were two beings better suited to each other than ourselves," she wrote from Richmond to Mobile in January 1824:

> The world speaks in vain of *Time* & *Distance*—they have no more influence over *my* feelings than the wind that passes over the rock. But—you know me *well* my love, my love indeed at once my greatest strength— my greatest weakness—& be it so—Let me hush this voice of my heart, let me soothe it by a remembrance of some tender word of affection, that has flowed from your lips, and let its acknowledgment, be the tear that now trembles in my eye.[75]

Solomon married three months later; Ellen remained single until her death in 1884. Her complex, effusive passion for her brother was a sign that the "happiness" so desired was not a simple state but a condition of emotional reward. Nothing in the longing for personal connections precluded loyalty to Judaism. The expectation of self-gratification might bypass piety, however, and, if incompatible with faith, displace it.[76]

Indeed, the demands of time-bound, human selves seemed to intensify among young people. Reasoning, now independent and critical, along with feeling, acquisitive and expansive, loosened the ties of children to past religious rules. Even so, they did not enter interfaith marriages as free agents. Power relationships between the Protestant majority and religious minorities formed the hidden but persuasive framework of personal decisions.

For years, civility had forged even-tempered, sometimes warm personal ties between Protestants and their neighbors. Mathew Carey drew Protestant admirers by his writings on political economy. Lyman Beecher borrowed Carey's ideas on manufactures for a sermon in 1820; one of Beecher's parishioners sent Carey a copy "with sincere esteem, & gratitude for your patriotic efforts."[77] Privately, Catholic and Jewish women made intimate Protestant friends. Rebecca Mordecai, Jacob's wife, felt so close to one neighbor in North Carolina, Eliza

Kennon, that she named her fifth child for her in 1809. The affection was returned. The same year, Sally Kennon, Eliza's daughter, wrote to Rebecca's stepdaughter Ellen that "tho' we are not lovers, my beloved girl, we are what is better, friends."[78] In 1817 Rachel Mordecai could not have missed the irony of her argument to dissuade her brother Moses from marrying a Christian: is she a "Sally Kennon, is she a Mary Long, is she in short a woman capable of comprehending your sentiments, & of appreciating your worth?"[79] Rachel invoked the uncomplicated cordiality of the Mordecais and Kennons to avert Moses' intermarriage. Her distinction between acceptable and unacceptable women mirrored her discrimination of safe and unsafe ways to mix with gentiles. Wishfully, Moses' romance might seem more palatable if it resembled the family's bond with Sally Kennon. Yet Rachel was clear-sighted and must have known that civil friendships lay the groundwork for interfaith marriages.

Once acquaintance was replaced by the prospect of kinship, the social border between Protestants and minorities became an unpredictable place. Sometimes a Protestant man drifted into a Catholic or Jewish family and, without fuss, married the daughter. Just so, Isaac Lea began calling on Frances Carey early in 1819. By August 1820 her father wrote in his diary that "Henry, Patty, Isaac Lea, & all our children [were] ready to meet us" when the parents returned from a trip.[80] Nearly part of the family, Isaac wed Fanny without to-do. Her sister Maria "suggested the idea of Frances's marriage taking place tomorrow evening, instead of Easter week," Mathew Carey wrote on March 5, 1821. "I took an hour to consider of it—then I acquiesced." On March 6 he rose early and invited some friends. "The wedding [was] celebrated about eight o'clock."[81]

How different when a Catholic or Jew approached a Protestant family. Fearful of humiliating terms or rejection, Solomon Mordecai courted Caroline Waller anxiously in Mobile in 1824. "I do not apprehend that Mr. Waller will wish to exact any thing to which I shall not feel disposed to submit," he told a sister. All remembered Solomon's temptation to convert to Christianity in order to marry Anna Tennent of Philadelphia in 1821. The engagement ended when Anna's parents refused Solomon's suit. Now he hoped not to be "the child of disappointment" again.[82] This time he won a bride. But Protestant cultural dominance was never far from view, and Solomon approached the Wallers as a suppliant. In the parents' generation, interfaith friendships had an egalitarian temper. Social distance made it unnecessary to probe prejudices and fears. Thoughts of marriage, in contrast, frayed good manners and exposed how much some had to seek social entry from others. Even then, intermarried outsiders accepted self-doubt and demeaning negotiation for the kind of reward Rachel Mordecai imagined for Solomon when she pictured him a "happy husband."[83]

Enlightened parents and their children were not unrecognizable to each other. Old and young alike were forthright, determined people, not afraid of unfamiliar things. The children, though, turned reason and feeling away from public service—the defense of religious tradition—and toward the self. Eager for gratifying lives, they took risks and fielded conflicts that stirred moral issues along with practical ones. The rise of this expansive temper might be seen as an expression of Romanticism. Yet in these families there was no Romantic revolt.[84] The change in values was gradual and, in the end, qualified, as love of family and commitment to religion continued to bind the generations.

Getting Married, Raising Families

In the later nineteenth century, newspapers carried wedding announcements telling who performed weddings and composed bridal parties. Formal and stylized, the notices nonetheless hinted at clerical approval or family feelings. Earlier American papers ran mainly commercial and political news. But private sources cast light on interfaith weddings and the households they produced. Priests and ministers performed mixed marriages. So complex were families' ensuing religious arrangements, however, that habits took shape outside institutions. The intricacy of these commitments appears in three families: the Blaines and Ewings on the Pennsylvania-Ohio border, the Careys and Leas in Philadelphia, and the Mordecais in Richmond, Raleigh, and Mobile.

In 1841 James Gillespie Blaine, eleven years old, spent the summer with his Ewing cousins—Philemon, Hugh, and Tom—in Lancaster, Ohio. Philemon had just stayed with the Blaines in Brownsville, Pennsylvania, and Tom planned to accompany James back home.[85] Because they were cousins, there was nothing unusual about the visits, except that James was a Protestant, the Ewing boys Catholics. Their respective Catholic mothers, Maria Gillespie and Maria Boyle, had been married by priests in 1820 to Protestant men. Maria Boyle Ewing's Catholicism deepened; around the time of James's arrival, her letters were filled with news of priests, first communions, and a nun's gift of rosary "beads," which "I *sometimes* say," she told her daughter humbly, "in the *proper spirit*."[86] Maria Gillespie Blaine was also pious, but she had agreed to raise her sons Protestant, though her daughters Catholic. In mixed-faith families, dividing children by gender was sufficiently common for a later Catholic tract to answer a rhetorical question about the permissibility of the practice with the words, "emphatically no."[87] Perhaps Maria Blaine sent James to Ohio to absorb the spiritual flavor of her cousin's Catholic home. Maria Ewing heard gossip later that fall that "Mr. Blaine was preparing to *come into the Church!*"[88] Whether he converted is unclear, but his wife may have hoped similarly to persuade their son by exposure to their Catholic kin. Religion aside, the Ewings and Blaines had much in common. The fathers, Thomas Ewing and Ephraim Blaine, were Whig politicians, and all, Catholic and Protestant alike, were proudly Irish. "I boast upon my descent," the Ewings' daughter Ellen professed in 1854. In 1884, when James G. Blaine—still a Protestant—ran for president, his cousin Tom told him "your Donegal and Londonderry blood will carry you through."[89] The Lancaster and Brownsville households handled the religious issues raised by the 1820 intermarriages quite differently. All regarded themselves as family nonetheless.

Behind these settlements, questions remain: why did priests consent to perform these weddings, and how did the couples decide on their children's religious training? Catholic clergy felt "compelled," Archbishop Carroll confessed in 1802, "for fear of greater evils to lend our ministry to their celebration."[90] In canon law, "grave scandals" born of cohabitation were one hazard; so was the "peril of perversion" of faith risked by marriage before a civil magistrate or Protestant minister. Catholics could be excommunicated for any of these choices. But, following Jesus, the church "left the ninety-nine sheep in the desert to seek the one that was lost" and granted dispensations from canonical impediments to retain its flock.[91] *Disparitatis cultus* (marriage to an unbaptized person) and *disparitatis fidei* (marriage to a baptized non-Catholic) appeared early in American parish records as canonical reasons to oppose marriages. *Angustia loci*, a scarcity of Catholic bachelors nearby, was one reason for a dispensation: the church must avert, a later treatise explained, the "indecorousness" of women "wandering about in search of a husband."[92] In 1820, Maria Boyle lived one hundred miles from the diocesan see of Cincinnati, in a town with no resident priest, in a household headed by her aunt's Presbyterian husband. It must not have been hard for the priest performing the rite to decide that the obstacles to a Catholic match merited Maria a dispensation.

Why her family wished a Catholic wedding also requires thought. Both Maria and her aunt Susan, who raised her, were baptized Catholics; but Susan's husband, Philemon Beecher, was "a strong Scriptural Presbyterian," in one biographer's view.[93] Maria's widowed father, Hugh Boyle, lived nearby in Lancaster, however, and as a married woman Maria began housekeeping in a home Boyle owned.[94] Father and daughter were close enough for him to support her Catholicism. Nor was Thomas Ewing in a position to question Maria's kin. Early American mixed marriages were not alliances of stable and equal families. Often one partner, seemingly alone, approached a future family and inevitably joined it on its own terms. Reared in the Ohio backcountry, Ewing had left home at age twenty in "search of adventure," he recalled, working as a laborer in a saltworks from 1809 until 1812.[95] He studied law with Philemon Beecher beginning in 1815 and soon rode the circuit in Fairfield County, so successfully that in 1830 he won election to the United States Senate. In 1820, though, the year of his marriage, he was not far removed from his legal apprenticeship to Maria's uncle. Of Presbyterian background, Ewing left no sign that he pushed for a Protestant wedding.[96]

Formally, the Ewings remained Catholics. But Thomas's Protestant roots influenced the family, to the point that the boys and girls seemed nearly as religiously divided as their Blaine cousins. Thomas directed his wife in 1831 to supervise the "lads" in their study of Peter Parley readers. Training conscience to avoid "idle & evil habits" was not un-Catholic; but the "system" of building self-control reminded Thomas of his own instruction by his mother and sisters in "a poor log hut."[97] Meanwhile Ellen, the only daughter, went to school at the Georgetown convent of the Sisters of the Visitation in Washington. William Tecumseh Sherman, her foster brother and future husband, got a secular education at West Point, as did Thomas Ewing, Jr., at Brown University. The boys' relaxed Catholicism made it seem natural that Tom fell in love with a Protestant, Ellen Ewing Cox, in 1854.

His mother, sure "there is no hope of her being convinced of her error and embracing the truth," mourned Tom's exposure to "the danger of heresy and error."[98] When he married Ellen in 1856, apparently without her conversion, the spiritual variety in this ostensibly Catholic family was visible to all.

The Ewings' history, along with the story of their Blaine relations, contains characteristic features of early American interfaith families. Unafraid of innovation or personal differences, couples still wanted clergy to perform weddings and their children to be religiously educated. Anyone could foresee, however, that parents' diverging values would play through households. Tension was inescapable, yet family loyalty was a potent salve. The Ewings were unusual because they did not let intermarriage become a straight path to Protestantism. Their cousin James Blaine was more typical. Marrying a Congregationalist in Maine in 1850, he later gained a political name as a foe of "Rum, Romanism, and Rebellion."[99]

Similar commitments to religion and family appear in the lives of Mathew and Bridget Carey and their children, especially Frances, their fifth child, and her husband Isaac Lea. The wedding of Fanny and Isaac in 1821 at St. Augustine's Church, Philadelphia, was an ecumenical affair. Mathew Carey identified the company in his diary: "Mrs. Leslie, Ann, Patty, Mr. Lea, Harriet M., John Lea, S. Bell, Maria, Eliza, Susan, Henry, Mr. Elmonic were present." Most came in family groups. Henry, the Careys' oldest son, brought his Protestant wife Patty, her mother, Mrs. Leslie, and Patty's sister Ann. There was the bridegroom and his brother John, Quakers by birth; the bride's sisters—Maria, Eliza, and Susan—filled out the party. The priest seemed untroubled by his role. "Mr. Hurley," Carey wrote, "S. Bell, & A. Leslie, each sang a song" after the service over food and wine.[100] Michael Hurley, pastor of St. Augustine's, was an old friend who sometimes dined with the Careys.[101] Whatever the formal grounds of the dispensation, personal loyalty must have helped sway the priest. Besides, Hurley had officiated at Henry's mixed marriage in 1819. Neither the Careys' family circle nor their standing in the church appeared damaged by the children's weddings to non-Catholics.

This cordiality was not simply a cheerful face for a ceremony that caused private distress. The family's Catholics and Protestants continued to mingle on close terms. Two months after Fanny's wedding, her father, worried by the ugly factionalism in St. Mary's parish, "went to the meeting [there] with I. Lea."[102] Perhaps Carey hoped to interest his son-in-law in Catholic politics. Lea did not appear again in family records as Carey's religious ally. But his children, raised Protestants, comfortably visited their Catholic kin. Henry Lea, age twelve, stayed at his grandparents' country house in 1837. "Grandpa comes out to Strawberry Hill in the morning before breakfast & takes his breakfast out there," he told his parents; "when he is not going to Germantown or any place out of his way we go in with him" to Philadelphia.[103] Mutual business ventures further bridged religious distances and secured family bonds. Even on his honeymoon, Lea answered Carey's questions about the Pittsburgh economy: the young couple visited "important manufactures" and relayed commodity prices.[104] Once home, Lea entered the Carey publishing business. He formed a series of partnerships with Mathew and his sons, Henry and Edward, before his retirement in 1851. All, too, had Irish blood. Thomas Gibson, Isaac's grandfather, emigrated from Ireland to Pennsylvania and married a Quaker in 1751. Whether Gibson was Catholic or Protestant is unknown. But Lea's Irish forebear lent sincerity to the good wishes Isaac sent his father-in-law in 1821 on the occasion of Carey's proposed trip to Ireland, "your own native country, & the country of other warm and generous hearts."[105] Enlightened tolerance sustained good feeling in this religiously divided family. Liberality, however, was well supported by common social interests and traits.

Despite this friendliness, the Leas decided not to bring up their children as Catholics. Mathew Carey Lea (born 1823), Henry Charles Lea (1825), and Frances Lea (1834) received a moralistic education, only vaguely Protestant and unaccompanied by church membership. Instructed at home by an Irish-born tutor, the boys kept notebooks of their studies. In 1834, Henry recorded a story called "La Promenade," most likely his own work but maybe transcribed. Its characters John and Arthur, the first cruel and the second kind, set out to do mean or good deeds. "I hope," Henry concluded, "that John will live to learn that a walk in the country does not want charms to those who look for pleasure without causing pain."[106] This utilitarian ethic, focused on increasing happiness and decreasing sorrow, was backed up by the Bible. A workbook titled "Bible Studies," dated 1838, contained accounts of creation, the patriarchs, and Israelite kings. God's providence was one lesson; Henry also reviewed the moral choices facing Jacob in his relations with Esau and Solomon when he loved foreign wives.[107] Booklets on religion, however, were outnumbered by secular subjects: mathematics and science (algebra, geometry, chemistry, botany, conchology), languages (Greek, Italian, French, German), history, literature, even jokes. The boys' education reflected their father's passion for science and art. Isaac's work in the Carey family business paled in personal importance next to his avocations. In 1852, on his way to publishing nearly 300 works on minerals, rocks, and shells, Lea received an honorary degree from Harvard for his contributions as an amateur naturalist. He bought almost 200 Italian paintings the same year.[108] Although Isaac did not dismiss moralism, he wanted his children to value knowledge and beauty as well.

The match between the boys' studies and father's interests does not quite explain how the Leas, married by Father Hurley, arrived at their concise, even spare, religion. The children's curriculum required deliberation, and the absence of Latin makes it seem that someone, probably Isaac, wished to distance the scholars from the Catholic Church.[109] Still, the father's will might not have prevailed without conspiring circumstances. Like Thomas Ewing in Ohio, Lea approached the Careys without fortune or, except for a brother, close kin. Cast in the role of petitioner, he nonetheless walked away from his in-laws' Catholicism because of the temper of the Careys' domestic relations. Frances Carey Lea, too, was an accommodating person. When the Leas visited the eighteenth-century homestead of Isaac's grandfather near Brandywine in 1849, "my good wife," he reflected, "to whom this was all new was interested for our sake as well as in this quaint old building."[110] Hospitable to Lea family lore, Fanny left no countervailing record of intimacy with her siblings to keep her from acceding to her husband's views. Eliza, her older sister, appeared in their father's diaries when she accompanied their parents to Mass; she was the only child to marry a Catholic, Thomas Baird, in 1822. Henry and his wife, Patty, joined St. Mary's Episcopal Church in Burlington, New Jersey, around 1840. High Church and Roman-leaning, the parish was a middle ground between the couple's childhood faiths.[111] Maria, Edward, and Susan, who never married, were consistently, yet not demonstratively, Catholic. Very often, bonds among siblings were as influential as relations with parents in determining who would intermarry and what kind of religious practice the couple would choose. Fanny's ties with her Catholic sisters and brothers did not seem persuasive enough to deflect her from the liberal path her husband laid.

A sense of being family remained. In 1910, Henry Carey Baird,

Eliza's son, wrote a letter of condolence to his nephew, a son of Henry Charles Lea. The elder Lea had died the year before, and Baird recalled the friendship the cousins struck up in Philadelphia in 1840. "My good aunt" Fanny had invited Henry Baird to come from Pottsville to spend the summer, and the two Henrys hiked in the countryside in search of botanical specimens. Baird "became intimate with your father" after he began living in the city with his uncle Edward in 1841.[112] Fanny and Eliza were the only children of Mathew Carey who had children themselves. Henry Lea became a Unitarian; Henry Baird was Catholic. Each outcome made sense in light of the values of their Carey grandparents.

The Mordecais, quite differently, did not assume the children's Christian spouses would become part of the family. The distance between Jew and gentile must have seemed a barrier to amiability. This is why they were unprepared for the loyalty of their Christian kin. When Moses married Margaret Lane in 1817, Rachel spoke as if he were lost: "you tear yourself from us" to live with "strangers."[113] The logic recurred when he died in 1824. All believed his death would end their relations with the Lanes, even though his second wife, Nancy, Margaret's sister, was within a month of delivering his posthumous child. Rachel took "comfort" that "our brother's poor little orphans," Margaret's three children, would be raised by Caroline Mordecai. This was Moses' wish. "Their father requested," his brother Samuel wrote, "they should be sent to Warrenton at a proper age, knowing that with Caroline they would find another parent."[114] Plans changed after Ellen Mordecai arrived for Nancy's confinement. "I was a little surprised to hear of your intended visit to Raleigh," Rachel told Ellen, but "it is very satisfying to perceive in [Nancy] indications of attachment to our family, & I should take pleasure in encouraging it."[115] Soon George Mordecai, living in Raleigh, informed Samuel that the baby's birth had "good effects" on Nancy's "spirits." "The other children continue to enjoy good health and are much pleased with the toys you sent them."[116] None of Moses' children went to Caroline, and it is puzzling that George, single until 1853, did not marry the widow, so attentively did he serve his brother's household as guardian.[117] Over the years, a mixed-faith clan of extraordinary complexity took shape, bound together by a sense of kinship itself. This appeared when Nancy identified herself as a Mordecai, and Ellen and George, followed by Rachel and Samuel, accepted her view.

One reason that it must have been hard to imagine gentiles as kin was that interfaith weddings almost never took place in Jewish family circles. Such marriages occurred far from home, literally and figuratively, and were clouded by shame. Young men commonly withheld their plans from relatives until shortly before the service. Solomon Mordecai in Mobile told his father by letter after the fact. Opening with "how warm, how filial, how devoted my feelings toward you are," he had assumed that his sister Ellen, living in Richmond with Jacob, had passed on news about her brother's romance. Besides, there was "so much of uncertainty whether our union would take place" while his father-in-law equivocated, "that I preferred saying nothing." Solomon had not been "sensible of the pain" he caused and now sent "my apology" for this "error of judgment."[118] But contrite rhetoric could not erase his earlier cowardice.

He must have known, too, that views of intermarriage in the Jewish community mirrored his father's distress. His sister Rachel's wedding to a Jew, Aaron Lazarus, in 1821 had been a joyous event; the *hazzan* (cantor) of Richmond's synagogue performed the service in the presence of the area's leading Jewish families at Jacob's home, Spring Farm.[119] Solomon, sensing that no mixed marriage would win similar approbation, marginalized himself by his silence. In fact, however, there was some leniency in Jewish attitudes that might have served Solomon if he wished a Jewish ceremony. Because there were no ordained rabbis in America until the 1840s, laymen determined communal policies and presided at circumcisions, weddings, and funerals. They understood traditional law, but the system's democratic temper favored exceptions. When Jacob Mordecai's own mother, an English-born convert and widow, sought a second marriage to Jacob Cohen in 1782, the Philadelphia synagogue denied them permission: a *kohen*, member of the priestly class, could not wed a convert. Ester Mordecai and Cohen were married anyway by a dissenting layman. Jacob Mordecai himself cut corners. In 1838 he officiated at the wedding of a son of a Jewish father and a Christian mother. Although matrilineal descent meant that the young man was not Jewish without conversion, Jacob left no sign that he insisted the bridegroom take this step.[120] Early American Jewry most likely judged marriage to a gentile a more serious breach than these accommodations. Conversions of gentiles to Judaism for the sake of marriage did occur.[121] But Solomon Mordecai was reluctant to examine his plans honestly, and without his initiative, no compromise with Jewish authority could be struck. He turned away from the Jewish community because he assumed Jews turned away from him.

Presumably a Protestant minister married Solomon and Caroline Waller, although the Mordecais' letters were typically silent about who performed the family's mixed weddings. For the Jewish spouse, the presence of Christian clergy must have been an unpleasant reminder of apostasy, most comfortably overlooked. Two facts, though, seem clear: ministers did not require the Jewish partner's conversion and willingly performed marriages. The baptisms of intermarried Mordecais, long after their weddings, show that becoming a Christian first was not obligatory. Caroline and Solomon, married in the 1820s, received the sacrament in 1834 and 1859 respectively.[122] Evangelical hopes must have encouraged leniency. When the Mordecai family sought clergy for baptisms, ministers quickly replied, as if thoughts of the conversion of the Jews were not far from mind. This was true in 1859, when a daughter and son-in-law of Solomon in Mobile wished to have their two children received in the church. The mother "desired *private* baptism," and, bypassing "Mr. Leecock who approves the public observance," another minister came to the house to bless the children in "Sol's chamber."[123] Most likely, Protestant clergymen approached baptisms more eagerly than intermarriages. Baptism secured souls; mixed-faith weddings just opened doors to spiritual change. But ministers seemed to review requests for weddings from interfaith couples in light of conversionary expectations, and friendliness drew new families toward Christianity.

Their children became Christians, often in a haphazard yet persuasive way. The Mordecais and their spouses left less evidence than the Ewings or Leas that they planned their children's religious instruction. Sometimes the result was vague knowledge, verging on ignorance. The minister who baptized Solomon's grandchildren spoke to his daughter Suny, her aunt Ellen reported, about her responsibility as godparent: "She to my surprise shed tears, thanked him & told him she wished he *would* teach her what religion was, for she knew nothing about it—what a speech for a child in the presence of a mother who says she has been for *20* years in the Methodist church!"[124]

Perhaps Solomon and his wife let Suny's training slide because, on the one hand, there was nothing to discuss and, on the other, it was too painful. The idea of Jewish self-hatred overstates Solomon's feelings. Judaism, however, was "noise and confusion" to him, and it must instinctively have made sense to raise his children as Christians.[125] Though not without guilt. In early America, there was an element of sad fatality to the absorption of the descendants of Jewish-gentile marriages in Christian culture.

In these families, the children's piety need not be lukewarm. For the children of Solomon Mordecai, Christian fervor entered the household through their extended kin. Their baptized aunts, Jacob's daughters, especially carried the gospel. Caroline Mordecai nearly suffered "derangement of intellect" due to "the displeasure of our dear father" over her baptism, Rachel wrote in 1834, and moved to Tennessee to get away. But she later lived in Mobile.[126] Ellen, also a Christian, spent time in Mobile as well. In 1859 she prayed that their brother Solomon would "have all the Holy Light he can so that if possible your dear Uncle," she told her Christian niece, "may *feel* the true church & enter it."[127] The Christian presence in the Mordecai family remained surprisingly secret. Ellen sent religious news in "my Christian letters," marked by a cross, to Ellen Mordecai, Moses' daughter in Raleigh, even then fearful that by "*possible* mischance they be left in the *folds* of the family letters & are sent on—oh how *frightful* to think of!"[128] The family's Christians were not unknown, however, to each other. Christians by conviction encouraged children who were Christians by default to think about salvation. This made the rearing of Jacob Mordecai's Christian grandchildren almost a family endeavor.

Intermarriages among the Mordecais reveal an unhappy side of mixed-faith families. Disappointment, anger, secretiveness, and shame punctuated their relationships. The family's Christian conversions raised the same feelings. In either case, the instinct to read crossing communal boundaries as betrayal was a response as old as Judaism. Even so, the thousands of letters the Mordecais exchanged attest to their family loyalty. True, Christian spouses appear less often as correspondents than subjects of comment, but as such they were asked after and remembered as kin. So, too, just as being Whigs or Irish laced Protestant-Catholic families, Southernness helped bind the Mordecais' Christians and Jews. In 1856, Jacob's son Samuel published *Richmond in By-Gone Days, Being Some Reminiscences of An Old Citizen.* Benign and nostalgic, the memoir meandered through chapters on "Races and Balls" and "Cemeteries." "Two Parsons and Ne'er a Church" chronicled the construction of sacred buildings: Baptist, Episcopal, Presbyterian churches, "and a Synagogue."[129] As a young man, Samuel had been sufficiently prominent in the Beth Shalome congregation to deliver occasional orations; now in his old age, he was an Episcopalian.[130] It was residence in Richmond that most comfortably joined the ends of his life. Slaveholding was part of Southernness. Jacob Mordecai was the largest Jewish slaveowner in the area by the 1820 census.[131] Although none of his descendants was a vocal Confederate, neither did any question slavery. Common attachment to a place and its mores must have lent calm to the ongoing, if muted, turmoil in the family's religion.

Two constants appear in the interfaith clans of the early republic: religion and family. Unlike the Enlightened generation, mixed-faith families behaved as if choice and change were part of observance. Religious solutions in their households, subtle and varied, effectively, if not intentionally, permitted spiritual migrations. This was the legacy of Enlightened liberalism: cosmopolitanism that once stood beside traditional practice now reshaped faith. It was love of family itself that contained dispersion of kin.

Not all family experiences were the same, however. Cultural power, manifested in the elusive quality of respectability, was a fixture in interfaith homes. It is hard to imagine Jews or Catholics forgetting that their Protestant relations belonged to America's dominant religious group. Children who grew up in the interfaith households of the early republic returned as adults to questions of religious identity that stretched back to parents and grandparents.

Descendants

Interfaith couples, like other nineteenth-century American families, produced many children by our standards, and each child must have reacted to intermarriage in a unique way. But it is possible to discern commonplace stories. Caroline Cohen, a granddaughter of Jacob Mordecai, calculated in 1913, for example, that only five of Jacob's huge progeny remained practicing Jews.[132] Beyond one family, a composite portrait of the grandchildren and even great-grandchildren of the Enlightened generation may be drawn. The descendants voiced liberal ideas echoing their forebears' civility. They did so as Protestants, however, and identified freedom as a Protestant message. Raised among mixed-faith kin, they seemed eager for simplification, often marrying cousins. Together, young couples settled into a part of the Protestant world that was socially comfortable and intellectually consonant with the Enlightened heritage of individualism and tolerance. Full amnesia, though, was impossible, and they carried on strange dialogues with their Catholic or Jewish pasts. This was true for three individuals reared in interfaith homes, all married in 1850: Henry Charles Lea, James Gillespie Blaine, and Ellen Mordecai Mordecai.

In 1903, Henry Charles Lea (1825–1909), Mathew Carey's grandson, became president of the American Historical Association. A committed Unitarian, Lea was by profession a historian of the Catholic Church. His first book was *Superstition and Force* (1866); others followed, including *An Historical Sketch of Sacerdotal Celibacy in the Christian Church* (1867), *History of the Inquisition in the Middle Ages* (1887–88), and *History of Auricular Confession and Indulgences* (1896). His biographer believed in 1931 that Lea treated Catholicism fairly because his mother, Frances Carey, had absorbed her husband's Protestantism without fuss. Her "liberalism supplied an important background for the work of her son," which offered "no opportunity for any valid attack from the Catholic church."[133] The key word was "valid." Catholic critics of Lea were outspoken, and *Lippincott's Magazine* refused to publish one manuscript, "an excellent one, of course," because the journal was "disinclined to offend our Catholic readers."[134] Beginning with his earliest scholarship in the 1860s, Lea depicted Catholicism as hostile to "equality, freedom of conscience, liberal education, self-government, and, in short, all the forces which constitute progress and modern civilization."[135] "An infallible church" was "immovable," "sacerdotalism" deterred "human progress," and "loose-jointed and shambling" logic led prelates to think "arrogant assertion to be equivalent to proof."[136] These opinions were not unusual in Protestant America. But Lea's dismissal of the church, couched in history, seems unexpected from the grandson of a leading partisan of American Catholicism.

How did Lea arrive at so public and ideologically framed a critique of the Catholic Church? The answer is nearly as puzzling as the question: he agreed with his grandfather, with the crucial exceptions of perspective and tone. Mathew Carey had a vision of republican Catholicism rejecting an authoritarian past. "This people never will submit to the regime in civil or ecclesiastical affairs that prevails in Europe," he declared during the St. Mary's controversy in 1821.[137] He would have been distressed by nineteenth-century Catholicism's ultramontane direction, typified by the Syllabus of Errors of 1864 and the pronouncement of Papal Infallibility in 1869.[138] He was no more a friend of the medieval church than was Henry Charles Lea.

Carey was as dedicated and hopeful, however, as his grandson was censorious and detached. Educated to focus on ethics as religion's core, Lea made decisions that confirmed his connection with genteel Protestantism. He married his cousin Anna, Isaac's niece from Cincinnati. One partner in his publishing business was another cousin on his father's side. Close friends included William Henry Furness, Philadelphia's first Unitarian minister, and his son Horace Henry, a Shakespeare scholar. Civic-minded like Mathew Carey, Lea urged reform of municipal politics in the 1870s, a cause with an elitist flavor.[139] In 1901, Henry Baird, Lea's Catholic cousin, sent "by my grandson a reproduction of the engraved portrait of our Grandfather which was published in a Dublin magazine in 1784." Six years later, Baird again wrote to say that for "fifty years, less three months, I have pursued, with an enthusiasm worthy of our common grandfather, the study of economics."[140] Lea's replies, if any, have not survived; but for him, veneration of Mathew Carey played no comparable role. The interfaith marriage of Frances Carey and Isaac Lea permitted their son's migration to Protestantism. Here, he identified his grandfather's liberalism with the Protestant faith. Yet he still traveled back by the circuitous route of historical research to examine Carey's Catholicism. The absence of comment in Lea's papers on the obvious connection between his work and descent makes it seem that his turn to this past was as privately difficult as it was unavoidable. Growing up in an interfaith family forced questions of identity. The settlement Henry Lea devised was to become a Protestant student of the Catholic Church.

James Gillespie Blaine (1830–1893) similarly embraced his Protestant heritage. His Catholic mother, sisters, and Ewing kin did not keep him from the Protestant path his father prescribed. In 1850 he married Harriet Stanwood, moved into her family's house in Augusta, Maine, and became "close friends," in the words of a biographer, with his pastor at the First Congregational Church.[141] He knew he left something behind. Inviting his mother in Pennsylvania to visit in 1857, he asked, "will you venture into this Puritan land?"[142] But for Blaine, no Christian creed had a decisive advantage. He approached "the love of God, whom he saw not," the biographer wrote, "through love of man, whom he had seen."[143] Nor did he close all doors to Catholicism. His daughter Alice boarded nearby in 1869 at St. Catherine's school. When she married in 1883, Father Murphy of Augusta gave her a picture of Jesus. The Blaines were friendly, too, with their Catholic relations. After the Civil War, Ellen Ewing Sherman and her family lived only one door away in Washington, where Blaine and William T. Sherman held high posts in government. When President Garfield was shot in 1881, it was Ellen who called the carriage to drive to the White House with Harriet Blaine.[144] Rachel, the Shermans' daughter, was Alice Blaine's close companion. She had a small hand in the crisis during the winter of 1882–1883 that called the Blaines' Protestantism into question.

Two stories unfolded concurrently: Alice's engagement to a Catholic and her sister Margaret's temptation to convert to the Catholic faith of her grandmother Blaine. Probably Alice met John Coppinger, an Irish-born officer in the United States army, through the Shermans. Her mother left "Alice at General Sherman's," she characteristically told Margaret, "receiving officers in a fraternal manner."[145] Engaged in December 1882, Alice was soon married at home in Washington by a priest, following her conversion to her bridegroom's faith. Margaret, in Paris, was taken aback: "I was awfully surprised to hear that the wedding was to be Catholic, did not suppose Father would go so far as to allow that. Is Alice's conversion in the least a matter of conviction or merely of convenience to Coppinger? If she cares to she will get very much attracted to her new religion, and I have no doubt make an exceedingly devout Catholic."[146]

The events, doubtless stirring discomfort, proceeded without trauma. Alice "is marrying a charming, lovable man," her mother reflected. "The service," on February 7, 1883, "was all in English, and was very brief, but impressive, and as soon as it was over, the ribbons were dropped, and congratulations commenced."[147] Perhaps strangely, the key difficulty with Alice's marriage was that it distracted the Blaines from Margaret's religious crisis abroad.

"Why did you send that cablegram?" Margaret reproached her father for delegating friends to take her away from her convent school just days before Alice's wedding. "It was like a thunderclap this morning as I was contentedly studying my French lessons to be summoned to the salon, and met by that small patch of blue paper."[148]

The Blaines had every reason to fear their daughter's conversion. Arriving at the convent in November, Margaret, seventeen years old, complained that her uniform was "not fashionable" and, everywhere, "those watchful eyes were fixed upon me." But on January 28 she wrote home:

> Oh these dreadful religious doubts, one may laugh as they please when all goes smoothly. . . . When one is in a tight place, one has need of faith keen and sharpedged. . . . [I] fear I shall go with the tide and take a step that I shall regret forever. Then I am equally afraid that I am missing my chance, and that I ought to do now, what will certainly be much harder to do in the future. . . . When I first came I thought a priest about the most detestable being on earth, but I acknowledge that now when I compare them with Mott, and his domestic troubles, I find them a relief and a security.[149]

A reader of Margaret's diary could have predicted Catholicism's appeal. "I have read little, remembered less," and "I am very self-absorbed and selfish," she wrote a month before she enrolled, by her choice, at the convent school.[150] This was a young woman who inscribed Dorothea's creed from *Middlemarch* in her journal: "Widening the skirts of light, and making the struggle with darkness narrower."[151] Idealistic and frustrated, Margaret turned away from the Catholic Church, however, nearly as quickly as she had approached it. "As to Catholicism," she told her father on February 5, "don't give yourself a minute's worry." Returning to school, she would tell the nuns "that I have promised you and that they may as well give up all desires on the subject."[152]

In an era when American wealth could afford convent training abroad for bright, uncertain women, Margaret's experience was not unique. But as the capstone to the Blaine family's interfaith history, the drama contained elements with Enlightenment roots: the father's distress, the mother's republican logic, and the daughter's invocation of her grandmother's memory. On paper, James G. Blaine was silent, with the crucial exception of the rescuing telegram. His Protestantism, betraying its fragility, could abide one daughter's conversion in order to marry, but not a case of conscience in a second child perhaps tempted to become a nun. It was Harriet Blaine who voiced the liberalism that long permitted risky marriages; now she used it to defend the Protestant fold. "I am a great believer in the rights of reason, the privilege of thinking for yourself," she professed to Margaret just as James sent the cable; "I shall be woefully disappointed should you consent to any obligations which fetter the intellect."[153] Margaret, acquainted with her Catholic kin, was unprepared for the furor over her contemplated change of faith. "In fact it did not seem to me that you would have any extraordinary objections to going back to the religion of my grandmother," she informed her father. "But your cable changes the face of affairs."[154] In 1890 Margaret married a Protestant, Walter Damrosch, a well-known orchestra conductor.

Three years after Margaret's wedding, Blaine's Protestantism received final confirmation when his funeral took place at Washington's Presbyterian Church of the Covenant.[155] His religious commitment had shown little sign of conflict except for its defensive edge, the consequence of his mixed religious past. Not deeply pious, Blaine, like his wife, seemed confidently to have identified freedom with the Protestant faith. Reminders of the family's Catholicism, however, could not be suppressed. William Tecumseh Sherman, cousin by marriage, told Blaine in 1884 that he would decline the Republican presidential nomination to guard his family from anti-Catholic slurs. In 1886 Blaine openly censored the priest who secretly married his son James, only seventeen, to a Catholic. The death of Mother Angela Gillespie, another cousin and the first American Superior of the Sisters of the Holy Cross, came a year later. Blaine was "much pleased," his wife repeated to their sons, that the young men "of your own volition" attended her funeral: "Vicarious attention of this sort meets his heartiest approval."[156] Indirection was precisely the way Blaine preferred to deal with the Catholicism of his kin. Less lucky than Henry Lea at keeping his Catholic roots from reappearing in the immediate family, Blaine, like Lea, wore his Protestantism as armor to deflect his heritage. Neither man was as religiously adventuresome as his grandparents or parents, most likely because both carried the wearying baggage of decades of compromise at home.

In the same way, the Mordecai descendants reacted to their family's swirl of intermarriages, conversions, and clandestine evangelism with an instinct for simplification. Although nearly all of Jacob's progeny were formally Christians, some anchored identity in love of family itself, without heed to faith. In 1912, Ellen Mordecai Mordecai (1820–1916), Moses' daughter, recalled a religiously composite past in *Gleanings of Long Ago*. After the death of Margaret, her mother, in

1821, the children "had three mothers, for our aunts were as mothers to us all."[157] No doubt Ellen meant Nancy, Harriet, and Tempe Lane, Margaret's sisters in Raleigh. But at Jacob's Spring Farm outside Richmond, on visits as long as two years, there were "Aunt Laura," "Aunt Eliza," and "Aunt Emma."[158] "Grandma," Rebecca Mordecai, "would come up every night after we were in bed to hear us our prayers."[159] Ellen never said that the Mordecais were Jews or the Lanes Christians. When she looked back, kinship surpassed religion in importance. Her sister "and I still survive, old women, but loving each other, and loving the past, and loving the young ones who have grown up around us."[160] In her life as well as her thoughts, Ellen used domesticity to circumvent religious vexation. In 1850 she married her cousin, Samuel Mordecai of Mobile, son of her uncle Solomon. The child of a Jewish father and Christian mother, Samuel matched Ellen exactly. Their marriage choice was a statement that to be a Mordecai was as crucial as a decision to embrace either one of the family's religions.[161]

Attachment to family was a common theme in interfaith histories. But perhaps a woman of the time would have been more inclined than a man to let reverence for kinship edge aside public faith. Indeed, John Brooke Mordecai, Ellen's nephew, was both a family antiquarian and an outspoken Christian. This was Jacob's great-grandson, the descendant of his tenth child Augustus (1806–1847) and Augustus' Christian wife, Rosina Young. In 1923 John delivered a "Layman's Protest" against "Some Modern Teachings" at Richmond's St. James Episcopal Church, where he taught a Bible class. The speech questioned the right of "a small group of intellectuals to lead us into veritable jungles of theological and scientific discussion."[162] "Every man has a right to his own private beliefs; but no man while holding a position of authority in a Church is justified in publicly asserting beliefs that are contrary to the doctrines of that Church." "Modernists" seeking "to gratify the intellect of a scholarly few," Mordecai argued, "are starving the souls of the many."[163]

Clearly part of the debates of the 1920s over such questions as evolution and biblical authority, the address told a family story as well. John Mordecai was a serious Christian. Rather than send him on a path to spiritual indifference, his interfaith forebears produced a discerning and pious man. Still, Christianity was his choice, despite his acquaintance through genealogical interests with the family's Jews. It was the intermarriage of his grandparents that first raised the question of religious preference and presented Christianity as an option. John Mordecai, taking this route, ended up far from his Jewish roots, yet also strangely near. The voice of Jacob Mordecai, contending with Charleston's Jewish reformers in 1826, may be heard in John's quarrel with modernism. "We, too, love truth," John professed in 1923, "and it is high time that the laity, especially we mothers and fathers, raise our voice in solemn protest." Erudite and impassioned, he cited sources ranging from Paul the Apostle to Aldous Huxley to defeat "new and dangerous teachings."[164] Here again was Jacob's impatience with Judaism's "visionary and destructive" faction.[165] No theory of heredity is needed to observe that religious polemicism was a Mordecai family tradition.

Descendants of couples intermarrying in the early republic were complicated people, but they were not often bold. Henry Charles Lea, James G. Blaine, and Ellen Mordecai, all growing up among mixed-faith kin, tried to wrap themselves and their relations in Protestant mantles. Perhaps stirred by flight from confusing childrearing or by eagerness for Protestantism's legitimacy, they made definite religious decisions, seemingly to quell doubts. Even then, their Catholic or Jewish roots could not be kept from view. The inheritance they received from parents was the need to manage a specific kind of past.

The origins of their families' intermarriages in the years before 1830 lay in commonplace conditions of republican culture. For Americans generally, religious traditionalism stood in balance with cosmopolitanism and civility. No more surprising, it was self-seeking individualism—the pursuit of happiness—in the children of Enlightened parents that tipped circumstances toward mixing and tolerance, now within households. Faith, liberalism, and family, all standard American themes, produced interfaith marriages. Although the children of the early families were inclined to reject the uncertainty of their backgrounds, interfaith marriage itself did not slow. But by the mid-nineteenth century, the religious environment had changed. Jews and Catholics were organized, and mixed marriage was much debated. Couples now made their decisions in the midst of public discussion.

Conversations about Interfaith Marriage

Discussions of interfaith marriage in America began as early as the weddings themselves. *Arthur Mervyn* (1799–1800), by Charles Brockden Brown, was the first American novel to depict a mixed marriage. This story of a country boy, who must learn to decipher Philadelphia's deceptions without yielding to its corruptions, makes relations between men and women into moral symbols. Arthur is acquainted with evidence of ill will. A "rude, ignorant, and licentious" servant girl had seduced his widowed father, and the forger Welbeck impregnated the mysterious Clemenza with an illegitimate child.[1] Now Arthur himself must choose a wife: either the innocent Quaker, Eliza Hadwin, only fifteen years old, or Ascha Fielding, a Jew. A woman of "superior age, sedateness, and prudence," Ascha is "dark and almost sallow," as "'unsightly as a *night-hag.*'"[2] And she has a past. She was married in London to a man greedy for her father's fortune, who abandoned her when the business failed. Yet for all this, "'no creature ever had more power to bewitch.'" *Arthur Mervyn* ends with the anticipated marriage of Ascha and Arthur, "the happiest of men."[3]

The connection between Brown's fiction and the facts of early American interfaith marriages was hardly simple. A resident of Philadelphia, Brown must have understood the city's cosmopolitanism that permitted these marriages to flourish. His novel also exhibited psychological realism when it portrayed the allure of the exotic and forbidden. When Arthur kisses Ascha fervently, with "a filial freedom and affection" for a beloved he calls "mamma," Brown communicated how difference and proscription may fuel romance.[4] His insight, however, did not penetrate ethnic stereotypes. Swarthy, foreign, sadly marked by experience, Ascha resembles the mythic Jew. Although Brown was an unconventional Protestant, he unskeptically mirrored the image of Jews held by the cultural majority. Yet social accuracy was not his deeper goal. *Arthur Mervyn* was a parable about America, and the choice between Eliza and Ascha was a figure for national alternatives: to keep the republic insular and pure or to admit the unfamiliar. During the nineteenth century, American views of mixed marriages changed, but the literary interplay of reporting and symbolism, visible here, did not. Public debates were nonetheless influential, affecting both the way Americans thought about their religious differences and how interfaith families behaved.

Sustained discussion of interfaith marriage in America began in the 1840s. It coincided with the growth of immigration, institutions, and channels of public expression among Catholics and Jews. Thoughts about interfaith families were part of broader dialogues about what it meant to be Catholic or Jewish in America. Ideas circulated within each faith community, including the wide sphere of Protestantism, much more than across religious lines. Prejudice and apprehension framed each group's separate conversation.[5] By the 1880s, the tempers of American Catholic, Jewish, and Protestant opinion were clearly distinguished. This was the key development of the mid-century era, not only for public culture but for families. Because couples of the period did not break away from religious practice, the tone of talk about interfaith marriage, whether by clergy or neighbors, became either a stumbling block or moral support. Which affiliation a family chose was much affected by how friendly people were. Now intergenerational religious stories of parents, children, and grandchildren unfolded in a more sharply pluralistic setting.[6]

Catholics worried about protecting community, Jews debated issues of descent, and Protestants barely spoke of mixed marriage. But how uniform was opinion within each group, and were there alternative, secular conversations? A comparison of prose statements, mainly by clergymen, and fiction by women writers picks up dissonant notes within communities. Even more, a sensationalized romance in the popular press signaled that religious viewpoints, though dominant, were not uncontested.

Official Opinions

Pastoral letters, sermons, magazines, and advice books transmitted ideas about interfaith marriage from religious leaders to the faithful. Intended to describe and guide behavior, this literature seemed unable to penetrate impressions and arrive at facts. There was little agreement, most basically, on how commonplace mixed marriage was. The first sustained Jewish periodical, the *Occident,* reported in 1845 that "many of our people intermarry"; in 1866, it called the practice "epidemic." The editor of the *Israelite* judged the subject "useless" in 1880, however, because such couples were "exceedingly few."[7] The Catholic bishop of Denver declared in 1889 that "the utter depravity of mankind was brought about by mixed marriages" and mourned their "great increase." Most of these unions were invalid, because dispensations enabling them were "rarely" given.[8] A canon lawyer disagreed: permission could be "obtain[ed] for the mere asking!"[9] Protestant journals, rarely discussing intermarriage directly, did not calculate their frequency. Their allusions to "unsuitable," "offhand," and "runaway" matches nonetheless added to the sense of marital disorder.[10] Then as now, reasonable estimates of rates of interfaith marriages were nearly impossible to obtain. Discrepancies in the sources are not cause for censure, however, but are reminders that denominational writings were ideology, determined as much by the fears and goals of the clergy as by social demography. Oscillating between denial and panic, public statements by Catholics, Jews, and Protestants dealt with intermarriage in ways that reflected each community's preoccupations.[11]

For American Catholic leaders, interfaith marriage became a sign of the threat to Catholic integrity posed by a religiously diverse society. Sacred order, all along, was at stake. But over time, blame for apostasy shifted from the deficiencies of Catholics to their contact with nonbelievers. Around 1800, Archbishop Marechal of Baltimore castigated fathers who say they "are too overcharged with temporal affairs" to have "time to spare for the purpose of instructing your children." He did not look further than parents who "made no prayers, received no sacraments" to find the reason that "children walk in the way of perdition."[12] In contrast, John Purcell, Archbishop of Cincinnati, divided his attention in 1853 between "the dangers we fear from without" and the evils "realized from within."[13] He understood that two Catholics were capable of "marrying in haste and ruining at leisure." Too often they "went to be married where they were not known," spent the wedding night "in sinful excesses," and did not "say the Rosary, or go to Church and to Communion together."[14] Purcell devoted most of his pastoral letter, however, to mixed marriages. These families risked "treating the religion which is false like the religion which is true" and "teaching children by parental example to be indifferent to the truth, or falsehood, of religion."[15] Now the errors of non-Catholics appeared alongside the immorality of Catholics as challenges to faith. Sharply conscious of the church's boundaries, Purcell undertook to defend them, explaining the canons on intermarriage, conditions of dispensations, and petitions to reverse excommunications for unlawful unions. This rhetoric sought real and symbolic effects: to deter intermarriages and to draw the line between Catholics and others.

The sacraments, in the prelates' view, infused grace into fallen nature; without the church's blessing, humankind persisted unredeemed. This link between the supernatural work of the priesthood and any hope of restoring natural virtue helps explain why anxieties about unsanctified marriages, performed without Catholic clergy or a nuptial Mass, continued to rise. In 1882 Bishop Michael O'Farrell of Trenton planned to focus his first pastoral letter on education. This was a compelling subject: two years later, American bishops at the Third Plenary Council issued a *"command"* to parents to "procure a truly Christian education for their dear offspring" and ordered each parish to support a school.[16] O'Farrell decided to begin his instruction not with parochial schooling, however, but with the family instead. "All society rests upon the family," and "if the family ties be loosely joined or easily broken, society would lose its consistency and cohesive power, and soon relapse into barbarism and anarchy."[17] Although mixed-faith couples were the theme of the letter's third section out of four, O'Farrell began his lament in part two, on the marriage sacrament. The church looked with sadness on Catholics who "seek to be united in marriage outside her pale, and by others than priests." "Truly," he judged, "their conduct must be considered as sacrilegious, as manifesting a contempt for their Church, and a complete disregard of her sacrament."[18] The words "sacrilegious," "contempt," and "disregard" evoked an image of the church besieged by worldliness and indifference. Here the non-Catholic party was more the occasion of sin than its cause. Either way, Catholicism stood vulnerable in America, and, by O'Farrell's logic, if families did not honor the sacraments, civilization would decline.

Parishioners might not be swayed by grave predictions about society's future, so the clergy catalogued disorders in interfaith households as well. Not only did young lovers resist their parents, but sometimes, according to Archbishop Purcell, ambitious elders "force[d] their sons or daughters, to marry against their will" for the sake of social advancement.[19] Once married, mixed couples contended with unnatural gender relations. A Catholic wife could not find "a representative of the Lord" in her Protestant spouse, Bishop Joseph Machebeuef of Denver wrote in 1889. "For how can a devoted Catholic wife be subject to her Protestant husband in all things!"[20] Subordination to heterodoxy strangely led to abandonment. Raising children, the Catholic mother finds "the whole burden of this religious and moral training laid on her." Worse, she may be "hampered by prejudices." Machebeuef concluded: "What guarantee has she," because Protestants allow divorce, "that she will not be put aside one day by her non-Catholic husband?"[21] This picture of the Catholic wife, paying dearly for yielding to temptation, drew on ideas about women's weakness as old as Eve. Indeed, the phrase "peril of perversion," current in canon law to denote the risk of intermarriage for orthodoxy, carried sexual overtones conjuring thoughts of an elemental disruption of nature.[22] Yet clinging to Catholic truth in a hostile home, Machebeuef's ideal mother seemed, no less, like the American church. Contradictory and powerful, these meanings attached to the intermarried wife held a clear message: love the church, love your Catholic spouse, and be rewarded with a family made happy by its consonance with God's design.

American Catholic writers knew well that their teachings on family were part of a transatlantic discussion. For the European church, the advent of revolutions, secular states, and liberal society challenged clerical control of weddings and encouraged mixed unions. The Vatican issued successive instructions after midcentury that alternately proscribed interfaith marriages and systematized dispensations. In

1877, the Sacred Congregation for the Propagation of the Faith listed sixteen circumstances in which priests could perform intermarriages, guidelines that remained normative until Vatican II.[23] Some American prelates were frustrated by official ambivalence. In 1882, Bishop O'Farrell spoke approvingly of papal censure of intermarriage voiced in 1858, then tried to contain the damage of "more recent constitutions of the Sovereign Pontiffs [which] relax the severity of the canons in some degree": if now "mixed marriage may occasionally be allowed, this is only done for the gravest reasons and very reluctantly, and not without express condition of requiring pledges which have their foundation in the natural and divine law."[24] O'Farrell's testiness with Rome obscured the practical leniency of the American church. By the 1870s, at least some American dioceses printed dispensation forms, attesting to the frequency of their use. Even so, similar strategies for dealing with interfaith couples throughout Western Catholicism did not change the fact that American priests were obliged to honor shifting policies devised abroad.[25]

Nor could the clergy act freely at home. Catholic responses to mixed marriage occurred in an environment defined by inequalities. Often Catholics were the object of prejudice, not just crude nativism, but insulting assumptions. In the midst of publicity about secret marriages of minors performed by irresponsible clergy, the state of Massachusetts circulated a pamphlet in 1873 reiterating the need to check licenses and record weddings with town clerks. Addressed to "ministers, and others solemnizing marriages," the "others" specifically named were justices of the peace and clerks of Friends' meetings.[26] One copy, however, belonged to "Jos. M. Finotti, Cath Priest, Arlington," who wrote his name on the cover. Perhaps the document intended "ministers" to include priests and rabbis. But Finotti thought of himself as a "Cath Priest," and, by his signature, quietly resisted his invisibility in the text. Yet Catholics, too, held prejudices. John Purcell of Cincinnati praised Christian marriage by contrasting it with polygamy and divorce in the Hebrew Bible, permitted by God because of "the hardness of the hearts of the Jews, and to exhibit more clearly the superiority of the Christian dispensation."[27] Diminished on one side, Catholics instinctively reduced other opponents. Either way, no discussion of interfaith marriage escaped unkind presuppositions about outsiders.

At the same time, laments and warnings built community, at least

No.

Diœcesis Vincennopolitanæ.

*Per has præsentes testamur quod, perpensis adjunctis,
et vi facultatum a S. Sede Apostolica Ill'mo. ac Rev'mo. Episcopo die
11 Mensis Februarii anno. 1888, usque ad diem 11 ejusdem Mensis
1893, concessarum, et Infrascripto subdelegatarum, dispensavimus*

Thomam J. Brooks acath. bap.

et Helenam (Lyons) Dickey, Cath.

ab impedimento   Mixtæ Religionis

*ita ut valide ac licite matrimonium queant inter se inire; dummodo mulier
non fuerit rapta, vel si rapta fuerit, in raptoris potestate non existat,
iniuncta tamen congrua eleemosyna in pium opus ad arbitrium Ordinarii
eroganda.*

In quorum fidem has literas dedimus, die vigesimo

Mensis Julii   1888.

D. V' Donaghue

Cancellarius Diœcesis Vincennopolitanæ.

Revdo. Dno. E. Audran

---

3. Catholic dispensation form, Vincennes, Indiana, 1888, releasing the couple
from the impediment "mixed religions" and permitting the marriage of the
Protestant groom and Catholic bride to be performed by a priest. Courtesy of the
Archives of the University of Notre Dame.

---

rhetorically. If religiously promiscuous romance raised fears of Catholic vulnerability, the campaign against it cemented orthodoxy. Prelates believed that "a lamentable ignorance" of duty led to invalid marriages, and they took pains to enlighten parishioners.[28] Pastoral letters, often along with papal communications, were read in parishes. Bishop O'Farrell told priests to communicate his teachings to "churches where there are resident priests, on the Sunday immediately after its reception, and in the mission churches at the earliest opportunity."[29] In Cincinnati in the 1850s, Bishop Purcell wanted Catholic doctrine on family to be heard "particularly among the laborers on the public works, now so numerous."[30] Plans for oral transmission meant that even those who could not read, or at least did not read

English, might be reached. More literate Catholics found additional instruction in novels, periodicals, and advice books. Many of them were written by priests, but women also produced didactic texts. Lelia Hardin Bugg's *The Correct Thing for Catholics*, in its twelfth edition by 1891, addressed the aspiring middle class: it was incorrect "to spend more than can well be afforded on wedding festivities," yet correct "to have an elegant and costly reception if one's means permit."[31] On mixed marriages, Bugg adhered to canon law. Excommunication might be imposed, but dispensations could be obtained for "grave reasons." Only notes of unashamed practicality distinguished Bugg's manual from the pastoral letters. Though it was correct usage for "Catholics to marry Catholics," petitioners for dispensations should be prepared to pay "a tax for some charitable object."[32] Subtle differences aside, these varied forms of preaching reached into Catholic communities to bind parishioners doctrinally and, if heeded, socially as well.

Perhaps it is wise to be skeptical about whether Catholics who inclined to intermarry were sufficiently close to the church to hear its official voice. Yet if they listened, the message was clear. Threatened by the apostasy of mixed marriage, the church in America would triumph by its charity. Individual Catholics experienced this redemptive love in the form of forgiveness. Virtually every tract on intermarriage followed a pattern: censure of mixed families, reasons for dispensations, penalties for their neglect, conditions of penance. Reconciliation was the key. Full of fire and brimstone, writers initially pictured exclusion from the sacraments, denial of "churching" after childbirth, even excommunication. The difficulty of obtaining absolution was a deterrent as well. Bishop O'Farrell required public penance, "either by themselves, or by the priest speaking publicly at the Mass for them, shall [they] ask pardon of the congregation for the scandal and bad example which they have given."[33] Only bishops, not ordinary priests, were empowered to absolve. Still, the essential fact was that it was never too late to be restored to the church. This was made possible, the Bishop of Grand Rapids wrote in 1904, by grace expressed as love. The church asked priests to approach the wayward in the spirit of Jesus: "Mindful of the Savior's words 'There shall be joy in heaven upon one sinner that doth penance more than over ninety-nine who need no penance,' invite and help them to return to the home of their heavenly Father ever ready to receive them with open arms."[34] More commonly, the church was "the mother of the spiritual life," eager to protect "her children" from "loss of faith."[35] Now the welcoming figure of the "mother church," recognizable to every Catholic, replaced the image of the intermarried wife beset by her Protestant husband's biases and neglect. The Catholic literature on interfaith marriage was fundamentally hopeful. Nature would be restored and the church repaired, because Catholicism had the means to acknowledge repentance.

Jewish discussions of mixed marriage had much in common with Catholic writings. Again, interfaith families were part of a deeper dilemma: how a religious minority could maintain observance and transmit loyalty in a Protestant culture. Communal and family integrity were not dispassionate questions for Jews, nor did they air their views in a neutral climate. Similar conditions of Jewish and Catholic dialogues, however, did not erase differences. Catholics most typically dealt with interfaith marriage in pastoral instructions, uniform in doctrine and practical in temper; Jews, in rabbinic debates. Discourse focused on communal law, addressed mainly fellow rabbis, and admitted disagreements. A couple contemplating intermarriage heard much said and might see a way to make a Jewish life; but they found no uniform rules like those of the Catholic Church.

The rabbinic tone of public discussion grew along with the immigration of European-born rabbis and training of American clergy. During the 1840s and 1850s, the first decades of a sustained American Jewish press, the exchange of views remained lay-centered. Isaac Leeser, religious leader of Congregation Mikveh Israel in Philadelphia, must have depended on lay writers to help fill the *Occident* (1843–1869), which he edited. Dr. Simeon Abrahams of New York contributed "Intermarrying with Gentiles" in 1845. Censuring this practice for disrupting "well-established lines of ancestry" and eroding "the landmarks of our religion," Abrahams urged synagogues not to allow intermarried men "in any way to be countenanced or regarded as Jews." They must "not be permitted to purchase or hire a seat," "called to the reading of the law," or "reckoned to make Minyan," the ten men required for prayers.[36] Robert Lyon, editor of the *Asmonean* (1849–1858) in New York as well as the *Mercantile Journal,* publicized synagogue policies, in part for his readers' information but also because "some are deserving of adoption" more widely.[37] In 1855, he announced that Congregation Anshe Mayriv in Chicago did not admit intermarried men as members; in 1856, that Shearith Israel in New York would not inter these men in the Jewish cemetery, although the Reform congregation, Emanu-El, might do so "with the consent of the Trustees."[38] Key features of antebellum lay commentaries recurred in later texts: a moralizing tone, calls for strict measures, and portents of catastrophe. The "very existence of the Israelites as a separate nation" was at stake, Abrahams warned, anticipating future jeremiads.[39] Still, the Jewish layman took a practical view of mixed marriage. It was bad behavior, and synagogues had to take immediate steps.

An essay—"Who Is a Jew?"—in the *Israelite* in 1890 shows how the tone of Jewish writing subsequently changed. Its author, Bernhard Felsenthal, rabbi of Chicago's Sinai Congregation since 1861, approached intermarriage by examining the status of the children of mixed couples in Jewish law. Readers would have recognized a method of reasoning typical of the rabbis who produced the Talmud. His argument covered all possible circumstances: was any marriage of a Jew and gentile religiously valid? was the child of a Jewish mother a Jew? of an apostate? of a convert? First laying out the orthodox answers, Felsenthal, a Reform rabbi, gave a liberal response. Despite rejection of mixed marriages by *halakhah,* the body of Jewish law, bonds contracted "in accordance with the laws of the state" should be accounted "perfectly valid by Jewish rabbis and congregations, and the children in such families, if so desired by parents, should be recognized as Jews."[40] This conclusion could open the way to new policies. Interfaith families might join synagogues and raise their children as Jews. Nonetheless, there was an odd fit between Felsenthal's historically rooted, formalistic argument and progressive intent. In 1909 Isaac Moses, another Reform rabbi, addressed his colleagues "as a man who has faced the world" and particularly "bridal couples that came to him in the perplexity of their hearts, and to whom I could not come with authorities and with theories," but "with my whole human heart."[41] Moses was a renegade, dismissing tradition for sentiment and performing mixed marriages. After one such wedding in 1880, he fled Milwaukee at night to escape his angry congregation.[42] His radicalism aside, however, Moses discerned the distance between rabbinic rhetoric and the warm realities of interfaith romance. But debates on law and ritual remained the intellectual framework in which these marriages occurred.

Much talk took place within the Reform movement. After mid-century, Reform Judaism edged aside older orthodoxy and commanded better means of communication, particularly Isaac Mayer Wise's *Israelite,* than did newer immigrants. Liberal laymen were active in 1873 in founding of the Union of American Hebrew Congregations; but it was the graduation of the first class of rabbis from Hebrew Union College in 1883 and formation of the Central Conference of American Rabbis in 1889 that signaled the Reform clergy's professional arrival.[43]

Their debates often began with dilemmas involving ritual. Although Jewish identity traditionally passed through a child's mother, a Hartford rabbi asked the *Israelite* in 1862 if the son of a Jewish father and Christian mother could be circumcised at the parents' request. Thirty years' experience did not give him "the least clue to solve this problem in the affirmative."[44] Wise, the editor, waffled over the years. Many queries around 1880 provoked him to say that "where the mother confers any right on her offspring, the father certainly does in preference to her, if he acknowledges fathership."[45] Yet in 1899, at the end of his life, Wise argued so strongly for the talmudic basis of the maternal line, "irrespective of its father's race or faith," that he seemed by omission to reject patrilineal descent.[46] Perhaps Wise's equivocation stemmed from liberal Judaism's reluctance to impose orthodoxy on belief, or, more likely, his uncertainty about how far tolerance should go.

Free-form conversion ceremonies stirred related exchanges about accepting converts in connection with marriage. Much comment was provoked in 1860, when Rabbi Samuel Adler converted the Presbyterian wife of a member at Temple Emanu-El in New York. Without rabbinic court *(beit din)* or ritual immersion *(mikveh),* she made a pledge and said prayers, mainly in English, before the open ark.[47] Isaac Leeser spoke for orthodoxy when he denounced "false guides" who would devise such a "mockery of Judaism."[48] Isaac Wise overlooked irregularities in the rite to praise Adler for heeding the key *halakhic* requirement for conversion, sincere intent: "seeing that her motives were pure and disinterested, [he] instructed her some time in the principles of the reformed Jewish religion."[49] When the convert was a man, there were further words about the need for circumcision. After rabbis in Kansas City, Missouri, and Vicksburg, Mississippi, accepted uncircumcised men in 1890, the *Israelite* was flooded with letters, pro and con. Wise now took a conservative stand. We "act according to modern ideas to a certain extent; to a certain extent, however, we are Israelites," and "we do not subscribe to the *modus operandi* of the two rabbis."[50] Suspicion of conversion itself, particularly as an adjunct to marriage, underwrote dialogues about ritual procedure. In 1845 Isaac Leeser categorically rejected the conversion of spouses, because rabbis would be obliged to "suspect interested motives."[51] David Philipson, a Reform rabbi, associated conversion distastefully with Christian missions to Jews. Responding to "laymen" in 1890, he explained that Judaism "taught that a man's goodness will save him, no matter what his opinions may be," and hence did not seek converts.[52] Ambivalent at best about conversion, rabbis focused on ritual options, reaching no clear resolution about proselytes at any level of discussion.

Whether rabbis should officiate at interfaith weddings was debated as well. This, too, was a ritual issue, though oddly blending considerations of religious law and professional identity. Perhaps because most commentators agreed that these marriages were religiously invalid, discussion shifted to attributes of the rabbi's role: freedom and authority. "A rabbi enjoys perfect freedom of action; *the* rabbi is bound to certain obligations."[53] Rabbi Solomon Sonneschien of St. Louis explained that "the" rabbi must honor his congregational contract, as well as think, before blessing a mixed couple, that "the rabbi who lowers himself and his sacred office to such an act, prostitutes his ministerial dignity."[54] His 1880 essay contained at least two subtexts: aspiring American rabbis must take care to protect their authority, and their presence at mixed-faith weddings would lend false legitimacy, if not sanctity, to the practice. By 1909, when the Central Conference of American Rabbis passed its first resolution against interfaith marriage, their attention focused more closely on the tension between duty and freedom. The assembly rejected a text specifying "that a rabbi ought not to officiate at the marriage between a Jew or Jewess and a person professing a religion other than Judaism." Respect for individual conscience led to softened wording: intermarriage should "be discouraged by the American Rabbinate."[55] Either way, rabbinic thinking became increasingly self-referential. In social fact, some rabbis reported to the *Israelite* that they married mixed couples; most did not.[56] Jewish laymen may at times have officiated, since rabbis, unlike priests, possessed no special grace. All the while, the issue of rabbis performing mixed marriages commanded a rhetorical importance that made sense mainly in light of who the speakers were.

These dialogues on descent, conversion, and weddings can be summed up in positive or negative terms, both somewhat true. Beginning in the early centuries of the Common Era, rabbis produced briefs called *responsa* to guide religious practice; the American writings, exploring *halakhic* precedents, continued the tradition.[57] The method promised thoroughness, precision, and, like the *talmud* itself, the chance for many views to be heard. It also risked disunity and formalism. Breaking down intermarriage into its legal components skirted plain issues about behavior and consequences. To be sure, rulings about ritual determined if couples had access to communal privileges and might live a Jewish life. But the goals of marriage and hazards of mixed marriage easily got lost in texts on status and rites.

Carrying on these debates in a liberal environment brought surprising liabilities. For one, free discussion encouraged inconclusiveness. There were "no legal disabilities" for American Jews, the *Occident* stated in 1845, and fewer in Europe than in the past, yet liberty was a mixed blessing for policy.[58] At conferences, European rabbis were much divided over interfaith marriage. German leaders at Braunschweig tepidly approved it in 1844; they reversed themselves at Leipzig in 1869. All the while, reforming and orthodox parties increasingly parted ways. Dissension, or, seen more positively, Jewish pluralism, grew along with the opening of the ghettos. In the ancient world, the Talmud's arguments, though admitting diverse voices, reached points of resolution. These were closed, rabbinic dialogues in Palestinian and Babylonian communities of exile. In the nineteenth-century West, in contrast, scholarly authority was less persuasive, mutual respect less secure, and compromise, it seemed, more dispensable. Many American rabbis of the midcentury era had been trained in Germany. They brought their differences with them, and free speech in America favored their expression. Although Jews understood that mixed marriage was objectionable, little else about it was uncontested.[59]

More problematic, open debates were inevitably overheard. Conversations could not be kept to whispers within Jewish circles. At the same time that rabbis examined religious issues, they had to deflect anti-Semitism. In 1881, Goldwin Smith, a British-born humanist, made Jewish opposition to intermarriage the centerpiece in his image of Jews as conspiratorial, unprincipled, and unpatriotic. Smith told the *Nation* that Jews had "thrust" England toward war with Russia to advance "trivial interests and quarrels of their own," not, as they claimed, to halt pogroms. If Russian Jews were persecuted, this was "the consequence of the extortion" of Christians by Jews. Gentiles had a right to "guard ourselves against their tribal bias," for Jews make "race a religion" and hence are not "the very best of candidates for citizenship." "When the Jews lay aside tribalism and intermarry with their Gentile fellow-citizens, the conflict will gradually subside."[60]

Prejudice constructs arguments in ways that block easy refutation. When Isaac Wise responded to Smith in the *Israelite*, he was in a bind: he could not reject mixed marriages without confirming his opponent's stereotype or accept them without violating his principles, and, more dangerously, stirring unspoken gentile distaste for contact with Jews. Shrewdly, he faced Smith's innuendoes about Jewish character directly—"vulgar assertions," in his words—then denied the relevance of the concept of race. "The racial question was never discussed or considered by Jews, and intermarriage never was and is not now a question of races; it was and is now a question of religion."[61] This premise invited Wise to showcase his Reform view of mixed marriage, emerging in the shadow of the rabbis' exchanges on Jewish law. He worked hard over the years to cast Judaism as one religion among others; no longer conceived as a nation or people, Jews would be identified by their convictions. This made interfaith marriage a problem of disagreement. Wise lectured his congregation one Friday evening in 1879: "It is an element of disturbance in any family if spouses confess two different religions, and a cause of contention in the education of children."[62] Oddly, when he spoke of confessional differences, Wise's teaching sounded like the pastoral warnings of the Catholic clergy. He promoted his reasoning as the Reform creed, however, valuable for its modern temper, polemical utility, and persuasiveness for American Jews exposed to a Christian culture.

Discordances, finally, marked American Jewish discussion of mixed marriages. Wise's analysis of the issue as religious had the smooth logic of ideology, but seemed out of touch with the impassioned debates on ritual and law. The rabbis' hearts lay in examining the details of who was a Jew and how Jewishness should be acknowledged. If mixed-faith couples sought solutions within Judaism, they worked

out answers about conversions, weddings, and children within congregations. Local freedom and flexibility were advantages, but lack of
clarity about mixed couples' status was not. It could not have been
easy for interfaith families to find their way.[63]

Most Jewish-Christian couples chose to live as Christians, however,
for the sake of social advantage. Invisibility must have been their goal,
although prejudice at times upset their desire to blend in. The "exclusion of a lady from a hotel on Staten Island because she bore a Jewish name" was reported in the New York *Independent,* a Protestant
weekly, in 1880.[64] The "lady was not a Jew, and her husband, though
of Jewish descent, was a Christian in creed and received into Christian
society." The editor cast the incident as a case of mistaken identity
and poor judgment, because the hotel owner, a German, behaved
with "Christian intolerance." What was unusual about the article was
that it appeared in the paper at all. Silence was the characteristic
Protestant response to interfaith marriage. Indeed, the *Independent*
praised the husband for "very properly laugh[ing] at the affair as ri-
diculous," bringing it to a quick close.[65] Protestant society and intermarried couples harbored the same wish: that these families would
disappear.

It is almost impossible to find Protestant discussions of interfaith
marriage. Whereas Catholic and Jewish leaders worried about it publicly and frequently, Protestants did not. Despite the spectrum of
Protestant denominations and Protestant dominance of the secular
press, few sermons, essays, news reports, or advice columns mentioned mixed marriage.[66] Goldwin Smith's proposal to make families
the route to assimilation was not unique. But his idea seemed symbolic and, as phrased, unreal. It is hard to imagine that Smith would
welcome his own child's wedding to a Jew, or even conceive this might
occur.[67]

Yet such marriages clearly took place. Reasons for the discrepancy
between social fact and rhetorical neglect are not, on reflection, obscure. The Protestant majority gained much and lost little by quietly
absorbing interfaith families. In crude terms of numbers, Protestantism added households. Declining to mention strangers in their midst
protected an impression of seamless hegemony and exerted pressure
on mixed families to honor Protestant norms. Religiously, Protestant
evangelicalism cared more about adult choices than family origins
and might overlook a person's roots. Far worse to lament intermar-

riage loudly, admitting threat, than to manage it discreetly. Besides, disapproval of intermarrying could be presumed in Protestant circles, and fear of gossip or social ostracism would deter the less bold. This is a theory to explain the scarcity of Protestant discussions of interfaith marriage resting on three types of evidence: Protestant commentary on both religious minorities and marriage, private behavior, and texts mentioning interfaith romance.

Middle-of-the-road Protestants spoke of Catholics and Jews with nervous cordiality. The *Independent* (1846–1928)—founded by Congregational clergymen, open to other denominations, and published in New York—was one journal that registered religious diversity with acceptance, but not concessions. Protestant superiority was unquestioned. Not only did the paper tirelessly report progress in the conversion of the Jews, but in 1880 it credited "Protestant missions" with a "universal renaissance" of "modern science and pure Christianity." Even Catholics are "now very much like Protestants."[68] Still, there was an undercurrent of self-doubt. Edward Everett Hale, the respected Unitarian, examined whether biblical scholarship produced "insincerity in the pulpit." Rev. Charles Thwing, Disciples of Christ, wondered if there was a "passing of religion" among the young.[69] This soul-searching, surely sincere, still had the temper of ritual bloodletting, strengthening Protestants in the face of challenge. The *Independent* alternately surveyed Jews and Catholics with generosity or worry. It decried the Jews' expulsion from Morocco in 1860 and the German "war on the Semitic race," then recorded escalating numbers of Jewish university students without comment.[70] It praised Pope Leo XIII as a "reformer" who would appeal to "intelligent Catholics," all the while running fillers on the "rapid increase of the Celtic race" and expansion of the Catholic press.[71] The tone of editorial commentary was friendly; the cryptic facts, for Protestants, spoke for themselves. A divided mind did not preclude minority contributors. George Deshon, Catholic convert and priest, described Catholic missions in the summer of 1890, soon followed by Henry Pereira Mendes, rabbi of New York's oldest Sephardic synagogue, on "The Judaic Sabbath."[72] The paper adhered to cautious liberalism, based on the premise that, in America, Protestants would retain religious control.

Interfaith families did not have to dig deep to find a message for them: adopt Protestant standards. Rebecca Harding Davis, a popular writer, explained in 1890 that "submission to the American idea" was the duty of "foreigners." "It is time that [the American] asserted himself in this his true character and that he reminded his guests who refuse to submit to his laws and customs that here, the majority rules, and that he is the majority, and that he has still the power of wholly closing the door again them."[73] Davis's essay, "The Modest Naturalized Citizen," was an occasional piece for the Fourth of July. Not surprisingly, in the spring of the same year the *Independent* gave extended coverage to parochial schooling and reported on *talmud Torahs* in the fall. Education to maintain Catholic or Jewish traditions fit poorly into the Protestant vision of assimilation.[74] Any custom preserving differences was suspect. The Jews' "'mark of the Abrahamic covenant,' their Seventh-day Sabbath, their peculiar dietary rules, separate them from the rest of the people," the editors wrote. "They hold themselves apart from intermarriage."[75] A decade after Goldwin Smith, mixed marriage reappeared in criticism of Jews' "ostentatious freedom," which made them "as disagreeable and noisy as many Negroes are." A "modest" demeanor was the admission ticket to the mainstream.[76] Interfaith couples who listened to Protestants found instruction on culture instead of religion. As the faith of the majority, Protestantism was a way of life long committed to the malleability of character. Protestant writing implied that if interfaith families behaved like Protestants, religious issues would fall into place.

At the same time, a countercurrent of warning sent signals that the marriage market was hazardous. "Suppress differences" was the advice to mixed couples, but "avoid these romances" could more subtly be heard. The *Ladies' Home Journal,* begun in Philadelphia in 1883, addressed Christians and, quietly, Jews. Instructions on making "Christmas Decorations" in 1888 showed how to entwine flowers around a cross and *magen David,* without identifying the religious meaning of either one.[77] No reader, however, could miss the lesson that marriages contracted in haste and built on deception were in crisis. There were "runaway" matches brought on by impulsiveness. Women did not know whom they were marrying. "Offhand Marriages" in 1889 told the story of a girl who unwittingly wed an escaped convict. "How Girls Deceive Their Parents" exposed "men ever ready to take advantage of ignorance and innocence, or to encourage recklessness and impropriety," such as lying to fathers and mothers to hide questionable dates.[78] This cautionary litany about misleading appearances may be read as the reflex of a mobile and impersonal society.[79] It did not necessarily pertain to mixed marriage. Still, the articles gave plain advice: the best way to be sure about a suitor was to stick to men acquainted with your parents and friends. Prudence, if followed as a general rule, would steer young people away from interfaith marriages.

Publications could afford to preach indirectly because private opinion repeated their core thoughts: disapproval of intermarrying or, if need be, accommodation. Fear of gossip or of being shunned must have been a deterrent. Zebulon Vance, U.S. senator from North Carolina, anticipated possible scandal when, as a widower and Presbyterian, he married a Catholic in 1880. He confided to his fiancée: "My interview with the preacher Rev. Dr. Harding was the most interesting, as I was most anxious to know from him how my church people would take my marrying a Catholic. As I expected, he said at first it would produce a great shock, then a nine days wonder, and then it would all disappear and they would learn to love you without regard to your religion."[80] Here perhaps was a typical sequence of events: disbelief at the Protestant's poor judgment, then grudging acceptance of his spouse, though never her faith. A politician, Vance needed to think about his constituents' esteem. Age and power gave him confidence to proceed, however, where a young man might not. "If all the world should turn against me tomorrow," Vance reassured his future wife, "it would make no difference."[81] In fact, the barrier to intermarriage raised by anxiety often gave way to muted welcome into the Protestant world. Priests complained so frequently about ministers who married interfaith couples that it seems Protestant clergymen required few concessions. Churches then discreetly absorbed willing spouses. David Levy Yulee, the first Jewish member of the Senate, married a Christian soon after his election in 1845. When he died in 1886, he belonged to Washington's New York Avenue Presbyterian Church. How this transformation came about, spiritually or sacramentally, is obscure, and that is the point.[82] Quiet forbearance was the Protestant majority's most effective resource to exclude or, alternatively, include religious minorities.

Yet on a deep level, Protestants did not quite see interfaith families, at least not as real households. Perhaps power gave them the luxury of overlooking cracks in the Protestant edifice. Besides, denial of the problem was expedient, and custom contained the damage. But intermarriage was finally as invisible to Protestants as were religious minorities themselves. As long as observers could not distinguish Catholics or Jews from their stereotypes, real mixed-faith homes could not be imagined. Zebulon Vance delivered a speech many times in the 1870s and 1880s on Jews as "The Scattered Nation." It was philo-Semitic, a plea for tolerance. Jews, sounding much like the postbellum South, were praised as agrarian democrats in ancient times, and in later days for their "constancy, faithfulness and devotion to principle under the most trying circumstances."[83] Though "a lonely river in the midst of the ocean of humankind," Jews had no equal in "unmixed purity of blood" or "unbroken generations of descent." Even today "they marry within themselves entirely."[84] Vance was not a sheltered man. He lived in Washington, had a close Jewish friend, and a Catholic wife. But his image of the Jews as different and separate so overrode his experience that he stated strict endogamy as a fact. In Protestant writing, intermarriages, and Jews or Catholics who might enter them, appeared, if at all, as symbols. Ingrained habits of reading the Scriptures and history typologically contributed to this stylized manner of speaking. Vance's "Jews" were as much the Israelites he found in the Bible as they were his neighbors.[85] Nonetheless, the way Protestants folded intermarriage into moral tales had an affinity with their more frequent silence. Both impulses permitted doubt about whether mixed marriages were really occurring and verbally protected the integrity of the Protestant world.

All told, Catholics, Jews, and Protestants dealt with interfaith marriages in moods consistent with each community's traditions and temper. Catholics placed these families in a church-centered drama of sin and salvation. Jews debated how they challenged the rules and rites of descent. Protestants quietly offered them a place in the majority culture. From the viewpoint of couples, each faith's answer had elements that must have appealed and repelled. Catholicism offered doctrinal clarity and parental warmth at the price of submission. Judaism left room for discussion and local solutions, yet did not speak to families in an understanding or easily understandable way. Protestantism held strong cards of acceptance and respectability, for households willing to exercise selective amnesia. Clergy and, among Protestants, laymen were not the only voices to speak on mixed marriage. In all three groups, women wrote fiction that cast intermarried life in different, though not unrecognizable, lights.

Moral Tales

When authors of fiction create characters and plots, their principles encounter their culture's basic desires and fears. In nineteenth-century America, Catholic, Jewish, and Protestant writers listened to the concerns about interfaith marriage voiced in their respective religious communities. Their works reviewed doctrine, however, in everyday settings of ambition and romance, assimilation and conflict. These stories revealed the human complexity of mixed-faith families. But like the preaching in nonfiction, this literature was moralistic. Each author spoke, more or less self-consciously, as a Catholic, Jew, or Protestant, and formulated lessons for readers. Because women specialized in domestic subjects, even controversial ones, the writers were often women. Two novels and one short story show the temper of Catholic, Jewish, and Protestant writing: Mary Anne Sadlier's *The Blakes and Flanagans* (1855), Emma Wolf's *Other Things Being Equal* (1892), and Rebecca Harding Davis's "How the Widow Crossed the Lines" (1876).[86]

It was the intention of Mary Anne Madden Sadlier (1820–1903) to reinforce the teachings of the Catholic Church. Priests distrusted fiction, and Sadlier began her book by seconding their view. "I do not profess to write novels" encouraging "maudlin sentimentality, which is the ruin of our youth both male and female." As "one who has Eternity ever in view," she offered "practical stories embodying grave truths, [which] will be read by many, who would not read *pious books*."[87] Her prudence sustained an acclaimed literary career. Irish-born, she married James Sadlier, a Catholic publisher, in New York in 1846. She wrote for nearly fifty years and in 1895 received the Laetare Medal from the University of Notre Dame for her contribution to Catholic letters.[88] Yet the close fit between Sadlier's goals and those of the clergy did not mean that they told the same story. Pastoral letters placed interfaith marriage in the cycle of sin and repentance; Sadlier located intermarriage concretely in the immigrant's search for self-fulfillment.

True to its title, *The Blakes and Flanagans* is about related Irish families in New York. Tim Flanagan, a leather dresser, is the brother of Mary Blake, whose husband, Miles, owns a grocery store. Intermarriage is a tale of the second generation, and there are two parallel stories about sons and daughters. Henry, the Blakes' son, is driven by ambition. A lawyer who worships "the fashionable world," he views his parents "with contempt" and aspires eagerly to become a "prominent individual." He marries Jane Pearson, a Baptist, yet really raised in the "religion of dollars and cents."[89] She mirrors Henry's willingness to subordinate religion to advantage. "'Jane was not at all particular about religion,'" he assures his parents, and "'would as soon go to the Roman Catholic Church as any other.'"[90] Indifference allies quietly, however, with prejudice. Jane resists Catholic baptism for her first son until she thinks the Blakes might give him a generous gift; by then, the baby has died. Her other children grow up with "a wholesome horror of Catholicity" and stand "in the front ranks of the Know-Nothings, urging on the godless fanaticism of the age."[91] Through it all, Henry never leaves the Catholic Church, though in spirit he does. Success is his idol, and his mixed marriage, to Sadlier, is a pact with a Protestant culture devoted to the same worldly rites.[92]

What happens to Eliza, Henry's sister, is a woman's equivalent of his pursuit of self-interest: she marries for love. Her Methodist suitor, Zachary Thomson, explains to the Blakes that romance, without thought to religion, is sufficient. "'You know I love Eliza as well, aye, better than I do myself,'" and "'she could never love anyone else as she loves me.'"[93] Eliza shares, however, the vulnerability of Eve. On their honeymoon, Zachary persuades her to eat meat on Friday; soon she is attending his church. But as she dies in childbirth, still "not believ[ing] it possible that she was to die" and before the priest arrives, her soul is "overshadowed by the dark wing of despair."[94] Her children are raised in the religion of their stepmother, a Unitarian. Mary Blake dies of "a broken heart," followed by Miles. Henry turns to drink: "*mint-juleps, sherry-cobblers,*" and other "bacchanalian devices."[95] Both he and Eliza marry believing that religion can be accommodated to self-gratification. Yet clearly, to compromise Catholicism equals its abandonment.

Sadlier's melodramatic warnings so resembled some clerical texts that one wonders if sentimental fiction influenced church teaching. A pamphlet on *Mixed Marriage* as "the forbidden fruit for Catholics" predicted that the unheeding reader's children would one day be reared Protestants, never say a "Hail Mary," and die without last rites. "Hence, you may as well give your Rosary away to the Catholic child of another; it is of no use to you any longer."[96] Yet prose by priests and lay women such as Sadlier remained distinct. *The Blakes and Flanagans* paused from its preaching to consider motives. Although Henry's determination to rise and Eliza's desire for romance appear in caricatured form, Sadlier asked readers to see themselves critically. Nor did she speak only to young people, but their parents as well.

The Blakes' tragedy was predictable and, more happily, avoidable. Parents were responsible for their children's interfaith marriages. Even names—the Anglicized "Blake," against the Celtic "Flanagan"—hint at mistakes in Miles and Mary's home. "'Business! business!' is the grand affair with the Blake family." Money settles religious issues. "Miles Blake was never behind any of his neighbors when a collection was taken up, especially if it were for the building or repairing of a church," but he confesses and takes communion only once a year, "deeming that quite sufficient." He sends Henry and Eliza to the public school because it is "free of all expense."[97] The Flanagans, "good, old fashioned Catholics" whose "chief ambition was to bring up their children in the same faith," choose, in contrast, St. Peter's School.[98] Two of the boys grow up to be priests. Edward, another son, marries Margaret O'Callaghan. Husband and wife "had learned the same catechism in the same church" and "received the sacraments before the same altar."[99] When Margaret's father dies, he leaves his fortune of $26,000 to Edward Flanagan.

The Blakes and Flanagans took mixed marriage out of the church and into the family. The clergy could not quarrel with Sadlier's stern censure of impiety, but perhaps they picked up disconcerting details in the way she told her story. For one thing, so much attention to parenting diminished the clergy's role. Dr. Powers, the priest, correctly predicts the misery or contentment of the Blake and Flanagan children; but he cannot change bad behavior and weakly consents to remarry Henry Blake and his wife after their wedding by a Protestant minister.[100] More vexing, Sadlier quietly absorbed the materialism of the American dream that she overtly condemned. After all, it is Catholic faithfulness—marriage to the girl next door—that brings Edward Flanagan economic reward. Bypassing themes of grace and redemption, Sadlier shrewdly confronted ambition and hoped to make it work for the Catholic community.

To have Jewish women enter discussions of mixed marriage was more startling than to hear female Catholics. Baptism was enough to guarantee Mary Anne Sadlier membership in a parish and, in a way, to invite her opinion. But "the fact stares us plainly in the face," the *American Jewess* magazine mourned at its inception in 1895, "that in Jewish congregations married [Jewish] women are still debarred from membership."[101] This would seem to close the door completely to intermarried women. Jews recognized that women, like men, wed gentiles. Isaac Leeser urged girls in 1866 to "reject the outward glitter of the world" for "honest, hard working, plain-spoken Israelites."[102] He had insisted that "the Bible demands that the guilty *shall* be punished," and intermarried men should forfeit ritual honors and voting rights in the congregation.[103] What women should lose never came up: synagogues could not bar them from privileges they never had. Matrilineal descent made their children Jews, but they could not join American congregations. This tangled situation helps explain why *Other Things Being Equal* deviated from rabbinic discourse in style, insights, and conclusions.

Although Emma Wolf (1865–1932) was not the first Jewish woman to depict an interfaith romance, her novel was unprecedented in American fiction in rendering the sensuality that contested religious proscriptions. Herbert Kemp, a Unitarian doctor, follows Ruth Levice from San Francisco to a resort in the California mountains to propose marriage. While they row on the lake and her mother, the chaperone, sleeps in the boat, Ruth observes that his "flannel shirt, low at the throat, showed his strong white neck like a column from his broad shoulders, and his dark face with the steady gray eyes looked across at her with grave sweetness." Once "his fingers closed softly, tightly over hers," the extent of Ruth's temptation is clear.[104] *Other Things Being Equal* appeared in 1892, the same year the Central Conference of American Rabbis voted to recognize women's equality in the synagogue. "However, one suspects," in the words of one historian, that "the resolution adopted was little more than a pious wish."[105] When Jewish readers picked up Wolf's novel, they found, by contrast, a full-bodied contemporary woman. A native of San Francisco and unmarried, Wolf must have been familiar with the kind of courtship she described.[106] Her book challenged convention not only by its realism but by her willingness to confront key issues of the day: religious liberalism and women's role.

Like Sadlier, Wolf believed assimilation set the stage for interfaith marriage. This was one meaning of her title about the equality of "other things." Whereas Catholics held individualism suspect and shunned compromise with Protestant culture, Wolf's choice of the word "equal" conveyed how warmly Jews embraced American liberties, until the subject was marriage. "'I have always imagined myself just and liberal in opinion,'" Jules Levice appeals to his daughter, but "'I never thought you could leap thus far.'"[107] "'Inasmuch as all my life you have taught me to look upon my Christian friends as upon my Jewish,'" Ruth predictably counters, "'why can he not be my husband?'"[108] Reared alongside Christians, with "'the same schooling'" and "'the same elements of home refinement,'" Ruth imagines she and Kemp can succeed in creating a religious middle ground. An admirer of Jesus as "'a teacher of brotherly love,'" she can "'call myself a christian, though I spell it with a small letter.'" As for the children, "'I think the simple religion of love enough for childhood,'" Kemp reasons. Later, "'I should let them choose for themselves, as all should be allowed.'"[109] Wolf let readers know that Ruth would have to swallow anti-Semitism. Could "this lovely girl," Kemp wonders the day they meet, be the daughter of "the little plain-faced Jew?"[110] Argument and counterargument remained suspended nonetheless. To Jules Levice, the couple's future resembles being "'cut adrift from both sides'"; it is "'a grave experiment'" in the couple's eyes.[111] Mixed marriage could be interpreted in more than one way, once Jewish liberalism went that far.

Rabbis sensed the possibly short distance from reform to intermarriage, but they were less equipped than Wolf to diagnose a second cause of the weddings of Jewish women to Christians: their discontent. Ruth is attracted to Kemp because he gives her something to do. She visits his patients—a poor, crippled boy and a girl pregnant out of wedlock—to lend them moral support. No Jewish woman in the novel lives an imitable life. Ruth's mother suffers from "'hysteria'" because she indulges too much in society's "'continual gayety.'"[112] Her cousin Jennie marries a man observant enough to light a *yahrzeit* candle, but who seems otherwise "to have one idea,—the amassing of wealth."[113] Jennie herself is a "'spiteful chatterbox,'" in Jules Levice's words, although she defends herself against "'scandal-mongering'" by saying that "'in my life such things are not trivial, perhaps because my life is narrower.'"[114] Jewish women's benevolent work took off in the 1890s. The National Council of Jewish Women began, for example, in 1893. *Other Things Being Equal* was a commentary on the times: middle-class girls might well marry Christians, long accepting of charity work for women, if Jews did not recognize what amounted to a crisis in women's identity.[115]

Yet it was the empathy of Wolf's portrait of Ruth that most sharply distinguished her novel from rabbinic debates. The rabbis approached families through issues of ritual and law. Women were literally the bearers of tradition, but they were scarcely imagined as actors. In a much different portrayal, Ruth Levice was a contemporary type: a woman with liberal attitudes of uncertain limits and intelligence without outlet. *Other Things Being Equal* came close to defending interfaith marriage by admitting it was understandable. Letting your heart go out to Ruth opened the way to respecting her love.

Wolf framed her story in doubt, however, and did not end so far from the rabbis' views. The Reform clergy offered interfaith couples a hushed maybe. Conversion, patrilineal descent, and synagogue participation were all possible to varying degrees. At the same time, Wolf finally whispered, maybe not. As he lay dying, Jules Levice insists that Ruth marry Kemp: "'I believe—and my wife believes,'" the father tells her suitor, "'that our child will be happy only as your wife, and that nothing should stand in the way of the consummation of this happiness.'"[116] Does Ruth realize too late, however, that she sacrificed her heritage, symbolized by her father's death? "'You mean,'" Kemp asks his now-reserved wife, "'that you no longer love me,—say it now and have it over.'"

> "Oh," she cried in exquisite pain, "why do you tantalize me so—can't you see that—"
> She looked so beautiful thus confessed that with sudden ecstasy he drew her to him and pressed his lips in one long kiss to hers.[117]

Perhaps Ruth's husband misreads her silent confession as a confirmation of love. When Wolf returned to the theme of marriage in *Heirs of Yesterday* (1900), she rejected interfaith romance. Lilian Otis, hearing that her suitor is a Jew, pretends a "headache" to avoid him. The young man, Philip May, had resolved to be "'an individual, not a class'" and "'*to break the chain*'" to "'a slavish past.'"[118] Now he learns that he is still "'what our religion has made us'" and believes Jean Willard, who is also Jewish, will save him. "'Ah, you see, I cannot help myself—you must have become my religion—if you are Jewish, must I not too be Jew?'"[119] Fiction, for Wolf, was a flexible medium of inquiry. When she pictured mixed marriage in American Jewish society, she not only allowed readers to see it in connection with assimilation, anti-Semitism, and women's goals, but created rhetorical tools to let them change their minds.

Sadlier and Wolf, religious outsiders in Protestant America, spoke similarly about intermarriage in the end. Describing aspirations for inclusion, parental complicity, and the shadow of prejudice, they took the viewpoint of families looking in. Rebecca Harding Davis's "How the Widow Crossed the Lines" was also about boundaries. Its theme was division and its dangers for the nation, the opposite side of the coin, not surprisingly, from the newcomer's worry about mobility and the threat to tradition. Told in retrospect as "our sketchy recollections of war-times in the old border town" on the Ohio River, the story alludes to the Centennial Exposition of 1876, now going on.[120] Into this political tale of nationhood Davis folded themes of other conflicts: battles of religion and the sexes. Davis (1831–1910) was known for the spare style in which she depicted ordinary lives. "Life in the Iron Mills" (1861), indebted to what she saw growing up in Wheeling, West Virginia, began her literary career. Yet she did not seek to represent a single interest or class. Predictably, the narrator of "How the Widow Crossed the Lines" took an omniscient stance and constructed an allegory of reconciliation.

The widow who crosses the lines is a minor character. Euphemia Van Pelt is "enormously fat, ruddy, and from head to foot a flutter of lace, ribbons and glittering Turkish jewelry."[121] Passing from North to South, she runs the blockade below Parkersburg, West Virginia. "'I'm a Southern sympathizer,'" she announces in the parlor of her friend Mrs. Potter. "'Tea? Oh certainly. What lovely Leeds ware!'"[122] But Euphemia travels as far as the border with another widow, who has crossed other lines. The fiction began with the woman's attempted suicide in the Ohio River. Margaret is a Scotch-Irish "'girl from some hill-country in Pennsylvania,'" who had married the new school-teacher and bore a son, John Knox, named for the founder of her Presbyterian faith. Then she learned the man is both a bigamist and a Catholic. When he "'stole the child'" and headed south, she followed, until father and son disappear, and she despairs.[123] It is a sad narrative of deception, seduction, abandonment, and theft. In a way, Margaret symbolizes the Union, betrayed by the Confederacy. But the story is also about the challenge to Protestantism of immigrant faiths. "'I suspect Margaret forgave him for his other wife,'" says Mrs. Potter, who rescues her, "'more easily than for his Holy Mother.'"[124] Davis was not uncritical of Margaret's ignorant nativism. She had Margaret repeat mean platitudes, calling the Catholic Church "'the Scarlet

Woman, drunk with the blood of the saints.'"[125] The fact remains that Davis constructed the marriage as an illegitimate bond with a man in every way unfaithful. Nor did she develop it dramatically, but left it as a recollection of events offstage. To Rebecca Harding Davis mixed marriage was imaginable, but perhaps too unpleasant to describe head-on. Here was Protestant silence about interfaith families in a different form.

Davis's instinct as a writer to sidestep the marriage is especially intriguing in light of the story's autobiographical roots. Her parents, though both Protestants, had eloped in 1830 to elude the bride's disapproving father. Much like Margaret's fictional suitor, Davis's own father was an immigrant who wooed her mother in Washington, Pennsylvania. It was through her mother that Rebecca was related to the intermarried Blaine-Ewing clan. She boarded for three years in the 1840s with "Aunt Blaine," her mother's sister, while she attended Washington Female Seminary. She must occasionally have seen her distant cousin James G. Blaine, a year older than she, who lived in Brownsville nearby. A Protestant like his father, James had a Catholic mother and sisters. Although Davis and her husband were Episcopalians in 1876, the year she portrayed the widows, she must have heard about the recurring mixed-faith matches among the Blaines and their Ewing kin. Her son's notorious affair with a Catholic was still in the future. A celebrated author and married man, Richard Harding Davis became infatuated with Bessie McCoy, a dancer, in 1908; the press sensationalized the details until his divorce and remarriage in 1912. Rebecca died in 1910; but it is safe to say that in this family she must have known more about mixed marriage than she let on.[126] Mrs. Potter of the story reduced Margaret's history to terse words: she "'courted and married'" and "'had one child.'"[127] Davis did not permit readers to see intermarriage as a human experience and instead sketched a myth of defilement.

Her decision to limit interfaith romance to symbolism was consistent with Protestant habits of writing. Ascha Fielding of *Arthur Mervyn,* meant by Charles Brockden Brown to connote sensuality and experience, was a livelier character than many in later tales of religious mixing. In *Hope Leslie* (1827), a story of two sisters in Puritan New England, Catharine Maria Sedgwick stressed the gulf between truth and error by making the Indians Catholics. Hope, one sister, weds an Anglican who will moderate Puritan rigor; Faith, captured by the Indians, marries in the tribe. First horrified that Faith is lost "'to the christian family,'" Hope is consoled that "'she bows to the crucifix'": "'any christian faith was better than none.'"[128] This thought did not erase the contrast, however, between the redemptive promise of Hope's marriage and Faith's interracial, interfaith bond. "'My sister married to an Indian,'" Hope gasps, "shuddering as if a knife had been plunged in her bosom."[129] As schematically, *Lady Alice* (1849), by Jedediah Huntington, made a love affair between an Anglican and Catholic a vehicle for judging the legitimacy of the Roman Church. A product of the Oxford Movement in America, the book projected disputation in the form of questionable passion. Should Alice Stuart, piously High Church, marry the Catholic Fred Clifford? In the story, Fred converts to the Church of England before he marries the girl. In life, Huntington, an Episcopal priest, and his wife became Catholics soon after the novel appeared. Either way, *Lady Alice* was about Huntington's romance with the Catholic religion, much more than about doctrinal conflict at home.[130] Catholicism appeared in Protestant fiction as the countervailing faith. The embodiment of religious quarrels in interfaith couples seemed incidental to the metaphysics at hand.

There were exceptions. In the same year that Davis published "How the Widow Crossed the Lines" in Philadelphia, George Eliot in London completed her philo-Semitic masterpiece, *Daniel Deronda*. No reader can doubt the depth of feeling between Deronda, the peer's adopted son who discovers that he is a Jew, and, beautiful and tragic, Gwendolen Harleth. The novel had an ideological level, examining Zionism. But Eliot did not simply manipulate symbols through romantic attachments. *Daniel Deronda* was her last work, and it grandly revealed the luxuriant realism of the Victorian novel.[131]

England was not America, however, and Rebecca Harding Davis was less concerned about probing her characters than making sure her lesson was plain. The lines of section, faith, and gender all need to be crossed and hard feelings healed. Hearing that her husband, Peter Brodie, joined the rebellion, Margaret plans to slip into the South with "Widow Van Pelt." Soon she learns that Peter is dead; she finds her son in a convent. He has "carefully-brushed hair and neat clothes." "The sister understood her, though she did not say a word. 'Tut! tut! that was a trifle,' she said. 'You would have done just the same. We are all His children,' crossing herself, whereat John Knox crossed himself too."[132] "'They *are* good women,'" Mrs. Potter, accompanying Margaret, confirms. It is not just the instinctive caring of women that brings harmony to Catholics and Protestants, but the love, refined by loss, of women who suffer alone. "'When I was looking for my boy,' she says to the sister, 'it was of the Child Jesus I thought, and of His mother.'"[133] Catholicism honors the Mother's sacrifice, and the nuns' vows imitate Mary's life. In 1876, so many American women had given their sons that the image must have appealed to Davis as common ground. When "John Knox crossed himself," his mother, in spirit, does so, too, making the lines she crosses those of Calvary itself. Conflict and bitterness become tolerance and reconciliation. Back home with her boy, she is "a devout United Presbyterian still, though when she tells John Knox of his namesake she 'doubts but that he was a hard man, and not as well acquainted with the Catholics as them whose opportunities have been better.'"[134]

Could a self-respecting Protestant female writer conclude her tale, though, without a wedding? Enter, again, the other widow, "larger and airier than ever," Mrs. Van Pelt. Although hard to imagine at the altar, she is "the bride of an ex-Confederate general," most recently seen seated "on the grand stand to witness the Southern tournament" at the Exposition in Philadelphia. A woman of principle—"a rebel still at heart"—part of her wartime errand was to save her motherless nieces and nephews, "'eight children running wild this blessed day over the plantation'" in Louisiana.[135] Her marriage reunites North and South in a home. Davis's plea for religious peace was absorbed in her vision of sectional concord, sealed by the Protestant icon, the family. It was a Protestant household, and stood in contrast to Margaret's seduction. Whether Davis worried that she had to hang her moral lesson on the clownish Euphemia cannot be said. This was the widow honored by the title, however, not the one who had given her heart to a Catholic. Davis made more than a bow of respect to Catholicism, but mixed marriage remained taboo.

The intricacy of the tale suggests how the process of writing stories pulled together thoughts on religion and family. Protestant writers skirted interfaith marriage in nonfiction, and in fiction they often used mixed families as symbols for something else. But when an author as serious as Davis made these households integral to plot and meaning, she could not hide her feelings: offer charitableness to outsiders, but stop short of intimacy at home. Neither she, nor Sadlier and Wolf, contradicted male leaders of their religious communities. All three advised readers of the hazards of mixed-faith romance. At the same time, the women's fiction showed that intermarriage was not just a matter of perverse instincts or errors in judgment. It was an understandable part of American freedom to aspire and love, and, more basically, to choose and change. Empathy between readers and characters made interfaith marriage seem natural in nineteenth-century culture, if not accepted.

Newspaper Romances

Despite the subtle tolerance found in fiction, almost nowhere in the decades after 1840 did American interfaith couples hear encouraging words. This was a religious society, and inherited rules remained influential. Indeed, institution-building by Catholics and Jews gave new life to precepts that helped demarcate each community from its neighbors. Renewed pressure to marry within the fold was a predictable correlate of the multiplication of faiths. But there was dissent. Stories of individual self-creation, encased in religious scruples in fiction, might shed their moralism. Near the end of the century, the popular press began to sensationalize romances that broke all bounds.

"Cupid Conquers," the headline read in 1878: "Race and Breed and Kindred All Succumb."[136] The Cincinnati *Enquirer* reported the elopement of Helen Wise as a fairy-tale-come-true. The facts were simple. Isaac Mayer Wise, the respected rabbi, forbade his daughter to see her suitor James Molony, an attorney and Christian. On pretense of visiting her cousins, Helen left the house, met Molony, was married by a Unitarian minister, checked into the Galt House, "and the deed was done." The newspaper transformed the event into romantic comedy. "It was a runaway match, one of the good old-fashioned kind," ancient as the day "Love first laughed at locksmiths." The article's section headings resembled captions of a silent-film melodrama, not far in the future: "Not to Be Reported"—"Reported"—"The Bride"—"The Groom"—"The Families." Comparing this provincial match with the splendid recent wedding in England of Hannah Rothschild ("the wealthiest maiden in all Israel") to Earl Roseberry (her "lordly Christian wooer") added to the glitter. With puckish fun, the feature implied that mixed marriage was not a weighty matter. More bluntly, the *Enquirer* took the lovers' side. "Public sympathy will ever go out to the lovers in such cases," unless the sad time comes when "Youth and Love shall be no more, and worse than chaos has come to a passionless world." The couple's happiness took precedence over counterclaims by family and religious tradition.

The appearance in print of brash sentimentalism showed that moralism was not unopposed. That the paper dared publish this flippant piece meant that it trusted readers to see the joke. Belief in love at any cost must have been gaining a following; the *Enquirer* helped legitimate the view.[137] Still, a pleasure-seeking ethos was not as instinctively respected as the report said. Anti-Semitism was recruited to win readers' sympathies for the couple, because the humor was at the rabbi's expense. "It would, perhaps, be only justice to all parties to say that Dr. Wise is known to entertain liberal views on all subjects, though discouraging the intermarrying of any sects," the paper interpolated. Here was gratuitous information, unless embarrassing Wise was the goal. Highlighting his entrapment in contradiction, the article slid over how the event made fools of the Molonys, who "were in ignorance of the course [James] had taken" and "also objected to his choice on grounds of sect." Now, it turned out, both families were distressed. Approval of the doctrine "cupid conquers" was qualified if the lovers were your kin. The feature could safely be published, however, without fear of provoking readers, because it sounded like fantasy: the bride "pretty, if not beautiful," with "pearl pendants in her ears, and a gold breast-pin," the groom "a picture of manly beauty." Without question, many nineteenth-century interfaith couples married for love. But in the *Enquirer,* clever writing embellished the acceptability of romance. Dreams of undaunted passion sold papers. The real lives of families were more complex.

With the appearance of a secular viewpoint, a way opened to families to turn away from religion altogether. Before the turn of the century, however, they rarely took this path. Attachment of mixed-faith families to religious communities remained the norm. When families approached churches or synagogues, they did not make free choices based on perceived advantage; couples brought personal histories with them to their weddings. Even so, American interfaith families now made their religious decisions in a setting of intensified public discussion about what they should do, having already taken a step most people agreed they should not.

CHAPTER THREE

The Strange Intimacy of Piety and Politics

By the middle of the nineteenth century, interfaith marriages were nearly commonplace among American politicians, and although Washington was hardly a typical town, its mixed-faith families may introduce similar households of the era. Judah Benjamin and David Yulee, U.S. senators from Louisiana and Florida, both Jews, wed a Catholic and Protestant, respectively, in 1833 and 1846. Stephen A. Douglas and Zebulon Vance, Protestants and senators from Illinois and North Carolina, married Catholics in 1856 and 1880. This inclination to intermarry in civic circles is not surprising. Republican government was committed to Enlightened ideals, and politicians as naturally took liberties and worked compromises in their private lives. Socially, Washington was a tolerant place, accustomed to pleasure-seeking and the pursuit of self-interest. When Virginia Clay, a senator's widow, looked back in 1904 to her days as *A Belle of the Fifties*, she recalled the capital's fashions, concerts, and masquerade balls. Principles did erect barriers, but the disputes were political. The southern "mess" where Clay dined met in a boardinghouse run by a kinswoman of a wealthy man of Jewish descent. But religion evoked no comment from Clay. The southerners focused on keeping "Free-soilers, Black Republicans and Bloomers on the other side of the street."[1] In this world, interfaith marriages appeared in Clay's memory as jewels in the crown of international diplomacy. Baron Alexandre de Bodisco, the Russian ambassador, wed a young woman from

Georgetown, and his successor married a girl from New Haven; a widow from Mississippi became the wife of the delegate from Sardinia.[2] Liberalism did more than absorb these mixed marriages: it embraced them with provincial pride.

Yet there were hints in Clay's memoir that she had forgotten how important religion was, even in political families. When the daughter of the Sardinian envoy and his southern-born wife died, much later, in America, she had a Catholic funeral at the cathedral in Memphis. So, too, David Yulee's Protestant bride, Clay gossiped, was "so devoutly religious that her piety caused her friends to speak of her as 'the Madonna of the Wickliffe sisters!'"[3] Nor was Clay blind to ethnicity, particularly once the glamour of the capital was removed. A refugee in Savannah after the war, she was welcomed by the city's Jews. "For an hour Miss Martha [Levy] had been busy presenting her friends, both Christian and Jew, when, one after another, came Mr. Cohen, Mr. Salomon, Dr. Lazarus, and Dr. Mordecai. At this remarkable procession my risibles proved triumphant." Clay could not resist: "'And is Haman here, too?'"[4] On the surface, *A Belle of the Fifties* was a breezy retrospect, in which liberalism smiled on intermarriage as an adjunct of freedom and a reward of success. The book's details, however, attest to religion's continuing presence. Washington families did not let inherited disapproval stop mixed-faith romance. But if they were anything like Virginia Clay, they were well acquainted with their Bibles, not above prejudice, or, more positively, not above piety either. They wanted to marry as they pleased and practice their religion as before; in short, to have their cake and eat it.

This all-too-human story unfolded in America between roughly the 1830s and 1880s, the same time that each religion set out its position on interfaith marriage. Practical tolerance of mixed families among laypeople advanced arm in arm with the clergy's public misgivings. Seemingly on a collision course, these trends might amicably intersect. This was an era of institution-building, and intermarried couples who wished an affiliation—as most did—had a greater chance than ever to find a church or synagogue, providing its membership policy was friendlier than its rhetoric. It was in the Catholic Church that families met the warmest welcome. Or more specifically, this was where Catholic wives found a congregational home. Despite soul-shaking homilies against out-marriage, Catholicism adopted women wed to Protestants as domestic evangelists. So shrewdly did the church sense that women increasingly had charge of family religion that it much slowed the drift toward Protestantism of interfaith households in its province. Easygoing husbands, often politicians, left matters of faith to their wives. Here, the private alliance of state and religion was an arrangement between the sexes. More deeply, women agreed with men that pious traditions could be made to serve love, and husbands appreciated their wives' religious devotion. In neither case did sacred and secular part ways in interfaith homes.[5]

We can concentrate on the much-repeated story of the mid-to-late nineteenth century—the marriages of Protestant politicians to Catholic women—without forgetting that not every intermarried man was a Protestant or in politics, nor all wives Catholics. Households of political husbands and Catholic wives are important because they show clearly how liberalism and piety stood side by side. Uncommon families—in one case a failed marriage, in another an observant Jewish wife—highlight the traits of more typical homes by contrast and remind us that no single norm prevailed. Patterns visible in the early part of the century reappear in this era. Liberal parents produced intermarried children, while bonds of family restrained dissent among kin. But there were also new trends. Now, at times, mixed families were the result of second marriages of established men, or the conversions to a different religion of older women. Intermarriage was not marginal to this culture, a rebellion of the young, but an expression of core premises about the acceptability—and limits—of individuality in families.

Washington Courtships

Despite Virginia Clay's memories of Washington's gentility, the nineteenth-century capital was not much of a place. Charles Dickens called it a "City of Magnificent Intentions" in 1842, "broad avenues that begin in nothing and lead nowhere."[6] Underdevelopment did not preclude urban problems: poverty, crime, inadequate schools, and, until 1862, slavery. Only gradually did officeholders bring their wives and children with them during seasons of government activity. In 1845, about a third of the members of Congress had their families in town. Many, bowing to the uncertainties of politics, lived in boardinghouses or hotels. The perpetual work of paying calls, occupying women especially, was like getting to know new people all the time.[7]

Why interfaith romance flourished here is plain. In this transient society, men and women of different backgrounds literally rubbed shoulders at levees and balls. Tradition or where you came from may have seemed less important in the republican city than who you wished to become. Yet religion was not forgotten, true as all this was. Washington's mixed couples were much driven by secular motives, but they still compromised faith, rather than dismissed it. How families juggled self-fulfillment and spiritual commitment may be seen in the marriages of three senators: Stephen A. Douglas, Zebulon Vance, and David Levy Yulee.

As Stephen Douglas (1813–1861) lay dying during the first spring of the Civil War, he and his young wife Adele (1835–1899) renegotiated the religious issues they held in balance throughout their four-year marriage. Adele, a strong Catholic, twice called the bishop to baptize her husband and administer last rites. But even on June 2, the day before his death, Douglas sent the prelate away. This was not because he was a confirmed Protestant. One historian calls his beliefs "nebulous," though "he leaned toward the Baptists"; another says he was "nominally a Congregationalist."[8] Perhaps he was drawn to both. Born in Vermont, Douglas had to have been exposed to Congregationalism. Later, his first wife was a Baptist from North Carolina, and so were their sons. Yet the deeper truth was that he never let religion make his decisions, and he refused to begin now. No politician, not even a Democrat opposed to the nativists in the Republican party, would consent to be married in 1856 by a priest—as Douglas was—unless he made religion secondary, privately, to feeling and, publicly, to the sectional crisis. Douglas held on stubbornly to his spiritual coolness to the very end. His widow, however, once alone, struck a compromise with the Protestants. He had died in Chicago, his adopted home, and although Adele wished for a Catholic funeral in Washington, Illinois officials resisted. Militia units, mercantile associations, trade unions, benevolent societies, and Freemasons walked with the casket in Chicago. There were no religious rites; Bishop Duggan, whom Douglas had dismissed, gave a brief eulogy at the grave. Though Douglas had no doubts about who he was, religiously speaking, the politicking surrounding his burial grew out of the crisscrossed loyalties of his interfaith marriage.[9]

There are two explanations for how Douglas met Adele Cutts, each one plausible because it reflects either secular or religious interests that in the long run held them together. The New York *Evening Post* told readers the couple became acquainted at the home of Douglas's Democratic colleague Jesse Bright.[10] Here, perhaps, they recognized that mutual advantage would support attraction. Adele's dowry was her elegance. Tall—"one of the queenliest" women, in Virginia Clay's memory—and "with the regal manner of a princess," she had so little money that "she once complained to me poutingly of the cost of gloves."[11] Her father, James Madison Cutts, was a bureaucrat, Second Comptroller of the Treasury; but the family was well connected, and so Adele was received. Dolley Madison, her great-aunt, lived with the Cutts family until her death in 1849. Never mind that Ellen, Adele's mother, came from a family of aspiring Irish Catholics, whose name appeared as "O'Neale" in the writings of Ellen's son, in later histories as the anglicized "Neale."[12] Even Millard Fillmore, presidential candidate in 1856 on the Know-Nothing ticket, communicated privately with young women who had Catholic kin. In 1850, as president, Fillmore sent a Bible to Adele's cousin Martha Cutts as "a slight testimony of his regard," accompanied by a note of thanks for "the beautiful purse."[13] Good breeding and style opened doors in Washington society, with marginal regard to religion or wealth. This would permit the reported introduction of Douglas, a recent widower, to Adele Cutts in Senator Bright's parlor. Personal chemistry then sealed the bond. Douglas—fortyish, lonely, and memorably short—fell for a statuesque woman not yet twenty-one; Adele responded to his position and power. The New York paper's account, consistent with the secular mind-set of Washington politics, had credibility and may well have been true.

More unexpectedly, Douglas's niece may have been friends with Adele around 1850 at the Academy of the Visitation in Georgetown. Neither came from a fully Catholic family. Adele's father was Protestant, though his children were Catholics. It is unlikely that Adelaide Granger, daughter of Douglas's only sister in upstate New York, was a Catholic at all. The Visitation Academy was known nationally for its rigorous and genteel training. The receipt sent to Douglas's brother-in-law in 1853 by Sister Mary Bernard, the school's treasurer, itemized Adelaide's lessons in piano and French.[14] Politicians, often Protestants, were inclined to patronize the academy because of its location. A letter to "dear uncle" from Adelaide, thanking Douglas for a book, makes it seem he took an interest in his niece's education, enough to suggest the convent school where she, perhaps, en-countered Adele.[15] This version of the Douglases' courtship forces a subtle reading of their marriage. Typically, contemporaries and histo-rians noted how the new wife made the widower and his house pre-sentable. Dressed for one costume ball as Aurora, "radiant in the pale tints of the morning," Adele brought luster by her poise and attentiveness to an eminent man.[16] Her work as emissary of good taste, however, obscures not only her piety but also her husband's re-gard for religion, seen in his approval of the Visitation Sisters. Even if the Douglases married for love and ambition, Catholicism was laced closely into their lives.

Their intimacy with Adele's church was apparent, for better or worse. The Douglases were perceived as a Catholic couple. The Re-publican press naturally excoriated Stephen for fellow-traveling. Adele, though, became in a small way a Catholic heroine: Mrs. Henry Miller of Raleigh, a stranger, approached her in 1860 as "also a mem-ber of the Catholic Church to which I have heard you are likewise at-tached."[17] Hearsay about the family's religious preference was consis-tent with their actions. Necessarily with her husband's consent, Adele made contributions to their parish, St. Aloysius, and to Washing-ton's Catholic charities. Far bolder, they chose a Catholic education for Douglas's sons, Robert and Stephen, seven and ten years old, re-spectively, when their father remarried. The boys had lived in North Carolina with their mother's family—Baptists—after Martha Douglas's death in 1853. Now they entered Gonzaga Seminary in Washington and later Georgetown College. On matters of child-rearing and, implicitly, religion, Douglas trusted his young wife's judgment. His will, dated September 4, 1857, made her guardian, should he die: "knowing her to be the best person in the world to per-form this sacred trust," she "shall have the possession, control, and education" of his children until they were twenty.[18] Friends warned him during the presidential campaign of 1860 to take the boys out of the Catholic school.[19] But, irreligious himself, Douglas showed no ambivalence about committing them to an unpopular institution. Raising Catholic sons made sense in the context of his marriage.

The profound consequences of the decision surfaced in the life of Robert Martin Douglas. Although what became of Stephen, Jr., is un-clear, Robert became a leading Catholic, despite his early Protestant-ism, impious father, and mixed-faith home in a city enamoured of politics. He was a main speaker at the Catholic Congress, convened to meet along with the World's Columbian Exposition, in Chicago in 1893. "Colonel R. M. Douglass [*sic*] of Greensboro, N.C.," the Baltimore *Mirror* announced, "spoke of 'Trade Combinations, Strikes and Arbitration.'" "He had no sympathy with the red-handed rioter," yet equally "dwelt at length on the evasion of taxes by the rich."[20] In 1913, now in his sixties and in poor health, Robert opposed a constitutional amendment to permit use of the Protestant Bible in public schools, for which James Cardinal Gibbons, reigning prelate of the American Catholic Church, thanked him by letter. Piety was the foundation of his advocacy. When he passed through Cleveland as a young man of twenty, Robert stopped at the cathedral for morning Mass. Once married, he made sure his son and eventual law partner, Martin Francis Douglas, received a Catholic education: St. Mary's College, Georgetown, Catholic University, before finishing with a law degree at the University of North Carolina.[21] What Stephen A. Douglas would have thought of this religious legacy can only be guessed. Consenting to the Catholic training of children did not require imagining them as Catholic adults. Hindsight suggests, however, how a Protestant boy became a Catholic man: the stepmother's fervor, the father's assent, backed up by the clergy's patience.

Washington's priests dealt with the Douglases in the 1850s with consistent friendliness. Even if Stephen's vague Protestantism was a strike against him, his prestige, combined with deference to Adele's faith, reconciled the church to the match. Priests not only married them, but baptized and buried the infants Adele bore in 1858 and 1859 and urged Catholic schooling for Douglas's sons.[22] "Fr. Maguire, accompanied by Fr. Rector," the parish records of St. Aloysius noted, called at the house to recommend Gonzaga. Adele, at first, favored a classical course: "Still after a few words, she determined to send Robert and Stephen to us."[23] The Catholic Church opposed mixed marriage; yet in practice, it compromised and awaited results. Even Adele's brother, James Madison Cutts, Jr., who traversed a wider religious arc than she, relied on the church's elemental loyalty to its flock. Cutts was less fond of his Catholic than of his civic, and implicitly Protestant, heritage. A graduate of Harvard Law School, he stressed his Puritan forebears in genealogical notes compiled late in life. When he delivered a paper at Washington's Columbia Historical Society in 1898, the theme was his kinswoman, Dolley Madison.[24] To his mind, having Stephen Douglas as a brother-in-law further secured his foothold in the mainstream. Cutts told the story of the oath that Douglas, on his death bed, administered to him in 1861: "'I J. Madison Cutts, son of J. Madison Cutts, nephew of President Madison do most solemnly swear that I will support the Constitution and Laws of the land and maintain the interests of my family.'"[25] The intermarriages of Cutts's father and sister permitted him to let wishes construct his past: in imagination, he was heir to Puritans and patriots. This, seen positively, was a half-truth and picked up on how the capital's civic culture served as common ground for couples of different faiths. But Catholicism, no less, retained its hold. "Reared a Catholic," Cutts included in the genealogical manuscript, and when his granddaughter married in 1904, a priest performed the rite.[26] Although freedom and compromise, taken for granted in politics, spilled over into Washington's interfaith families, religion remained a bedrock they chose not to dismiss.

This formula does not mean that couples married for the sake of liberty. Rather, loosening the ties of tradition allowed self-gratification in matches serving vanity, ambition, or passion. If the Douglases' motives may be guessed, Zebulon Vance (1830–1894) left a full picture of his infatuation with Florence Martin. They met in the blue parlor of Riggs House in Washington soon after Christmas, 1879. Vance had been widowed a year, and grief must have brought them together. "I have seen black garments so constantly," Florence confessed with a young widow's impatience, that "I fairly cry out for sunshine and colors!"[27] Sharing their loneliness was soon superseded by sharp feelings. "I am a middle aged man," Vance began, "with a heart in which many emotions slumber—some that I fancied dead or at least overlaid by care and ambition or selfishness. I never dreamed that I could have them all renewed again."[28] His attraction, all-encompassing, was visceral. "I am *heart hungry* to see you," he confided in March 1880; two weeks later, "I am *hungry* again to tell you how much I am in love with you!"[29] Coming from a man known for his enjoyment of food, Vance's equation of missing Florence with unsatisfied appetite underscored the pain of their separation. More explicitly, "I am almost crazy over allusions to your wedding garments." He begged her to send a bit of the fabric.[30]

Martin returned his emotion, though in tamer rhetoric. "I never intended to remarry," but "now you see you have changed the whole color of my life." Laughing at herself, "Here I am nearly forty and dead in love!"[31] Although Florence was Catholic and Zebulon Protestant, they became engaged early in February 1880, not yet acquainted two months. Hard smitten by love, they were old enough to recognize the religious problem, but assumed they could manage it. Florence was concerned her religion might damage Vance's Senate career. But on February 24 he replied, "I beg you not to trouble yourself about [it] for a moment."[32] He realized later that her worry about him concealed misgivings about herself, the seed of possible future regret that "you had not judged wisely in marrying a Protestant," he inferred shrewdly, and in "going to live in an intensely Protestant community."[33] Initial fears about public opinion—not ungrounded—were replaced by sobering self-awareness of the couple's own prejudices. How little religion could be severed from romance came to light as they planned the wedding.

Composure vanished when Vance learned he had to make a pledge to the priest who would marry them. At the news, "my heart stood still with fear & agony! What was it, I asked myself again & again, I had to promise except to love & cherish her until death?"[34] Private feeling should be enough, were it not for the designs of the Catholic Church to meddle in families, robbing them—non-Catholic husbands especially—of their freedom.

A thousand fears came upon me, and there rushed before my imagination all the stories I had heard from childhood about the diabolical craft of the priests in entrapping people by taking advantage of their passions, their loves and hatreds and what not; and how in every divided household the priest came between man & wife, dethroning him and sowing distrust between him and the wife of his heart.

Vance sensed that he might be heeding rumors whispered by ignorant people: "stories I had heard from childhood." Even so, he was sure that "there is a great difference between your church and mine in this matter of personal liberty." Protestants "would turn from me with contempt if they thought I had surrendered that conscience for any motive other than honest conviction."

The crisis might have been foreseen. Its root was the religious seriousness of both Zebulon and Florence. For the full twenty-five years of his first marriage, Vance resisted his wife Hattie's prayers that he profess Christianity. Her death brought a change of heart. "I learned with great pleasure," a friend wrote just after New Year 1879, "that you have confessed Christ, and connected yourself with the 2nd Presbyterian Church of Raleigh, N.C."[35] Not a zealot, Vance was a churchgoer, reading the Bible before he left his Washington boardinghouse one Sunday and then "so happy in church that I joined the choir in singing a familiar old hymn."[36] His belief that the Catholic Church "does not agree with mine as to the sanctity of the Sabbath day" was worrisome; but "I *know* we will agree in welcoming its quiet hours," making their separate peace.[37] He could be detached from religion. Florence should read Johnston's *American Politics,* he urged in one letter, where he also spoke easily of Emerson and concluded with advice to build up a library: "You ought to be collecting one for Harry," her son.[38] A lawyer-turned-politician, Vance might be expected to take his faith with a grain of salt. Florence, in contrast, took a pious viewpoint more consistently. Zebulon chided her for studying "metaphysics" to the neglect of the book he gave her on government.[39] In the spring of 1880, as their discussion of her Catholicism dragged on, Florence's good manners predictably frayed. "All the people of North Carolina couldn't [fret?] me about my religion," she said in temper; "for to tell the truth I have a most unchristian contempt for their doctrines."[40] At bottom, each one harbored disdain of the other's religion. This was not unusual for Protestants and Catholics in America, but it was a problem if they were in love.

Perhaps the couple's elemental distastes were never fully resolved. The Catholic clergy stepped in, however, to calm Vance's distress. What he found he had to promise—to let his wife practice her religion freely and raise their future children in the church—was less crucial than his discovery that priests were reasonable men. As soon as he heard of the pledges, Vance turned to friends who knew Catholics. One was "intimate" with Archbishop Gibbons of Baltimore.[41] Although Gibbons had been the first bishop of North Carolina from 1868 to 1873, Vance knew him only by reputation as a "courteous gentleman," and he now requested an interview. The meeting went well. "He recd me kindly and explained everything fully." Vance left convinced that he risked no "dishonor" by a matrimonial oath, which he could take "cheerfully, as I told him, & keep it like a Christian gentleman." Coming from a white southerner, the language of chivalry signaled how deeply contact with Catholicism touched his self-respect. But if the Catholic clergy, too, consisted of honorable men, he did not "object to the priests of your church visiting you. On the contrary I have already invited the archbishop to visit us when we go to housekeeping & he has promised to come on the first notice of that interesting fact!"[42] Vance coped well with the Catholic Church as long as he felt in control. It was important to him to line up the priest for the wedding. "Please give me the address of the clergyman whom you desire to perform the ceremony," he asked just before leaving for Louisville, Florence's hometown, "and I will write to him and engage his services."[43] Though Vance extolled family privacy, free of church intrusion, he dealt comfortably with priests conceived as fellow gentlemen. Archbishop Gibbons was in truth a distinguished man. No less, the prelate's patience and cordiality to the senator showed insight into the deep fears of Protestants who married Catholics and willingness to smooth the way for mixed-faith relationships already sealed by love.[44]

The Vances' marriage in June 1880 still did not yield a Catholic legacy to match the descendants of Stephen Douglas. Although Harry Martin was raised Catholic, Zebulon's four sons were grown up, and the couple had no children of their own. Vance, a firmer Protestant than Douglas, did not drift toward his wife's church. The result was a friendly truce. Zebulon's birthplace in the Smoky Mountains was as much a Catholic wasteland as his wife might have imagined. When Florence, apparently alone, visited his "tribe of poor kin" in September, she wrote plaintively to her husband, "I could not live in Asheville" because "there was no church here." "I *must* have church," she insisted fretfully; "It is dreadful to be without it."[45] This helps explain why Vance ran twice for reelection to the Senate, dying in office in 1894. With many Catholic institutions, Washington was a city where Florence could be happy. After 1889, when Vance underwent surgery, they spent more time at their home outside Asheville. Here, even he compromised spiritually and attended a Baptist Church, the only services nearby. When Florence spent the summer of 1890 alone at the North Carolina coast, she may have been in search of a Catholic parish.[46] Through all, Zebulon did not betray his pledge to the priest. He permitted his wife and stepson to practice their faith. In this limited sense, the marriage was a victory for the Catholic church. Affection sustained the arrangement. When Florence worried during their engagement that their passion might cool, Vance replied: "As you feel toward your church, so have I the same faith in your love."[47] Religion and romance might unexpectedly and angrily come into conflict, as Vance, in honesty, knew. But in their household, two faiths and mutual regard coexisted amiably on the whole, as his simile presumed.

The wedding of David Levy Yulee (1810–1886) and Nannie Wickliffe in 1846, the earliest of the three senators' matches, shuffled the terms of the religious equation. But again, marriage proscriptions were overridden by longings of the self. To all appearances, David Yulee was a man of supreme ambition. John Quincy Adams, as a member of the House, railed in his diary about Yulee as an upstart in the nastiest terms. In 1842, he was "the Jew Delegate from Florida," then still a territory; another time, "the alien Jew Delegate from Florida" with a rumored "dash of African blood."[48] These scurrilous words measured the disdain of a Yankee champion of antislavery for a man—to Adams, a greedy, unprincipled Jew—rich in human chattel. In November 1845, Yulee spent $7,180 at a slave auction in St. Augustine, purchasing twenty-four men, women, and children ranging in age from seventy-five to two. His wealth far exceeded that of his father, Moses Elias Levy, who owned three or so slaves when he emigrated from St. Thomas to the U.S. mainland in 1818. The dowry of Nannie Wickliffe brought slaves as well. [49] Yulee's marriage seemed the capstone to aspiration. He became one of Florida's first senators upon its admission to statehood in 1845, then petitioned the legislature to change his surname from "Levy" to the exotic "Yulee," somehow connected with his Sephardic ancestors in Morocco.[50] Did Nannie succumb to his spirited self-creation? She was a woman of idealism and passion. "'I pity those who have no country to love or to fight for,'" she professed fervently after secession.[51] Yet clearer than her motives was how well the match worked as political alliance. Charles Wickliffe, her father, was formerly governor of Kentucky and a member of John Tyler's cabinet, like Yulee, a southern Whig. David and Nannie—one of "three graces," society's pet name for the Wickliffe sisters—perhaps met at a Washington function.[52] Common slaveholding interests, sectional loyalties, and politics promoted the marriage, over the objection that Yulee was a Jew.

Yet what kind of Jew he was made all the difference in determining his relationship with his wife and, strangely crucial, with his family of birth. Unlike Douglas and Vance, Yulee seemed eager to absorb his wife's creed, which put him at odds with his father. It was a convention of the time that wives should purify husbands morally, so it is hard to measure the depth of David's plea for Nannie's spiritual aid. "I have felt this was no place to begin my reform," he reflected in Washington in 1848, because "love of human praise is fatal to faith." "With your approbation," he wished "to retire from [the Senate] upon the expiration of my term, with the purpose of providing a comfortable home here for my family, and joining my dear wife in assisting each other to secure a happy home hereafter."[53] His profession was, on one level, sincere. In the 1860s, he recalled in private notes that he had left Judaism for Christianity by the 1830s. A Jew to hostile eyes, Yulee may have thought of himself as a Christian. Once married, he bought Christian books at his wife's request, and they attended Presbyterian Church, though he declined to be baptized.[54] Evidences of Christian loyalty were bound up in other stories, however, of romance and power. As newlyweds, David and Nannie, acclaimed for her piety, discoursed at length about doctrine. "I believe with you," David affirmed, "that there is but one way of approach to God": "a true christian faith & humility, and a rational submission of ourselves to God with faith."[55] His words need not be doubted to see that they were a route to intimacy to a wife preoccupied with godly things. But the reflective letters did not continue, and Yulee's interest in spiritual growth competed with politics. After he lost reelection in 1851, he imagined Stephen Douglas "enjoying the busy scenes of Washington life," he wrote from Florida to his Democratic colleague, in contrast to his own "quiet happiness of rural retirement and repose." But his heart was in the political melee—to which he devoted the next three and a half pages—and he won back his Senate seat in 1855.[56] Although Christian commitments united the Yulees at home, they did not change David's life as much as he had once foreseen.

Nor did he let troubled relations with his father cast a shadow on his public face as a shrewd and driven man. This, however, was the family's core religious conflict and the subtext to Yulee's marriage. Much like his son, Moses Elias Levy (1781–1854) was a canny entrepreneur who became so rich, particularly in Florida land, that he left an estate of more than 42,000 dollars. He was also a reader of great breadth: less often classic Jewish texts than books on kabbalah, mesmerism, and millennial prophecy. In correspondence with leading Jews and Christians, he elaborated a philosophy of Jewish millenarianism. Again and again, he condemned the "doctrine of individualism": "Self government is a heresy against the nature or man and the Bible, nay it infuses atheism."[57] With the same energy, he dismissed the clergy, Jewish and Christian: "The Bible is true & the teachers are false."[58] Like her father, Levy's daughter Ramah wrote in September 1854, not knowing that he was already dead, "I worship my Creator in temples erected for Christian worship as you often have done, for I have no temple worthy to dedicate to him, but my heart is firm in my people."[59] Soon the time of false prophets would end, Levy believed, and "Christians (*spiritual* Israel) will ask Israel to establish a theocracy."[60] In a twisted way, his logic echoed the Christian expectation that Jesus' Second Coming would be preceded by the conversion of the Jews. But Levy unquestioningly saw himself as a Jew, and though it is easy to see how a man so precariously situated on several religious margins produced a Christian-leaning son, why their relations were tempestuous is equally plain.

In Nannie, Levy found a woman of intense devotion: a kindred spirit. His father felt "affection for my wife," David recalled in 1868. More strongly, Levy closed his single surviving letter to Nannie, "farewell faithful mirror of my affection & mind."[61] Yet affinity led the father to manipulate the couple. We "will be much rejoiced at any manifestations of sympathy upon your part in our feelings," Yulee replied from Washington in 1849: "But in respect to our religious views & conduct you must consent to have us unquestioned & responsible only to God—who we pray will in the fullness of his mercy enlighten and guide our hearts."[62] What Levy envisioned religiously is unknown. David's resistance, though, was just one episode in a sad history, reconstructed in the son's marginal notes to letterbooks of Levy's correspondence that Yulee compiled after the war. Although "Mr. Levy knew of his sons having adopted a different faith" before, "it was not till 1836 that the climax of his hallucinations of mind took place that he commenced to repudiate his sons Elias & David." "Letter of P. S. Smith 1841," David recorded, "on which is endorsed his assertion that David is no longer his son since he became a Lawyer."[63] Few callings, presumably, were more combative and unspiritual than the law. But even after "our separation," Yulee helped Levy in business, and they met and partly reconciled in 1845. Renewed friendliness did not survive the quarrel about the Yulees' religion. At Levy's death in 1854, his will left each son $100, his daughters everything else.[64]

Were the Yulees really a mixed-faith family, and, if so, was this at all like the Protestant-Catholic households of their Senate colleagues? From the viewpoint of doctrine, David was a Christian, though his letters to Nannie focused on ethics—"love of our neighbors"—and spoke of Jesus in a solitary reference as "a model of a perfect man."[65] Yet without overreading, it is possible to see Yulee's persistent, disquieting dialogue with his father, and his father's memory, as a private struggle with his Jewish roots. During the war, Union troops burned the Yulees' plantation on the Gulf Coast at Homosassa, and later he was jailed for a year. It was in defeat that David tried to assemble Levy's diary and letters, and finally settle the will. This was dreary business, since it was "our father's peculiar religious views & theory of life, which had unhappily broken up the family, & scattered & alienated its members."[66] But, through the work, Yulee must have thought hard about himself. Levy's unconventional Judaism entered his son's life as a barely detectable presence in normal times. Now Yulee lost the reassuring props of a self-made man and returned to thoughts of his father. It is doubtful that Nannie shared, or even knew much of, David's labors over the letterbooks. While apparently Nannie was no fool, she had little to do with his Jewish memories. The distance between them was a mark of an interfaith marriage.

The Yulees, like the Douglases and Vances, belonged to a world in which there were many reasons to marry that edged religion aside. Washington epitomized America's romance with freedom and selfhood. Here it made sense to wed for social advantage and personal reward. Yet even if religion did not guide marriage choices, it remained part of families. The question is how. The Catholic Church seemed able to offer interfaith households a structure in which to function as religiously mixed homes. Priests assisted the Douglases and Vances at crucial junctures, not in a disinterested way, but neither with the presumption that Protestant husbands would yield to Catholicism right away. Tolerance, evangelicalism, and, critically, an institution squarely facing mixed marriages had appeal in an era when couples seemed eager for public religious ties. True, the submerged conflict in the Yulee family grew just as much from David's deep questions of identity as from the cool propriety of the Presbyterian Church. But no middle ground appeared for this Jewish-Protestant couple, who seemed never quite settled. Outside Washington, Catholicism repeated the same successful arrangement: the church nurtured Catholic wives and children, and waited for the conversions of Protestant men.

Converts and Their Husbands

Not all religiously mixed families began with marriages. Some became interfaith households because of subsequent conversions to Catholicism of Protestant wives. Self-fulfillment, the promise of liberal society, often took the form of seeking mundane rewards—romance, for one, or status—at the expense of religious rules. Secularism was not the temper of the age, however, in any simple sense. Self-assertion might be expressed as religious commitment. A conversion experience as a matter of rededication was integral to Protestantism. But when the penitent embraced Catholicism, spiritual urgency, in Protestant eyes, must have seemed like rebellion. Male converts to Catholicism who were heads of households invariably brought wives and children with them into the church. For women, the family consequences were more painful. Autonomous enough to become Catholic and raise their children in the faith, wives acquiesced almost silently in their husbands' continued Protestantism. No less, the husbands watched anxiously as their wives changed in unexpected ways.[67] This was the experience of Sophia Dana Ripley, Anna Barker Ward, and Wilhelmine Easby-Smith, who converted, successively, in 1847 or 1848, 1858, and 1862.

Sophia Ripley (1803–1861) and her husband George had a reputation as social radicals. By the winter of 1847–1848, when Sophia became a Catholic, they had lived at the Brook Farm Community outside Boston for six years. Although George, a Unitarian minister in the 1830s, was well known for his Transcendentalist leanings, Sophia, too, signed Brook Farm's Articles of Association in 1841. Their goal, to make economic equity and education available to all, led the group to ally itself with the Fourier movement in 1844. Charles Fourier's theory was an elaborate plan for social reconstruction, and the reformers were now busy with publicity and conventions. But something else was happening quietly at the farm. "We are beginning to see wooden crosses around and pictures of saints," a staunch Protestant was said to report irritably to a visitor, "and I suspect that rosaries are rattling under aprons."[68] Some, including Sophia, were studying church history. George, however, by one account, did not think it was "your old Fathers nor even your Dante" that brought her to Catholicism: "It was Isaac at his bread board while you peeled potatoes."[69] "Isaac" was Isaac Hecker, a deeply spiritual young man who sampled Transcendentalism before entering the Catholic Church in 1844.[70] Perhaps he and Sophia did talk, in a less one-sided way than George supposed, as they worked. Soon she was a Catholic, too.

Contrary to the nervous gossip about Romanism, Sophia's conversion made sense in light of Brook Farm's purpose. The community sought a total change of society and spirit. "I long for action," George wrote Isaac Hecker in 1843, "which shall realize the prophecies, fulfil the Apocalypse, bring the new Jerusalem down from heaven to earth, and collect the faithful into a true and holy brotherhood."[71] This wish for a devout, common life pursued with a view to the past instead of the future, in an ancient institution not new ones, led easily to Catholicism. Sophia believed the church offered her the chance for "a sanctified heart." One Sunday in 1848, she had "a clear revelation of myself," she confided to her cousin Charlotte Dana, also a convert: "I saw that all through life my ties with others were those of the intellect & imagination & not warm human heart ties; that I do not love anyone & never did, with the heart & of course never could have been worthy in any relation."[72] With the help of "my Blessed Director," she would learn "obedience" to the rule to love God and neighbor, "not with the heart you have *not* my child, but with the heart you have."[73] George, a decent man, understood that Catholicism held answers for his wife. In 1862, on the first anniversary of Sophia's death, he thanked Charlotte for arranging a memorial Mass. "You know that it has always been my wish that such a faithful Catholic heart should enjoy, to its fullest extent, every rite & promise which the good motherly Church affords to those who look to her for blessings."[74]

These, however, were retrospective thoughts of a man still grieving. Sophia's conversion had in fact set a barrier between husband and wife, difficult particularly at first. Sophia eagerly told Charlotte in July 1848 that Orestes Brownson, a friend and convert, was writing "noble letters" to George on "the process of his conversion," at once "full of manly strength, but tender & patient as a woman's pleading."[75] But George remained devoted to Fourierism, though now in a sober mood. Failing financially, Brook Farm was sold late in 1847, and the Ripleys moved to New York. "When you see any of our [divine?] ones of Brook Farm," George wrote sadly to a Boston friend, "tell them not to forget me."[76] Sophia struggled with his continuing activism. *"My Father,"* her confessor, "told me, rather to my disappointment," she confided in Charlotte, "that I must by all means go to the Fourier Festival, as 'the companion of my husband,' though of course he should prefer I would not."[77] The next year, George went to work for Horace Greeley's *Tribune,* and his involvement in Fourierism declined with the movement itself. He warmed, occasionally, to Catholicism. In 1857, writing an entry on *Agnus Dei* for *Appleton's Cyclopedia,* he asked to see one of these prayer aids, "put it on with perfectly childish delight, & would not lay it aside on any account."[78] Still, George was not a Catholic, declaring sympathy in 1865 with the "liberal Unitarians."[79] "There"—to Catholicism—"he could not follow her, could not even agree with her, and they tacitly decided not to mention it any more than necessary."[80] This twentieth-century estimate cannot be documented, yet it rings true. Many years after their wedding in 1827, Sophia's conversion precipitated the Ripleys into an interfaith marriage. They coped, it seems, by forbearance.

Husbands as well as the converts restrained their disagreements. By common measures, Samuel Gray Ward underreacted to his wife's conversion. Apparently traveling alone, or perhaps with their children, Anna Barker Ward (d. 1900) became a Catholic in Rome in 1858. Samuel, in his biographer's words, "remained silent." "There is nothing to suggest that this step, extreme for the daughter of a Quaker, bothered Ward particularly. He could hardly have felt in strong sympathy with it, although, in accepting it gracefully, he was expressing a theological tolerance not uncommon in Unitarians like his father."[81] Perplexed negatives—"nothing to suggest," "could hardly have felt"—indicate Ward's tight self-control, if not the liberality inferred here. His actions help fill in the message. He "provided his wife with a Catholic chapel on the grounds" of their country house in Lenox, Massachusetts.[82] Altogether, these gestures speak of the conflicts of a man long married: disbelief mixed with acceptance of his wife's decision, no longer framed securely by intimacy.

No conversion is simple, but for Anna Barker Ward, becoming Catholic had an element of liberation. Self-reliance should not have eluded a woman of wide experience and bold friends. A Quaker from New Orleans, Anna was on close terms with Margaret Fuller and Emerson when she married in Boston in 1840. It may have been their insistence on selfhood, however, that instilled her doubts. "I sail under orders & you are my authority," she wrote to her father-in-law, Thomas Wren Ward, in 1851. "I wonder, if after all, I am 'a woman of authorities,'" she reflected again. "Do I get all my ideas from you & Sam?"[83] Other signs, too, gave hints in the 1850s that Anna wondered who she was. This was a difficult decade. In 1849, the Wards leased the farm in the Berkshires where they had experimented with pastoral living; back in Boston, Samuel became the American agent of British bankers, once his father's job. Margaret Fuller died in 1850, and soon, so did the Wards' daughter, Mary. Invalidism pursued Anna. In 1855, she told her father-in-law of a "severe neuralgia attack."[84] Friends living in Germany were "astounded" in 1857 to "find you in Europe so soon again," without her husband and seeking health.[85] So close to her father-in-law that she addressed letters "my dear father" and signed "your attached daughter," Anna must have been moved by news of his final illness preceding his death on March 4, 1858. But the loss of "my authority" seems, too, to have freed her. In Rome, she became a Catholic the same month.[86]

Although Samuel's response is obscure, other Protestant men involved with Anna withdrew to a safe emotional distance. Perhaps their postures and her husband's were similar. Emerson drafted a letter in early May to "lament the chance-wind that has made a foreigner of you—whirled you from the forehead of the morning into the mediaevals, again." He did not send it. Excising his disapproval, he stressed, true to his philosophy, the preeminence of character over sect: "how supremely unimportant the form under which we celebrate the Justice, Love, & Truth,—the attributes of the Deity & the Soul!"[87] This kept a bridge open between them, but at the expense of letting Anna know how he really felt. Jacob Barker, "thy fond father," wrote often from New Orleans to "my much loved daughter." Yet only once, in 1863, did he mention Anna's religion:

> I was rejoiced at thy success in relation to the new institution. I think the Catholics have done more good to the world in their efforts to enlighten the rising generation & relieving those in want, than all the other sectarians together. Yet I object from the bottom of my heart to some of their religious dogmas particularly to that which supposes our heavenly father has any authorized agents to represent him on earth. He is fully competent to do his own work & is always present.[88]

Here was the honest, equivocal view of a Quaker, then in his eighties. But Catholicism seemed, by its neglect, a painful subject to him, better suppressed to protect their affection. By contrast, the famed singer Jenny Lind wrote engagingly to her friend. Surely "with your warm feelings and earnest desire after perfection how natural it was that *Christ* should grow deeper and deeper into your heart," Lind observed in February 1858, during Anna's spiritual "struggle." Not a Catholic herself, Jenny warned "not to expect more of the church on earth than she really *can* give."[89] Her letters showed none of the caution, however, of Anna's male friends and kin. To all appearances, Samuel and Anna approached each other with care. This was deeply engrained in genteel post-Puritan culture overall. It appeared in the perfect poise of Charles Eliot Norton's note to Samuel in 1900: "I have just heard of Mrs. Ward's death. I clasp your hand for an instant in silence."[90] Still, the instinct to contain and channel feelings came to the fore when the Ward household of aging Transcendentalists became an interfaith home. Religiously, the Wards parted ways. But domestically, patience managed to keep the family from breaking.

Creating rules to keep the peace was not just a Yankee trait. In Alabama, "religious discussions had never been allowed in the home" of William Russell Smith, one daughter remembered.[91] This Protestant father seems to have kept his Catholic wife on short rein, until the memoir continues: the children were raised Catholic, religious artwork covered their walls, and priests came to dinner.[92] How could silence about religion be reconciled with crowded reminders of Catholic activity? How, similarly, could Samuel Ward say so little to Anna about Catholicism and then build her a private chapel? Each wife's conversion rent her family spiritually. Households did cope. But whether the terms of reconciliation were logical did not matter so long as the truce made sense to them.

The conversion of Wilhelmine Easby-Smith came at such an inopportune time that there must have been reason in her madness. By January 1862, when she became Catholic, the war had scattered her family. Wilhelmine was living in a hotel in Tuscumbia, Alabama; her husband, a Confederate colonel, nearby at camp. Two younger children were with her. A daughter was at convent school in Washington, D.C., her oldest stepson in the army, and two more stepchildren with kin. Years later, she told a daughter that her decision was "the most severe blow that ever befell your father."[93] Fearful, Wilhelmine said nothing of her intent until the night before she entered the church. Yet her conversion might have been foreseen. The child of Episcopalians, she studied at the Academy of the Visitation in Georgetown. She taught a class on church history at the Smiths' Episcopal parish in Tuscaloosa after her marriage in 1854, and, like many swayed by the Oxford Movement, was convinced that historical authority belonged to the Catholic Church.[94] It was the war, however, that seemed to dislodge and finally embolden her. This, certainly, was how she felt as it progressed. In 1864, William explained to Confederate officials that his wife was "greatly disturbed" by news of her daughter and mother, both behind Union lines in Washington since 1861. When no pass arrived to travel north, Wilhelmine set off without one; the South's Provost Marshall, not wishing "to send a guard after her," still threatened to "take such steps as will bring her back."[95] In the same mood of uncertainty and then resolve, Wilhelmine, one imagines, determined two years earlier to become a Catholic. Her family's wartime dispersion was an essential condition of her conversion, though not its cause.

William Russell Smith's reaction to his wife's spiritual step may have been similar to the Provost Marshall's to her flight: bring her back. Hearing the news at her hotel, he paled and "went out," Wilhelmine recalled, "shutting the door with enough force to make me understand how deeply he was offended."[96] Smith was not, like many Protestants, ambivalent about Catholics. A Know-Nothing politician, he publicly opposed them. In 1856, he delivered the nominating speech for Millard Fillmore, the party's presidential candidate, at its convention in Philadelphia. Little wonder that Wilhelmine worried in 1862 that William might wish to separate, or that she was relieved when he returned. She recalled: "What a wonderful battle he must have fought with himself that night! And I knew that only his great and abiding love and respect for me could (under God) have ever brought him to accept the bitter draught that my action must have been for him."[97] Her memory may have overdramatized the moment. After all, Mamie, their oldest child, was already enrolled at the Visitation school. Soon William closed letters to his daughter with reminders to give "obedience to the sisters."[98] Yet the fact is that his wife's conversion divided their family far more profoundly than did the war. Equally, marital contention was surprisingly brief. With the exception of the grown son of Smith's first wife, children and stepchildren were now baptized Catholics. So was Wilhelmine's mother, Agnes. Writing to her son-in-law, Agnes praised William's "catholicity" and called him a "christian."[99] But he did not become a Catholic, and the Smiths proceeded as an interfaith family.

Strong and conflicting feelings surrounded all these wives' conversions. Each woman, driven by her convictions, made a bold and independent decision, all the while apprehensive of her husband's displeasure and eager for his religious change of heart. The men not only stood their ground, but restrained what must have been dismay at a choice that loosened family intimacy and allied their households, in the view of most Protestants, with a proscribed faith. Considering the emotional stakes, explosive fights were rare. Conversions unfolded in families with almost ritual solemnity, at least in the historical record. Three conditions eased the passage. The first was commitment to family: married twenty, eighteen, and eight years, respectively, the Ripleys, Wards, and Smiths faced religious disagreement within frameworks of domestic habit and caring. Gender, secondly, caused, then eased problems. Women of this class possessed real freedom, though not enough domestic power to make husbands Catholics. Still, in a culture believing women to be pious and men worldly-wise, it must have seemed natural to have wives be the devoted Catholics in interfaith homes. When the three husbands, pursuing careers in journalism, business, and law, showed modest religious interest, they conformed as neatly to social expectations. Last, the Catholic Church stood by. The wives, as converts, welcomed the church's presence, and the husbands did not reject it.

Interfaith Families and Their Church

What were the homes of Catholic wives and Protestant husbands like, and on what terms did they meet the Catholic Church, and the church them? The seven mid-century couples that lived as Catholics approached the church by varied routes. Female converts came by choice as adults. Of the women raised Catholic, only Esther La Rose, marrying Joel Chandler Harris in Savannah in 1873, grew up for certain with two Catholic parents, though Florence Martin Vance may have as well. Others came from religiously mixed homes. Ellen Ewing Sherman and Adele Cutts Douglas, both wed in the 1850s, did as their mothers had done: they took Protestant husbands.[100] Daughters who set up mixed-faith households like those of their childhoods must have done so with a comfort eluding the converts, who faced their husbands' distress and their own guilt at dividing their homes. All, however, lived with liberal-minded men focused on down-to-earth goals, pursued often in politics, and the religious outcomes of the marriages were the same. Catholic mothers reared children in their religion, with the fathers' acquiescence and the church's support. The solution worked well because it matched deep traits of mid-century Victorian culture: women's piety and men's restrained spirituality, mediated by their common taste for institutional life.

It was the religious dedication of women that anchored their families' Catholicism. Although a mother's zeal might be embellished in her children's recollections, this was less an act of mythmaking than a index of the respect her commitment stirred. When Anne Easby-Smith, a sister in the Society of the Holy Child Jesus, looked back in 1931 at her childhood in Alabama, she pictured her mother ministering to their black neighbors: "It was, in fact, her custom, if she knew that a child was dying, to baptize it, and many a little white soul took its flight to heaven from her tender arms, or soon after her sweet voice had coaxed it to sleep." To Anne's mind, her mother's seriousness contrasted with her father's playfulness. "She made her children love their Faith"; he "could lay aside his innate dignity for the amusement of his children."[101] The centerpiece of memory was the mother's Catholicism. Family emotions, the source of memoirs like Anne's, grew intimately with the women's Catholic convictions.

Often wives were prepared by Catholic educations to establish pious homes. Anna Barker, though raised a Quaker, had attended a convent school in New Orleans. Three others studied in Georgetown at the Academy of the Visitation. Adele Cutts, Wilhelmine Easby, and Ellen Ewing all had Protestant fathers employed by the government. Adele and Ellen were Catholics; Wilhelmine, an Episcopal girl in a convent school.[102] William Tecumseh Sherman, Ellen's foster brother and future husband, laughed almost cruelly at the cloister. "You did not tell me how you were pleased with the nunnery," he wrote in 1837 from West Point; "it must be a very dull place."[103] But this was the view of an adolescent boy. The sentimental piety of Catholic academies more likely appealed to girls. "Farewell to My Convent Home" was the title Esther La Rose gave her final composition in the late 1860s at Acton-Vale school in Quebec. Love of Mary, figurative

mother of the convent, converged with reverence for motherhood itself. Although Esther anticipated missing "the chapel, the place of
calm repose" where she "partook of the life giving bread," she returned happily "to my mother, my own tender mother whom I so tenderly love." Even more, "Mary, my mother, shall always accompany
me; her smile shall cheer the clouded path of life."[104] The essay was
not unique in Esther's schoolgirl papers. Drawings of hearts, flowers,
crosses, and communion cups accented the resemblance between love
of God and romance with a man.[105] Quite naturally, women so
trained made Catholicism the cornerstone of their adult homes.

They did so with the consent of Protestant husbands. Behind Catholic Church attendance, schooling, and charitable work were quiet
struggles of couples who never quite saw eye to eye. Converts—
women who adopted an unpopular religion on their own—were especially grateful for domestic peace. Coming home from a trip alone in
1852, Sophia Ripley told her cousin Charlotte that it "seemed to
George & myself as if we were beginning life together again," and "I
assure you it is very pleasant." She sounded relieved. Her husband, no
churchgoer in the 1850s, still had radical Protestant sympathies, and
despite his occasional willingness to accompany his wife to convents
and Mass, their beliefs stood between them. Without children, hers
was "a strange sort of lonely life," where she did not "hear a Catholic
word spoken from morning to night."[106] No couple could avoid some
sense of alienation, which was covered, but not erased, by compromise.

Yet families were sustained, most powerfully, by wives' hopes for
their husbands' conversions. Women prayed, cajoled, and searched
for signs of a change of heart for many years. Rationally, Ellen Ewing
must have known that William Tecumseh Sherman was uninquisitive
about faith, because he had lived with her family since boyhood.
Posted with the army in Charleston in 1842, he reported to Ellen that
he heard a Presbyterian and Catholic preach, and visited the synagogue. "This you see in answer to your question. I [torn] say little else
than that to be a soldier and a [professing?] christian is somehow incompatible."[107] Cump mellowed for a time after the wedding. Perhaps
heartened that he walked her to Mass and gave her a crucifix, Ellen
pleaded in earnest. My "prayer and hope," she began in July 1855,
"are that you may not only die a Catholic but that you may live
many a long year in the [true church?] & enjoy [much?] of the faith

which availeth such satisfaction." In September she urged again: "The desire of seeing you a christian is the hope of my life and in death it will not desert me."[108] Some men fulfilled their wives' dreams. William Russell Smith and later Joel Chandler Harris became Catholics on their deathbeds in 1896 and 1908; so did Ellen's father Thomas Ewing in 1871.[109] But Cump was not one of these. Faced with his inattentiveness, Ellen increasingly saw his separate interests as a reproach and his independence as desertion. Pregnant in 1859 for the fifth time in a decade, Ellen, home with her parents in Ohio, challenged Cump, working in Kansas: "Have you never wondered what the child might be—have you no preference as to the name it may bear?" Soon the war took him physically and emotionally farther away. "It is not that I think the dear children we now have will fail to take an absorbing & appreciative interest in your part in the present history of the country," she wrote caustically when their son dreamed about his father in 1864, "but it makes me heart sick to feel that sense of loss that every such memento awakens in my heart."[110] Her peevishness about Cump's disengagement was not simply about his religious indifference. Still, his rebuffs of Ellen's evangelism must have made his autonomy more galling. The family, even then, never gave up. The children called a priest to administer last rites when their father died in 1891, three years after Ellen's death. It was less crucial to family harmony for interfaith couples to worship together than for them to believe that one day they might.

The Catholic Church supported the matriarchs' aspirations. Nuns and priests were devoted to the husbands' conversions. "Sister M[ary]. C[atherine]. & I are uniting in the Thirty Day's prayer for him," Sophia Ripley confided to her cousin in 1848. Hopeful again in 1857, she inferred that "Mr. Ripley misses & needs Father H[ecker]—inexpressibly, & we have no idea when he will be able to return."[111] Sophia did not imagine the interest of Isaac Hecker, old friend and now priest, in ministering to Protestant men. When he corresponded with Anna Barker Ward in the 1860s, Hecker communicated Catholic news, at times particularly for the ears of her husband Samuel. Had Anna read a recent article on St. Augustine? Hecker was sure Ward, too, "would find something to his liking in it."[112] Even when not intent on conversion, priests visited interfaith households on friendly terms. Theodore Ratisbonne, superior of a French religious order to convert the Jews, left his calling card in the 1870s at the Wards'

Boston home. In turn-of-the-century Washington, "our house was always open to priests," a daughter of Wilhelmine Easby-Smith recalled, "especially if they were strangers in the city."[113] The cordiality of the church had to be gratifying to Catholic wives. Separated by their faith from their spouses, the women were nourished by contact with the church's representatives, especially those who promised spiritual repairs for marriages.

Protestant husbands might well have been resentful for the same reasons. It would not have been hard to suspect a priest of conspiring with your wife to ensnare your soul, particularly in a Protestant culture already anxious about Catholicism's subversive designs. But in fact, husbands were rarely distressed. William Russell Smith, banning family religious debate, still did not resist his children's prayerful wishes that "dear Papa was a Catholic" and behaved as "the soul of courtesy to all guests," including priests.[114] In 1896, Joel Chandler Harris wrote from Atlanta to instruct a daughter at St. Joseph's Academy to thank Sister Bernard for "praying for a special favor for me": "I think I know what it is, and the idea is growing more pleasing to me everyday." Soon he began to study with a priest for baptism, but then put it off, perhaps finding it too much "to root out of the mind," he told his little girl, "the prejudices and doubts and fictions that have been educated into it."[115] William Tecumseh Sherman came closer to stereotypical fears of manipulation. When Ellen nagged him in 1872 to call on Cardinal Manning in London, Sherman gratuitously reminded her that he was "not a Catholic," yet would be victimized "because they make use of [such visits] for their purposes, not mine."[116] He did speak with Manning, however, much as he had paid respects on his honeymoon in 1850 to Bishop Hughes in New York and welcomed San Francisco's archbishop to his home there on New Year's Day 1854.[117] As the freethinking father of a large Catholic family, Sherman eyed his wife's Catholic allies as instinctively as he might have scanned a landscape for ambush. What is noteworthy is not that he chafed, but that he tolerated the church. The question is why.

The husbands tended to be liberals, comfortable with diverse views, even at home. William Russell Smith championed an ideal of civilized letters. The Sisters of the Visitation might teach that "mythology is all fiction," he warned his daughter in 1866: "But it is still very important to study and understand the subject, as it is part of polite learning; without a knowledge of which you could not enjoy or appreciate the greatest and best poets."[118] A poet himself, Smith recruited literary playfulness to lace family bonds made vulnerable by religious disagreement. "The Honey-Moon," a sonnet composed for the couple's fourteenth anniversary in 1868, pictured their love—the honeymoon—"as bright as she was wont to be on that espousal night."[119] It was not just a sentimental but a clever poem, each line marked in the margin by a successive year of the marriage, a sign of how important humor could be in keeping potential quarrels in check. Jokes sparred with the temptation to be dogmatic. One day in 1896, Joel Chandler Harris laughed about his mixed marriage after Esther got dirty scrubbing the stovepipe, and she told him to go find a clean wife. He explained to their daughter: "I answered that the Church does not allow divorces. The reply was that I was not a Catholic—to which I answered that having become (as it were) a brother-in-law of the Church, with the hope and expectation of a closer relation when I felt good enough, I felt bound to conform to the rules in so far as I could. Well, it was a great time."[120] Another time, when Esther caught him discussing the Middle Ages with their son Julian, it was Julian who launched the witty reply: "Mother, don't you trust us with the church?"[121] Catholic wives would not have been wrong to sense elements of defensiveness and dismissiveness in this lightheartedness about faith. Humor was one expression of the liberal's instinct to keep all creeds at arm's length, except tolerance itself. Less deeply, husbands were more easygoing about religion than their wives. This helped keep marriages together.

The spouses' differences in mood were not rooted absolutely in their natures as men and women or Protestants and Catholics, but in the way traits of gender and religion blended in this milieu. True to contemporaneous myths about the sexes, these men were more worldly than their wives. Like classic Protestants, they circumscribed their piety as they went about their everyday business. Politics seemed to match their instincts, and their taste for civic life began early. Looking back in 1892, William Russell Smith remembered that he owned Bible and hymnal as a boy, yet most prized Mason Weems's *Life of Washington*—"the greatest man that ever lived": "WEEMES. Ah! happy boy! to become the absolute owner of WEEM's Washington, at the age of ten years."[122] Joel Chandler Harris, a Georgia teenager during the sectional crisis, demonstrated political wit in a schoolboy satire of Lincoln. Posing as "Obadiah Skinflint" writing to "Meester Abraham Linhern," he let the president know that he "naimed mi old shepe killin cur Abe."[123] Civic culture, which gave both men principles, was rough and combative, built on contests of opinion, leavened with humor. This temper helps explain why husbands of Catholics finally shrugged their shoulders at domestic religious divisions. In politics, disagreement was not fatal, and nearly all of the men had political ties. William Smith, Stephen Douglas, and Zebulon Vance held elective office. William Tecumseh Sherman's name circulated repeatedly for the presidency after the war. Journalism, the focus of others, was bluntly partisan in this era. George Ripley wrote for the New York *Tribune,* and Samuel Ward helped establish the *Nation,* both Republican. Joel Chandler Harris worked for the Atlanta *Constitution,* one voice of the "New South" creed.[124] Simply more interested in the polity than the church, husbands turned a deaf ear to their wives on occasion.

It is still hard to believe that the men's composure alone sustained their patience with years of Catholic training for their children, visits from priests, and church socials on their lawns. Behind the husbands' neat liberality was a less manageable attraction for the family religion, not so much because the faith was Catholicism, but because its practice was the way of the household. William Tecumseh Sherman, most testy of all about his Catholic obligations, was also most enmeshed. So often did he distance himself verbally from "your church" that he protested too much: he betrayed his uncomfortable intimacy with Ellen's religion.[125] Formally, he was a Catholic. Baptized by a priest as a boy at his Catholic foster mother's insistence, he married and died with the sacraments. Growing up with a Protestant foster father who ran his wife's Catholic errands, he behaved much the same when he married the daughter, yet grumbled more.[126] Family bonds and habituation to things Catholic pulled him toward the church, at the same time that his spare moralism pushed him away. Even then, perhaps he feared he would succumb to religion in the end. Although it does not seem Sherman was conscious enough on his deathbed to consent to the last rites arranged by his children, worry that he might weaken spiritually must have spurred his irritability over reminders of Catholicism in his life. Sherman was caught in a web of religious ambivalence, where the bait was his Catholic family. If he saw how much he encircled himself by his choice of wife and tolerance of her faith, his frustration might have been deeper still.

On most occasions, however, husbands seemed more nourished than threatened by family piety. Thoughts about their own convictions had small chance to surface in busy Catholic households. Mothers, such as Wilhelmine Easby-Smith, set a fast religious pace, "making the altar breads, playing the organ and leading the choir, even serving tables at picnics."[127] A family's single biggest commitment, though, was to raise Catholic children. Parents patronized Catholic academies and colleges. Mamie Easby-Smith, oldest daughter of William and Wilhelmine, spent about seven years at the Visitation convent in Georgetown, until her mother brought her home to Tuscaloosa in 1868, "after," in her father's words, "so long an absence."[128] Sons of the Douglases and Shermans studied with the Jesuits at Georgetown, and Julian Harris planned to attend Frères Maristes College in 1890 while he stayed with his mother's parents in Quebec.[129] Apparently, intermarried parents agreed that it was worth parting with their children for the sake of Catholic training, often at young ages and for extended times. This was an era when many prosperous parents favored boarding schools. Sending children away diminished the day-to-day cohesion of families and, in mixed-faith homes, may have strengthened each child's attachment to the church. Yet fathers, party to the selection of Catholic institutions, resisted this conclusion. Happy about the gentility of the Catholic curriculum, they ignored its consequences for piety. William Russell Smith expected Mamie to come home "an elegant and accomplished lady."[130] Joel Chandler Harris instructed Julian in Canada that "you must learn to talk French." Far differently, Esther nagged their son to go to confession.[131] Whether Julian's Canadian trip was intended to be exposure to French-speaking society or immersion in Catholic culture depended on who was asked: father or mother. Behind the consensus about Catholic schooling of interfaith parents were distinct subcurrents of interpretation about what the spiritual outcome of this upbringing would be. Fathers were comfortable raising Catholic children, but not too Catholic.

The men's quiet dissent most influenced the rearing of sons, particularly firstborn. Although gender did not strictly determine how much contact children had with the church, boys were less bound than girls by their mother's religion. Most dramatically, the oldest sons of two converts did not become Catholics, while their younger siblings did. Thomas Wren Ward, Anna's child, and Sidney Binion Smith, stepson of Wilhelmine, were in their teens when the women converted around 1860. Like their fathers, the boys remained Protestants.[132] Manhood, it seemed, conferred freedom of religious choice; yet being oldest also brought pressures from fathers. Joel Chandler Harris coolly approved Julian's enrollment at the "French School" in Quebec, but warned that his son must soon "begin the business of life," and "no youngster who has any promise of a career can afford to bury himself in Upton, or in any other country place."[133] Internal cleavages such as these rarely fractured families openly. If anything, they revealed unspoken agreement that women and men might be Catholics of different kinds.

The presence at home of diverse expectations makes it all the more striking that the children commonly remained devout Catholics. One daughter and five nieces of William Russell Smith became nuns. Tom Sherman, so bitterly in his father's eyes, was a Jesuit. The other Sherman children married Catholics, and, although the Harrises' sons and daughters equally wed Protestants, most of them raised Catholic families.[134] Even Thomas Wren Ward, who at age thirteen in 1858 avoided conversion with his mother, stayed in the shadow of the church. Marrying a Catholic, he tried for decades to reconcile his "search for contact with God" with his "old prejudice" against Catholicism, until he converted in 1940.[135] Memories verging on myths gave lives Catholic meaning. Anne Easby-Smith's 1931 biography of her father was essentially a conversion narrative, honoring his final enlightenment and brightened by tales of their kin's conversions and religious vocations.[136] The grown children of intermarried parents did not think of themselves as the offspring of mixed marriages, but as people raised Catholic. From the Catholic standpoint, this must have measured the success of their upbringing. The church had a hand in the process in a quiet yet steady way.

The Protestant imagination easily pictured Catholicism as preying on naive women and children. Emerson fully shared these suspicions. Father Hecker "converted Mrs. W[ard]," he wrote in his journal, "and like the lion that has eaten a man, he wants to be at it again, and convert somebody."[137] Not surprisingly, this nervous view of a rapacious church embellished the facts. Priests and nuns who befriended interfaith couples had evangelical intentions, but did not hide them. Patience, not scheming, was the mood of the church. Its parishes and schools, as if branches of a solid institution, sent a message of reliability: grace was ever within reach of anyone who sought it. It did not matter that Joel Chandler Harris was not baptized by his original in-structor. "Father O'Brien died before he had the happiness of receiv-ing his old friend [Harris] into the Church."[138] Father Jackson, with-out fuss, performed the rite instead; the priests shared the church's authority. Both parents in these households, Protestant and Catholic, accepted the proximity of church and family. With feelings at home never quite settled, Catholicism's constancy must have been valued. The families survived, even flourished, because their wish for partner-ship with the Catholic Church was met by Catholicism's willingness to submerge censure of mixed marriage in evangelism.

A Failed Marriage

So many families juggled dissimilar views that unhappy couples were exceptional. Incompatibility, however, holds lessons. In 1845, Natalie St. Martin Benjamin left her husband, Judah, in New Orleans and took their two-year-old daughter to live in Paris. Although Judah vis-ited annually, the Benjamins did not share a home until months before his death in 1884. Was this marriage any more miserable than, say, the Shermans', who often lived apart and endured low-pitched bicker-ing? Benjamin's biographers agree the match was sad. At the same time, value judgments shape their standard of failure. In 1906, Pierce Butler, believing "marriages between persons of different faiths are rarely wise," might have anticipated the Benjamins' separation. Rob-ert Meade measured by conventional domesticity in 1943 when he blamed Natalie for "ignor[ing] her wifely duties." Marrying up into the Creole gentry, in the eyes of Eli Evans in 1988, was the source of Judah's "lifelong humiliation."[139] How much preconceptions of mar-riage and women affect these conclusions carries a warning to ap-proach marital failure with care. Plainly, the Benjamins' long separa-tion at least bespoke diverging interests, if not acrimony. Late in life, Judah, normally guarded, gave evidence of regret. Thinking of himself "over fifty years ago," he advised a niece involved with a man disliked by her family to beware "the impatience and rashness which are so natural at your age and which may prove fatal to your happiness."[140] Whether it was a troubled relation in an absolute sense, at best the Benjamins' marriage rested on civility, not intimacy. Here, the ques-tion is how much the religious distance between Jew and Catholic was at fault.

The Benjamins left few helpful documents. As the Confederate Secretary of State, Judah burned his wartime correspondence before fleeing Richmond in 1865. In his last year of life, he swore to a would-be biographer that he never "retained a copy of a letter written by me," and "no letters to me by others will be found among my papers when I die."[141] "So affable and uniformly courteous," in one historian's words, he was also intensely private, "remarkable all through life for having no close friends."[142] There are no letters by Natalie and their daughter Ninette, even in French; after "so long in Paris," Benjamin observed, "they have almost forgotten their English."[143] With all this, a theory is still possible about how the Benjamins' backgrounds strained the marriage. Neither one was religious enough, at least not in a sense that a compromise about faith might be reached. A Jewish writer in 1904 called Judah a "race Jew," not an observant one.[144] Just so, Natalie was a French Catholic by culture, whose piety inhered more in customs than doctrines. Curiously premodern by instinct yet nearly secular by habit, they could not find an institutional bridge—most readily, the Catholic Church—to draw them together. Particularly in a time of pious routines, the Benjamins had too little religion.

Socially, they were a great deal alike, and this helps explain why they first came together. Children of immigrants, both were upstarts in the slaveholding world. Natalie was born in Charleston after her parents' flight from slave violence in Santo Domingo. When she married in New Orleans in 1833, her dowry included two slave girls and some cash. Her father had done well as an insurance broker; with a foothold in the urban bourgeoisie, he was still not a planter. Judah was born on St. Thomas, grew up in North Carolina and Charleston, and arrived in New Orleans almost penniless in 1828.[145] To historians, the romance with Natalie had a fairytale quality. Hired to teach her English, Benjamin won "a Creole princess," in one writer's words; "a belle of the Creole type," to another.[146] This story of boy-makes-good by marrying into the elite was, however, insubstantial. Natalie was so little entrenched in New Orleans that she chose to spend most of her life in France. Judah lived in London from the fall of the Confederacy until 1883. When it became clear that the federal government would not prosecute former rebels, he might have returned to "secure a large practice in New Orleans," but "preferred to remain in England."[147] Most southerners mourned their lost cause; Benjamin built a new career in British law. "His task always seemed to be to erase the past, not to retain it."[148] Not only were Natalie and Judah both members of the South's ethnic minorities, but they began life on each group's social margins and never quite settled in. Some instinctive recognition of this restlessness in each other may have helped the romance to flower, although the same transiency in the long run also worked to push them apart.

Mobility did not preclude involvement in family, although the St. Martins-Benjamins were an interfaith clan strangely without anchor in a viable marriage. Instead, the couple's relationship seemed sustained by their common bonds with extended kin. Natalie and Judah's ten-year residence with her parents in New Orleans was not simply a matter of cost-saving or French custom. When she left for France, Judah still lived with his in-laws in the city. On weekends at Bellechasse, his plantation, "one guest who came so frequently as to be almost a member of the household was Benjamin's father-in-law, Auguste St. Martin, a delightful old gentleman who entertained the young people with tales of the bloody slave insurrection in Santo Domingo."[149] There St. Martin met Judah's widowed sister Penny, who had arrived from South Carolina to keep house in Natalie's absence, and, until her death in 1847, Judah's mother Rebecca. Natalie's younger brother Jules was important to the family as well. In the 1830s, the Benjamins nearly acted as parents to Jules; Judah and Jules shared a house in Richmond during the war. Gradually, much of the family drifted to Europe. St. Martin spent his last years in Paris with his daughter. Judah, in London, faithfully assisted his kin in New Orleans.[150] At least as measured by co-residence, this was a close family. Judah adopted Natalie's relatives more than vice versa, not surprising for a Jew seeking entry into Creole society. Nor was all happy in his own circle, since Judah had little contact with his father, who had been separated from his mother for many years. Yet on the whole, differences between Catholics and Jews did not deter amiability. Warm feelings among their kin should have smoothed the Benjamins' way in marriage.[151]

Despite this social foundation, their relations became entangled in myths verging on lies. Most romances contain elements of fantasy: lovers project idealized images of each other and their future together. But for the Benjamins, wishes repeatedly outran possibilities. Judah was ever "Philippe" to Natalie. Philip, his middle name, appeared on

4. Père Lachaise Cemetery, Paris, burial place of Judah Benjamin in 1884. Placed in the crypt of his wife's Catholic family, Judah was identified in the cemetery records by his Christian-sounding middle name "Philippe." Photograph by Eleanor Rose.

their marriage certificate and, at his death, he was Philippe in the burial records of Père Lachaise cemetery in Paris. In conversation, this is what she called him, not Judah, from which the word "Jew" derives.[152] Her habit may have gratified his desire for assimilation, yet his dream had a different flavor. He imagined a tranquil and prosperous home, so much that he "tried to hide his domestic troubles," one biographer remarks, "even from his family and intimate friends."[153] Three times in America he built or refurbished lavish houses, hoping to please his wife. The first house at Bellechasse, in one historian's view, had "the splendor of a Southern fantasy."[154] But he soon tore it down to erect a grander one for $28,000. After reelection to the Senate in 1858, he outfitted a Washington mansion "to hitherto undreamed-of magnificence," Virginia Clay recalled, to induce Natalie to return. Its elegance could not prevent her social failure. The "much-talked-of lady" arrived from Paris, accompanied by reports of "rumored delinquencies," then snubbed the southern delegates in favor of the French legation. "Then, Arab-like, the lady rose in the night, 'silently folded her tent and stole away' (to meet a handsome

German officer, it was said), leaving our calls unanswered, save by the sending of her card, and her silver and china and crystal, her paintings, and hangings, and furniture to be auctioned off to the highest bidder!"[155]

Judah did not relinquish hopes of family glory even then. Anticipating retirement in the 1870s, he constructed a home in Paris for $80,000 for Natalie, Ninette, his son-in-law, and himself.[156] He was more a workaholic than socialite, and the houses, no doubt sought as status symbols, also reflected the longing of the bourgeois for domestic peace. This, however, was a prospect from which Natalie repeatedly fled. Judah never became "Philippe," nor Natalie a composed wife. Their stories about themselves, told in words and mortar, did not ring true.

The Benjamins' struggles with insubstantial impressions were not unique in interfaith families. Some stories began when family members instinctively obscured their differences by rhetoric. This is how Judah became Philippe. Other tales arose to explain why anyone would wed an outsider of questionable origins. Whispers circulated about the high-placed forebears of self-made men who married well. David Yulee's grandfather, it was said, was vizier to the Sultan of Morocco, perhaps even straying, exotically, from Judaism to Islam.[157] Families could not control gossip, even stories starting in their own circles, and it was easy for prejudice to twist already-murky accounts. The Benjamins lived under this cloud. During the war, Judah's detractors spread word that Yale University had expelled him for stealing in 1828 and, as malicious, that he was a "eunich." Perhaps it was Natalie's supposed infidelities, much discussed, that gave rise to suspicions of his sexual failure.[158] Certainly most public figures are open to unfriendly talk. But it is hard to imagine anyone more vulnerable in Protestant America than a Jew and a Catholic, married to each other. Benjamin was frustrated by sensationalism until the end of his life. Writing from London to an old friend in 1878, he apologized for "a terribly egotistic letter," but he wished "to separate the real facts from the absurd exaggerations sometimes seen in the newspapers."[159] Imagination, it seems, is called into service to explain social anomalies. Interfaith families and their critics all looked for ways to make sense of unexpected matches. But it is possible to lose hold of conjugal feelings amid dreams and slanders, particularly if the marriage bond, like the Benjamins', is fragile to begin with.

The couple's religious commitments can barely be discerned in this series of myths. Successive biographers of Judah Benjamin, in 1904, 1906, and 1934, used the identical phrase to describe Natalie: "devout Catholic."[160] The repetition, offered without elaboration, suggests they knew little. She and her daughter were married by priests, and Judah received last rites. But there is no record of prayer, parish activity, or friendliness with clergy. On the contrary, Natalie seems to have dressed, flirted, and carried on illicit liaisons, as the gossip charged. Judah's acquaintance with Judaism is just as indistinct in the historical record. When he hurriedly left Yale, he forgot his Hebrew Psalter, a book a mother might pack for her son, which the boy might open or not.[161] Rabbi Isaac Mayer Wise recalled meeting Benjamin in Washington in the 1850s. "He had a confused notion of orthodox Portuguese Judaism," Wise wrote in his *Reminiscences,* a judgment hard to weigh because the Reform leader thought all orthodoxy was muddled. In Richmond during the war, Benjamin was a good friend of Gustavus Myers, president of the Sephardic synagogue. "If he did attend" services, one scholar infers, he "would have been a celebrated visitor" and "would have been 'called up to the reading of the law.'"[162] This is true, but also speculative. Much note is taken by historians that Benjamin was "the first acknowledged Jew elected to the U.S. Senate."[163] He did not live a Jewish life, however, and how loyal he was to Judaism can only be guessed.

It may be that religion had little to do with the Benjamins' difficulties. But if so, the combination of Catholic and Jew seems, at first glance, the root of their problems. The only such couple identified for this study, they were also unusually troubled. Jews and Catholics both stress ritual practice, in contrast to Protestants who focus on doctrines. Ways of doing things may be harder to compromise than habits of thinking. What made matters worse was that Judah and Natalie were more conventionally religious than actively so. Each one took being Jewish or Catholic for granted; neither had an interest in communal life. They were marginal to the evangelical culture of the mid-century decades, where women championed piety, men respected their wives, and institutions welcomed families, even intermarried ones. Their instinctive hold on religion seems more traditional, more European than the American norm, though oddly manifested in day-to-day indifference. They did not use religious commitment to bind their family, as so many of their intermarried contemporaries did. Inattention to sacred habits might be inconsequential in a more secular society. But the Benjamins were out of step with mid-nineteenth-century America, and it is not surprising that they ended up separated and abroad.

Because their marriage was exceptional, it brings commonplace patterns into clearer view. Mixed-faith households of the era flourished when they were most like their contemporaries. This was a gender-conscious and institution-oriented culture. Families composed of Catholic wives who embraced their church with the acquiescence of Protestant husbands were not so far from other fervent women, disengaged men, and inviting places of worship. Suppose, however, the wife was Jewish and wished to live a Jewish life. Here, if she was successful, was another anomaly: Judaism was neither as feminized nor evangelical as contemporary Christianity. The Benjamins' cool relations highlight the importance to mixed marriages of pious activity. An observant, intermarried Jewish wife, as unusual, can underscore the influence of gender.

The Rabbi's Daughter

The newspaper report of Helen Wise's elopement in Cincinnati in 1878, cast as the myth "cupid conquers," contained an accurate subtext: this was an American story.[164] Not only did love dupe tradition, but the girl was the central actor. Judaism was prepared for every circumstance except this. American rabbis debating *halakhah* assumed Jewish descent required Jewish mothers. Biological and formal roles, however, did not grant women privileges; almost nowhere in 1878 were women members of synagogues. Even more, intermarriage, to the rabbis, equaled apostasy. This was the prevailing lesson of the Hebrew Bible, and American men who married out, such as David Yulee and Judah Benjamin, supported the case. In this world, Helen's determination to raise her children as Jews must have been, to say the least, a surprise. More deeply, she was behaving like intermarried Christian women, and stranger still, Judaism accommodated her. She must have been protected by the power—and forbearance—of her father, Isaac Mayer Wise. Here nonetheless was rare evidence that Judaism, too, bent to American mores shaped by the initiatives of women.

"From early childhood my mother took me to the Plum St. Temple," Helen's daughter Iphigene recalled, "where I sat in the straight-

5. Plum Street Temple, Congregation B'nai Yeshurun, Cincinnati, Ohio, consecrated in 1848, where Helen Wise Molony continued to attend services after her intermarriage in 1878. Isaac Mayer Wise, Helen's father, was rabbi of the congregation from 1854 until his death in 1900. Courtesy of the Jacob Rader Marcus Center of the American Jewish Archives.

backed pew with my feet not touching the ground."[165] Understandably, "this did not endear me to services." But Iphigene and later her husband "always regarded ourselves as Jews." They were married by Rabbi David Philipson, her grandfather's old friend, at the Wise family farm in 1916.[166] Iphigene's Jewishness was the work of her mother. A "gentle, sensitive, artistically gifted woman" in the eyes of her daughter, Helen, like all Wise's children, "adored their father to the point of worship." She "felt a sense of guilt for embarrassing him, who was always underfire for his Reform Judaism, by marrying out of the faith." Somehow Helen reconstructed bridges to her family. Her brothers corresponded with her after her marriage. In 1886, she wrote a story, "True Love Falters Not," for the *American Jews' Annual,* published by her mother's kin. It was not about intermarriage, but about the match of Emily Heavenrich and Robert Stern, approved by Emily's father, as pious as his name.[167] Discreet, repentant, or both, Helen situated her children in the Jewish community. In high school, "all my friends were Jewish," Iphigene remembered. This was after the family moved from the house of their Presbyterian grandmother to the farm of their Jewish one, following the death in 1900 of Dr. Wise. Perhaps Helen and her father never reconciled fully, and she had to wait until then to go home. Even if true, her return completed her Jewish self-identification rather than began it. Isaac Mayer Wise did not bar his daughter from services, and his granddaughter grew up thinking of herself as a Jew. Like intermarried Catholic wives, Helen led her household religiously, and her husband—and father—went along.

James Molony risked the disgrace of a clandestine marriage to win Helen, but he was undemonstrative about religion. He was "an indifferent Presbyterian" in Iphigene's memory, the son of "a Catholic who left the church when he came to the U.S. and married a Presbyterian." Leaving the family's spiritual care to his wife, Molony practiced law and pursued politics. At one time he was Assistant Prosecutor of Cincinnati's Hamilton County.[168] When his daughter in turn chose a husband, she found a man like her father. Gilbert Bettman "cared deeply about government and politics," serving as Attorney General and Supreme Court Judge of Ohio. In neither generation was division of interests by gender absolute. Helen Wise Molony, serious about Judaism, was no less "an avowed feminist and strong worker for Woman's Suffrage" whose name appears "on a bronze plaque in the lobby of the Hamilton Cy. Court House." Looking back, Iphigene felt her own "life was all politics," and she remained "active in the Republican Party" after Bettman's death. The fact remains that it was women, particularly in her mother's time, who took charge of religion. Helen's status in her father's congregation must have been marginal, without a Jewish husband to anchor her. Still, she made her marriage work religiously by allying herself boldly with Judaism. In this, she resembled other American women intermarrying in the mid-century decades. Among Jewish women her story seems unique, however, made possible by who she was.

Probably in no interfaith household were relationships simple. Kin had to visit and revisit internal rifts and conflicting expectations. Yet most families of the era, formed between the 1830s and 1880s, functioned well within a predictable framework: the religious leadership of wives, bolstered by the cooperation of husbands and assistance of institutions. Varying temperaments of religious communities had an impact on families. The Catholic Church was especially nurturing, because it offered clear policies, evangelical goals, and, most crucially, time. But Protestantism and Judaism, too, responded to the attraction of mixed-faith couples to organized faith.

Yet it is reasonable to wonder how long this pattern, linked to timebound values and tastes, might persist. Suppose women became less driven by religion, and families grew less interested in church or synagogue ties. Suppose interfaith couples, well-read and unconventional, stopped listening to the clergy and devised their own philosophical answers. At the turn of the twentieth century, new public discussions of interfaith marriage appeared, focusing less on faith and practice and more on ethnicity, conceived as race, and assimilation. This shift in thinking was a sign that the ways families chose to live were changing, too.

CHAPTER FOUR

The Uncertain Limits
of Liberalism

In 1908 President Teddy Roosevelt attended the American premiere of Israel Zangwill's *The Melting-Pot* in Washington, and he was enthusiastic about its message. "God is making the American," the play's hero proclaims, here in "the great Melting-Pot where all the races of Europe are melting and re-forming!" Grateful for the president's acclaim, Zangwill called Roosevelt the "ideal spectator" and dedicated the drama to his "strenuous struggle against the forces that threaten to shipwreck the great republic."[1] Zangwill presented his grand theme of human unification through the love story of Vera Revendal and David Quixano, both Russian-born immigrants to New York, Vera a Christian and David a Jew. The "call of our blood through immemorial generations" prohibits the match, David's uncle warns. But the hero's counterargument prevails. "Fires of hate" of the Old World will be replaced by "fires of love" in the New. Taking Vera's hands in the closing scene, David instructs her to "cling to me till all these ghosts are exorcised, cling to me till our love triumphs over death."[2] Whether Roosevelt approved of intermarriage as policy or simply liked Zangwill's optimism may only be guessed. Either way, his excitement made him a typical viewer. *The Melting-Pot* was popular with theatergoers and appeared many times in print. Americans, it seems, were finally comfortable with the idea of interfaith marriage.

Beneath Zangwill's vision of "God's crucible," however, were currents of skepticism about social mixing that his audiences likely shared. This was a scientifically minded age, and theories of race, genetics, and eugenics now seconded religion's long-standing disapproval of interfaith couples. In the play, Vera calls Jews a "race," commonplace usage at a time when cultural traits were often traced to biology. The name "Mendel Quixano," David's uncle, echoes Gregor Mendel, the founder of modern genetics. Nor would careful listeners miss the resemblance between Quincy Davenport, the drama's unashamed anti-Semite, and Charles B. Davenport, a eugenicist who would help found the Galton Society to promote white racial purity in 1918. "I'll send as many Jews as you like to Germany," Quincy jokes: "I'd even lend my own yacht to take 'em back."[3] All these allusions to race and descent did not add up to a coherent case against interfaith marriage, seen here as miscegenation. Zangwill's details nonetheless evoked current scientific and pseudoscientific debates. If the "crucible of love" was to work its magic, the playwright confessed quietly, the vessel would have to melt down the objections of science.[4]

In most ways, *The Melting-Pot* was a perfect mirror of American thinking about interfaith marriage at the turn of the twentieth century. Although few public figures championed mixed-faith romance, more and more spoke casually about families divided by religion. Some judged intermarriage worth risking for the sake of social harmony or self-fulfillment. Others were less fearful of religious discord at home than of rising rates of divorce, women's employment, and abortion. Such tempered opinions might be heard alongside shrill debates about the biological roots of civilization. Here customs and beliefs were conceived as byproducts of race. Religious differences, grounded in nature, could not be resolved by human will. Intermarried couples sacrificed not only their own happiness but the species' vitality, since racial mixing, most theorists agreed, produced degeneration. Fatalism and pessimism entered conversations with the language of race, and Americans commonly applied biological words to culture. Even then, most citizens shared at least some of Roosevelt's bright faith in the republic. They listened at one moment to visionary predictions such as Zangwill's, and the next to eugenic forecasts of doom. It must have been easy for the public to have ambivalent feelings.

Interfaith marriage was a theme in three public discussions in America between the 1890s and 1920s: exchanges about race, initiatives in denominational policies, and the circulation of personal reminiscences. Often these dialogues seemed to have little relation to one another. In popular science, religious law, and literary retrospects, readers encountered dissimilar vocabularies and logic. Religion no longer dominated debate on mixed marriage; Americans sifted through arguments from various authorities. Anthropologists, biologists, and popular authors were among those who spoke persuasively. The culture of the era, precisely because of its complexity, required intellectuals and their audiences to judge for themselves.

More subtly, over time interest in interfaith marriage diminished altogether. The literary equation of domestic happiness and national harmony in *The Melting-Pot* in 1908 would be unlikely a decade later. This was because newer conceptual categories—among them race, institution, and self—edged aside the family to become social lenses on which Americans relied. Certainly people still spoke about intermarriage, and couples formed mixed-faith households. But religious differences in families became increasingly just one cultural issue among many.

"Can the Ethiopian Change His Skin or the Leopard His Spots?"

In Western society, mastery and fear advanced together during the nineteenth century. Scientists explained natural processes, and bureaucrats helped colonize native peoples. These gains underscored the power of physical laws and the range of human differences, and shaded exploration with a sense of vulnerability. When white peoples turned to the Bible, they found Jeremiah's prophecy about the intransigency of dark-skinned men and their beasts.[5] But increasingly it was science, not religion, that seemed to hold answers. Racial theories grew in what one scholar calls an atmosphere of "scientific uncertainty and confusion."[6] Ironically, the more contradictory and impenetrable the ideas, the greater their usefulness to polemicists and the more persuasive their mystique. Discussions of racial mixing only occasionally led to the specific question of interfaith marriage. Nonetheless, the strange blend of determinism and panic in racial thinking was one backdrop for reflections on mixed-faith romance.

By the end of the century, the words "race" and "racial" belonged to common parlance and, like most widely used terms, their meanings were vague. When the weekly *American Hebrew* polled sixty-four prominent Christians in 1890 about the roots of anti-Semitism, their answers distinguished problems caused by religion and race. "Is this prejudice not due largely to the religious instruction that is given by the Church," the Jewish newspaper asked, stirring "adversion, if not loathing for members of 'the despised race?'"[7] "Anti-Jewish prejudice is not at all religious," one Catholic editor typically replied, but "wholly racial and commercial."[8] His answer deflected blame from Christian doctrine to personality and business conflicts, presumably conditioned by Jewish behavior. Less clear were the connotations of "racial." John Burroughs, a writer, equated race with natural inheritance. The Jew "is too tough to be digested and assimilated by the modern races," he judged; prejudice was "irradicable." More perplexing, many respondents traced hatred to "race antipathy," yet expected feelings to improve with "general education and enlightenment."[9] Here "race" was not simply a matter of genetics but almost the equivalent of "culture." This usage made sense at a time when scientists still widely accepted the premise that environment might permanently alter heredity. Still, one historian notes that "race, culture, language, nationality were jumbled together in even the most respected works."[10] Leading Christians consistently pictured interfaith relations as interracial in the explanations of anti-Semitism they gave to the *American Hebrew.* There was little consensus, however, on exactly how races combined biological and social traits.

Nor did logic dictate the commentators' views on heredity and mating. Sex would seem to gain importance as a determinant of culture once religious communities were defined as genetic ones. This was the Jim Crow era, and it is easy to imagine public outcry over miscegenation of any kind. But in fact, the *American Hebrew* survey evoked few thoughts on interfaith courtship. One man repeated Goldwin Smith's charge, now a decade old, that Jews caused anti-Semitism by refusing to intermarry. The Jew "must violate one of the fundamental regulations of his race," the president of Tufts College advised, "and take his wives from the daughters of the land." Very differently, a minister revealed the unspoken links between prejudice and romance. Christians go to summer resorts "to get rid of as many of the inharmonious things of life as is possible," wrote Rev. Alvah Hobart of Yonkers; they wish "that their daughters shall have such a circle of acquaintances as will insure a pleasing termination to the summer vacation."[11] To say that Jews and gentiles were separate races might open serious speculation about the consequences, physiological and social, of interfaith matches. Instead, the *American Hebrew*'s respondents offered hackneyed prescriptions and notes on customs. Whereas the rhetoric of race could erase any chance of adjustment and reconciliation in mixed marriages, this lack of intellectual rigor left space for varying applications of racial theories to interfaith dating.

The importance of racial ideas resided less in their specific content, however, than in the habits of thinking they nurtured. Self-styled racial scientists began with the judgment that religion was inadequate. Take note of the author's "distrust in the efficacy of religion and morality," urged the editor of the first American printing of *The Inequality of Human Races* (1854) in 1915.[12] Retrospect exaggerated the religious skepticism of the French writer of this popular classic, Arthur de Gobineau. Less vehement than his editor, Gobineau said simply that Christianity was "filled with proofs of this indifference to the outward forms of social life."[13] He turned to sociobiology. But at whatever pitch, religion remained under fire. Josiah Nott of Alabama, Gobineau's contemporary, believed the races were separate species with no common ancestor in Adam and Eve. His *Two Lectures on the Natural History of the Caucasian and Negro Races* (1845) contained an "outspoken denial," one scholar writes, "of the omniscience of Moses," the Pentateuch's author in the eyes of the faithful.[14] Disdain of religion became shriller over time. In 1916, Madison Grant mocked "old-fashioned theologians" in his best-selling eugenic tract, *The Passing of the Great Race*. Now Christianity was the enemy of civilization. "Mistaken regard for what are believed to be divine laws and a sentimental belief in the sanctity of human life," Grant declared, "tend to prevent both the elimination of defective infants and the sterilization of such adults as are themselves of no value to the community."[15] Readers did not have to reject religion altogether to see that race science raised new questions about interfaith marriages and offered new experts to consult.

Their language was seductive because it suited a heterogeneous environment. At times ethnic communities, eager for acceptance, claimed membership in the "white" race. Yet as often Americans registered their sense of differences by identifying many "races." The French, Germans, and Poles, though all Catholics, were distinct "racial groups," an Irish priest wrote in 1928, echoing everyday speech.[16]

Jews, however, were the race par excellence. Theorists lauded racial purity, and, as outsiders in Christendom, Jews figured strangely in these writings nearly as race heroes. As early as 1854, *Types of Mankind* cited "the comparative purity of the blood of the Israelites down to the time of their dispersion" and "perpetuated, in an extraordinary degree, through all their wanderings, and under all their oppressions, down to the present day."[17] The authors were American gentiles, Josiah Nott and George Gliddon. Maurice Fishberg added in 1911, "we have those Jews who take great pride in the purity of their breed." "Prevailing opinion" is that Jews "have maintained themselves in absolute racial purity for three or four thousand years." Fishberg, a Jewish ethnologist, understood that scientific praise was a double-edged sword. Many Americans "see a peculiar peril in the prospect of indefinitely harboring an alien race which is not likely to mix with the general population." He argued for the Jews' racial impurity "due to intermarriage and proselytism" in order to show their capacity for assimilation.[18] No matter which side one took in conversations about Jewish genetics, however, the terms of debate were imbalanced. In a world where everyone seemed to have a racial identity, Jews were somehow more of a race than others, scrutinized with wonder and suspicion.

The literature on race, in sum, claimed the authority of science, yet was hardly value free. Its arrogance was matched by its indefiniteness. The frequency and the effects of miscegenation, for example, were subject to dispute. Gobineau speculated that "the human race in all its branches has a secret repulsion from the crossing of blood"; Madison Grant believed as strongly in our "perverse disposition to mismate." Predictions of degeneration from race mixing made it seem that most theorists instinctively took Grant's side. Even then their opinions varied about which racial strain would suffer decline. Josiah Nott, one historian reports, was certain in the 1850s that "any racial mixture weakened the superior stock." Ignatz Zollschan, an Austrian Jewish doctor read in America in the 1910s, forecast deterioration on both sides. The "interbreeding of totally different nations produces a bastard type whose character is far below the level of either parent." Fishberg's *The Jews* mirrored the confusion of public discussion. First listing some distinguished offspring of interfaith parents, Fishberg then linked intermarriage with the disappearance of "darker, shorter, and brachycephalic types" and, more broadly, with the "process of decadence" among Jews.[19] These contradictions within and among theories may have been less important, however, than the mood the writings stirred: that miscegenation was unfortunate and commonplace. Armed with statistics and illustrations, race scientists repeated the substance of what religious leaders had been saying about interfaith marriage for many years.

Who was listening? Were exchanges about race strictly a highbrow conversation? In the style of the sciences and social sciences, the terms of analysis were abstract. It would have been hard to discern clear lessons for yourself in arguments about race instincts and degeneracy. But a theoretical tone did not preclude popular interest, and some writers were adept at weaving racial ideas into down-to-earth tracts. This was especially true of Jews, perhaps because race theories, focused on the fate of human groups, had an unexpected affinity with Judaism's traditional loyalty to a community of descent.

Two pamphlets published in New York during World War I show the way racial logic entered Jewish polemics. Bloch Publishing Company, founded by kin of Isaac Mayer Wise, issued an English translation of Ignatz Zollschan's *Jewish Questions: Three Lectures* in 1914. The Viennese author was well known for *Das Rassenproblem* (1912); the lectures spoke more specifically of Jewish accomplishments, prosperity, and intermarriages. On the last subject, Zollschan phrased his diagnosis in racial language, his policy ideas in political terms. The Jews of Western Europe courted "racial chaos" by intermarrying. "It is therefore not impossible that Judaism may be disbanded in the near future—to be more precise, when the amelioration of the lot of the Jews will enable them to spread themselves still more." Zionism was the answer. When the options were "to preserve the Ghetto" or "to abolish the diaspora," there was no contest: "The first alternative can only mean a continued morbid existence."[20]

Rabbi David De Sola Pool as thoroughly blended biblical, pastoral, and scientific arguments in *Intermarriage,* a tract distributed by the Jewish Welfare Board to soldiers and sailors in 1918. Leader of Shearith Israel in New York, the city's oldest Sephardic Orthodox congregation, Pool seemed to try everything to communicate with young Jewish men. He anchored his biblical exegesis in a contrast between the legitimacy of Abraham's sons, "Ishmael, the son of a strange wife, and Isaac, the son of a Hebrew wife." In the present day, he warned that "domestic division and disruption" were inevitable in "a divided home."[21] Racial language appeared throughout. "Race memories" separated intermarried husbands and wives. "Pride of race" was the root of "the fundamental instinctive desire for Jewish survival—the instinctive protest against Jewish extinction." As the occasion demanded, Pool ended his tract patriotically. Just as we "have been ready to devote our all, even our lives, for our nation," so the Jewish people has "the right to claim the loyalty and the self-sacrifice of every individual Jew."[22] Pool's lesson could not have been more traditional: don't intermarry. But he made his point in a hodgepodge of old and new rhetorics, including racial, that he must have judged compelling in his time.

This prevalence of racial language in popular writings suggests that readers were familiar with theories of biological descent. Indeed, nearly every Jewish periodical ran articles on genetics. Rabbi Max Raisin wrote "Magic Circle of Race Integrity" for the *Israelite* in 1909; Dr. Recliffe Salaman contributed "Jews a 'Recessive' Race Type" to the *American Hebrew* in 1910.[23] Yet these and similar newspapers spoke at other times about being Jewish in terms unrelated to physiology. Education was a prime concern of the *American Hebrew*. "The Duties of Mothers to the Religious School" and "The Religious Training of Children" implied that Jews were not so much born as made. Homes entered the discussion to be censured for their failure to nurture faithfulness, because parents, one rabbi scolded in 1910, too often take "the side of secularism, materialism, and irreligion."[24] Whether the families were racially pure never came up. Attention to Jewish schooling in the *American Hebrew,* consistent with the nation's can-do spirit, did not displace race theories, just bypassed their gloomy tangles.

In an age of proliferating ideologies, religious instruction was not the only project to distract Jews from racial thinking. Like the advocates of education, the American Zionist women who founded the Hadassah organization in 1912 were less concerned with inherited conditions than future promise. True to the organization's goal "to promote Jewish institutions and enterprises in Palestine and to foster Zionist ideals in America," the *Hadassah News Letter* in the 1910s reported initiatives such as health care abroad and youth groups at home. Racial concepts, ranging from instincts to degeneracy, were not part of the women's vocabulary. Intent on creating a new Jewish homeland, they sidestepped deterministic views.[25]

White Protestants heard a similar blend of rhetorics. Relations between race theorists and conventional Protestants were tense from the beginning: eugenicists defending Anglo-Saxon or Nordic purity disdained Christianity as ineffectual. This did not keep Christians from adopting racial concepts. The Congregationalist *Independent,* published in New York, called Jews "a race" and anti-Semitism "race prejudice" in 1890.[26] The pieces they chose betrayed anxiety about racial mixing. Sui Sin Far told her story in "A White Woman Who Married a Chinaman" and "Her Chinese Husband" in 1910. Divorced by her philandering white husband, Far was rescued by marriage to a kind Chinese man, only to see him murdered for intermarrying by his intolerant countrymen.[27] W. E. B. Du Bois spoke about interracial marriage the same year. "A white man of the South writes to me: The crux of the race problem is intermarriage," Du Bois began. He urged readers to "avoid hysteria," not "to dogmatize" where science was uncertain, and focus instead on "education and social justice to both races." Citing state laws prohibiting interracial marriage as "wicked devices," he brought unusual realism to the debate on miscegenation.[28] The *Independent* overall was less bold. Its periodic discussions of race and marriage conveyed concern without drawing conclusions. Readers were free to think for themselves, but encountered emotional signals more often than intellectual guidance.

It was Catholics who tried most systematically to restrict the use of race concepts, yet even they slipped into the prevailing jargon. Reasons for the church's wariness are clear. Its anti-modernism, culminating in the encyclical *Pascendi Dominici Gregis* in 1907, made it look askance at science. Races themselves were part of the natural order, to be superseded by grace. "It is the Church not of one race or one nation," declared the American bishops in 1919, "but of all those who truly believe in His name."[29] The bishops' Pastoral Letter initially limited the meaning of "race" to biological groups. The "Negro and Indian" are "races less fortunate in a worldly sense."[30] In the course of the teaching's seventy-five pages, however, "race" acquired overtones that were cultural and moral. The bishops lined up the way people differ—"in race, tradition, and language, in national temper and political organization"—as if these were all social traits. They borrowed "race suicide" from popular speech to describe the "selfishness" of birth control use.[31] Catholics acquainted with the Pastoral Letter must have felt comfortable with these eclectic connotations of "race." Despite the church's resistance to secularism, it absorbed the language of the time.

What finally makes it so difficult to measure the influence of racial ideas is the challenge of matching texts with readers. Who read academic geneticists and ethnologists, or the high-pitched, often vicious eugenicists? What kinds of Jews subscribed to the *American Hebrew,* or Protestants to the *Independent?* Were any of these readers the same ones who picked up *Popular Science Monthly* with its unexpectedly similar array of themes: "Euthenics and Eugenics," "The Future of the Human Race," and "Is the Christian Religion Declining?"[32] Turn-of-the-century discussions of race occurred in the context of the rise of the mass media. Readers can no longer simply be identified with an institution—say, a church—and its literature. Instead, consumers of ideas may well have dabbled in varied writings. What can be said is that virtually everywhere they found the concept of race. Race affects us, Henry Fairchild wrote in 1926, "because we are animals."[33] Yet another eugenic tract, Fairchild's *The Melting-Pot Mistake,* championed anti-immigration laws in a tone of provocation and foreboding. Oddly balanced between biological determinism and a strategy for redemption, the book was representative of race theories. It was also typical in how little it said about sex. Racial ideas implicitly turned interfaith romance into miscegenation. The writings about race avoided sexuality, however, almost puritanically. Their nervousness about degeneracy nonetheless preached that mixed marriages were socially irresponsible. Not surprisingly, the clergy agreed.

Rules and Exceptions

In contrast to the recurring debates about race progress, two American religious groups, Reform Jews and Roman Catholics, reached conclusions in the early twentieth century about how to handle interfaith marriages. The ruling of the Central Conference of American Rabbis (CCAR) in 1909 and the Code of Canon Law of 1917 were results of denominational discussions reaching back to the mid-nineteenth century. Along with institutional triumph, however, were evidences of defeat. Both groups forbade interfaith marriages at the same time that they devised policies to accommodate mixed couples. In an age when secular viewpoints such as science competed with faith, how many respected the authority of the rabbi or priest enough to do what he said? Who, for that matter, heeded the minister? Protestants' awareness of intermarriage as a threat grew slowly in the shadow of the other religions' decisions, as they woke up with surprise to their own decline.

The passing of the CCAR resolution on interfaith marriage was a moment of high drama. In 1907, the professional body of Reform rabbis decided to put the issue on its agenda. All knew that rabbis had written much on the subject; now, however, one increasingly heard laymen, Jews as well as gentiles, praising mixed households as the key to social harmony. One rabbi spoke at the 1908 conference in Michigan, just months before the American premiere of Zangwill's hit play *The Melting-Pot,* which epitomized the pro-intermarriage spirit. During the year before the 1909 convention in New York, rabbis writing in the *Israelite* tried to counter Zangwill's vision. Little wonder, as the *Israelite* reported, that the session on marriage at Temple Beth-El was "looked forward to as probably the most interesting and vigorous meeting of the conference."[34]

"Early in the afternoon the vestry room of the temple was filled, and rear aisles crowded, largely by women who had come to hear the subject discussed." The audience listened to two papers. Both rabbis took the Reform position that the distinction between Jews and others "was not difference of race, but of religion": "Intermarriage has become purely a religious question." The discussion, led by Rabbi Isaac Moses, then began with a joke. "'What do you think will happen if the rabbi refuses to marry such a couple of Jew and non-Jew?'" Moses asked. "'They will go to another rabbi,'" called a rabbi from the floor, "and the audience broke into laughter."[35] "Meanwhile rabbis, eager for the long-awaited discussion of the subject, had crowded into the front of the room to take part in it." Suddenly, one rabbi made a motion to close debate, and "after a surprised silence," it passed by a vote of thirty-four to thirty-three. "The discussion for which the rabbis had traveled far and primed themselves well was ended before it began." Behind the scenes, a committee drafted a resolution. Its strong initial wording—"mixed marriage is prohibited by the Jewish religion" and "a rabbi ought not to officiate"—was toned down. A milder statement, "mixed marriages are contrary to the tradition of the Jewish religion and should be discouraged by the American rabbinate," passed on the last evening by forty-two votes to two.[36] Why fifty-three rabbis who attended the conference did not vote is unclear. Many, perhaps, had gone home.

This remained the sole CCAR discussion of interfaith marriage until 1935. The turmoil on the floor in 1909 reflected unsettlement among the rabbis, and the resolution's vagueness marked it as a compromise. At bottom, the rabbis were unsure of their own authority. As liberals, Reform rabbis wished to allow individual conscience to judge tradition. But they also constituted a professional association inclined to dictate its members' conduct. Curtailing debate and approving nebulous wording permitted them to stay on the fence between freedom and conformity. The modesty of the resolution also allowed them to avoid the possible shame of being ignored. What will a family do, Rabbi Moses continued, if the rabbi refuses to perform an interfaith wedding? "They will, if the father is a prominent Jewish layman, engage a prominent Jewish judge to perform the civil ceremony in a public hall." Although the CCAR action began in response to a real social issue, it soon became entangled in the modern dilemma of religion's authority.

Private doubts accompanied public confusion, making the intermarriage resolution seem even less like a bold stroke than a shot in the dark. Even Rabbi David Philipson, presiding officer at the conference, was prey to self-questioning. A member of the first graduating class at Hebrew Union College in 1883, he now keenly felt Reform Judaism's vulnerability. Two times in his journal, in 1905 and 1906, Philipson wondered if "the reform movement is a colossal failure," because, as different critics said, it "detached itself from catholic Israel" and could not keep the Jew from remaining "aloof in but too many instances from his religion."[37] Diffusing these worries, he next confided that "doubt oppresses me" whenever he preached at a Reform service held on a Sunday or attended congregational dinners that made temples "social amusement centers not the homes of spiritual uplift."[38] Threats from outside the Reform movement were as menacing as signs of internal decline. Convinced that "the future of Judaism in America will lie in the hands of the descendants of Russian Jews," he feared "the future looks dark" unless the Orthodox were saved from superstition by "the doctrines and teachings of reform." Anti-Semitism, too, challenged "our mission to be scattered through the world to be a light to the nations": "Let us confess it, we are not wanted; the peoples resent our presence; they are envious of Jewish ability."[39] A month after the 1909 meeting, Philipson replied confidently in the *Israelite* to Orthodox critics. The intermarriage ruling displayed no "equivocation or evasion"; "as a conference of liberal Judaism, it could no further go." Yet privately, he must have felt like an "old war-horse of reform," the name he gave a friend.[40] Seen in the context of Philipson's diary, the CCAR marriage policy was a gesture of an aging movement.

More shocking, rabbis shared in the practical tolerance of mixed marriage that permitted it to flourish. When Israel Zangwill married a gentile in 1903, David Philipson sent them a gift. "Dear Dr. Philipson," Edith Zangwill wrote from her honeymoon in France, thanking him for the pretty vase.[41] The rabbi's willingness to let civility override censure was not unique. The *Israelite* raved in 1909 that Sir George Faudel-Phillips in London flaunted "decencies and proprieties" by attending his son's wedding in a church. Showing Jews that "he does not care what they think of him," he should resign as president of Jews' Hospital and Orphan Asylum. But the *Israelite* sensed this was unlikely.[42] The peer's disregard of communal standards was a token of their waning power. A Mr. Stern in New York, the article continued, did not give up his presidency of the Jewish Orphan Asylum when his daughter married a Christian, although he did step down as trustee of Temple Emanu-El. Not even communities of the immigrant poor, most of them Orthodox, resisted intermarriage effectively. "In the congested districts of New York," Ignatz Zollschan reported in 1914, "marriages with the surrounding elements, such as the Irish and particularly the Italian, occur with growing frequency." There were some conversions of spouses or at least circumcisions of sons. "But the vast majority of mixed marriages taking place in New York City are devoid of any of these ceremonies," wrote Maurice Fishberg in *The Jews*. "Most of them are satisfied with a civil ceremony, while the rich have either a Rabbi or a Christian clergyman."[43] The CCAR resolution was the tip of this iceberg. Although Philipson was truthful when he said its wording proscribing mixed marriage was as decisive as possible for a liberal organization, equivocation in practice was prevalent.

At the same time, rabbis cleared a path bureaucratically for interfaith couples. Standardized forms and up-to-date manuals streamlined the process of conversion prior to marriage. In 1845 Isaac Leeser had flatly rejected these conversions, saying they could not represent disinterested commitment.[44] It must have seemed by the turn of the century, in contrast, that they were Judaism's best hope. Among the papers left by Isaac Moses as rabbi of New York's Congregation

Ahawath Chesed Shaar Hashomayim is a blank conversion document for women, dated 1906: "Miss" so-and-so appeared before "the undersigned Rabbis" and "expressed her determination to join the faith and people of Israel, and to live in all respects as a Jewess."[45] Soon the CCAR *Minister's Hand Book* (1917) nearly confessed that conversion was an adjunct of romance: it placed the "Conversion Service" just before the "Marriage Ceremony." One of its seven questions for converts, echoing the Catholic marriage pledge required of the non-Catholic spouse, focused so much on progeny that the candidate's own sincerity seemed incidental. "Should you be blessed with children," the *Hand Book* instructed rabbis to ask, "do you agree to rear your children according to the Jewish faith?"[46] It was a short step to admit that conversion before marriage might be dispensed with altogether. Interfaith weddings occurred at Temple Beth El in Detroit in the 1910s after couples signed a simple promise: "We, the undersigned, hereby pledge ourselves that in case children should be born of our marriage, we will, to the best of our knowledge and ability, rear them in the Jewish faith."[47] The existence of measures to accommodate mixed-faith romance does not mean that the CCAR resolution was hollow. Probably no rabbi felt good about intermarriage. Even so, institutionalized recognition of interfaith dating must have made its official prohibition seem less severe.

All things considered, the rabbis' legislation did not initiate greater regulation so much as quiet neglect of an impossible question. The CCAR did not follow up its ruling with new programs to deter intermarriage. Rather, it shifted focus from Jewishness as a birthright to Jewishness as an acquisition, as if to say that if descent could not be monitored, perhaps commitment might. Beginning in 1911, the CCAR helped to produce a series of Sunday school texts. David Philipson, representative of the CCAR, filed copies in his papers of the correspondence of Rabbi George Zepin, who oversaw the project. "We are training children in becoming 'good Jews' and 'good men,'" Zepin explained to a prospective author.[48] Teenagers were especially targeted. One rabbi who read a draft of a Confirmation manual praised it for being "well within the grasp of every fourteen-year-old boy and girl." A man from Seattle, volunteering to write, told Zepin that "we can best hold the older pupils by engaging them in a course of study which requires as hard work and as much concentration as does their work in high school or the earlier classes in the university."[49] Perhaps all hoped that better education would, by extension, encourage endogamous marriage. No one stated this logic, however, and another interpretation is equally likely: Reform rabbis wished to hold onto the families they had without worrying too much about the ones being lost.

By the 1920s the *Israelite* rarely spoke of the biological boundaries of the Jewish community. Family purity, the subject that brought out eager rabbis and spectators in 1909, received little comment compared with public issues. There was much to discuss. At a conference in 1921, delegates of the Union of American Hebrew Congregations and Temple Sisterhoods heard results of a survey on the state of American Judaism sent to 160 rabbis and laymen: "First, ignorance; second, skepticism and indifference; third, a dearth of inspiring leaders and teachers and unsatisfactory organization of the synagogue."[50] The Jewish press elaborated. Should women be ordained to fill empty pulpits, the *Israelite* asked? Should Communist sympathizers be tolerated? How should anti-Semites be answered?[51] Institutionally focused, the *Israelite*'s commentary presumed that American Jewry could be equated with synagogue members. Admission of widespread disenchantment, however, was evidence that this was hardly the case. Among those on the margins of affiliated Jewry were interfaith families, now invisible in public rhetoric. The *American Hebrew* did run a column called "The Melting Pot." But its subtitle, "Sketches, Impressions and Comment," gave its content away: poems, humor, and household hints.[52] This cozy melting pot of Jewish domesticity obscured the difficult question of mixed marriage. Although the CCAR policy remained on the books, there is little to suggest that it changed lives.

The Catholic experience was similar. Clarification of the church's position on interfaith marriage did not lead to predictable results. Of the 2,414 canons included in the 1917 Code of Canon Law, 129 legislated on marriage and four of these focused on mixed marriage. These began with the decree that "the Church most strictly and everywhere forbids marriages between a Catholic and a person enrolled in an heretical or schismatical sect." For "good and weighty reasons" a couple might obtain a dispensation, however, provided conditions were met: the Catholic promised to resist error and convert the spouse, and both partners agreed to be married by a priest and raise their children as Catholics.[53] In 1946, two Jesuit authors praised the Code as "a complete system" that replaced "old rambling discussions," and the sharp provisions for intermarriage seemed part of its rigor.[54] This was the first synthesis of church law since the *Corpus Iuris Canonici* completed in 1500. Ordered in 1904 by Pope Pius X, the new codification was the work of a commission overseen by Pietro Cardinal Gasparri. Observers expected the project to take twenty-five years, considering the quantity of legislation enacted over three centuries in response to religious schisms, political revolutions, and social change. But Gasparri, both a scholar trained in canon law and a papal diplomat skilled in church politics, expedited the process of research, review, and synthesis and submitted the finished document to Pope Benedict XV in 1917. He must have taken a personal interest in the canons on marriage, because he was the author of a two-volume *Tractatus Canonicus de Matrimonio* (1892). Still, his brilliance as a systematizer could not keep mixed-faith families firmly bound to the church.[55]

Part of the difficulty was that Catholic law remained complex. Interfaith couples were so dependent on priests to navigate the system that many seemed reluctant to seek church sanction at all. Although Monsignor Joseph Selinger offered point-by-point explanations in *A Catechism on Pledges* (1930), some must have sounded like double-talk. Legitimate reasons for granting dispensations were not determined by common sense but consisted of sixteen "canonical reasons" listed in an instruction from Rome in 1877. Little wonder Selinger advised Catholics in mixed-faith relationships to "go to a priest, consult with him and follow his instructions" and told priests where to find the needed Latin texts.[56] Which marriages the church judged valid was even more tangled, yet sometimes crucial. *Ready Answers in Canon Law* (1934), a manual for clergy, explained. Before the 1917 Code, marriage between a person baptized in any church and someone unbaptized was invalid because of the impediment "disparity of cult." The Code, in contrast, in effect discounting Protestant baptism, saw the same marriage as a "valid natural contract." The consequences for remarriage differed. "In 1916," the text began hypothetically, John, a baptized Lutheran, married Mary, non-baptized, before a judge." Divorced in 1930, "John now wishes to marry a Catholic girl" and can do so "because his first marriage was null and void." But if John had first married in 1918, the legitimacy of the marriage required that the case go to the Holy Office in Rome to clear the way for a Catholic wedding.[57] The process of securing a dispensation was "irritating to many Protestants," another Catholic advice manual confessed.[58] The difficulty of working with the Code, synthethized but not simplified, may have been one cause.

Yet the church must equally have known that any coolness of mixed-faith couples to Catholicism was part of a broader spiritual malaise. The Pastoral Letter of 1919, the first communication from the American bishops since 1884, should have been triumphal: the American church was so strong institutionally that the pope rescinded its mission status in 1908. Instead, the bishops mourned "the decay of positive belief," saying "that unbelief is so common, that firm and definite teaching of Christian truth is so often replaced by vague uncertain statements, and that even these are left to individual preference for acceptance or rejection."[59] Perhaps the bishops chose the tone of a jeremiad, exaggerating failings, to shame Catholics into obedience. Yet its list of the sins of families was substantial enough to make them seem real: the prevalence of birth control, acceptance of divorce, and public ambitions of women.[60] Such widespread disregard of church teaching helps explain why intermarriages continued without dispensations and the blessings of priests. *Casti Connubii,* the encyclical on marriage issued in 1930 by Pope Pius XI, lamented that today "the sanctity of marriage is trampled upon and derided," and interfaith marriage, both as symptom and cause, was part of the problem. Catholics who "rashly and heedlessly contract mixed marriages" fail "to make their marriage approach as nearly as possible to the archetype of Christ and the Church." Wearily, the encyclical added that this church teaching "appears in many of her documents."[61] Repetition was apparently needed because not all laypeople listened.

At the same time, mixed marriage figured less prominently in Catholic discussions. Like Reform rabbis, priests systematized intermarriage and then turned away. Although the church had asked for pledges as early as the eighteenth century, now the wording was standardized. John O'Brien, a college chaplain, included the text in *The Church and Marriage* in 1934. "'I, the undersigned, not a member of the Catholic Church,'" the vow began, concluding with promises required by canon law to permit the spouse and children to be Catholics. Praising the church's pragmatism, O'Brien saw pledges as evidence that "she does not bury her head in the sand, ignoring unpleasant realities."[62] Seen differently, the church shook its finger at the same couples it welcomed. Pledges did allow the church to pigeonhole the problem. Contraception, abortion, and divorce were prime domestic threats in the clergy's eyes. The Pastoral Letter of 1919 did not mention interfaith marriage. *Casti Connubii* gave the subject three paragraphs, beginning with number 82, among 130.[63] Nor could the church afford to be preoccupied with families. Cardinal Gasparri, as the Vatican's secretary of state, was disturbed by the American race riots of 1919 and instructed the bishops to address "the problems of the black population." Seeking a compromise with Mussolini throughout the next decade, he and the dictator signed the Lateran Pacts in 1929. For a prelate trained in canon law, diplomacy was a burden, as witnessed by Gasparri's repeated efforts to resign. But the pressure of the times seemed to restrict choice and force accommodation, no less on domestic issues such as mixed marriage than on questions of state.[64]

Both Jewish and Catholic intermarriage policies, in sum, were part of the ambiguous story of twentieth-century religion. Well organized on paper, faith communities faced obstacles: clerical self-doubt, lay indifference, secular distractions. Bureaucracy was a sign that Jews and Catholics had made it institutionally in America. Clarity and efficiency, however, could not guard commitment. Yet strangely enough, tightened Jewish and Catholic standards affected Protestants. Requirements imposed on intermarried Protestants by religious minorities were a wake-up call that the days of Protestant hegemony were numbered.

To this day, Protestants think far less about interfaith marriage than do Jews or Catholics. One Methodist minister in Ohio, interviewed by a rabbinical student in the 1980s, did not know that his denomination had passed a resolution in 1960 discouraging religiously mixed families. At seminary, "beyond a five minute comment in one of his classes, [intermarriage] never came up."[65] Such Protestant policies as appeared were delayed reactions to minority initiatives. In 1948 the Episcopal Church went on record that it "earnestly warns members of our Church against contracting marriages with Roman Catholics under conditions imposed by modern Roman Catholic canon law." Presbyterians, Baptists, Lutherans, and Disciples of Christ issued similar wording within the next five years.[66] On the whole, Protestant dominance, evangelicalism, and individualism blunted awareness of mixed marriage. When it occurred, the same traits led Protestants to expect that a non-Protestant spouse would quietly honor the family's religion.

Their confidence began to erode around the time Jews and Catholics codified their policies. Perhaps Protestants finally saw that minorities were determined to resist assimilation. This insight had to be especially unnerving after the First World War, when, in one historian's words, "the indexes of [Protestant] denominational vitality show a prevailing downward trend for the next ten years."[67] Declining church attendance, diminished contributions, and fewer volunteers for missions made Protestants feel vulnerable and led to suspicion. "At a good will seminar of Protestants, Jews and Catholics held recently at the University of Illinois for the purposes of removing needless sources of friction," a priest reported in 1934, "a Protestant spokesman" identified the Catholic "Church's marriage laws as a source of such antagonism." To this man, pledges were "'a crafty device whereby the Catholic Church ensnares many of our members into her fold.'"[68] He could imagine losing Protestants through marriage. Still, his admission of weakness was muted. The account appeared in a Catholic book, and official resolutions from Protestant clergy to avoid Catholic marriages had not yet begun. Systematic Catholic dispensations shook the Protestant pedestal by the 1930s, but not much.

Protestant discomfort with Catholic rules was nonetheless a small sign that the Code of 1917, as well as the CCAR resolution of 1909, had some influence. These censures of interfaith marriage carried the moral authority of organized religion. To varying degrees, they controlled church and synagogue procedures affecting mixed couples. Both policies aspired to stop intermarriage, however, and here there was no evidence of success. Inattentiveness of the laity was not new; intermarriage had a history in America. The difference now lay in the clergy's mood. Compared with Jewish commentary on anti-Semitism or apostasy and Catholic reactions to fascism or divorce, discussions of interfaith marriage seemed perfunctory by the 1920s. With these families alternatively condemned, slighted, and discreetly managed, it is safe to say that couples got conflicting signals from community leaders. That is, if families listened at all. Early twentieth-century partners in interfaith marriages spoke in a way that presumed their autonomy and implied they did as they pleased.

Immigrant Autobiographies

Few life experiences were more memorable at the turn of the century than coming to America, and immigrant writers often published their own stories. Although these were tales of transformation, how they depicted their interfaith marriages was puzzling. "I was born, I have lived, and I have been made over," Mary Antin began *The Promised Land* in 1911.[69] Jewish and Russian-born, Antin had wed a Protestant in Boston in 1901. Her marriage would seem a key episode in her makeover, but instead she omitted it from the book, cutting off the narrative at the end of her girlhood. This was the norm. By one writing strategy or another, immigrant authors turned their real intermarriages into literary nonevents. Family relationships that epitomized the romance of adventurously trying something new were slighted. On reflection, reasons for speaking guardedly of households are not hard to guess: perhaps mixed marriages were too controversial, too private, too painful. Another answer to the mysterious sidelining of domesticity lies in the autobiographical form. These books were about the self. Marriage was a subtheme in the main story of growing individuality. Now the pieces fall into place: eager for self-fulfillment, the writers disregarded tradition and intermarried, only to learn in the mirror of their own writing that family was incidental to who they wished to be.

Autobiographical writings by immigrants exemplify the self-assertive spirit that coexisted in the early twentieth century with the determinism of racial theories and legalism of religious policies. Jews especially produced memoirs treating intermarriage. Along with Antin's *Promised Land,* there were Ludwig Lewisohn's *Up Stream* (1922), Elisabeth Stern's *I Am a Woman—and a Jew* (1926), and Anzia Yezierska's *All I Could Never Be* (1932). Although none was as popular as *The Promised Land,* reprinted thirty-four times, all were read widely.[70] In them Americans found intermarriage portrayed as one choice in the life of an intelligent adult, neither glorious nor trouble-free. Turning private life into public information, the books disengaged interfaith marriage from cosmic dramas of racial degeneration or spiritual damnation. Anyone considering a mixed marriage might be heartened by this unadorned view.

Authors began their accounts in a mood of leave-taking, knowing that emigration meant giving up old ways. Fathers were symbols of the past, but no two were the same. "'Now I am free,'" Elisabeth Stern thought with bitter relief when she saw her father in his coffin. Loyal to a kind of Judaism he "brought to the twentieth century from the fifteenth," he "would destroy everything in his life, the very happiness of his children, that it might not be, in one small observance, unhonored."[71] In contrast, Mary Antin's father was not a villain but a hero. Raised an Orthodox Jew in Russia, where "his body was starved, that his mind might be stuffed with useless learning," he now believed in "atheistic doctrines." Because of his openness, he "brought his children to school" in America "as if it were an act of consecration."[72] Antin left strict Judaism behind with her father's blessing. More subtly, Anzia Yezierska understood that the past followed her in disguise. When the gentile she fell in love with quoted from the Bible, she recognized "her father as he might have been in a new world."[73] This echo of her heritage seemed quickly lost, however, in a chronicle of selfhood. The man, a college professor, offered to help the young immigrant with her writing. "'For art is the climax of human experience,'" and "'perhaps I can have the great happiness of helping you to a realization that *you are*, and *what you are*.'"[74] Although the semblance of her father which the writer found in her American lover expressed a profound truth about the private sources of creativity, the focus of Yezierska's fictional autobiography remained the future, not the past.

What is most striking about the books is the strength of the writers' personal voice. The speaking "I" dominated the stories, no matter how complicated they became. The title *I Am a Woman—and a Jew* signaled unmistakably what Stern's 1926 memoir was about. Remembering a time when "the new feminism had not begun to be discussed," Stern knew even then that "I had a certain knack that [her husband] had not, of knowing people, understanding them." Working "was how I would 'express my personality,'" and interspersed with childrearing and relocating for her husband's career, she had held too many jobs to count.[75] More to her surprise, her father's death taught her that "in that inner self that cannot change, I belong to my people." Loss of her father as an opponent brought her back to her roots. "I hungered for the comfort of some religion, some way in which my father and his philosophy of life would be near to me and my life."[76] She imagined that the search for identity would be wide open; now it took a Jewish turn, as she made friends with a Reform rabbi, worshiped with the Orthodox, and listened to Zionists. Through all, Stern's literary form was a monologue, oddly solipsistic given the numbers of her co-workers and kin. Readers heard about her social circle at second hand, because its importance lay in relation to herself. She was riveted by the problem of who she was.

In the midst of unpredictable self-discovery, marriages seemed oases of contentment. Brief sketches of domesticity highlighted its happiness. For Ludwig Lewisohn, becoming an American was mainly an experience of loss. "Alienation from my own race" began when Lewisohn, a German-Jewish boy in South Carolina in the 1890s, attended a Methodist church and "accepted Jesus as my personal Savior." "If ever the child of immigrants embraced the faith of the folk among whom it came—I was that child."[77] But his conversion was transient. Discriminated against first as a Jew and then a German during World War I, Lewisohn denounced "Christian-capitalistic civilization" as a "tribal tyranny" loyal only to "base-ball and the prohibition of wine, love, speculation and art."[78] *Up Stream* charted his progressive isolation. The exception was his marriage in 1906 to the first of his three gentile wives. "We sat on a bench under the bare poplars with all the stars of heaven for our own," he wrote idyllically.[79] Despite later disillusionments, he warmly remembered this.

Elisabeth Stern entered her mixed marriage with more guilt, but she pictured it as peacefully as Lewisohn did his. The "happy marriages have no chroniclers," she reflected. "They grow like great trees, deep-rooted, year after year, quietly."[80] She knew her choice betrayed Jewish tradition. Her cousin Simeon's wedding gift was a "little jade god" that came with a note echoing the biblical prohibition against "Strange gods."[81] Her father cut her off, and when her mother came alone to visit, she brought dishes from home. "I cannot describe her coming, its heartbreak." "My husband was so dear to her, so tenderly kind"; but "they were strangers," and "my little baby was a Gentile baby in her arms."[82] Nor did Stern and her husband always agree. Interested in "religious observances" as "psychological manifestations, as mirrors of the human mind," he favored letting their children sample them freely. For herself, "there was always the need of something into which to pour my whole soul," and "I wanted them to feel their kinship with my people, with my family anyhow."[83] Yet all these issues did not shake Stern's perception of the amiability of her marriage. "The only two people who did not seem to be troubled by religious distrusts, religious animosities were my husband and myself."[84] *I Am a Woman—and a Jew* is a memoir filled with struggle, except at home.

Such unequivocal declarations of happiness provoke mistrust by their excess. Sometimes doubt is justified. Lewisohn began an affair with Thelma Spear in 1921 or 1922, just as he was writing *Up*

Stream. The liaison continued until his wife Mary agreed to divorce, after much heartache for all, in 1937.[85] If real difficulties at some point exploded rosy images of interfaith love, they could inspire a countermyth of inevitable failure. This is how Anzia Yezierska's frustrated affair with the philosopher John Dewey became a tract on racial barriers. He, classically, was the great man, America's favorite sage, sixtyish and married when they became intimate during a research project in 1917; she was an aspiring writer in her thirties, divorced and with a child. He loved her Jewish "'intensity,'" she recalled when she fictionalized their story in 1932, and saw their bond as part of "'this interracial symphony'" now taking place: "'Our whole history is one of assimilation.'"[86] But soon he asked for his letters back, the relationship apparently still unconsummated. The man with the "cool, sane face" and "clear, disciplined intellect" returned to "his kingdom of books."[87] "For thousands of years, his race and hers were fearing, mistrusting, hating, and fighting each other," Yezierska mused sadly in *All I Could Never Be.* "Was it a wonder that the ancient battle had thrust its shadow of doubt and fear between them?"[88]

Did Yezierska issue a rebuttal on mixed-faith love to the other immigrant authors, or is her tale of romantic trauma the exception that proves the rule? Anguished, graphic, and informed by racial theories, the novel departed from the optimism of her literary peers. But the similarities among the memoirs were more numerous. All were based on experience and depicted private relationships with a circumspection perhaps natural to autobiographers. Even Yezierska suppressed the facts behind her fiction; until scholarly sleuthing in the 1970s, her liaison with Dewey was just a rumor among family and friends.[89] All the books, too, took interfaith romance for granted as one event in the immigrant's self-creation. Although Yezierska spent far more time than the others describing her love, her story did not end there. Once the professor was gone, the novel's heroine wrote fiction, organized workers, and found contentment with a Russian artist. The affair was painful, but no less a cherished part of herself.

Viewing society through the eyes of one person was the basic reading experience of the immigrant narratives. This may have been a matter of literary technique, but more likely a sign of a contemporary mood. Strangely, at the same time that Americans listened to racial determinism, they picked up books celebrating self-construction. In these, seeking one's identity was nearly a duty, and authorities who guarded tradition were brushed aside. Her Orthodox father dead, Elisabeth Stern befriended a rabbi with "a quick, boyish friendliness that was winning, irresistible." Tact was his watchword: "With a subtle courtesy, he seldom discussed our faith with my husband, except when the subject was brought forth by some one else."[90] To Stern, this man perhaps seemed typical of the new gatekeepers of Judaism, who honored self-fulfillment even if acquired at the community's expense. His respect for her eager quest for identity made him an ally—a "delightful friend," not a censor.[91] No other author spoke of a rabbi, as if public tradition meant too little to bother to mention it. Either way, the writers willingly sacrificed the past for the sake of experience, and all chose to express themselves in interfaith romance.

It is important to keep in mind that autobiography becomes apology when publication exposes private life to public view. This might in fact be the author's intention, but may equally occur in the minds of readers sensitive to emphases the writer does not see. The early twentieth-century stories by Jewish immigrants affirmed self-seeking, not quite as a good thing but an inevitability nonetheless. Interfaith marriages might be expected routinely and no longer would be riveting news.

Interfaith Marriage Moves to an Inside Page

As subject and symbol, interfaith marriage lost visibility after World War I. The enthusiastic reception of *The Melting-Pot* in 1908 and furor a year later over the Reform rabbis' vote seem echoes of a passing era. Newer viewpoints skirted mixed-faith romance. As race theorists debated crossbreeding, they oddly omitted mention of families and sex. Reform Jews and Catholics pigeonholed intermarriage as they turned their sights outward to public events. Autobiographers reduced their marriages to one episode in complicated lives. The question is not simply why Americans worried less about interfaith romance, but why they paid less attention to families.

By the early twentieth century, any number of domestic problems dwarfed religious differences. Indeed, families no longer seemed bastions of order so much as mirrors of social disintegration. The nineteenth-century love affair with domesticity was coming to an end, and going with it were distress over intermarriage as a threat and attraction to mixed couples as a symbol.[92] *Little Ships* (1925) by the Catholic author Kathleen Norris (1880–1960) pictured the family in trouble.

"So all the little ships come sailing home across the sea," Tom Cunningham sings at the close of this novel about a third-generation Irish clan.[93] The homecomings were generally sad. Tom returns to San Francisco from his travels as a sailor as an alcoholic, a "pleasant egotist," in the eyes of his cousin Kate, "not sincere even with his mother."[94] His sister Ellen reveals her secret wedding at age seventeen to a man in his thirties—married on the day of their child's birth. Who would be surprised that she reacts to her mother's broken heart with "light-hearted indifference," or that her husband soon resists his daughters' Catholic schooling because "'the nuns are going to make bigots of them'"?[95] Their brother Martin marries a woman whose "passion for martyrdom" led her to take a private vow of chastity, and their sister Cecilia becomes a nun against the wishes of a father who denounces "'all this foolishness about entering, and vocations, and all the rest of it!'" Convent life, even in the loyal Catholic view of Norris, is "minutiae glorified."[96] Yes, there is hope for the Cunninghams. The siblings' cousin Kate, a librarian who marries hard-working John Kelly, finds happiness as a woman "beloved, building a home, bearing children."[97] But the book ends soberly. Recalling "the dear, dear children," the narrator sees "in their places these somewhat disillusioned, somewhat hardened, somewhat saddened men and women, so soon to be grey, to be feeble and alone, to vanish as completely as those same dear busy ignorant children had!"[98]

In the midst of tales of self-indulgence and self-denial, interfaith romance appears in two stock subplots. Cecilia's love affair with a rich Protestant before she enters the convent contains a conventional moral: do not let status-seeking seduce you to jeopardize faith. Like Mary Blake in Mary Anne Sadlier's *Blakes and Flanagans* in the 1850s, Cecilia's mother, Mollie, promotes her daughter's crush on Dion Taylor. Musing on "future complications of 'the promises' Dion must make regarding the children, and the details of the ceremony," Mollie "did not realize that she was chiefly fearful that Cecy's religion would cost her her admirer; she honestly thought her apprehensions came under the head of piety, and she was mournfully proud of them."[99] Soon Dion dumps Cecilia, and the plot moves on, in contrast to Sadlier's novel, where Eliza Blake came to regret marrying a Protestant before she died in childbirth without last rites.

While Cecilia mourns Dion, Tom Cunningham falls for Babette Garberg Newman, a married woman he met in Paris with "thick black hair cut short over her ears, and giving an almost Egyptian look to her seriously smiling face."[100] He announces his intent to marry Babette to his parents, though her divorce is not final. His father asks:

> "Is she a Catholic?"
> "She's a Jewess. Her uncle is a rabbi."
> It was said. They knew the worst now. The storm could only break over him. Tom mentally bowed his head to it, and felt some spiritual emotion corresponding to the closing of eyes.
> "Oh, no—no—no!" Mollie moaned in the silence. "Oh, my God!"[101]

Behind the melodramatic moment lay the real problem: again, the mother's ambition. Mollie had packed Tom off to Paris because she feared he might marry his poor cousin Kate. Predictably, her snobbery produced Babette instead. But no matter. Babette returns to her husband, Tom descends into drink, and there is no interfaith marriage.

It is not surprising that the twin evils of status-seeking and mixed marriage, standard themes of nineteenth-century Catholic immigrant fiction, had a role in *Little Ships*. Literary convention and human nature must have conspired to retain a place for a classic character such as Mollie Cunningham, eager to fit in and move up. What is new is that Norris dealt quickly with these moral dangers. Deceptiveness, insensitivity, poor judgment, and excesses of piety or skepticism: these are the corrosive failings of Mollie's children. Next to them interfaith romance may have seemed a small matter. Facing these faults head on, readers found the family besieged by its own decay. *Little Ships* was a classic domestic novel chronicling reasons for the decline of the genre.

But there was also an unexpected bright side to this picture. What seemed like a grim family saga to a moralist like Norris might be turned around to reveal Mollie's children's self-assertion. Neither virtuous nor often happy, they nonetheless behaved with modest regard to their parents' wishes and in that sense enjoyed freedom. The disintegration of the Cunningham family from one viewpoint was the children's liberation from another. Their greater range of choices did not have to mean an end to family, as it seemed in *Little Ships*, but might produce different kinds of families instead. Unlike the cozy circle of Mollie Cunningham's memory, where common faith sealed affection, households of the new generation might be individualistic and open-ended, though also impermanent. Couples inclined to experiment could sample the ideas of scientists, clergy, and popular writers. While the erosion of moral certainties made writing domestic fiction more challenging, there was plenty of advice available to the young peers of Mollie's children. What Kathleen Norris mourned as family failure might be opportunity in their eyes.

Fitting Religion into Complicated Lives

From the beginning, interfaith marriages in America raised issues about weddings. Mathew Carey sat up late in 1819 worrying about who would perform the ceremony when his son took a Protestant wife. Happily, all soon agreed. Two days later Carey's old friend, Father Michael Hurley, officiated at St. Augustine's Catholic Church in Philadelphia. Headaches multiplied for Rachel Berenson and Ralph Barton Perry in 1905. Because Ralph's father opposed his son's marriage to a Jew, Ralph hoped to avoid the "embarrassment" of a wedding in Boston without his father by planning a "quiet affair" abroad.[1] This suited Rachel, already in Europe studying art. She urged Ralph to consider St. Mildred's Anglican parish in London, "a very beautiful *tiny* little gem of a church just right for a *tiny* little wedding."[2] Daughter of a freethinking father, Rachel knew little about Judaism; her older brother Bernard, the art critic, had been baptized a Catholic in 1891. Now Bernard's circle of left-leaning aesthetes cared less for tradition. "The B[ernard]. B[erenson].'s and 'their kind' haven't a grain of sentiment about such things," Rachel complained; most marry "in the Registrar's Office." Bernard's "horror" of ceremony helped keep him away from his sister's wedding, and she confessed that "to be married without a single one of my own flesh and blood is *pretty hard*."[3] Yet technically it was easy to marry in St. Mildred's; only two weeks' residence in the parish was required and publication of the banns. Juggling family opinions and personal preferences, Ralph and Rachel, a Protestant and a Jew of sorts, became husband and wife on August 15 in England's established church.

The Perrys' creative solution was part of a culture where how to mix customs at the altar was only one question facing interfaith couples. American society at the turn of the twentieth century was increasingly open-ended. Did marriages need to be solemnized at all, or was the Registrar's Office sufficient? Who should decide—the parents or the couple?—and should clergy have a voice besides reading vows? As religion's authority diminished, a young woman like Rachel relished her freedom, "the rich spiciness of the whole idea—being mar-

6. Ralph Barton Perry and Rachel Berenson Perry, during World War I. Courtesy of Ralph Barton Perry III.

ried quite in our own way—with just a little tang of the adventurous about it."[4] Even so, she chose to marry in a church. St. Mildred's, one of "lots of dear little chapels in London," lent the event a "sacred" tone and must mercifully have diverted the couple's attention from their families' divergent opinions: his father's strict Protestantism, her brother's idiosyncratic Catholicism, her parents' residual Jewishness.[5] No one among them was indifferent to religion, and there was no quarrel with Rachel's wish for a traditional wedding. Yet only Ralph's father attended services routinely and had conventional views. For the others, art, philosophy, literature, and politics, along with religion, contributed to personal decisions. The appeal of St. Mildred's was that its building was tasteful and its policies were liberal. The church had no private meaning for either Rachel or Ralph. After a honeymoon on the English coast, they headed home to Cambridge in time for the fall term at Harvard, where Ralph taught philosophy. In September he received a letter from his father, written "in the calm of resignation," accepting the marriage. On the same day George Perry sent Rachel a note addressed to "my dear daughter" conveying his "blessings."[6] The crisis of the wedding past, religion in family conversations returned to being just one topic among others.

The Perrys were not like American interfaith families of earlier decades. Mid-nineteenth-century households allied themselves with religious institutions and raised their children in the faith. In contrast, couples who married around 1900 were less interested in public religion or, for that matter, producing large families. They lit votive candles, consulted astrologers, and visited Palestine, but often did not join a synagogue or church. Their small numbers of children and willingness to divorce may have been both a cause and consequence of their free-form religion: parents modestly committed to transmitting their heritage to their children were more likely to experiment, and slim contact with religious authorities gave families latitude to do as they pleased. In this trend toward religious privacy, the attitude of women was crucial. Once, intermarried Victorian mothers had kept children and husbands connected with communities. Now, wives with liberal educations and career goals were less focused on faith. In none of these traits—outgoing wives, declines in births, or rises in divorce—did interfaith families differ much from their peers. Moralists on all sides, from clergy to eugenicists, mourned the family. But their laments were hasty, and families persisted, even if smaller and more susceptible to change. These were the kinds of households where early twentieth-century intermarried kin worked out their religious commitments.[7]

A clear story may be told about interfaith couples who married between the 1890s and World War I. Progressive wives were comfortable with intellectual openness at home, and this encouraged a range of religious expressions. At the same time, the era's popular culture thrived on news of romantic scandals—affairs, divorces, sexual deviance—to the point that religious differences of husbands and wives raised fewer eyebrows. All this worked to free interfaith families from convention. Loyalty to traditional faiths declined; but family feeling, including a sense of common religious interests, remained.

A New Kind of Wife

No magazine reader in 1900 could fail to recognize a Gibson girl. In drawings published everywhere, Charles Dana Gibson rendered the new temper of American women. Dressed in shirtwaist and skirt for golf or low-cut gown for husband-hunting, she exuded fitness and pluck. Flirtatious, she was also outspoken and could surely give a suitor a hard time. Behind Gibson's light-hearted sketches were real changes. Some young women sensed their talents and wanted to make a difference in the world. What kind of mothers would they make, if they married at all? Would they shepherd their children to church, or to galleries and meetings? How might they behave in interfaith marriages? Rachel Berenson Perry, Julia Collier Harris, and Rose Pastor Stokes, all married between 1897 and 1905, thought about religious differences in their households in the context of who they wished to be.[8]

"O mighty scholar—may all the muses of classical antiquity attend thy steps," Ralph Barton Perry wrote playfully to Rachel Berenson (1880–1933) during their courtship in 1903.[9] Graduating from Smith that spring and beginning Radcliffe's master's program in Classics, Rachel was looking for a vocation. Her brother Bernard (1865–1959), famous for his knowledge of Renaissance art, was her conscience. "You have left me no loophole of excuse for not making something of myself," she closed a self-probing letter to him in 1901. Her choice seemed to lie between "teaching and criticism." She could see that teaching Greek would be "laborious and uninspiring";

study of antiquities promised to be "so absorbing—so elevating." There were doubts: "Who am I that I should undertake to interpret such wonderful things?"[10] But misgivings did not block her studies. In 1904 Rachel went "to Athens to study at the American School of Classical Archeology for a year," Ralph remembered late in life in autobiographical notes.[11] What he forgot was her adventurous spirit. During the summer of 1905, while they negotiated about a place for the wedding, she chased Greek art across two continents: Constantinople, Naples, Florence, and Paris. At one point she hoped they might marry in Italy, then visit classical ruins together.[12] In a modern mood, Rachel assumed that her wedding need not end her personal plans. Even their decision in favor of St. Mildred's, designed in the seventeenth century by Christopher Wren, fit in with her involvement in art. But did aesthetics so fill her horizons that her aspirations edged religion aside?

The daughter of Jewish immigrants who arrived in Boston from Lithuania in 1875, Rachel was comfortable in Christian society. "Unconsciously we follow the customs and folkways of our neighbors," Bernard reflected in 1944, and "aspire to be no less American than other Americans."[13] At the time of Rachel's engagement, the Berensons conformed to Christian routines. "Church in the morning for which I find myself in no mood," Rachel grumbled in her diary in Athens in February 1905. Two months later Ralph sent her "A happy Easter to you!" after a holiday meal with her parents in Dorchester.[14] Albert, Rachel's father, prepared the way for accommodation. A militant modernizer, "he read lots of Voltaire to Rachel & me when we were tots," her sister Bessie recollected. His cronies advertised their impiety by eating ham sandwiches within sight of Boston synagogues on Yom Kippur. Albert forbid his wife, Judith, to attend services, and although she resumed Jewish practice after his death, Bessie recalled that she "read the new testament & even Mary Baker Eddy."[15] Even then, the Berensons were not without Jewish identity. Bessie did not see her courtship by a rabbinical student during the summer of Rachel's wedding as an extraordinary event. "He's rather nice," she confided to Ralph, "but I'm not a bit interested so I fear I won't be a little rabbiess."[16]

Rachel left no evidence of being troubled by these religious crosscurrents. The youngest child, she was a latecomer to family conversations. Bernard, the oldest, more clearly recorded his views. Because he paid for Rachel's education and directed it, something of her mind-set may be inferred from his. Culturally, he was a Christian. "To-day everybody who has been brought up as a European, no matter in what country of the earth, is the product of that culture, that civilization which under the name of Christianity absorbed nearly all worth preserving that was left over of the Judeo-Hellenic-Roman world; and acting both as a nucleus and as a leaven, has shaped mankind for good and for evil, into what we are now."[17] His baptism as an Episcopalian in 1885 and then as a Catholic must have helped secure his intimacy with his beloved literature and art. He had few second thoughts about assimilation. Assessing Russian-Jewish writers in 1888 for the *Andover Review,* he happily predicted that they "will doubtless adopt Russian" as a language and "become part and parcel of Russian literature."[18] Later, after Rachel's death, his opinions became more nuanced. It was just before he went into hiding in 1943 in Florence, his home for seventy years, that he professed the identity of Western and Christian society. Now, however, he also saw his Jewishness unmistakably, not simply because he was "the enemy for whom and with whom there were no possible pacts," but because "Jews never lose faith in life." Like himself, "they live on, and enjoy life."[19] A complex religious personality forfeits simple faith. The "emancipated Jew" retains "little except a vague Deism," he wrote in 1944, though for himself, doubts did not blunt his elemental "awe before the universe."[20] He was Christian by taste, Jewish by heritage, pagan by sensibility.

Rachel, neither a product of Lithuanian Jewish schools nor a survivor of Nazism like her brother, approached Christian culture more naturally. But she, too, embraced it aesthetically, not piously, and without denying her Jewishness. Smith and Radcliffe colleges, with traditional curriculums and obligatory chapel, put her in touch with Christianity. Athens deepened her acquaintance with the West's "Judeo-Hellenic-Roman" roots, although at least one Sunday she slipped away from the students going to church. "Take my church service on the hill," she confided to her diary, "back of the stadium."[21] Ralph's father's rejection of Rachel pushed her Jewishness back in her face. "It is an almost unbearable thought that *I—I—I—me misera—* should be the cause of a good man's misery and pain," she appealed to Ralph from Constantinople. "I can't quite believe it—I mean—it doesn't seem real to me, his prejudice. My mind tells me it ought not to be pampered & sympathized with but my heart tells me all sorts of other things—that you are the dearest hope of his life & anything that touches that must be the ideal he has painted in his mind."[22] In this mix of reactions—hurt, disapproval, and empathy—Rachel never questioned that, strictly speaking, she was a Jew. Yet if this was her past, she hoped for a broader future.

Full of curiosity, Rachel showed little of earlier women's devotion to institutional piety. Instead, she resembled Ralph religiously, and because American men had long had the option to be intellectually free, it was the difference in her that changed them as a family. Ralph Barton Perry was a rigorously moral man who prized America's Christian heritage. "Let every right thinking and feeling man put on record his detestation of Anti-Semitism," he wrote privately in the 1940s, then named his remedy: "To inculate the *Christian-Democratic Code* of humanity, so that every sort of mass hatred and discrimination, will be intolerable."[23] Here, differently phrased, was Bernard Berenson's equation of Christianity and civilization. For this philosopher, religion was a wide-open concept, consistent with "ethical principles of prudence, justice, and good-will," Perry argued in *The Moral Economy* (1909), and healthier if disengaged from sectarian "partisanship."[24] Personal piety was not needed. In 1930 he recalled "an intense adolescent religious experience," and he had planned to become a minister after graduating from Princeton in 1895. Studying with William James at Harvard led "from faith to criticism," however, and in philosophy he "found a way in which I might think freely and still 'do good.'"[25] It is not surprising that Ralph courted Rachel at a time when he equated religion with the best in art, literature, and morals. "The Berensons love you very much," Bessie assured Ralph as a soulmate in 1905, and they spent an afternoon in Boston viewing an exhibit of Monet's paintings.[26]

Yet for Rachel, marriage closed doors as well as opened them. One was vocational. "How far away your Greek world must seem," exclaimed Mary Berenson, Bernard's wife, as Rachel set up housekeeping in Cambridge. Soon Mary wrote that "the Common Lot has overtaken you." Rachel was pregnant. By 1910 Mary told Rachel to leave her two sons in Florence while "you & Ralph could make a *scappatura* to Greece or Rome, which would do you both a lot of good I am sure." But instead of revisiting sites of her early hopes, Rachel and her boys arrived in Florence in 1911 for "a splendid rest."[27] The new woman's career goals were fragile. This did not mean that Rachel returned to the path of nineteenth-century wives and took up church or synagogue work. Sailing to meet his family in Italy in 1912, Ralph noted the name of a minister in his diary who led shipboard services. No mention of churchgoing appears in the Perrys' papers again.[28] A public philosopher, Ralph championed tolerance and community. Rachel had a role in this ethical enterprise as a faculty wife, but the generalized language of philosophy nearly shut a second door—on her Jewishness. Visiting Bernard in 1953, Ralph made inquiries about the Berensons' childhood religion.[29] There is no record that he had asked about this before. Surely Rachel conspired to obscure her background, though not erase it. A month before her death she brightly told Ralph about a play she saw "on the rise of a young Jew from the slums to the highest pinnacle of the New York bar."[30] Still, she paid a toll of ethnic invisibility by her eagerness to meet her husband on the wide ground of liberal culture.

Here was a modern story, in any case: free-thinking wife matched with like-minded husband. Their differing backgrounds erected no visible obstacle to happiness, and they were content to transmit the core of Western values they shared.

Julia Collier (1875–1967), a Methodist from Georgia, might have been a sister to Rachel Berenson, so close were their ambitions. "My mother had planned, from my early childhood, that I should support myself as a designer and illustrator," Julia remembered; "she felt that all her girls should be trained to care for themselves."[31] Her mother Susan's intent betrayed the anxiety of an orphan who must have felt lucky to wed a man who became mayor of Atlanta. But her viewpoint was also a sign of the times, and Julia spent four years in Boston studying art. The future unraveled in 1897. Susan died at age forty-two, soon followed by her husband. Julia returned home to raise six younger brothers and sisters. In October she married Julian La Rose Harris, who helped with the children. He gave her career an unexpected turn. A journalist at the Atlanta *Constitution* at the time of the wedding, he sparked her interest in newspaper writing. "I could have had no more experienced or brilliant mentor than he." Julia "was one of the few women correspondents present" at "the signing of the Versailles Treaty" in 1919; she covered the Scopes trial in 1925.[32] She got to know leading writers: H. L. Mencken, Sherwood Anderson, Sinclair Lewis, Margaret Mitchell. This was not the vocation Julia had anticipated, but in it she became a powerful figure.

She took charge of the religious difference between herself and

Julian in the same self-assured spirit. Julian (1873–1963) was the oldest child of Joel Chandler Harris and his wife Esther; he was raised Catholic, though pressed by his father to temper his faith. Now Julia considered her options. She seemed to think briefly about conversion. An acquaintance, Mrs. Burke, "and her mother accepted Mr. Burke's religion and she is now the most devout of Catholics," she confided to Julian in June 1897.[33] That fall she enrolled her brothers at Sacred Heart Seminary in Sharon, Georgia, perhaps on the advice of Julian's mother. Yet she came only so close to Catholicism before backing away. Priests performed the weddings of four of Julian's siblings, none of whom married Catholics; not so for Julia, wed at home by a Methodist minister. Her reticence did not keep her from bowing to Catholicism occasionally. With her son Charles (1899–1903), she recited "Now I lay me down to sleep" when "the Catholic bell tolled for six o'clock." A priest baptized Pierre (1901–1904), named for Julian's Catholic grandfather. Still, when each of the boys died, she called a Methodist minister to conduct the funerals at home.[34] In every case, Julia was the decision maker who marshaled ministers and priests. This did not need to end churchgoing. Julian told an acquaintance in 1925 that "I attended the Methodist church with Mrs. Harris until a preacher uttered so many bigoted and intolerant sentiments she decided not to attend further." It did not take much for an independent woman like Julia to give up organized faith.[35]

It was her cosmopolitanism that exposed southern prejudice and helped sustain her once she rejected Protestant churches. She had lived in Boston and in the 1910s divided her time between New York and Paris, writing for a syndicate anchored by the New York *Herald*. But there was a dark side to her success. Looking back at the years after her sons died and siblings grew up, she recalled being "empty-handed." She became a writer "to fill this void."[36] Even then she was lonely. How "absurd" for Julian to work fifteen hours a day, she complained to her mother-in-law from Paris in 1920, "especially as we have no children & I am so entirely cut off from everybody I care for."[37] Sometimes guilt was her companion. After Pierre's death she recorded eighteen pages of notes on his health and treatments from birth. "I was in a nervous, feeble condition" during pregnancy, she began; his decline seemed her fault. In 1949 she drafted a reminiscence "About My Mother" as part of her "reparation" for being "unresponsive, stubborn, rebellious" as a girl. "Life is so pathetic," Julia reflected at seventy-three: "she is dead and gone these fifty years and few now recall her existence, for she was an orphan and an only child, and I, the eldest of seven, am the only one who has a clear conception of her personality."[38] Episodes of collapse punctuated Julia's career. A "complete breakdown forced me to resign from the editorial staff of The Chattanooga *Times*" in 1937. She spent time at a sanatorium in 1902, wintered in Florida for her health in 1906, and took "six months' rest" in the early 1930s.[39] She sensed that work diverted her from the sad thoughts that brought her relapses. Nowhere in the cycle was there religion of a kind that offered consolation.

Most likely Julia learned to throw herself into her work by watching Julian. "He never sees anything of Paris except the streets between the two offices," she reported home.[40] This was the life his father had wished. "I frequently catch myself mapping out a proud career for you," Joel Chandler Harris confided to his son in 1890.[41] Ambition may have helped displace faith. "I have been accused of being a Catholic—I am not," Julian explained to a correspondent in 1925, conceding, "My family is a catholic family." He had changed since childhood. The "Lord is almighty," he wrote at sixteen, mourning his brother Linton; we must "pray that he may have mercy on the souls of the departed."[42] Perhaps the deaths of his sons strained belief. A memorial poem to Charles, clipped from the *Constitution* and saved, suggests this was so. "Oh, there never is no preachin' in any thunder-tone, / Can sing a song to the sorrow of a heart that's lost its own!"[43] Grief, careerism, Christian intolerance: all must have led Julian to deny his religious connection. In each case Julia shared his perspective.

Yet the Harrises were professionals who knew how to turn their private quarrels in positive directions. Their commitment to ethics seemed to grow as they left conventional religion behind. As joint editors in the 1920s of the Columbus, Georgia, *Enquirer-Sun*, they battled the "ignorance, bigotry, intolerance, and graft" of the Ku Klux Klan, as one observer put it, in "the heart of the lynching belt."[44] Their co-owner was Tom Loyless, already attacking the Klan in Augusta and known for exposing the anti-Semitism of the murder trial and eventual lynching of Leo Frank near Marietta in 1915. Politics at the *Enquirer-Sun* heated up in 1921 when it reprinted the New York *World*'s "famous *exposé*" of the Klan. When "we found out that not a single newspaper in the State of Georgia was going to run the series," Loyless recalled, and that the Klan "was going to sue every newspaper in the United States" that did, "we wired the New York *World* and asked them to send the series to us."[45] Julia became associate editor when Loyless left in 1922, and she extended the paper's targets beyond the Klan's anti-Catholicism, anti-Semitism, and racism. "Mrs. Harris has been especially active in the *Enquirer-Sun*'s campaign against the barring of evolution teaching," reported its managing editor. She "hurled some convincing argument at the fundamentalists," while Julian satirized a bill in the legislature meant to keep evolution out of the schools.[46] This was a sign of how political the editorials were, and how dangerous. "We charged the present governor, the commissioner of agriculture, the attorney general, the state game warden and several minor officials with being Kluxers," Julian wrote; caught in lies, they confessed. The paper ran the Klan out of Columbus, but not before enemies threw sand on their presses and threatened to bomb the Harrises' apartment. Already $39,000 in debt by the middle of the decade, they had to sell the *Enquirer-Sun* when the Depression began and did not finish repaying their creditors until 1951.[47] Yet their work won recognition: they received the Pulitzer Prize for journalism in 1925.

It was Julian who insisted that the Pulitzer committee cite Julia. He accepted the prize, along with the honor of membership on the Advisory Board of Columbia's Pulitzer School of Journalism, "with the stipulation that his wife, Julia Collier Harris, share them equally with him." He praised her publicly "as a trained newspaper woman, as fearless as she is intelligent."[48] Privately, he must have seen that they found most in common in this work. It seemed natural to use religious terms to describe the campaign. Julia called their efforts "crusades," a black newspaper welcomed a "long promised awakening," and Catholic prelates commended "valiant service" to the faith.[49] These phrases stretched familiar words to cover an ethical cause pursued independently of churches. The *Enquirer-Sun* was one of a few southern papers to "capitalize the word Negro," remarked the Chicago *Bee*, a black weekly. "Absolutely this is a small concession," but in today's South it "represents a literary courage of sufficient importance to constitute such a paper an oasis in an intellectual and moral desert."[50] The difference in the Harrises' religious backgrounds was unimportant in light of their interest in decency.

For them as a couple, Julia's transformation was crucial. Julian, taught by his father to take stock of the world and succeed, lived a typical Victorian boyhood. What Julia grew up to expect in the 1890s was more complex. Once she quit churchgoing, however, they took a path shaped by their careers.

In contrast to the quiet religious adjustments in the families of Rachel Perry and Julia Harris, the marriage of Rose Pastor (1879–1933) and James Graham Phelps Stokes was headline news. The papers worked hard to explain why a millionaire chose a poor Jewish immigrant. "J. G. P. Stokes to Wed Young Jewess," announced the New York *Times* in April 1905; the Philadelphia *Record* piqued curiosity by the title "Proud of Ghetto Bride." Leaving Rose without a name, the reports made Graham's proposal seem an act of benevolence. Apostasy was the diagnosis of the *Hebrew Standard*: Rose was his "Christianized bride."[51] Graham himself rejected any thought of distance between them. "Dear Mother, I am very fond of Rose, a wonderful peace fills my soul as seems in itself to prove the divine." Her passion for social justice made her "Christlike." "I don't know where to find another Christian who is truer to the teachings of her Master," he confided to his mother. He repeated it to the *Times:* "She is a Jewess as the apostles were Jews—A Christian by faith."[52] Rose subscribed cautiously to the fiction. She wrote privately to her "dear darling Saint." When she wore a cross at her wedding in St. Luke's Episcopal Church in Noroton, Connecticut, she nodded her acceptance of Christian culture. Yet anyone acquainted with this "Israelitish maiden," as Graham's aunts saw her, might have wondered just how firm a foundation Christianity would be for their marriage.[53]

The issue was less her Jewishness than her work. Courting socialism by the time of her marriage and embracing communism later, Rose believed labor defined identity. "We are conscious participants in a world-wide conflict," she lectured Graham in 1925. "In the very nature of our respective backgrounds, it was inevitable that you should place yourself on the side of capitalism, I, on the side of the workers."[54] Written just after she moved out of their house, in the tense years following the Russian Revolution, her view of their difference was doctrinaire compared with earlier hopes. In 1905 it seemed they might struggle together as reformers for "applied Christianity," Graham's term for socialism.[55] Yet all along Rose clung to her roots. Fearful that marriage into wealth would cause alienation from her class, she returned briefly to factory work during her romance with

Graham. Going to work as a writer in 1903 for the *Jewish Daily News* had been liberating after twelve years as a cigar maker, beginning at age eleven. Now upward mobility seemed like entrapment. The poverty of her mother and six stepsiblings kept her mindful of harsh realities. Some of the children had lived in orphanages and foster homes; at least one still did in January 1905. They came to Rose all her life with reports of illness and unemployment, seeking help. She had to ask Graham to continue his stipend to her mother after their divorce. All this marked Rose as a paradoxical kind of "new woman": she sought a vocation that was not a bourgeois career.[56]

Strangely then, her work made an ally of her "Comrade-lover" at the same time that it drew the line between them. Their religious views had a similar effect. Graham was an unusual Christian. He did not care for churches; "my faith," he explained publicly in 1903, "is something that is between my God and me."[57] Individualism in the Stokes family did not equal quietism. In Graham's time, his unmarried aunts Olivia and Caroline exemplified the clan's commitment to the stewardship of wealth. Devoting their lives to philanthropy, they gave great sums, earned in business by their Presbyterian grandfather and father, to black education and housing. Elsewhere in the family the freedom of the rich combined with the Stokeses' moral fervor to produce more questionable legacies. William, Olivia and Caroline's brother, married and divorced a Cuban Catholic and later wrote eugenic tracts such as *The Right to Be Well Born* (1917). Graham had something in common with both sides. Like his aunts, he believed Christianity enjoined social betterment, and he followed their special interest in race when he helped found the National Association for the Advancement of Colored People in 1909. Like his uncle, he proposed to the woman he pleased. Offbeat, the family perhaps was sincere when it told the press "Miss Pastor is an ideal woman, loving, true, tender hearted, gentle and intellectual."[58] She fell into line most comfortably with them behind a radical Jesus. Chasing the moneychangers from the Temple, Jesus used "methods of sensationalism and emotionalism," she tried to persuade Graham's brother Anson in 1916, "though His main method of propaganda was of the 'orderly constructive' type."[59] Written during Rose's activity in demonstrations over access to birth control information, this was a private argument about the nature of the Stokeses' Christianity.

Rose cited Christian concepts in good conscience because her Jewishness was self-defined. She blamed her mother's unhappiness on Anna Pastor's submission to Jewish custom. "Yet so bound by tradition was my mother," Rose reflected not long before her own death, "she would not marry her Polish lover—out of the faith and against her father's will."[60] The Pastors may or may not have been observant after they emigrated to Cleveland in 1890. As Rose silently gave up ritual, however, she did not leave Jewish circles. Her friends in New York after 1903 belonged to the "intelligentsia of the Lower East Side": Zionists, socialists, Yiddish authors. Marriage did not end Jewish contacts. She spoke uptown at Temple Emanu-El in 1906 and wrote a column for the Yiddish-language *Jewish Daily Forward*. In 1915 the Council of Jewish Women contributed to her speaking tour; she asked Atlanta's Jewish Educational Alliance to produce her play. Caritas, the Stokeses' island off Connecticut, became an interfaith commune, hosting Rose's large family as well as gentile socialists and their Jewish wives.[61] There were limits to Graham's empathy with Jewish radicalism. By 1913 he seemed tired of the rhetoric of class and rowdiness of class struggle. He "feels that he is not specifically fitted for that kind of work in the movement," Rose noted when he stayed home from a garment workers' strike. In 1925, after she left him, he lashed out, "you have brought nothing but shame to me in the use you have made of the cottage," furnishing "a place of recreation for ingrate enemies of America such as you had there before."[62] Although his resentment was not specifically anti-Semitic, his bitterness measured the distance between her radicalism and his: class-conscious, international, if need be violent, instead of paternalistic and familiarly American in its attention to race. The two were close enough to their separate ethnic backgrounds to jeopardize domestic peace.

Yet it was Rose's work as an agitator that ended the marriage. She labored in an unacquisitive spirit. "I have devoted the greater part of my life to humanity," she informed Graham in 1926. "I have no regrets but because of my devotion neither have I any means."[63] She seemed to accumulate ideology instead of material rewards. A communist in the 1920s, she thought in political terms. Each of us is "a soldier in a hostile camp," she told Graham, making their divorce "the visible symbol of a spiritual cleavage deep as life itself—sharp as the struggle you would have me deny." Graham, borrowing the language of bourgeois domesticity, seemed to prove her point. "'Political differences' have little if anything to do with our trouble, Girlie"; it comes from "your wholly selfish determination to disregard my feelings in our home."[64] But she did not really hear him and dreamed of moving to Russia. A friend exclaimed in a letter, "What if at last we may go on to Russia!" In 1933 she advised Jerome Isaac Romaine, the communist she had married, to bring up his son in the doctrines of communism, not religion: "Jerry boy needs to grow up over there."[65] Rose herself died of cancer during radiation treatment in Germany, five months after Hitler became chancellor.

At the outset of the Stokeses' romance, their socialist commitments brought them together. Rose's growing militance and Graham's retreat turned the same principles into a wall. To neither one was religion important enough to affect their deteriorating marriage.

Men who experimented with ideas and dismissed personal piety were not new in America at the turn of the twentieth century. But women who were like them were. In interfaith marriages, wives and husbands increasingly found common ground in their work, and church or synagogue affiliation seemed dispensable. Even then, spirituality did not disappear. Free-thinking in fact encouraged religious experimentation.

One's Own Way to Heaven

It is surprising at first to find astrology, numerology, and palmistry in progressive households. Overtures to Zionism, Christian Science, and the mysticism of Kahlil Gibran are unexpected, too. There is a logic, however, to the dual focus of interfaith families on secular ethics and unconventional faiths. As people who thought for themselves, they chose their own values. Issues of orthodoxy, community, and descent were of little concern. This perspective will disturb anyone who wishes to preserve a coherent tradition. Still, interfaith families were not crudely irreligious and sought ways to approach the unseen. A sampling of their individual answers may be found in the practices of five couples who married near the turn of the century.[66]

Reliance on mediums to interpret the occult was nearly commonplace in these homes. Julian and Julia Harris turned at times of personal crisis to readers of the stars, palms, numbers, and letters. After Julian left the army in 1919 an astrologer warned that success at the moment was unlikely. Alice Jennings of Atlanta, a specialist in "Character Analysis" and "Vocational Guidance," did a reading of Julian's hand soon after the Harrises sold the *Enquirer-Sun* in 1929. A decade later, during Julia's rest cure at a sanatorium, "Elaine" composed numerological charts for husband and wife. Assigning a number to each letter of Julia's name, Elaine concluded that Julia's "expression number" was eleven, the same as Hitler's. "I'm proud to know you— wish Hitler's manifestions of power were more like yours."[67] Presumably the Harrises took the readings seriously, because they commissioned them repeatedly and filed them away. But there was no sign that they subscribed to a philosophy of the occult. If anything, their curiosity about symbols was akin to their fascination with folklore. Julia edited a book of Roumanian tales in 1917; she enjoyed Louis Ginzberg's collection of *midrash* issued as *The Legends of the Jews* (1909–1928). These legends, she reported to Julian, "abound in miraculous amplifications" to stories that are mere "skeletons" in the Bible. She thought he would be interested because "you used to read the *Talmud*."[68] Like Joel Chandler Harris, who spun "Uncle Remus" tales from southern myths, his daughter-in-law and son loved popular literature, without quite taking it seriously. Perhaps they approached spiritual readings of physical objects in a mood that similarly blended appreciation and doubt.

Much as the Harrises paired militant liberalism and casual mysticism, Charles Sanders Peirce (1839–1914) and his wife Juliette pursued philosophy along with astrology, fortune-telling, and spiritualism. Though Charles was the brilliant founder of Pragmatism, rumor marred his life. Said to be atheistic and immoral, he lost his academic position—teaching philosophy at Johns Hopkins—soon after his second wedding in 1883. True, he had done little to hide his five-year affair with Juliette during his marriage to his first wife Zina. True, too, Juliette encouraged innuendo by vague answers about her past. Was she an exiled Hapsburg princess, as she claimed, or, as some guessed, a French courtesan? In the midst of impropriety and mystery, the religious distance between Charles and Juliette, discussed by no one, must have seemed unimportant. Raised a Unitarian, he had become an Episcopalian; she must have been a Catholic as a native of France.[69] Together they settled into domesticity most surprising for its normalcy. Juliette made gifts for his family: a dress and pillowcases for his mother in 1884, a plum pudding for his brother in 1891 and pillows in 1902.[70] Charles wrote philosophy, despite career obstacles, and from beginning to end insisted that religion, to be valuable, must be explained. A justification of faith "fails to be philosophy while it appeals not to the head, but only to the heart," he noted critically in a review of *The Secret of Swedenborg* in 1870. "Musement"—philosophical reflection—stirs us "by the beauty of the idea [of God] and by its august practicality," Peirce argued boldly in "A Neglected Argument for the Reality of God" in 1908.[71] Sectarian differences between husband and wife must have mattered little next to the restless energy of Charles's speculations.

Indeed, with conventionality thrown to the winds, any and all spiritual experiences might be welcome. It was Juliette who acted most freely. Pictured at her death in 1934 as a "slight, foreign lady," a "harmless but a strangely queer person," some neighbors in Milford, Pennsylvania, would remember that she told "fortunes with the famous pack of cards that belonged to one of the ladies of Napoleon's court" outside a local theater during the World War. She maintained a veneer of respectability. "Every cent received," the newspaper reported in 1918, "goes for war relief work."[72] Yet her intimacy with the paranormal was more than a civic performance. She was interested in astrology. In 1894 Ellen Hopkins, founder of the New York School of Applied Design for Women, had forwarded to Juliette a reading by "Mrs. Nott the astrologer." Despite "*much* treachery" in your family, the seer reassured, "you will be in every way *happy.*"[73] Later, after Charles's death in 1914, Juliette's strange behavior cast more light on her views. She declined to bury his ashes, against family wishes. By telegram and letter, his sister Helen urged Juliette to inter his remains in the family plot in Cambridge, Massachusetts. Helen had politely agreed to "the cremation service" in Jersey City "by all means as you have planned it." Still, "if you like it we could have a little service in the chapel of the cemetary here or a burial service at the grave so that relations & friends can gather." The proposal seemed disingenuous. Reclusive, Charles had few acquaintances, and Helen and Herbert, his remaining siblings, were disinclined to go out of their way. They would not be at the cremation service, Helen wrote: "I am too old."[74] More likely the real issue was decent burial. Perhaps Helen foresaw Juliette's decision: to keep Charles's ashes on her mantle, until they were buried with her.[75] Did his relics help Juliette communicate with his soul? To think of her as a spiritualist may verge on caricature. Even so, the cards, readings, and now the display of his ashes all point to her familiarity with the occult.

There is no evidence that Charles, so strange in his own way, was bothered by Juliette's excursions in invisible realms. In contrast, Richard Harding Davis (1864–1916) worried about the seductiveness of mediums, just before he fell in love with a woman who induced him to perform private rites. Son of the writer Rebecca Harding Davis and nearly a folk hero himself as an adventurer-author, Davis completed *Vera, the Medium* late in 1907. It was a rescue fantasy that must have colored his encounter with a vaudeville dancer, Bessie McCoy, the following spring. Vera's virtue—and dilemma—is her innocence. Employed by a man who uses every trick to dupe customers of Vera's crystal ball readings and rappings, Vera sees the deceptions yet still believes in her power. "'I am a priestess! I am a medium between the souls of this world and the next. I am Vera—the Truth!'"[76] Winthrop, a rising star from Geneva, New York, and now New York City's District Attorney, meets Vera with a divided mind: enamoured of her sincerity and lured by her imperiousness, he disdains her clairvoyance. His sisters will rehabilitate Vera; they are "two of the best women God ever made." The story ends when the medium flees with Winthrop from a rapping. In the waiting car, "as he threw out his arms, with a little sigh of relief, she crept into them and pressed her face to his."[77] It is hard to believe that Davis wrote *Vera* before meeting Bessie, so true to life was the tale. Repelled by the tawdriness of the stage, he made Bessie retire after their marriage in 1912. The fiction was also subtly anti-Catholic, and Catholicism was Bessie's religion. It would not take much for Richard to imagine himself Winthrop from Geneva, a Calvinist hero, saving the girl from the "mummeries" devised by her self-interested manager, so like the Protestant stereotype of a manipulative priest.[78]

Life, however, was more complicated than art. Any chance that the Davises would honor religious convention collapsed by the time of the wedding. It was painful for Bessie to marry outside the Catholic Church, but she had no choice if Richard was the groom. Little seemed left of his Protestantism except nativism, not only his fear of Catholic duplicity but his distaste for Germans "with Hebraic features" who figured in his stories.[79] The unlikelihood that Richard might agree to be wed by a priest was probably matched by the unwillingness of the church: his divorce from his first wife came three weeks before a judge performed the ceremony for Bessie and him.[80] Even then the civil wedding was not a prelude to secularism. On every trip abroad that Richard made as a reporter he lit votive candles in Catholic churches. He wore Bessie's St. Rita's medal and a scapular in Europe during the war. Unconnected in Richard's eyes with Catholic tradition, his habits resembled fetishism, sacralized by their meaning for his wife. His list of amulets was eclectic: "I have your charm around my neck, and all the pictures, and the luck-bringing cat, and the scapular, and the love you give me to keep me well and bring us soon together."[81] With tradition in his hands, his appropriation of Catholic symbols did not have to dislodge his prejudices. Priest were cowards, he intimated to Bessie in 1914. They "all had run away" from the Vera Cruz cathedral when U.S. troops landed; "I had to hunt up the candle, and pay the money into the box marked for that purpose."[82]

In contact with Richard and away from her church, Bessie's Catholicism grew intellectually ragged. She was attracted by Christian Science, characterized by a hostile contemporary as a "supplementary" faith for "female neurasthenics." Because Christian Science offered no life-cycle rites and required no exclusive commitment, a Catholic like Bessie could dabble at will. Healing, not doctrinal rigor, in the eyes of the same analyst, was its "effective form of suasion." Beliefs that matter is a manifestation of spirit and positive thoughts can change circumstances made Christian Science, to this skeptic, akin to "witchcraft."[83] Bessie was no witch, but Christian Science fit into the Davises' taste for cultivating spiritual forces. Richard seemed inclined toward pantheism. "When we walked in the woods," Bessie recalled after his death in 1916, "he liked me to wear a gown that would harmonize with the colors of the woods."[84] Even more mysteriously, newspapers intimated that though dead, he was not really gone. The Los Angeles *Examiner* reported "The Grave Defying Romance of Richard Harding Davis and his Dancer Wife" in 1917. Five years later, when their daughter was seven, the New York *Herald* asked, "Does Richard Harding Davis Guide the Daily Career of Little Hope?"[85] Here was a series of unorthodox forays, ranging from petty magic to vague spiritualism. The importance was less the collection's variety than its source: the authority of the self. Bessie sounded conventional in 1919 when she advised women to "yield to the idolatry of the man you love."[86] But when she—and Richard—acted on this view religiously by making their own preferences the basis of practice, the spiritual outcome was untraditional indeed.

More surprising than the odd way religion punctuated the Davises' marriage was the infatuation of hard-headed Rose Pastor Stokes with Kahlil Gibran. "I am so glad you have found a heart of authority to which you will listen," declared her friend Olive Dargan in 1923, the same year Gibran published *The Prophet*.[87] Feeling so close to Rose that she addressed letters to "beloved," and Rose in turn called her "precious," Olive encouraged her friend as early as 1920 to find "spiritual hope" in the "life beyond."[88] She shared Rose's politics: America's resistance to the Russian Revolution was "a piece of colossal fiendishness." Yet Olive's communism did not exclude faith. "O, there is no other happiness."[89] Gibran became the agent of Rose's awakening, and their interest in drawing was the bridge between them. A Lebanese-born Christian, he gained fame in America for the lyric mysticism of his writings and sketches. He praised Rose's art, and Olive agreed. "The spirit is there," she said of a portrait: "'Spirit' is your particular preserve, dearest, and isn't that a proper vengeance for one who doesn't believe in it?"[90] Olive was right that Rose met Gibran with divided feelings. She believed he was "a truly great man," yet in 1926 she still closed a letter to Olive, "Thru life and the nothingness beyond." Intellect resisted sensibility, though for a moment Rose thought she would follow Gibran's advice and "withdraw for a few months from my general activities and concentrate on drawing." In the end, art offered a peaceful private space. She wrote for the public good, she said during her cancer in 1931. "Art? That is my 'salvation,' in a sense," something for herself.[91]

Was her encounter with Gibran a religious experience? Clearly Rose achieved some spiritual focus. As surely, he did not overturn her unbelief. She attached herself to his faith, and art must have helped carry emotions connected with him forward in time. Conflicted and episodic, her spirituality was nonetheless personally important. It seemed unrelated to the dichotomies of her marriage: Jewish-Christian, proletarian-capitalist. Its poor fit with ideology, however, attests to its genuineness. Rose must have been more surprised than anyone to discover her sense of the transcendent.

It is significant that this happened in the 1920s. War accelerated the search for new faiths. Juliette Peirce's public readings, Bessie Davis's Christian Science, and the Harrises' consultations all began during or soon after the war. Now Ludwig Lewisohn (1882–1955), too, returned to Judaism through his own form of Zionism. "Not everyone need go upon so long a pilgrimage" before repenting, he advised in *Israel* in 1925.[92] Born Jewish in Berlin and yet an eager Methodist in South Carolina as a boy, he married Mary Crocker Childs in 1906 in a Unitarian ceremony. Both writers, they had literature in common. Leaving Mary in 1923, however, helped Ludwig reclaim his roots. His new love, Thelma Spear, was the child of a German-Jewish father and Christian mother. In Jewish law this made her a gentile; Ludwig, measuring by his own needs, cultivated the fiction that she was a Jew. On their way to Palestine in 1924, a rabbi married them in Poland. Perhaps Ludwig failed to tell the rabbi, who issued him a religious divorce *(get)* from Mary, that he was still civilly married. How he persuaded the same rabbi to see Thelma as Jewish, the other condition of the wedding, is anybody's guess. Together they dreamed Jewish dreams. Thelma included a "Jewish Portrait" in her thin book of poems, privately printed, *First Fruits* (1927). Ludwig, childless in his forties, longed for a baby to raise as "a serenely conscious Jew." Theirs was "a Jewish house," he confided to a friend, "without religious hocuspocus."[93] The qualifier was essential: Ludwig's Judaism was all his own.

Only a minority of American Jews were Zionists in the 1920s, and Lewisohn dissented even from them. He had little use for assimilated Jews, such as he had recently been. For himself, spiritual return required touching Palestine physically. As he approached Jerusalem from Egypt in 1924, "The forty years' journey is made in a day."[94] Clearly moved by the landscape of the patriarchs and prophets, he rejected what he saw as the Zionist plan "to establish a peasantry on the soil of Eretz Israel." Communalism, agriculture, spoken Hebrew: all these presumed that Judaism anchored an ordinary folk culture. Jews must not "go to Zion and be a folk like other folks"; we "go to Zion to be ourselves." "We do not desire renationalization in the romantic sense." The uniqueness of the Jews was their complexity. Armed with "original moral qualities"—as "rebels, destroyers, seekers of abstract justice"—"we master and possess the cultures of the West" and "what we contribute belongs to us and also to mankind."[95] This vision of selfhood without isolation was eloquent, if heterodox, and Zionists struggled to keep Lewisohn in the fold. It was a trial. He patronized rabbis. "Do be a good Zaddik," he addressed a Rochester rabbi when he asked the man for a favor.[96] His love life was embarrassing. The tempest surrounding his marriage in 1940 to Edna

Manley, including Thelma's hysterical appearance at the wedding, could mean "he will be finished for us Zionistically," worried Rabbi Stephen Wise.[97] Often interfaith couples investigated religious alternatives discreetly. Lewisohn cut a path through the Jewish world for all to see.

Interfaith families were not the only early twentieth-century Americans to seek meaning in the stars or on their ancestral soil. But because they were less closely tied than the average household to churches and synagogues, personal, often offbeat practices were unusually important for them. Belief was commonly qualified by unbelief, not surprising in this century. On the whole, though, the new spiritual routes were invigorating to an extent that couples were comfortable leaving conventional faiths behind. There were so few children in these five homes—in fact, only two—that the issue of transmitting faith, to all appearances, almost never came up.[98] Small families, whether the product of accident or choice, helped sustain adults' freedom because religious schooling was not a pressing need. Let there be no mistake: these couples were capable of training their own children ethically. A Julian Harris or Rose Pastor Stokes had not only idiosyncrasies but moral visions—just no one to teach at home. Even so, this was a difficult time to hold onto spirituality of any kind. Turn-of-the-century Americans loved scandal, and family trials gained perverse legitimacy when they titillated the public.

A Taste for Misbehavior

Perhaps from the beginning of history, one of the attractions of mixed-faith liaisons was that they were forbidden. Romance feeds on mystery and danger; desire gains an edge if the beloved satisfies and threatens at once. Prohibitions, keeping unacceptable behavior in view, work to lure no less than inhibit. In America around 1900, the balance of commentary on interfaith marriage shifted from censure toward sensationalism. Gossip, the press, and movies still scolded departures from respectability yet clearly were infatuated with daring acts and capitalized on alluring tales. Popular media and their audiences, though performing rituals of disapproval, could not get enough of illicit love. The interfaith affairs of three men—Charles Sanders Peirce, Richard Harding Davis, and John Dewey—show how what was once notoriety might become fame. This was peculiarly a man's story. "New women" of the era asserted their selfhood in practical accomplishments; men tested their freedom in risky romance.

Although the affairs of Peirce and Davis were nearly identical, cruel gossip damaged Peirce in the 1880s, while two decades later Davis was a popular hero. Each fate was a sign of its time. Their first wives were well-bred, intelligent, and sexually indifferent. Marriage to Zina Fay (1836–1923) in 1862 fit well with Peirce's background. He was the son of a Harvard professor; she, the daughter and granddaughter of Episcopal priests. Zina devoted herself to public projects and took a feminist slant. Advocating city planning for Washington in the *Atlantic Monthly,* she blamed men for the capital's disarray: only "the genuine masculine insensibility to both beauty and order could possibly have produced such a result."[99] Eroticism was her enemy. Ideally, marriage was platonic, and punishment for adultery should be "death or prisoning for life."[100] Cecil Clark (1877–1955), who married Davis in 1899, generally agreed. Rumor had it that she informed Richard before their wedding, "We will simply be as brother and sister."[101] There was much to bind them together other than sex. Children of wealthy Protestants, they met where their parents summered on Cape Cod. He had his writing to keep busy, she her art, always a serious competitor to Richard for her attention. Their divorce in 1912, in one biographer's view, meant little to Cecil except that "she could now concentrate on her primary passion—painting."[102] For Richard, leaving Cecil must have felt like rejecting his mother, Rebecca: both women were talented and masterful. Guilt kept him from telling Rebecca about his failed marriage before her death in 1910. Davis, like Peirce, had married the girl next door. He woke up to find that a choice once promising security was now stifling.[103]

The second wives, Juliette Pourtalai Peirce and Bessie McCoy Davis, were exotics. Juliette (1857?–1934) wove impenetrable stories of her royal birth abroad and exile to America. After Zina left Charles in Europe in 1875, he fell in love with Paris, consuming French novels, studying French wines, and dressing like a dandy. Juliette "reflected the glamour of that world," one scholar writes.[104] The shameless openness of the Peirces' five-year affair broadcast their disregard of American norms. Decades later, Bessie McCoy (1887–1931) aroused Davis by her peculiar magic. When he first saw her on the New York stage, she danced with impassioned abandon. "Her hair flies in loose flax around her face," reported the *Evening Journal.*

Figure 7. Bessie McCoy, dancing in "The Echo," 1911, just before her marriage to Richard Harding Davis. *Metropolitan Magazine,* November 1917.

"Her face flickers with changing moods."[105] More sprite in her role than girl, Bessie wrapped real life, too, in fantasy. Romance was her language. Before loving Richard, "I did not know then that there were secret melodies in the heart," feelings "born of romance, of love, of those perfect days that lie between the first and the last great days which bind the heart of a woman forever in the tender foils of their memories."[106] The ability of Juliette and Bessie to stir the imagination was the source of their power. Juliette inspired confidence, to the point that the commonsensical women in the Peirces' circle came to accept her stories as true.[107] Far from being pale opposites of Zina and Cecil, the second wives were also commanding. Religion—Juliette's presumed and Bessie's professed Catholicism—went nearly unnoticed among other fabulous traits. Yet, not surprisingly, the love affairs raised eyebrows.

Within two years of his marriage to Juliette, Charles Sanders Peirce lost his last regular job. Fired by Johns Hopkins in 1884, he resigned under pressure from the U.S. Coast Survey a year later. Like most scandals, the charges were vague: immorality, drunkenness, misuse of funds. Timing, however, helps solve the puzzle. Charles's affair, under way when he went to Johns Hopkins in 1879, had been tolerated along with his drinking and extravagance. It was the divorce and re-marriage—his willingness to make his sins public—that brought re-prisals. "The supposition is," whispered an enemy at Hopkins, "that the marriage last summer made no change in the relations of the parties." Worse, "Mrs. P (2) has begun to cultivate Mrs. G's ac-quaintance."[108] To have Mrs. Gilman, the president's wife, receive Juliette socially condoned impropriety. "Divorces are so common nowadays," lamented the *Ladies' Home Journal;* the *Independent* judged it "difficult to estimate the stupendous magnitude of such an evil to human society."[109] Predictably in this climate, Johns Hopkins did not renew Charles's contract. The president kept the most damn-ing reason to himself: unfitness to oversee "the guidance and instruc-tion of young men."[110] Soon the Washington *Post* targeted the Coast Survey with the headline, "Intoxicated—Demoralized," continuing, "Prof. Hilgard and Others Charged with Being Drunk in Office." The congressional investigation of the agency could not reasonably cite Charles's domestic irregularities, but suspicions of deviance now clung to him. "There is little doubt that his inability to obtain fitting employment after 1885 can largely be blamed on these two events," his biographer says.[111] By 1897, destitute, Peirce was stealing food. Hurtful words, circulated in private and shouted in print, exacted harsh punishment for stepping morally out of line.

The infatuation of Richard Harding Davis with Bessie, in contrast, enhanced his career. Luck and image-management played roles; so did changing times in the form of the yellow press. Although Richard's family was every bit as stuffy as the Johns Hopkins faculty, he tried to live the part of his adventurer-heroes. During every war—Spanish-

American, Boer, Russo-Japanese—he raced to the front as a reporter. In 1908 he could safely risk disclosure of his passion for Bessie because love suited his larger-than-life personality. Hearing her sing, he told *Collier's* readers, "I am now, with the rest of the world, kneeling at her feet."[112] Shock might have replaced amusement in his audience were it not for a fortuitous tragedy. In 1911, Richard's only sister, Nora, married, at age thirty-eight, the Anglican chaplain to the King of England. Within months police caught the man in a homosexual act, "an unprintable offense," one newspaper said, and, in Britain, a criminal one.[113] Sailing to England, Richard's job was to rescue his sister. This buoyed his public image, in need of support since Cecil began divorce proceedings in 1910. Next to poor Nora, too, he appeared "merely conventionally unhappy."[114] Yet the essential fact is that the press loved these stories and by its attention tacitly excused the newsmakers' moral failings.

The media revealed its double standard in a New York headline about Nora's husband: "Farrar Scandal Only Whispered in London." What the British suppressed sold papers in Manhattan, giving the *World*'s seeming concern for decency a hollow ring.[115] Privacy, too, was a victim to prying eyes curious to know why love goes wrong. As newspapers reported the painful turns in Cecil's divorce suit, they lured readers with sentimentality. The Cincinnati *Commercial Standard* mourned, "Divorce from Author Ends Childhood Romance." With emotion and excitement as standards of value, however, new love readily replaced old. This made it possible for Richard and Bessie to gain a respectability that eluded the Peirces. Bessie, instinctively kind, warmed the hearts of reporters. When she asked Richard to treat fifty poor mothers and their children to a trip to Coney Island on her wedding day, the papers inflated the number of mothers to five hundred. Even after Richard's death in 1916, Americans were charmed by the Davises. The *Metropolitan* printed "The Love Letters of Richard Harding Davis to Bessie McCoy Davis" in 1917, along with a sweet photograph captioned, "The latest picture of Bessie McCoy Davis and her daughter Hope."[116] Not only had Bessie survived the publicity of Richard's illicit passion to become a Madonna-like figure—she flourished.

There is an obvious difference between relishing a star's heartaches and dealing with your own family problems. Infidelity and divorce, intriguing from afar, are painful at home. Even so, the press's sensational coverage of love's trials and triumphs eroded traditional morality, and this had incalculable social effects. Once finding romantic happiness became the preeminent goal, the self measured decency. Someone might remember the issue of interfaith marriage if a religious clash threatened domestic peace. Otherwise prohibitions could be ignored. This shift in popular outlook was not sudden and, even today, is not complete. But the contrast between the Peirces' banishment and the Davises' love affair with reporters was a measure of change.

The secrecy of the affair of John Dewey and Anzia Yezierska in 1917–1918 is the exception that proves the rule. Almost sixty, many years married, and internationally respected, Dewey could not have tolerated the circus atmosphere surrounding the Davises. Nonetheless, a thinly fictionalized version of their story became Yezierska's novel *All I Could Never Be* (1932). Imprudent love was marketable. What was hidden in life might flourish in print.

Yezierska (1880?–1970), an aspiring writer, approached Dewey at Columbia to help her find work. Apparently, the ensuing relationship was never consummated, but the emotions were real. Swooning in the novel in a dreamy "mood of contentment," Fanya Ivanowna wishes Henry Scott would visit her room in the "ghetto." When he appears unexpectedly, the characters enact a fantasy of symbolic disclosure and embrace. "'I want to see your ghetto and see it through your eyes,'" he implores. "'There's richness and color for you,'" he exclaims; "'your people,'" the Jews, have "'intensity.'" Later, "his hand fumbling her breast," she realizes that "instead of a god, here was a man." Turning away, she blames herself for this "bitterest failure—the failure to hold a great friendship, a great love."[117] Anzia, speaking through Fanya, did not mistake Dewey's mood. Around the time of their liaison, and mainly then, he wrote poetry. The subject was not always love, but when it was, the lyrics were personal. "Whate'er, howe'er you move or rest / I see your body's breathing / The curving of your breast / And hear the warm thoughts seething."[118] He, too, believed he knew why the relationship must end. "Who makes, has. Such is the old old law." He belonged to Yankee culture and to the wife and children who were part of it: "What I am to any one is but a loan / From those who made, and own."[119]

At the same time that these two people of unusual self-understanding probed their feelings, they acted practically to keep their connection from view. As the relationship cooled, Dewey returned Anzia's letters. They have since disappeared. Dewey erased most records of his personal life, neither saving his correspondence nor writing an autobiography. Against this background, his casual disposition of the poetry manuscripts seems strange. A colleague at Columbia with an office near Dewey's in the late 1920s rescued some poems from the wastebasket. When Dewey changed offices in 1939, the professor inheriting his desk found more there.[120] Perhaps tossing some poems was part of his systematic destruction of personal papers. But he kept others longer, maybe out of lingering ambivalence about the romance or, more speculatively, a half-formed wish for discovery to ease secret shame. Yezierska played an equally complicated game of mixing discretion and revelation. Although few readers could have recognized Professor Scott of *All I Could Never Be* as John Dewey, Yezierska marked the book in a way that he had to see himself: she included one of his manuscript poems in the text. It was a private signal in what she hoped would be a popular book. She had written for Hollywood movies in the 1920s and must have thought that the clandestine love of a latter-day Puritan and vibrant Jew would sell.[121]

In fact, the novel did not do well. A brilliant analysis of the psychology of mixed-faith romance, *All I Could Never Be* was too realistic, ending not with the gratification but the frustration of desire. Like extramarital affairs, interfaith marriage is by traditional standards forbidden, and Yezierska made the connection. No less was Henry Scott, to Fanya, a "symbol of all she could never be"—a man of "culture, leisure, the freedom and glamor of the 'Higher Life'"—but all she could never have, so long as he was married.[122] Alien and unattainable, these qualities underwrote his appeal to her, as well as the reverse. He loved her as an offspring of inchoate "generations of stifled words," now "reaching out *through you*" to become "luminous, slow-revolving, ordered in rhythm."[123] In romance fiction the seductive plot line of "opposites attract" commonly ends with the subversion of prohibitions. Yezierska, in contrast, had science explain that racial barriers between Jew and gentile could not be crossed after centuries of "fearing, mistrusting, hating, and fighting each other."[124] This was a sobering message that would not have gripped readers who hung on sensational news.

The culture of scandal in this way predetermined the weak showing of Yezierska's story about Dewey. It was just not racy enough. No less important was how fiction and fact intertwined. Not only did Yezierska readily put her experience in print, but the display of marital irregularities in the media gradually decreased their shock value and pushed back the bounds of acceptability. This gave interfaith families more space to decide what kind of families to be.

Family Ties

In public rhetoric, the dark side of fascination with impropriety was fear of moral collapse. Routine infidelity, rising divorce, low birthrates—worrisome traits of the modern family—fed anxieties about the future of the home. Casual acceptance of interfaith marriage added to the pessimism. In reality, the forecasts of doom were one-sided. There were happy as well as sad tales among mixed-faith kin. Indeed, to ask if religious differences hurt or helped marriages slights a crucial fact: how little inherited faiths guided these families at all.

It is risky to cite unsuccessful children as evidence of troubled marriages. Children in some measure make themselves. Two children in these families, however, James Lewisohn and Hope Davis, began life with few emotional advantages, and neither did well. Jimmy, born in Paris in 1933, was the illegitimate son of Ludwig Lewisohn and Thelma Spear and the only child Ludwig fathered. His rearing was chaotic. A series of custody trials shuttled him between father and mother after Ludwig married Edna Manley in Baltimore in 1940. Sexual abuse of Jimmy by his mother came to light in court; once she won custody, she left him for a time in an orphanage. Pretending to shoot his mother on his father's wedding day, he really killed his own wife in 1975. Thelma recognized that their life would make "a good Hollywood film."[125] For her son, it was a tragedy. Circumstances were only slightly brighter for Hope Davis. Only a year old when her father, Richard, died in 1916, she appeared in magazines for a few years as a charming toddler. "She enjoys having her picture taken," one caption noted.[126] Soon her father's literary reputation, dependent on his swashbuckling personality, "gathered dust, like an Eastlake chair in grandmother's parlor," and Bessie and Hope moved to France. Orphaned by Bessie's death in 1931, Hope married a French neighbor who lost his wealth during the war. She committed suicide in Maine in 1976.[127]

It is impossible to disentangle religious issues from the other burdens carried by Jimmy and Hope. Ironically, although both sets of parents were interfaith couples, Judaism and Catholicism, respectively, may have given the children some anchor. Ludwig Lewisohn was fervently Jewish; his last wife, Louise, who helped raise Jimmy, was Jewish, too. After Ludwig became the first full professor at Brandeis University in 1948, the year of its founding, Jimmy entered as a freshman in 1952. More speculatively, Hope and Bessie may have returned to the mother's Catholicism after settling in a Catholic country. Hope's marriage would have sealed the choice. Yet religion was neither the downfall nor salvation of these children, just one more factor in families shaped by shallowness and caprice.

One unexpected gesture of family feeling did touch Hope Davis. Cecil, her father's first wife, offered to adopt Hope when she was left alone as a teenager after her mother's death.[128] Not surprisingly, Hope refused the overture of a woman she had never met and had no reason to like. The fact remains that Cecil perceived Hope as kin, despite the divorce and lack of blood tie. At a time when families seemed vulnerable, Cecil's offer was evidence that kinship was not dead, just self-defined.

Indeed, family memoirs proliferated during the same decades that the public consumed headlines about the domestic traumas of the famous. Although Americans keenly tracked breaches of respectability, they celebrated kinship as well. Descendants of nineteenth-century interfaith parents recorded stories of cherished forebears and sprawling clans. Ellen Mordecai and Caroline Myers Cohen published memoirs and genealogies of the Mordecais just before World War I. The Depression, stirring renewed interest in core values, produced a shelf of histories. In 1931 and 1932, Anne Easby-Smith issued *William Russell Smith of Alabama,* C. Wickliffe Yulee recalled "Senator Yulee of Florida," and Henrietta Clay, granddaughter of Benjamin Gratz, read "Bits of Family History" to the John Bradford Club of Lexington, Kentucky.[129] When the audience was neither readers of regional magazines nor neighbors meeting to chat, it was simply family. "Not Confidential but Written for Family Only" was the way Philemon Tecumseh Sherman, once "Cumpy" as the youngest Sherman son, marked his typed "Reminiscences of Early Days." Looking back in 1940, he captured the interplay of his parents' military and Catholic commitments. When his father insisted that the Jesuit Pierre De Smet be Cumpy's godfather in 1867, this was not an ordinary priest but a fearless "blackrobe" ministering to Indians. Philemon ended with his father's death in 1891: generals and admirals carried the casket, while his brother Tom, by then also a Jesuit, conducted the service.[130] Memoirs like this normalized the compromises and idiosyncrasies of interfaith households and, circulating among relatives, strengthened connections. "Given to me by Uncle Cump, July 1941," noted Eleanor Fitch on the document's cover. The taste for honoring lineage that inspired recollections is a sign that healthy twentieth-century interfaith families may be found.

The Harrises of Georgia, for one, formed an intricate extended family. Relations were not always idyllic, but they managed their differences well. Between 1895 and 1911 all six of Joel and Esther's children, raised Catholics, wed Protestants. In this they duplicated their parents' interfaith marriage, and the best known couple in each generation epitomized the norm of the time. Esther kept her household close to the Catholic Church; Julia and Julian pursued religion on their own and minimally then. Yet among the Harrises more broadly Catholicism remained the family religion. Some were more attached than others to the faith. Evelyn and Lucien, Julian's younger brothers, belonged to the Knights of Columbus at the turn of the century, and in the 1950s Evelyn was still friendly with prelates.[131] Joel Chandler Harris, Jr.—"Sonny Boy" in letters to his mother during World War I—was less serious. He wrote home from France on stationery headed "Knights of Columbus, War Activities," perhaps to reassure Esther that he visited the services for soldiers sponsored by the church. He admitted to being a "rapscallion," yet one who "found it ridiculously easy to live a clean life—even if not a very religious one."[132] As the years passed, Catholicism seemed like the family umbrella: some stood squarely under it, others at the edge, Julian not at all. Esther, living until 1938, set a tone that made this possible. When "children become men & women," she wrote, "they have a perfect right to their views."[133] Where differences of opinion divided, mutual affection filled gaps. Into old age the siblings used pet names. Lillian was "Bill," and she wrote to Julian and "sister" in 1926 to congratulate them on the Pulitzer Prize. "Millicat" (Mildred) was "shocked" that "Bubba Ju" (Julian) forgot her birthday in 1954: "Wish I could forget it."[134] The names must have taken them back to their childhoods at "Wren's Nest," their parents' home in Atlanta's West End.

Measured by lifelong correspondence, the siblings' memories of good times far overrode issues of religion.

Like many contemporaries, the Harrises were interested in recording their history. In part this was because they were a literary family, although Julian's brothers worked in businesses such as insurance and public relations. Writing about kin involves more, however, than having a way with words. Julia Collier Harris seems to have moved into the family's inner circle after she published a first-class biography of her father-in-law in 1918, *The Life and Letters of Joel Chandler Harris*. Securing her place was probably not her intent. Bright, childless, and married to a workaholic, she would welcome an absorbing project. Still, the result was that she gained new intimacy with her in-laws by studying their papers and brought them honor by a creditable book. In a family with several sisters and sisters-in-law, by 1920 Julia was the only "sister" among the nicknames.[135]

Years later Julian and his brother Evelyn labored over more memoirs. Their writing was important less for literary reasons than for the cooperation it seemed to elicit between Joel and Esther's least and most pious sons. Confusion from the beginning about the purpose of Julian's book helps explain why he never finished it. In 1946 the New York publisher E. P. Dutton asked him to write an "autobiography." "You have had an interesting life," observed the company's president Elliott Macrae, "and have been involved in important international problems." But in the very next paragraph Macrae inadvertently muddied the waters. "I remember so well, during my childhood, when Father used to read to us from UNCLE REMUS." He had just bought a first edition: "If I send you the copy, would you mind writing a few words in it and refer to your father?"[136] The Atlanta *Journal*, looking for a headline, said more bluntly that the real interest was Joel. "Joel Chandler Harris, as His Eldest Son Remembers Him" was the title the newspaper gave to an early extract published in its magazine.[137] No wonder Julian had trouble with the book. Both Macrae and the *Journal* stumbled on the truth that Julian, more than his siblings, was his father's child. Looking back, the story Julian instinctively found was a father currying his oldest for success, a taskmaster who cared greatly for Julian but was strangely cold. The manuscript pictured Joel correcting his son's prose and arguing with him about attending college. Julian said that his father never read

"Uncle Remus" tales to his children.[138] To make matters worse, he cast his recollections in dialogue, perhaps trying to honor his father's literary gift at the same time that he attempted to equal him. In his seventies, Julian found himself with thoughts of a father the public did not know and whom he still had no confidence he could match.

Six months after signing the contract with Dutton, Julian told a vice-president that initially he had trouble remembering events. As he wrote, however, "long submerged incidents and conversations came to the surface." Although he kept the tone light, it is easy to wonder if some memories were more problematic than forgetfulness. In June 1948 he returned the cash advance, "most unhappy" that "I have failed to carry out my agreement."[139] He assured Dutton that he would continue to work at a slower pace. He never got beyond his teenage years. Even then, the fragmentary manuscript should not be construed as a symptom of family failure. The Harrises were accomplished, and their love for each other was real. But the project must have underscored for Julian the complexities of relationships.

To celebrate Easter 1949, Evelyn produced a small book for family reading, "A Little Story About My Mother." The number of details that matched Julian's draft suggest that Julian passed his brother his notes. Both reported that their Canadian-born mother had encountered few blacks before her marriage in Georgia. They remembered that she called her husband "Cephas," after the Jewish historian Josephus, and that as children they had Jewish friends. Evelyn confirmed that their father never read "Uncle Remus" aloud at home.[140] There is nothing terribly startling in the idea that Julian and Evelyn shared materials, except that they were different kinds of men who generally steered clear of each other. In 1954 they had a tiff about whether Evelyn sent the bishop to call on his errant brother; denying the charge, Evelyn professed to be "trying desperately to not inject myself into my brothers' affairs."[141] Cautious of each other, they were not alienated, however, and their memoirs acquired the character of family projects. Lillian reacted to Julian's 1946 extract in the Atlanta *Journal* as if it was a common possession: "It was splendid & sounded so good & homey—made me a wee bit homesick for a little while until I realized we can never go back."[142] However the evolution of Evelyn's history related to the abandonment of Julian's, one brother seems to have lent his jottings to the other.

Mother-focused, Evelyn's reminiscence was a modern-day saint's life. "Father's life is so familiar to all," Evelyn began; he would write about Esther. His decision was grounded in a sense of affinity. The most seriously Catholic of her sons, Evelyn sketched a mother he must have revered. She was a liberal Catholic who would have understood the Holocaust just past, he believed, and Civil Rights on the horizon. She had admired their Jewish neighbors in the 1880s for "their loyal, devoted family life." When Evelyn came to her as a boy with a report of anti-Semitism, "she reminded me that Christ was a Jew, that the Blessed Virgin, whom mother revered with sincere devotion, was a Jewess." "And she cautioned us always to be as true to our Faith and as loyal to our parents as our Jewish friends were to theirs."[143] Like traditional hagiography, Evelyn's book crystalized incidents and aphorisms from Esther's life as moral instruction for her descendants. Faith and charity were virtues; so was family itself. Sticking together, despite differences, religious or otherwise, was a lesson Esther's children had learned.

The way Ralph Barton Perry and Bernard Berenson, as two widowers, dealt with the death of Bernard's sister Senda in 1954 tells a similar story of family commitment. In several ways the relatives were scattered. Only Ralph's son Barton lived in California when Senda had a stroke in Santa Barbara, where she and her sister Bessie kept house. Ralph had an apartment near Harvard in Cambridge, too far to travel to the funeral. Bernard was in Florence. Religiously, too, all followed their own paths. After retiring in 1946, Perry continued to speak and write on the ethical requisites of civilization. Berenson immersed himself in the foundations of Western culture. "I find both Homer and the O[ld]. T[estament]. inexhaustible in exciting interest," he wrote at age ninety-one in 1957. "I brood over them constantly, have flashes of revelation and turn to the text for confirmation."[144] Senda's funeral bowed slightly toward Judaism. Her body was cremated, not permissible in Jewish law, but a friend read "a few Psalms" at the grave.[145] The surviving brothers-in-law were united by a practical worry, however: Bessie. As early as 1909 Bessie suffered from "nerves gone wrong," in the words of Bernard's wife Mary; "nothing is so despairing."[146] Never marrying, she spent part of her middle age moving from relative to relative, until she settled with her widowed sister Senda. On the day Senda died she confessed to Ralph, "I am selfish now and think about myself and the loneliness that will come."[147] This was not a family, however, that abandoned each other.

In 1944 Bessie and Senda crossed the country to be near Ralph when he was critically ill with pleurisy. Now he returned the kindness. "I am grateful for the promise to keep close to Bessy," Bernard thanked him.[148] There had been no tangible connection between the Berensons and Ralph for more than two decades: Rachel Berenson Perry died in 1933. All behaved, nonetheless, as close kin.

Like most families formed by marriage, the Berenson-Perrys developed a common history. In 1954 these interactions, now memories, were the basis of Ralph's offer of aid. Although Bernard Berenson and Ralph Barton Perry were leading intellectuals, the exchange of ideas figured only modestly in their friendship. Bernard politely read Ralph's work after Rachel and Ralph married. He professed to get "pleasure & profit" from Ralph's *Approach to Philosophy* (1905), but came closer to the truth when he promised "to lend it to friends who like myself take an untechnical interest in thought."[149] He did not care for abstraction. So strong were Bernard's opinions and temper that his wife called him "'Mr. Crazy,'" and Ralph's visits to Florence went well because "he entered most intelligently into my world & its dreams," as Bernard brightly told a friend in 1928.[150] Harvard, where both men studied and Ralph taught, was a favorite topic. Ralph shared his Pulitzer Prize-winning biography of William James in 1937. "Evenings he read aloud to us," Bernard recalled: "What a delicious book for us old enough to have seen & perhaps heard the heroes of the first volume." Indeed, Bernard loved personalities. "We seldom touched on events or principles," he noted after Ralph went home in 1934; "we talked literature & people incessantly."[151] Putting these tastes together, it was natural that Harvard gossip held a special place. George Santayana, their teacher, tried in *The Last Puritan* to describe "a world he touched & could not penetrate," Bernard carped to Ralph in 1936. When Santanyana died two decades later, Bernard pronounced "Peace be to his ashes," yet added cynically, "Who will remember him or any of us now alive 50 years hence[?]"[152] For Bernard and Ralph, mutual acquaintances, and incidentally their ideas, came to anchor family ties.

Family also built common interests, and none drew more attention than the sons of Rachel and Ralph. Bernard, named for his uncle, and Ralph Barton Perry, Jr., called Barton, were the only children produced by the four Berenson siblings. Expectations for the future focused on them. "We are looking forward very much to seeing

Barton," Mary assured Ralph from Florence in 1929, "quite independent of whether he has a vocation or not towards a career connected with art." The same year Mary and Bernard began prolonged worry over how to save their villa and art from the insecurities of fascism, and for a moment Barton fit into a plan. "My own secret wish—mais Allah est le plus savant!—is that the difficulty about our wills may be solved by Barton," Mary told Rachel; "if he inherited the place it would not be liable to any tax at all."[153] Soon Rachel died of cancer at age fifty-three. Her sons, in a way filling her place, helped their father keep in touch with her kin. Bernard Perry accompanied Ralph to Florence a year after his mother's death. Moved by the visit, Ralph composed "a beautiful tribute," in his brother-in-law's words. "I read yr paper on Rachel aloud to Mary & we both were deeply touched by it."[154] It was Bernard Perry, again, who spotted the article in the New York *Times* in 1944 announcing "Bernard Berenson and Art Work Safe." Clipping it for his father, he clearly understood his bond with his namesake and the importance of family to all.[155]

Yet there were limits to the affinity between gentile and Jew, particularly in the Nazi era. This does not mean the clan failed as a family, only that some boundaries could not be crossed. Ralph's letter to Bernard on February 19, 1945, the first since the war began, was filled with news. He reported on his latest book, his sons' jobs, and Barton's children. For "these long years in which we have been separated," his "teaching has gone on continuously all year round, and I have been connected with a number of organizations, given speeches, written letters to the newspapers, etc., etc.—in short, trying to do what I could with my pen and lungs." Thankfully, "you and I are going to live to see the end of this dark chapter in human history and to get some peep into the next."[156] Ralph's warmth and decency could not bridge the distance between his safety and Bernard's vulnerability. Hiding in occupied Italy, Bernard wrote in his diary in August 1944: if arrested, "I might be captive not only as an alien enemy but as a 'non-Aryan' and sent to Lublin, if not killed first." His status divided him from gentile kin, including his wife who lived openly. As "a pure Aryan & immobilized invalid," he said after the liberation, "she had nothing to fear."[157] Family life returned to normal. "My brother-in-law Perry's visit for the whole of August was delightful," Bernard reflected in 1953.[158] Still, Bernard was not quite the cosmopolite he was before. He corresponded with Jewish relatives on particular interests.

Israel must not be dominated by "rabbinical zealots," he lectured Lawrence Berenson, an American-born cousin and his attorney. The country would be a "Yeshiva supporting drones who shake backward and forward mumbling prayers like Tibetan Lamas." Only as "the most powerful organization in the Near East" will Israel "render the Jew the self-respect that he suffers from lacking."[159] Ralph Barton Perry was not purposefully excluded from this conversation, but the letter to Lawrence was a reminder that no interfaith family lacks crosscurrents. Ralph and Bernard, on an elemental level still a Christian and Jew, might be close without being intimate.

Two features of interfaith families begun by marriages near the turn of the twentieth century stand out: the wide variation in their success at achieving happiness and the insignificance of denominational connections to their well-being. This assessment contains both bad news and good news, not only for the households involved but Americans generally. Once interfaith couples began to bypass religious institutions and the morals they taught, they were freer than in the past to make good on their wedding vows, or not. Though not quite bad news, the lesson was cautionary: intermarriage was hazardous, and responsibility fell squarely on families. The good news was also mixed, in the sense that religious liberals would be more likely than traditionalists to applaud emerging trends. Some interfaith families flourished in a freethinking environment. Even more, their reserved posture toward public religion seems part of a larger process that loosened Protestant dominance in the United States. Treating religious traditions as malleable, these households reflected a wider mood of tolerance. The extended Harris clan lived comfortably as Catholics, as did Ludwig Lewisohn and his wives as Jews. Others practiced no religion at all. Faithfulness as a matter of institutional commitment declined. But there were gains in individual choice and equality of faiths. These conditions could be spiritually invigorating and served many families well.

A World Turned Upside Down?

It is easy to caricature interfaith families formed around 1900 and decide their members were morally hopeless. Wives with professional interests, husbands with extramarital loves, children as afterthoughts: all seemed part of a self-seeking world. Clergy, as representatives of once-binding traditions, occasionally performed weddings or conducted funerals. More routinely, religion consisted of private rites to fan assurance or uplift. Though overstated, this sketch makes the presence of self-determination unmistakable.

Despite the temptation to believe that modernity is uniquely degenerate, the contest between desire and obligation is an old theme. From biblical times, moralists cited interfaith marriage as a cause of broken laws. The race theorist's pronouncement in the 1910s that "interbreeding" produces decline echoed the warning in Exodus that idolatrous wives "will turn your children away from Me to worship other gods." The appeal of the formula is its simplicity: marry endogamously, and all will be well. But the way intermarriages occurred in the early twentieth century explodes this logic, at least for our era. Men and women, claiming more autonomy than ever, were much changed before they chose spouses unlike themselves. Faiths acquired in childhood were so muted in households devoted to liberalism, say, or socialism that it makes little sense to speak of intermarriage as a blending of heritages at all. Mixed marriages did not undermine religious loyalty. Rather, tradition was a small factor in marriage decisions.

Scant traces of old-fashioned piety do not mean, however, that these interfaith homes bore no resemblance to earlier ones. Like all stereotypes, images of ambitious women and pleasure-seeking men betray the subtlety of change. Neither was the pursuit of private happiness new, nor were religious values now callously abandoned. The liberalism of the American Revolution sanctioned self-interest and guaranteed that interfaith couples would clash with rules designed to preserve tradition. By 1900 extramarital affairs and divorces represented brasher searches for gratification. But the essential problem—balancing self with family and community—was already part of the culture. Elements of religion persisted, too, if in unfamiliar forms. Judeo-Christian ethics inspired the crusading liberalism of Julian and Julia Harris and the socialism of Rose Pastor Stokes. Spiritualism and Christian Science had roots in mysticism. What was new was how boldly families devised their own answers. What is noteworthy is how often they did so with compassion.

The Discovery of Interfaith Marriage

In the years after World War II, Americans turned to interfaith marriage as if it were a new topic. "Fifty years ago," observed Episcopal Bishop James A. Pike in 1954, "it would not have been particularly important" to write his *If You Marry Outside Your Faith*. "But now the mixed marriage is one of the most common phenomena of our time."[1] Sociologists furiously gathered statistics. Still, "it is a matter of simple honesty to say," the authors of *One Marriage, Two Faiths* admitted, "that no one knows exactly how many mixed marriages" there are.[2] What was clear was that more and more Americans chose spouses without heed to religious authority. Pope Paul VI began his apostolic letter on mixed marriages in 1970 by recognizing "the natural right to marry and beget children," whether exercised in compliance with "Divine law" or not.[3] Although his respect for lay freedom reflected the spirit of Vatican II, his opening also bore testimony to the independent-mindedness of Catholics. This was a situation with deep historic roots. Mixed-faith families have made their decisions and religious bodies have responded for a very long time. Discussion in recent decades represents an awakening to a fact nearly as old as the republic: the self-determining temper of religiously mixed families.

It is ironic that these marriages provoked renewed comment just as they were eclipsed by more radical choices. For the first time in their history Protestant denominations issued resolutions on mixed-faith unions soon after 1945. In 1964, however, a study appeared called *Intermarriage: Interfaith, Interracial, Interethnic*, followed by an expanding number of titles on intercultural relationships of all kinds.[4] Interfaith marriage, touted by clergy and counselors as something new, was well established in comparison with Americans' other romantic preferences. It was, nonetheless, a powerful symbol. Tempted to mourn an imagined past of tight-knit families and revered faiths, many saw mixed marriages as evidence of division and uncertainty. Yet one day, it seemed, the nation became accustomed to thinking of differences as the American norm, and anxieties eased. Growing tolerance of interfaith marriage has been the most important development of the recent past.

This increased comfort with intermarriage is part of today's multicultural ethos. Within smaller circles of discussion, however, social science helped shift the tone about mixed couples from censure to explanation. Just about every writer after World War II cited reasons why interfaith romance was on the rise. The assertiveness of young people, falling age of marriage, dismantling of social boundaries, revolution in communications: references to trends such as these were standard in publications by clergy and social scientists alike.[5] Few initially liked what they saw, and the impulse to understand nearly drowned in disapproval. Statistics, in theory the handmaid of objectivity, sometimes made incredible claims that unmasked a researcher's bias. No one could mistake the slant of *Successful American Families* (1960) after reading that intermarriage correlated with divorce, low birth rates, academic failure of the children, and teen arrests.[6] Social science's instinct to fix problems increased the temptation to label mixed-faith families pathological. Counseling became a panacea and gave rise to books like *Intermarried Couples in Therapy* (1990).[7] Yet in the end, the uneasiness of observers with their subject could not contain the liberating effect of information-gathering, analysis, and discussion. In the late 1950s Conservative rabbis tersely stated why synagogues should restrict the privileges of intermarried Jews. The rabbis' inattention to sociology was a sign of their traditionalism overall. Mixed marriage was not permissible; there was little to discuss.[8] All around them, however, were Americans who might agree in principle but were eager to know why so many people broke the rules and what the consequences were. Gradually, explanations separated themselves from judgments, and information became empowering. Now a couple may plan its own future with *Weddings: A Complete Guide to All Religious and Interfaith Marriage Services* (1986).[9]

At the same time that academics, therapists, and clergy produced studies and advice books, religious communities reviewed their policies. Increasingly, Protestants realized that they shared the religious stage; they represented, Will Herberg wrote in 1955, "the anomaly of a strong majority group with a growing minority consciousness."[10] This was the background to their awakening to interfaith marriage. Immediately after World War II, denominations began to alert parishioners to the problem. Commonly, an organization issued a "public warning," as the Southern Baptist Convention did in 1951; "increased attention to education and counseling," the plan of the United Lutheran Church, was a typical solution.[11] Protestants said their "ideals of freedom and liberty" did not permit them to take steps beyond persuasion.[12] The anti-Catholicism framing their initiatives, however, made them seem less tolerant. Long-held presumptions that the Catholic Church was undemocratic, conspiratorial, and expansionist colored every Protestant discussion. For a century, interfaith couples who chose to be married by a priest signed pledges binding the Catholic spouse and children to the church. Now Protestants jumped on the Catholic system's unfairness. *If I Marry a Roman Catholic* (1945), a tract circulated by the Federal Council of Churches, was polite. It honored Catholics' "right under the freedom of religion to promulgate its teaching about marriage"; but "we are compelled in duty to those who look to us for counsel, to emphasize the fact that we of the other churches have freedoms and convictions that are inexpressibly precious to us."[13] Bishop Pike of the Episcopal Church was more provocative in 1954. The Catholics' "neat set of rules," "well-organized machinery," and "'Jim Crow' attitude toward the non-Roman party's Church" discouraged "even the most hardy and individualist souls from an optimistic 'we'll work things out somehow' approach." Pike proposed that both partners adopt a "spirit of inquiry" and agree on a church after free investigation. This was "the true solution," he said, with a dogmatism at odds with his rhetoric of liberty.[14]

While Protestant leaders defended their churches as repositories of freedom, interfaith couples went ahead and married. One Catholic study reported in 1956 that as many as one-third of valid American Catholic marriages involved a non-Catholic who signed the pledges; perhaps a quarter of the nation's recently married Catholics contracted invalid unions outside the church.[15] By the mid-1960s it was clear that competition between religious bodies was a less serious problem than the contest between organized faith itself and the laity's wishes. Robert Tucci, a Jesuit, identified the opponent as "culture." Ideally, the church honors culture as "the unity of the values of a civilization," Tucci explained at an interfaith conference at Notre Dame in 1966; but today the world contains "the danger of phenomenalism and agnosticism, and that of self-sufficiency." "Anthropocentric," modernity "rejects transcendence and places man at the center of the universe."[16] Why mixed marriages became frequent once people measured worth by self-gratification followed logically from Tucci's analysis.

This strong language did not lead Catholic policy toward rigidity and pessimism, however, but to compromise and reform. Vatican II (1962–1965) was the context of discussion, and conversations echoed the Vatican Council's commitment to ecumenism and lay rights. As if in response to Protestant cries of Catholic tyranny, scholars and prelates reviewed the obligation of the non-Catholic spouse. "The Church has to take into account the mind and the desires of other Christians if she really wants to build up a closer communion with them," advised Ladislas Orsy, a canon law expert. This practical thought had a philosophical foundation. "In modern societies, the source of faith has to be in the strength of the person."[17] The "conscience of the other partner is to be respected," declared the National Council of Catholic Bishops in 1971, at the same time that "the conscientious devotion of the Catholic to the Catholic Church is to be safeguarded."[18] Now only the Catholic entering a mixed marriage had to pledge faithfulness to the church; the non-Catholic simply had to know of the partner's vow.

All—council, pope, and bishops—agreed, too, that mixed couples should not face fixed canon laws. Each family deserved individualized pastoral care. Before Vatican II, *Marriage Legislation in the New Code of Canon Law* (1935) was a typical manual designed for "the clergy in parish work" and "the professor and student in the seminary."[19] Once the council shifted the emphasis of theology from permanence to dynamism and hierarchy to community, advice to priests changed. The Holy Spirit, the source of "all communion among Christians be it in faith, be it in charity, [is] by its very nature dynamic," Orsy wrote. "It cannot be forced by rigid legislation."[20] In practice, Pope Paul VI issued guidelines on mixed marriages in 1970 that "open the way to an improved pastoral approach," in the words of the American bishops. There was enough flexibility in the system for a priest to participate in a non-Catholic wedding if there was "a just pastoral cause."[21] Perhaps Catholicism's new spirit won the loyalty of mixed-faith couples more effectively; perhaps not. Either way, the church identified the issue of the hour as how to approach families.

Reform rabbis also saw interfaith marriage against a changing social background. "We live today in an age of options," observed Rabbi Irwin Fishbein in 1973. "We cannot compel Jews to marry Jews any more than we can compel Jews to be Jews."[22] This thought brought liberal leaders close to crisis. Every few years after World War II the Central Conference of American Rabbis reviewed the wording of its 1909 declaration of opposition to mixed marriage. In the meantime the number of conference members willing to perform these ceremonies inched up. Already in 1943 thirty-five percent of Reform rabbis married interfaith couples; in 1973 forty-one percent did so.[23] Differing opinions strained civility at professional conferences. In Minneapolis in 1962 one rabbi took the floor to say that "I saved a Jewish family" by officiating at an interfaith wedding. A colleague believed as strongly that such rabbis "are the ones who have opened the floodgates for mixed marriage on so large a scale."[24] Some grew tired of the wrangling. This "question comes up at our annual conventions every seven or eight years," complained Julian Morgenstern, retired president of Hebrew Union College: "There is much discussion, much parliamentary quibbling, but little or no progress."[25] Yet the issue was tenacious, because it struck at Judaism's identity as a community of descent in more than one way. Behind the question of whether Jews still chose to marry Jews was the deeper fear that Jews no longer wished to live as Jews at all.

Worries about principles, vulnerable leaders, continuing mixed marriages: these ingredients were so troublesome that Reform rabbis never devised a consistent policy. They took a painful step in Atlanta in 1973. By a narrow margin of three to two, the conference voted "its opposition to participation by its members in any ceremony which solemnizes a mixed marriage."[26] As liberals, they were anxious about restricting clerical freedom. But it was the rabbi's power that was really at stake. Debate revealed bitterness about "the pressures of powerful congregants" who asked rabbis to perform intermarriages. One speaker professed his determination "to lead my people, not to be led by them": "we rabbis are the last bastion in the struggle for

Jewish survival" in a "wilderness of deteriorating values."[27] Others, however, believed that the day of the rabbi's prestige was already past. "Let us stop fantasizing about influence we do not possess and power we do not have."[28] Sadly, laypeople now seemed the opponents, and more than one rabbi must have imagined himself like "Moses when confronted with the company of those who sought to usurp his authority."[29]

How quickly the conference began discussion of how to deal with the children of gentile mothers was a sign that the rabbis' official refusal to conduct interfaith weddings had little effect. In Pittsburgh in 1980 the CCAR broached the subject of patrilineal descent. Since the 1940s, the movement's religious schools had accepted the children of one Jewish parent. But students with Jewish fathers were not Jewish until confirmation, which functioned, the CCAR said in 1947, "in lieu of a conversion ceremony."[30] Three decades later, the rabbis took further steps to welcome the children. "Authentic Jewishness," one committee proposed, should depend "upon how the child of a mixed faith marriage is reared and educated." Conservative-leaning colleagues jumped on the wording: "It changed Judaism to a religion of faith from a religion of birth."[31] But the long-standing role of training in making the children of Jewish fathers Jewish meant that they voiced this objection too late. In the Reform sphere, choice already quietly coexisted with biology as the requirement for Jewishness, making the CCAR's 1983 resolution no surprise. The rabbis agreed to recognize "the Jewish status of the offspring of any mixed marriage" who performs "*mitzvot*": "appropriate and timely public and formal acts of identification with the Jewish faith and people."[32] This came close to normalizing the same marriages the rabbis declined to sanction.

The thought that the foundation of Judaism might to any extent be a voluntary community was startling. But in most respects the conference skirted the facts. Frustrated in 1973, Alfred Gottschalk, president of Hebrew Union College, charged his colleagues with dealing "with the symptoms here tonight and not with the cause." He asked them to study "the substantive issues of those factors in Jewish life, in Jewish education, and in Jewish society which have led to the acceleration of intermarriage."[33] A decade later, however, no closer to understanding mixed-faith couples, the rabbis coped by adjusting policies to fit popular choices. In their inability to penetrate the hearts and minds of laypeople they were not alone. Clergy of all faiths worked to reopen communication with families. But it was not that men and women had not heard about the problems of mixed marriages; they decided not to listen. This was a troubling conclusion for religious leaders, and they called for more data to solve the mystery.

A look at history provides answers. The struggle between freedom and religious tradition began with the American republic, and families were one place where the drama played out. When interfaith households broke with inherited teachings on marriage, they moved toward self-determination. Love, conviction, and prejudice vied with one another at home. But kinship itself proved tenacious and most often kept relatives together. In the process, interfaith families helped change American religion. Mixed marriages did not represent an attack on faith, but they were a challenge to institutions to take account of the crosscurrents of an open society. Religious curiosity, family loyalty, and a taste for the unexpected: these traits of interfaith families, seemingly so American, have woven their histories into the experience of the nation itself.

Appendix

Abbreviations Used in the Notes

Notes

Index

Appendix

The Interfaith Couples Studied, Listed in Chronological Order by Wedding Date

Names	Religions of groom and bride	Date of Marriage	Residence(s)
Moses Mordecai to Margaret Lane	Jewish; Protestant	1817	North Carolina
to Nancy Lane	Jewish; Protestant	1824	North Carolina
Benjamin Gratz to Maria Gist	Jewish; Protestant	1819	Kentucky
to Ann Shelby	Jewish; Protestant	1843	Kentucky
Ephraim Blaine to Maria Gillespie	Protestant; Catholic	1820	Pennsylvania
Thomas Ewing to Maria Boyle	Protestant; Catholic	1820	Ohio
Achilles Plunkett to Caroline Mordecai	Catholic; Jewish	1820	North Carolina
Isaac Lea to Frances Carey	Protestant; Catholic	1821	Pennsylvania
Solomon Mordecai to Caroline Waller	Jewish; Protestant	1824	Alabama
George Ripley to Sophia Dana	Protestant; Catholic	1827	Massachusetts, New York
Judah Benjamin to Natalie St. Martin	Jewish; Catholic	1833	Louisiana, London, Paris
Samuel Ward to Anna Barker	Protestant; Catholic	1840	Massachusetts, New York
David Levy Yulee to Nannie Wickliffe	Jewish; Protestant	1846	Florida
William Tecumseh Sherman to Ellen Ewing	Protestant; Catholic	1850	Ohio, Washington, D.C., Missouri, New York
William Russell Smith to Wilhelmine Easby	Protestant; Catholic	1854	Alabama, Washington, D.C.
Stephen A. Douglas to Adele Cutts	Protestant; Catholic	1856	Washington, D.C.
Joel Chandler Harris to Esther La Rose	Protestant; Catholic	1873	Georgia
James Molony to Helen Wise	Protestant; Jewish	1878	Ohio
Zebulon Vance to Florence Martin	Protestant; Catholic	1880	Washington, D.C., North Carolina
John Coppinger to Alice Blaine	Catholic; Protestant	1883	Kansas, New York
Charles Sanders Peirce to Juliette Froissy Pourtalai	Protestant; Catholic	1883	Maryland, Massachusetts, Pennsylvania
Julian La Rose Harris to Julia Collier	Catholic; Protestant	1897	Georgia
Ralph Barton Perry to Rachel Berenson	Protestant; Jewish	1905	Massachusetts
Graham Stokes to Rose Pastor	Protestant; Jewish	1905	New York
Ludwig Lewisohn to Mary Crocker Childs	Jewish; Protestant	1906	New York
Richard Harding Davis to Bessie McCoy	Protestant; Catholic	1912	New York

Family of William Tecumseh and Ellen Ewing Sherman

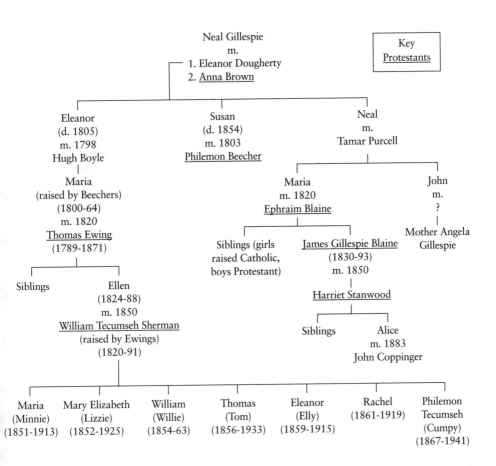

Family of Jacob Mordecai

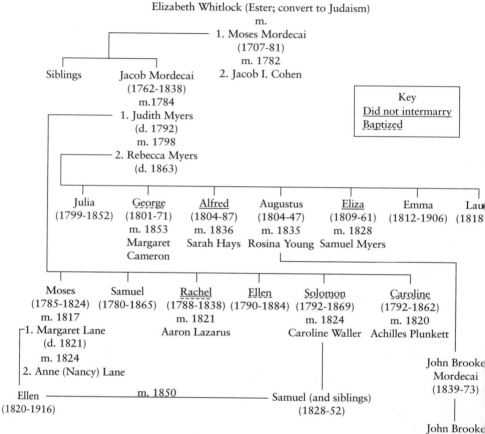

Elizabeth Whitlock (Ester; convert to Judaism)
m.
1. Moses Mordecai
(1707-81)
m. 1782
2. Jacob I. Cohen

Siblings   Jacob Mordecai
(1762-1838)
m.1784
1. Judith Myers
(d. 1792)
m. 1798
2. Rebecca Myers
(d. 1863)

Key
Did not intermarry
Baptized

Julia	George	Alfred	Augustus	Eliza	Emma	Lau
(1799-1852)	(1801-71)	(1804-87)	(1804-47)	(1809-61)	(1812-1906)	(1818
	m. 1853	m. 1836	m. 1835	m. 1828		
	Margaret	Sarah Hays	Rosina Young	Samuel Myers		
	Cameron					

Moses	Samuel	Rachel	Ellen	Solomon	Caroline
(1785-1824)	(1780-1865)	(1788-1838)	(1790-1884)	(1792-1869)	(1792-1862)
m. 1817		m. 1821		m. 1824	m. 1820
1. Margaret Lane		Aaron Lazarus		Caroline Waller	Achilles Plunkett
(d. 1821)					
m. 1824					
2. Anne (Nancy) Lane					

John Brooke
Mordecai
(1839-73)

Ellen ———————— m. 1850 ———————— Samuel (and siblings)
(1820-1916)   (1828-52)

John Brooke
Mordecai

Abbreviations Used in the Notes

AJA	Jacob Rader Marcus Center of the American Jewish Archives, Hebrew Union College-Jewish Institute of Religion, Cincinnati, Ohio
Chicago	Department of Special Collections, Joseph Regenstein Library, University of Chicago, Chicago, Illinois
Emory	Special Collections, Robert W. Woodruff Library, Emory University, Atlanta, Georgia
Harvard	Harvard University, Cambridge, Massachusetts
Huntington	Henry E. Huntington Library, San Marino, California
LC	Manuscript Division, Library of Congress, Washington, D.C.
NC State Archives	Division of Archives and History, Department of Cultural Resources, Raleigh, North Carolina
Notre Dame	The Archives of the University of Notre Dame, Notre Dame, Indiana
UNC	Southern Historical Collection, Wilson Library, University of North Carolina, Chapel Hill, North Carolina

Notes

Introduction

1. Leslie Woodcock Tentler estimates that as many as one-third of Catholics in parts of late nineteenth-century Detroit married non-Catholics, in *Seasons of Grace: A History of the Catholic Archdiocese of Detroit* (Detroit: Wayne State University Press, 1990), p. 100; Jacob Rader Marcus states that one-half of Jews in antebellum New Orleans intermarried, in *United States Jewry, 1776–1985* (Detroit: Wayne State University Press, 1989–1993), 1: 608. It is important to keep in mind that interfaith marriage rates, at any point in time, varied greatly by location.

2. Tom Sherman to William Tecumseh Sherman, Dec. 11, [18]77, box 3, folder 75, William Tecumseh Sherman Family Papers (CSHR), Notre Dame; Tom Sherman to W. T. Sherman, May 20, 1878, quoted in Michael Fellman, *Citizen Sherman: A Life of William Tecumseh Sherman* (New York: Random House, 1995), p. 378.

3. W. T. Sherman to Henry Turner, July 7, 1878, quoted in Joseph T. Durkin, *General Sherman's Son* (New York: Farrar, Straus and Cudahy, 1959), p. 53; W. T. Sherman to Ellen Ewing, Apr. 7, 1842, box 1, folder 103, Sherman Family Papers.

4. Ellen Sherman to W. T. Sherman, May 25, [1878], box 2, folder 144, Sherman Family Papers.

5. W. T. Sherman to James A. Hardie, Apr. 12, 1850, folder 1850, James A. Hardie Papers, LC. Ellen described Hardie's Catholicism in a letter to her mother, Maria Ewing, May 4, 1850, box 152, pt. 1 (letterbook, 1838–Oct. 15, 1851), Thomas Ewing Family Papers, LC. The italics in this and subsequent quotations appear in the original texts.

6. W. T. Sherman to Elly Sherman Thackara, Sept. 16, 1883, quoted in

Fellman, *Citizen Sherman*, p. 397. Although Sherman voiced this doubt about Catholic schooling for boys after the crisis over Tom, there is much evidence that he worried for years about the manliness of all three boys. See Fellman, pp. 117–21, 372–77, 397–98.

7. W. T. Sherman to Ellen Sherman, Oct. 14, 1863, quoted in Fellman, *Citizen Sherman*, p. 207.

8. Durkin, *General Sherman's Son*, pp. 34–35.

9. W. T. Sherman to Ellen Ewing, June 19, 1845 and Feb. 8, 1844, box 1, folders 105, 104, Sherman Family Papers. On Cump's Catholic baptism, see Ellie Ewing Brown, with editorial additions by Eleanor Sherman Fitch, "Notes on Boyhood of Philemon Beecher Ewing and William Tecumseh Sherman," unpaginated typescript, ca. 1932, box 7, folder 7, Sherman Family Papers.

10. Ellen Sherman to W. T. Sherman, May 25, [1878], box 2, folder 144, Sherman Family Papers.

11. W. T. Sherman to Thomas Ewing, June 17, 1844, box 154, Ewing Family Papers. On the Beecher and Ewing families, see "The Autobiography of Thomas Ewing," ed. Clement L. Martzolff, *Ohio State Archaeological and Historical Society Publications* 22 (1912): 3–54, offprint; Eleanor S. Ewing, "Ma Beecher," "Maria Boyle Ewing," "Neal Gillespie Chart and Note," and "Hugh Boyle," undated manuscripts and typescripts, Ellen Boyle Ewing Sherman Papers, Huntington.

12. Quoted in Eleanor Ewing, "Maria Boyle Ewing," typescript, Ellen Sherman Papers.

13. Maria Ewing to Ellen Sherman, May 1, 1854, box 152, pt. 2 (letterbook, Dec. 17, 1851–Aug. 2, 1854), Ewing Family Papers.

14. Maria Ewing to Ellen Ewing [Sherman], Nov. 1841, box 152, pt. 1, Ewing Family Papers.

15. Thomas Ewing visited Georgetown Academy at Maria's request to inspect it as a possible school for their children and relatives (Thomas to Maria, Mar. 5, 1831, box 16, folder 14, Sherman Family Papers). Ellen asked Cump to call on Archbishop Manning in London, Apr. 15 and May 28, 1872, box 2, folder 132, Sherman Family Papers. Whether Sherman's children and Protestant brothers clashed over calling a priest to administer last rites was the subject of contemporary controversy; see Fellman, *Citizen Sherman*, pp. 413–15. On Thomas Ewing's conversion, see Katherine Burton, *Three Generations: Maria Boyle Ewing (1801–1864), Ellen Ewing Sherman (1824–1888), Minnie Sherman Fitch (1851–1913)* (New York: Longmans, Green, 1947), pp. 191–93.

16. W. T. Sherman to Minnie Sherman Fitch, June 16, 1878, quoted in Durkin, *General Sherman's Son*, p. 52.

17. "Reminiscences of Early Days," typescript, 1940, p. 23, box 7, folder 1, Sherman Family Papers.

18. Peter Guilday, ed., *The National Pastorals of the American Hierarchy (1792–1919)* (Washington, D.C.: National Catholic Welfare Council, 1923), pp. 137–38.

19. Genesis 26.35. The English text for this and subsequent quotations from the Hebrew Bible have been taken from the *Tanakh: The Holy Scriptures* (Philadelphia: Jewish Publication Society, 1985). See also Genesis 27.46 and 28.1–9 on the issue of endogamy.

20. Deuteronomy 7.4. The complete passage (Deut. 7.1–5) names seven pagan nations proscribed because of their idolatry; see also Exodus 34.11–16 and Deut. 23.4–9. The Mishnah and Talmud widened the ban to include all non-Jews, but nineteenth-century rabbis occasionally wondered if marriage to other monotheists was permitted. See "Reform Judaism and Mixed Marriage," in Elliot L. Stevens, ed., *Central Conference of American Rabbis: Ninety-First Annual Convention, 1980* (New York: Central Conference of American Rabbis, 1981), 90: 90–91, 97, and M[oses]. Mielziner, *The Jewish Law of Marriage and Divorce in Ancient and Modern Times, and Its Relation to the Law of the State,* 2d rev. ed. (New York: Bloch, 1901), pp. 47–48. The Central Conference of American Rabbis, the professional organization of Reform rabbis, will be designated hereafter as CCAR, and the proceedings of its annual convention will be abbreviated *CCAR Yearbook.*

21. Ezra 9.11, 10.10. See also Nehemiah 13.23–31 and 1 Kings 11, as well as commentary by Gary N. Knoppers, "Sex, Religion, and Politics: The Deuteronomist on Intermarriage," *Hebrew Annual Review* 14 (1994): 121–41; Louis M. Epstein provides an excellent overview of the issue of intermarriage in the Hebrew Bible, in *Marriage Laws in the Bible and the Talmud* (Cambridge, Mass.: Harvard University Press, 1942), pp. 145–67.

22. See Mary Douglas, *Purity and Danger: An Analysis of Concepts of Pollution and Taboo* (New York: Praeger, 1966), and Sigmund Freud, *Totem and Taboo: Some Points of Agreement between the Mental Lives of Savages and Neurotics* (1912; rpt. London: Routledge and Kegan Paul, 1950), esp. chs. 1–2.

23. Malachi 2.10, 2.14, 2.11. Additional passages outside the Pentateuch warning against "alien" and "forbidden" women are found in Proverbs 2.16–19, 5.1–20, 6.24, and 7.1–5.

24. Deut. 23.4. Rabbinic commentators of the first centuries of the Common Era interpreted the ban against Moabites more leniently: if a Moabite woman converted to Judaism, her descendants could marry a Jew in the third generation. See "Reform Judaism and Mixed Marriage," p. 90. On laws governing a childless (levirate) widow, see Judith Romney Wegner, *Chattel or Person? The Status of Women in the Mishnah* (New York: Oxford University Press, 1988), ch. 4.

25. Ruth 1.14, 16.

26. Many commentators believe that the Book of Ruth was included in the He-

brew Bible to pose an implicit counterargument to Ezra; other scholars dismiss the narrative as an insignificant story because Ruth was unlike most gentiles. See Baruch J. Schwartz, "Ruth," in R. J. Zwi Werblowsky and Geoffrey Wigoder, eds., *The Oxford Dictionary of the Jewish Religion* (New York: Oxford University Press, 1997), p. 593. Even so, Ruth became the prototype of converts; see, e.g., Rabbi S. Shulman, "Mixed Marriages in Their Relation to the Jewish Religion," in Julian Morgenstern, David Lefkowitz, and David Philipson, eds., *CCAR Yearbook, 1909* (CCAR, 1910), 19: 327.

27. 2 Corinthians 6.14, 6.17, 7.1. Quotations from the Christian Bible have been taken from the Revised Standard Version.

28. 2 Cor. 6.14–16.

29. Ephesians 5.23, 25.

30. 1 Cor. 7.12–14. I infer Paul's concern with the stability of mixed marriages from the context of these passages. Immediately following his instructions to intermarried couples, Paul admonished the Corinthians that "every one should remain in the state in which he was called" (1 Cor. 7. 20). James A. Brundage warns, however, that Christian commentators have found Paul's cryptic teachings on mixed marriages "enigmatic" and that any reading should be advanced cautiously, in "Intermarriage between Christians and Jews in Medieval Canon Law," *Jewish History* 3 (1988): 28.

31. I have limited my discussion to Jewish-Christian relations because the Judeo-Christian tradition, broadly understood, defined the boundaries of religious life in America before World War I. Worldwide, Islam arose as a third religious community intimately connected with the other two. Mark R. Cohen offers a comparative analysis, including discussion of interfaith families, in *Under Crescent and Cross: The Jews of the Middle Ages* (Princeton: Princeton University Press, 1994), esp. pp. 129–33.

32. On Jewish marriage law, formalized during the first centuries of the Common Era, a 1980 Reform survey states: "The most significant change made during this [talmudic] period was the declaration of invalidity of mixed marriages" ("Reform Judaism and Mixed Marriage," p. 90). Marriages that had once been legally recognized, though proscribed, were no longer accounted legitimate. Although overlapping civil and canon legal systems coexisted in Christian Europe, the temper of the Theodosian Code on intermarriage was typical. See Cohen, *Crescent and Cross*, esp. pp. 34–35, and Brundage, "Intermarriage," esp. pp. 27–28.

33. Salo Wittmayer Baron, *A Social and Religious History of the Jews*, 2d rev. ed. (New York: Columbia University Press; Philadelphia: Jewish Publication Society of America, 1967), 11: 83. Scholars believe that interfaith relationships persisted, despite harsh laws, in the form of concubinage, common law marriages, and bonds ratified by vows said in the presence of lay witnesses.

34. Sander L. Gilman offers a compelling analysis of how power structures per-

ceptions, with self-destructive consequences for the powerless, in *Jewish Self-Hatred: Anti-Semitism and the Hidden Language of the Jews* (Baltimore: Johns Hopkins University Press, 1986). His analysis may be applicable to other subordinate communities in addition to Jews.

35. Proverbs 5.3–4. The literal translation of what appears here as "forbidden" is "strange."
36. Quoted in Brundage, "Intermarriage," p. 29.
37. The word "decadent" appears in Raphael Mahler, *A History of Modern Jewry, 1770–1815* (1971), quoted in Deborah Hertz, *Jewish High Society in Old Regime Berlin* (New Haven: Yale University Press, 1988), p. 223. Hertz discusses historians who make similar judgments on pp. 223–24.
38. The question appeared in "Napoleon's Instructions to the Assembly of Jewish Notables (July 29, 1806)," in Paul Mendes-Flohr and Jehuda Reinharz, eds., *The Jew in the Modern World: A Documentary History,* 2d ed. (New York: Oxford University Press, 1995), pp. 125–26. On the context of Jewish emancipation, see Raphael Mahler, ed., *Jewish Emancipation: A Selection of Documents* (New York: The American Jewish Committee, 1942).
39. Assembly of Jewish Notables, "Answers to Napoleon (1806)," in Mendes-Flohr and Reinharz, eds., *Jew in the Modern World,* p. 129.
40. Mielziner, *Jewish Law of Marriage and Divorce,* p. 24.
41. For example, Michael A. Meyer describes ambivalence about interfaith marriage at German and American rabbinical conferences, in *Response to Modernity: A History of the Reform Movement in Judaism* (Detroit: Wayne State University Press, 1995), pp. 134–35, 256–57.
42. Alban Stolz, *Mixed Marriage: The Forbidden Fruit for Catholics,* trans. and rev. by H. Cluever, 4th ed. (New York: Fr. Pustet, 1883), p. 11. Catholic commentaries on interfaith marriage developed in the context of repeated revolts against Catholicism as the state religion; see Owen Chadwick, *The Popes and European Revolution* (Oxford: Oxford University Press, 1981), esp. chs. 7–8. All religious groups in nineteenth-century Europe confronted secularism, egalitarianism, and a reforming mentality, which challenged inherited marriage laws.
43. Hertz, *Jewish High Society,* p. 217. A dramatic instance of the complicated motives behind multiple conversions and intermarriages in an extended family involves the Mendelssohns, beginning with the children of Moses (1729–1786), the Jewish philosopher, and including his grandson Felix (1809–1847), the composer. They belonged to the Berlin social circle described by Hertz. See Nancy B. Reich, "The Power of Class: Fanny Hensel," in R. Larry Todd, ed., *Mendelssohn and His World* (Princeton: Princeton University Press, 1991), pp. 86–99.
44. More than one couple belonged to these families: the descendants of Jacob Mordecai; the Blaine-Ewing-Sherman family; and the descendants of Joel Chandler Harris and Esther La Rose Harris. In general, I chose couples where neither partner converted to the religion of the other prior to mar-

riage. Until recently, Reform Jews termed a marriage preceded by a conversion a "mixed marriage," in contrast to an "intermarriage" where the gentile did not convert. See Michael Cook, "The Debates of the Central Conference of American Rabbis on the Problems of Mixed Marriage: 1907–1968," typescript, 1969, p. 4, AJA. The category "mixed marriage" has fallen into disuse as conversion prior to marriage has become more acceptable. Christians, less concerned than Jews about origins, have not considered marriages preceded by conversion to be interfaith marriages. I use the terms "interfaith marriage," "mixed marriage," and "intermarriage" interchangeably.

45. See, e.g., Sydney E. Ahlstrom, *A Religious History of the American People* (New Haven: Yale University Press, 1972), pts. 4–7; Jay P. Dolan, *The American Catholic Experience: A History from Colonial Times to the Present* (Notre Dame: University of Notre Dame Press, 1992), chs. 4–12, and Marcus, *United States Jewry*, vols. 1–4.

46. Will Herberg's analysis of the triple melting pot is more complex than mine, although I believe his theory can be adapted in a general way for my research. See *Protestant-Catholic-Jew: An Essay in American Religious Sociology*, rev. ed. (Garden City, N.Y.: Doubleday, 1960). Jenny Franchot offers a model for studying boundaries in the triple melting pot, in *Roads to Rome: The Antebellum Protestant Encounter with Catholicism* (Berkeley: University of California Press, 1994). Studies of tightly bound sects or ethnic groups tend to comment on intermarriage; see Christine Heyrman, *Southern Cross: The Beginnings of the Bible Belt* (Chapel Hill: University of North Carolina Press, 1997), pp. 139–42; Carl F. Bowman, *Brethren Society: The Cultural Transformation of a "Peculiar People"* (Baltimore: Johns Hopkins University Press, 1995), pp. 66, 382–83, and Robert Anthony Orsi, *The Madonna of 115th Street: Faith and Community in Italian Harlem, 1880–1950* (New Haven: Yale University Press, 1985), pp. 116–17, 125–26.

47. Maurice Fishberg, *The Jews: A Study of Race and Environment* (London: Walter Scott Publishing Company, 1911), p. 204. Marcus offers the estimate of less than one percent in *United States Jewry*, 3: 400.

48. Genesis 17.7, 23–27.

49. Although much has been written about religion and gender in America, families have received less attention. See Edmund S. Morgan, *The Puritan Family: Religion and Domestic Relations in Seventeenth-Century New England*, rev. ed. (New York: Harper and Row, 1966); Mary P. Ryan, *Cradle of the Middle Class: The Family in Oneida County, New York, 1790–1865* (Cambridge, Eng.: Cambridge University Press, 1981); and Anne C. Rose, "Religious Individualism in Nineteenth-Century American Families," in Peter W. Williams, ed., *Perspectives on American Religion and Culture* (Malden, Mass.: Blackwell, 1999), pp. 319–30.

1. Children of the Religious Enlightenment

1. [Ambrose Marechal], "Marriage," no date, no pagination, box 4, folder 21, CABA (Diocese of Baltimore Collection), Notre Dame.
2. [John Carroll], "Manuscript Sermon of Archbishop Carroll," Jan. 17, 1802, no pagination, box 1, folder 8, CABA, Notre Dame. Unusual spellings in this and subsequent quotations appear in the original texts.
3. On Carroll and Marechal, see J. Hennessey, "John Carroll," and T. E. Buckley, "Ambrose Marechal," *Dictionary of Christianity in America,* ed. Daniel G. Reid (Downers Grove, Ill.: Intervarsity Press, 1990), pp. 226–27, 704–05.
4. My analysis builds on two common premises about the Enlightenment: there was more than one temperament within the Enlightenment, and the American Enlightenment was generally more respectful of religion than its European expressions. See esp. Henry F. May, *The Enlightenment in America* (New York: Oxford University Press, 1976); May, "The Enlightenment and America: The Jeffersonian Moment," in his *The Divided Heart: Essays on Protestantism and the Enlightenment in America* (New York: Oxford University Press, 1991), pp. 161–78; and Sydney E. Ahlstrom, *A Religious History of the American People* (New Haven: Yale University Press, 1972), ch. 22. On religion in the European Enlightenment, see Peter Harrison, *"Religion" and the Religions of the English Enlightenment* (Cambridge, Eng.: Cambridge University Press, 1990), and David Sorkin, *Moses Mendelssohn and the Religious Enlightenment* (Berkeley: University of California Press, 1996). Cosmopolitanism, tolerance, and practicality were attitudes shared by many Americans who might not have read "Enlightened" texts. Use of the concept of a "generation" also requires care. Although Glenn Wallach argues that who constitute a generation is a matter of perception, in *Obedient Sons: The Discourse of Youth and Generations in American Culture, 1630–1860* (Amherst: University of Massachusetts Press, 1997), I look at a small number of individuals who were actually parents, children, and grandchildren in families that were close contemporaries of each other.
5. On the Catholic and Jewish communities in the early republic, see Randall M. Miller, "A Church in Cultural Captivity: Some Speculations on Catholic Identity in the Old South," in Miller and Jon L. Wakelyn, eds., *Catholics in the Old South* (Macon, Ga.: Mercer University Press, 1983), pp. 11–52; Patrick W. Carey, *People, Priests, and Prelates: Ecclesiastical Democracy and the Tensions of Trusteeism* (Notre Dame: University of Notre Dame Press, 1987); Jay P. Dolan, *The American Catholic Experience: A History from Colonial Times to the Present* (Notre Dame: University of Notre Dame Press), ch. 4; Jacob Rader Marcus, *United States Jewry* (Detroit: Wayne State University Press, 1989–1993), vol. 1; Myron Berman, *Rich-*

mond's Jewry, 1769–1976: Shabbat in Shockoe (Charlottesville: University Press of Virginia, 1979), chs. 1–4; James William Hagy, This Happy Land: The Jews of Colonial and Antebellum Charleston (Tuscaloosa: University of Alabama Press, 1993); and Lance J. Sussman, Isaac Leeser and the Making of American Judaism (Detroit: Wayne State University Press, 1995), esp. chs. 2–3. Among the extensive writing on early national Protestantism, the most helpful interpretation for comparisons with other religions is Nathan O. Hatch, The Democratization of American Christianity (New Haven: Yale University Press, 1989).

6. Jan. 10, 19, 21, Diary, 1810–1819, titled A Journal of Daily Occurrences, for Years, Beginning Anno 19—[sic] and Ending Anno 18—(Philadelphia: M. Carey, 1808), no pages, box 84-B, Mathew Carey Section, Edward Carey Gardiner Collection, The Historical Society of Pennsylvania, Philadephia, Pennsylvania (hereafter Carey Papers). This diary is unpaginated.

7. Jan. 19, Diary, 1810–1819, box 84-B, Carey Papers. On Carey's early life, see Mathew Carey, Autobiography (1835; rpt. Brooklyn: Eugene L. Schwaab, 1942), esp. letters 1–6, and Arnold W. Green, Henry Charles Carey: Nineteenth-Century Sociologist (Philadelphia: University of Pennsylvania Press, 1951), ch. 1.

8. Carey to [John Carroll], Mar. 27, 1791, box 84-A, folder "Mathew Carey Letters, 1791–1810," Carey Papers.

9. Oct. 18, 1812, Diary 1810–1819, box 84-B, Carey Papers. Earlier notes on church attendance, in order, are found on Mar. 13, 1791, Diary dated Feb. 1791, Jan. 1796, June 4, 1820, and Nov. 10, 1821 (hereafter Diary 1791, 1796, 1820–1821), p. 15; Apr. 2, 181[5], Diary 1810–1819; and Dec. 25, 1820, Diary 1791, 1796, 1820–1821, p. 154, all in box 84-B, Carey Papers. Carey married on Feb. 24, 1791. On his publication of Bibles and Catholic books more generally, see Carey, Autobiography, letter 11, and Mary Stephana Cavanaugh, "Catholic Book Publishing in the United States, 1784–1850," M.A. thesis, University of Illinois, 1937, ch. 1.

10. He noted fast days, e.g., on July 26, 1812 and Sept. 9, 1813, Diary 1810–1819, box 84-B, Carey Papers. On the wafer, see Bridget Carey to Mathew Carey, Dec. 20, 1799, typescript titled "Selection from the Letters of Mrs. Mathew Carey, 1796–1815," p. 8, box 84-B, Carey Papers.

11. Feb. 7, Diary 1810–1819, box 84-B, Carey Papers.

12. Mar. 7, Diary 1810–1819, box 84-B, Carey Papers. Comments on Smith and Malthus appear on July 22, 1820, Diary 1791, 1796, 1820–1821, pp. 58–59, box 84-B, Carey Papers. Isaac Lea, Carey's son-in-law, calculated the number of pamphlets Carey wrote in "Necrological Notice of Mathew Carey," Apr. 17, 1846, p. 10, Isaac Lea Papers, American Philosophical Society, Philadelphia, Pennsylvania.

13. Jan. 12, 1821, Mar. 2, 1821, Diary 1791, 1796, 1820–1821, pp. 165, 184, box 84-B, Carey Papers. He noted his participation in the Literary and

Franklinian Societies in the same diary, Mar. 14 and 19, 1791, pp. 16, 24–25.

14. Dec. 19, 1820, Diary 1791, 1796, 1820–1821, p. 150, box 84-B, Carey Papers. He wrote all of Sunday afternoon on Apr. 2, 181[5], Diary 1810–1819, box 84-B, Carey Papers.

15. Bridget Carey to Mathew Carey, Aug. 5, 1806, "Letters of Mrs. Carey," p. 39, box 84-B, Carey Papers. Her description of the revival appeared in the same letter on p. 38. On the Baltimore Cathedral, see her letter to her husband of Aug. 16, 1801, ibid., p. 18.

16. Bridget Carey to Mathew Carey, May 28, 1806, "Letters of Mrs. Carey," p. 34, box 84-B, Carey Papers.

17. July 22, 1820, Diary 1791, 1796, 1820–1821, p. 58, box 84-B, Carey Papers.

18. "A Catholic Layman" [Mathew Carey], *Address to the Right Rev. Bishop Conwell, and the Members of St. Mary's Congregation* (n.p., 1821), pp. 2, 1.

19. "A Catholic Layman" [Mathew Carey], *Address to the Right Reverend the Bishop of Pennsylvania, the Catholic Clergy of Philadelphia, and the Congregation of St. Mary's in This City* (Philadelphia: H. C. Carey and I. Lea, 1822), p. iv. The adjective "tumultuous" appeared on Dec. 30, 1820, Diary, 1791, 1796, 1820–1821, p. 157, box 84-B, Carey Papers. He recorded the priest's excommunication in the same diary on May 27, 1820, p. 234.

20. *Address to Bishop Conwell*, p. 3.

21. Accounts of the Carey children and their marriages appear in Green, *Henry Carey*, pp. 3–4, and Edward Sculley Bradley, *Henry Charles Lea: A Biography* (Philadelphia: University of Pennsylvania Press, 1931), pp. 22–32.

22. R[achel] Mordecai to Samuel Mordecai, Oct. 1, 1817, box 1784–1817, folder July–Dec. 1817, Jacob Mordecai Family Papers, Rare Book, Manuscript, and Special Collections Library, Duke University, Durham, N.C. (hereafter Mordecai Papers, Duke).

23. Rachel Mordecai to Moses Mordecai, Oct. 4, 1817, ser. 1, subser. 1.2, folder 13, Rebecca Mordecai to Ellen Mordecai, Oct. 8, 1817, subser. 1.2, folder 13, Jacob Mordecai Family Papers, Collection 847, UNC (hereafter Mordecai Papers, UNC). All Mordecai papers cited at UNC are located in series 1, "Correspondence."

24. On her role as *hazzan*, see Rachel Mordecai Lazarus to Ellen Mordecai, Oct. 7, 1821, cited in Berman, *Richmond's Jewry*, p. 103. I refer to Rachel Mordecai in the notes as "Rachel Mordecai Lazarus" after her marriage to Aaron Lazarus in 1821. On Sabbath travel and the availability of matzoh during Passover, see ibid., pp. 103, 102. Information on the Mordecai family may be found in Ruth K. Nuermberger, "Some Notes on the Mordecai Family," *The Virginia Magazine of History and Biography* 49 (1941): 364–73; Edgar E. MacDonald, ed., *The Education of the Heart: The Correspondence of Rachel Mordecai Lazarus and Maria Edgeworth* (Chapel Hill: University of North Carolina Press, 1977), pp. 325–34; Myron Berman,

The Last of the Jews? (Lanham, Md.: University Press of America, 1998); and Emily Sims Bingham, "Mordecai: Three Generations of a Southern Jewish Family, 1780–1865," Ph.D. diss., University of North Carolina, 1998.

25. Advertisement for the Warrenton Academy, quoted in Stanley L. Falk, "The Warrenton Female Academy of Jacob Mordecai, 1809–1818," *The North Carolina Historical Review* 35 (1958): 285.

26. Discussions of these authors appear in letters from Edgeworth to Rachel Mordecai Lazarus, Apr. 9, 1824 (Scott and Cooper), and Rachel Lazarus to Edgeworth, July 17, 1824 (Byron) and Oct. 21, 1824 (Sedgwick), in MacDonald, ed., *Education of the Heart*, pp. 55, 67, 69.

27. Rachel Mordecai to Ellen Mordecai, Dec. 12, 1813, quoted in Berman, *Richmond's Jewry*, p. 28.

28. Rebecca Gratz to Maria Gist Gratz, Feb. 16, 1832, *Letters of Rebecca Gratz*, ed. David Philipson (Philadelphia: The Jewish Publication Society of America, 1929), p. 142.

29. "A [Coreligionist?] of Richmond Virginia" [Jacob Mordecai], "Remarks on Harby's Discourse Delivered in Charleston (S.C.), Nov. 21, 1825, before the Reformed Society of Israelites on their First Anniversary," p. 21, AJA. Mordecai did not deliver his address in person, but sent it from Richmond to Charleston with relatives of his son-in-law Aaron Lazarus. See Berman, *Richmond's Jewry*, p. 105. On the Charleston reformers, see Gary Phillip Zola, *Isaac Harby of Charleston, 1788–1828: Jewish Reformer and Intellectual* (Tuscaloosa: University of Alabama Press, 1994), esp. ch. 5.

30. "Remarks on Harby's Discourse," pp. 3, 20, 4.

31. Ibid., p. 1.

32. "Remarks on Miss Martineau's Tract, entitled 'Providence as Manifested through Israel,' and on the Writings of the Rev'd Alexander Keith entitled 'Evidence of the Truth of the Christian Religion, derived from the Literal Fulfillment of Prophecy, Particularly as Illustrated by the History of the Jews, and by the Discoveries of Recent Travelers,'" Richmond, 1836, p. 16, in "Apologetics for the Old Testament," Rare Documents file, AJA. The manuscript uses two sets of page numbers; I have cited the numbers found in the upper corners of individual pages.

33. "Remarks on Miss Martineau's Tract," p. 6. Discussions of Ireneus and Origin appear on p. 11, of Tertullian on p. 25.

34. Rachel Mordecai Lazarus to Ellen Mordecai, Apr. 14, 1834, box 1833–1855, folder 1833–1836, Mordecai Papers, Duke. On Solomon's Hebrew lessons, see Berman, *Richmond's Jewry*, p. 104. The five children who were almost certainly baptized were Caroline (1834), Rachel (1838), George (1839), Ellen (prior to 1845), Solomon (1859). These events are documented, respectively, in Rachel Mordecai Lazarus to Ellen Mordecai, Apr. 14, 1834, box 1833–1855, folder 1833–1836, Duke; Berman, *Last of the Jews?*, p. 69; Ellen Mordecai to Solomon Mordecai, July 3, 1838, subser.

1.4, folder 71, UNC; [Ellen Mordecai], *The History of a Heart* (Philadelphia: Stavely and M'Calla, 1845); and Berman, *Richmond's Jewry,* p. 119. Ellen's *History of a Heart* can best be read as a conversion narrative. It was true in the sense that it is an account of her change of heart; but specific facts were often either vaguely stated or fictionalized. Other Mordecai children, such as Samuel, were buried by Christian clergyman; but whether they were baptized or not is unclear. Rachel was the only child of Jacob and his first wife Judith to marry a Jew; among the children of his second wife Rebecca, Alfred and Eliza chose Jewish spouses. Six of the thirteen children never married. Despite her Jewish marriage, Rachel thought seriously and painfully about conversion to Christianity in 1835 and was baptized on her deathbed in 1838. An account of Rachel's religious crisis and the family conflict it occasioned may be found in Ellen Mordecai to Solomon Mordecai, July 3, 1838, subser. 1.4, folder 71, Mordecai Papers, UNC.

35. "Sainted mother" appears in Ellen Mordecai to Solomon Mordecai, Nov. 12, 1817, box 1784–1817, folder July-Dec. 1817, Mordecai Papers, Duke. Rachel asked her stepmother to reason with Jacob during Caroline's conversion crisis of 1834; see Rachel Lazarus to Ellen Mordecai, Apr. 14, 1834, box 1833–1855, folder 1833–1836, Mordecai Papers, Duke. Naturally, Rebecca's own children felt more warmly about her than did her stepchildren. Her son Alfred addressed letters to "my dear mother," for example (Jan. 23, 1824, box 1822–1824, folder Jan.–June 1824, Mordecai Papers, Duke).

36. [Samuel Mordecai] to [Rachel Mordecai?], Oct. 18, and Rachel to Samuel, Oct. 19, 1817, box 1784–1817, folder July–Dec. 1817, Mordecai Papers, Duke.

37. Samuel Mordecai to Ellen Mordecai, Dec. 11, 1817, box 1784–1817, folder July–Dec. 1817, Mordecai Papers, Duke. The wedding had been held on Dec. 9 at the home of Betsy Hamilton, the bride's aunt.

38. Samuel Mordecai to Ellen Mordecai, June 2, [1836], box 1833–1855, folder 1833–1836, Mordecai Papers, Duke.

39. Rebecca Gratz to Maria Fenno Hoffman, Oct. 31, 1819, box 4, Rebecca Gratz Papers, Collection 236, AJA.

40. Rebecca Gratz to Maria Gist Gratz, Dec. 25, 1819, in *Letters of Gratz,* ed. Philipson, p. 21. Maria married Benjamin on Nov. 24, 1819. For information on the Gratz family, see ibid., pp. vii–xxiv.

41. [Rebecca Gratz] to Benjamin Gratz, Jan. 18, 1856, box 2, folder "Benjamin Gratz," Gratz Papers.

42. Rebecca Gratz to Maria Fenno Hoffman, Oct. 31, 1819, box 4, Gratz Papers.

43. Rebecca Gratz to Miriam Cohen, June 20, 1842, box 1, folder "Miriam Cohen, 1836–1862," Gratz Papers.

44. Rebecca Gratz to Miriam Cohen, Mar. 29, 1841, box 1, folder "Miriam Cohen, 1836–1862," Gratz Papers.

45. Rebecca Gratz to Miriam Cohen, Nov. 9, 1840, box 1, folder "Miriam Cohen, 1836–1840," Gratz Papers.
46. Rebecca Gratz to Benjamin Gratz, Aug. 21, [1812], in *Letters of Gratz,* ed., Philipson, pp. 4, 3.
47. Rebecca Gratz to Maria Gist Gratz, Jan. 6, 1834, in *Letters of Gratz,* ed. Philipson, p. 190.
48. Rebecca Gratz to Maria Fenno Hoffman, Oct. 31, 1819, box 4, Gratz Papers.
49. Rebecca Gratz to Maria Gist Gratz, [Apr. 1832], in *Letters of Gratz,* ed. Philipson, p. 145. On Gratz's involvement in Jewish educational and benevolent efforts, among them the Hebrew Female Benevolent Society (founded 1819), the Hebrew Sunday School of Philadelphia (1838), and the Jewish Foster Home (1855), see Dianne Ashton, *Rebecca Gratz: Women and Judaism in Antebellum America* (Detroit: Wayne State University Press, 1997), pts. 3–5. These did not preclude her nonsectarian causes, but emerged with the growth of the Philadelphia Jewish community.
50. Rebecca Gratz to Maria Gist Gratz, [Apr. 1832], in *Letters of Gratz,* ed. Philipson, p. 154.
51. Rebecca Gratz to Maria Gist Gratz, Aug. 4, 1820, box 3, folder "Mrs. Benjamin Gratz," Gratz Papers.
52. Rebecca Gratz, Last Will, June 16, 1865, Gratz Papers. She left $5,000 to Benjamin and $2,000 to her niece Miriam Cohen, who received the next largest bequest. After the individual gifts, the remainder of the estate went to her nephew and executor Horace Moses.
53. Rebecca Gratz to Maria Gist Gratz, Sept. 21, 1833; Gratz to Ann Shelby Gratz, Nov. 24, 1845, in *Letters of Gratz,* ed. Philipson, pp. 181, 319.
54. Rebecca Gratz to Miriam Cohen, Oct. 11, 1855, box 1, folder "Miriam Cohen, 1851–1855," Gratz Papers.
55. Carey, *Address to Bishop Conwell,* p. 3; "Remarks on Harby's Discourse," p. 2. Privately, too, study with Jacob became the Mordecais' attempted cure for apostasy. In 1823, after Gershon Lazarus, Jacob's step-grandson, took "the sacrament [of communion?] publicly," his father Aaron sent him to Jacob for instruction in Judaism (Ellen Mordecai to Solomon Mordecai, June 5, 1823, subser. 1.3, folder 29, Mordecai Papers, UNC; Ellen Mordecai to Solomon Mordecai, Jan. 15, 1824, box 1882–1824, folder Jan.–June 1824, Mordecai Family Papers, Duke). Jacob's children, however, sometimes spoke of his "researches" as almost a hobby (Ellen to Solomon, Jan. 15, 1824, Duke), and, in his "Remarks on Miss Martineau's Tract" (1836), Jacob voiced skepticism that he had an audience, because "the youthful have no inclination, the middle aged no time, and the aged no occasion for investigating the subject," in this case, Jesus' resurrection (p. 7).
56. Aug. 2, 1791, Diary 1791, 1796, 1820–1821, p. 29, box 84-B, Carey Papers.
57. Carey, *Autobiography,* p. 25. Although the autobiography was published in book form in 1835, the quotation appears in a letter in the volume dated

Dec. 12, 1833, originally appearing in *The New-England Magazine*. Perhaps self-consciously, Carey echoed Benjamin Franklin's values, well known in the early republic through the many editions of *The Autobiography of Benjamin Franklin* (1791).

58. Solomon Mordecai to Ellen Mordecai, Sept. 24, 1820, subser. 1.3, folder 18, Mordecai Papers, UNC.

59. Solomon Mordecai to Jacob and Rebecca Mordecai, Apr. 23, 1824, subser. 1.3, folder 34, Moredecai Papers, UNC.

60. Apr. 21, 1832, "European Journal," Apr. 16–July 13, 1832, Isaac Lea Papers.

61. Carey, *Autobiography*, p. 9. On changing relations between religion and the state in this period, see Ahlstrom, *Religious History of the American People*, pp. 379–80, and Joseph L. Blau and Salo W. Baron, eds., *The Jews of the United States, 1790–1840: A Documentary History* (New York: Columbia University Press, 1963), 1: 15–20. The demography of early national interfaith marriages rests on two factors: where minorities settled and whether religious boundaries were sufficiently open for interfaith marriages to occur. The Jewish case is especially clear because there were so few American synagogues and Jewish families (still fewer than 15,000 Jews in 1830). Before 1830 stable congregations were found in New York, Philadelphia, Baltimore, Richmond, and Charleston. This settlement pattern in part reflected the persistence of state churches (Congregational) in New England until as late as 1833 (Massachusetts). Jewish families that lived in New England did not intermarry, most likely because of the strength and insularity of Protestantism. The children, for example, of Moses Michael Hays, a wealthy Boston merchant who flourished around the turn of the century, did not intermarry; see Berman, *Richmond's Jewry*, p. 65. The first interfaith couple formed by marraige, not conversion, that I found in New England was Ralph Barton Perry and Rachel Berenson, married in 1905.

62. Quoted in Falk, "Warrenton Academy," p. 281.

63. Jacob Mordecai to Samuel Mordecai, Nov. 28, 1817, box 1784–1817, folder July-Dec. 1817; Ellen Mordecai to Solomon Mordecai, Jan. 22, 1824, box 1822–1824, folder Jan.-June 1824, Mordecai Papers, Duke. Jacob's weariness of operating the Warrenton Academy was another reason for the family's move. The school was sold in Nov. 1818; discussions of moving began, however, around the time of Moses' marriage. See also Samuel Mordecai to Rachel Mordecai, Nov. 6, 1817, box 1784–1817, folder July-Dec. 1817, Duke.

64. Caroline fell in love with Achilles Plunkett in 1814, but contended with her father over permission to marry him until 1820 (MacDonald, ed., *Education of the Heart*, p. 330). Her husband died in 1824; but she felt sufficiently at home in Warrenton to be baptized there, with the encouragement of friends, in 1834 (Rachel Lazarus to Ellen Mordecai, Apr. 14, 1834, box 1833–1855, folder 1833–1836, Mordecai Papers, Duke).

65. Benjamin's correspondence with Frank P. Blair touched political, financial,

and family subjects. See Benjamin Gratz to Frank Blair, 1833–1864, Gratz Papers. One of Benjamin's daughters (Annie) married a grandson of Henry Clay. See Henrietta Clay, "Bits of Family History: Paper Read Before the John Bradford Club, Lexington, Kentucky, December 8, 1932," AJA.

66. Rebecca Gratz to Benjamin Gratz, Mar. 7, 1819, in *Letters of Gratz,* ed. Philipson, p. 16.

67. Rachel Mordecai to Moses Mordecai, Oct. 4, 1817, subser. 1.2, folder 13, Mordecai Papers, UNC.

68. One family's history suggests that couples who migrated to the frontier earlier than the nineteenth century were more inclined to be intermarried than eastern contemporaries. Neal Gillespie, great-grandfather of Ellen Ewing Sherman and James G. Blaine, seems to have been a Scotch-Irish Protestant who wed a Catholic wife, Eleanor Dougherty, in Ireland and settled south of Pittsburgh in the 1760s. Her children were raised Catholics; when she died, Neal married a Protestant, Anna Brown. See slightly conflicting accounts of this story by Gail Hamilton [pseud. of Mary Abigail Dodge], *Biography of James G. Blaine* (Norwich, Conn.: Henry Bill, 1895), p. 53, and Eleanor S. Ewing, "Maria Boyle Ewing (1801–64)," "Neal Gillespie," and "Hugh Boyle," Ellen Boyle Ewing Sherman Papers, Huntington. The example indicates that frontier circumstances could be more important than generational differences in determining patterns of interfaith marriage.

69. The phrase "furious storm" appears in *Address to Bishop Conwell,* p. 4. Lea's words and estimate of the total number of pamphlet pages are found in "Necrological Notice of Carey," p. 15, 10, Isaac Lea Papers.

70. Rebecca Gratz to Maria Gist Gratz, Jan. 6, 1834, in *Letters of Gratz,* ed. Philipson, p. 190. The strenuous tone found in the writings of these two individuals correlates with the rising pitch of Protestant revivalism after the War of 1812. This is not to say that Protestant events caused a more impassioned religious style, but that members of all religious communities experienced a change in sensibility. On the postwar revivals, see Paul E. Johnson, *A Shopkeeper's Millennium: Society and Revivals in Rochester, New York, 1815–1837* (New York: Hill and Wang, 1978), and Mary P. Ryan, *Cradle of the Middle Class: The Family in Oneida County, New York, 1790–1865* (Cambridge, Eng.: Cambridge University Press, 1981), ch. 2. On Christian missions to the Jews, see Jonathan D. Sarna, "The American Jewish Response to Nineteenth-Century Christian Missions," *Journal of American History* 68 (1981): 35–51.

71. Feb. 24, Mar. ?, Mar. 16, 1791, Diary 1791, 1796, 1820–1821, pp. 7, 15, 21, box 84-B, Carey Papers.

72. Jan. 23, 1814, Diary 1810–1819, box 84-B, Carey Papers.

73. Ellen Mordecai to Solomon Mordecai, Oct. 19, 1817, box 1784–1817, folder July–Dec. 1817, Mordecai Papers, Duke.

74. Ellen Mordecai to Solomon Mordecai, Apr. 16, 1824, box 1822–1824, folder Jan.–June 1824, Mordecai Papers, Duke. Rachel's advice to Ellen ap-

peared in a letter on Aug. 23, 1823, subser. 1.3, folder 30, Mordecai Papers, UNC. The man Ellen turned down was John Plunkett, the son of Caroline's husband Achilles.

75. Ellen Mordecai to Solomon Mordecai, Jan. 1, 1824, box 1822–1824, folder Jan.–June 1824, Mordecai Papers, Duke. On the rise of a culture enamored of romantic love, see Karen Lystra, *Searching the Heart: Women, Men, and Romantic Love in Nineteenth-Century America* (New York: Oxford University Press, 1989). Although scholars are aware that such intense feelings were not limited to relations between husbands and wives, or even between men and women, the love of siblings has been little studied. Even in 1859, when she and Solomon were in their late sixties, Ellen could still write to a niece that "to look at my dear S—to know that affection long ago taught me almost to anticipate his wishes & his wants, to see that I have lost nothing of my heart's instinct and yet to have to leave him is *my cross* which I trust my savior may enable me to bear, and my beloved S. to endure until it please our Heavenly Father to comfort our hearts by bringing me back again" (to Ellen Mordecai [Moses' daughter], Mar. 11, 1859, subser. 1.6, box 1856–1859, folder 86, Mordecai Papers, UNC).

76. The emergence of the self as a presence in American religious life, not necessarily in conflict with piety but transforming it, is analyzed by Richard Rabinowitz, *The Spiritual Self in Everyday Life: The Transformation of Personal Religious Experience in Nineteenth-Century New England* (Boston: Northeastern University Press, 1989).

77. Frederick Wolcott to Mathew Carey, Feb. 21, 1820, box 89, no. 454, Carey Papers. Frances (Fanny) Wright, the free thinker, also admired Carey and wrote to him around 1820, box 89, letters numbered 434–48, Carey Papers.

78. Sally S. Kennon to Ellen Mordecai, Mar. 17, 1809, quoted in "Kennon Letters," *The Virginia Magazine of History and Biography* 31 (1923): 301. Information on the Kennon-Mordecai relationship is found in an earlier installment of the series of letters, ibid., p. 187.

79. Rachel Mordecai to Moses Mordecai, Oct. 4, 1817, subser. 1.2, folder 13, Mordecai Papers, UNC.

80. Aug. 25, 1820, Diary 1791, 1796, 1820–1821, p. 82, box 84-B, Carey Papers. According to Carey's diary, Lea began to call at their home on Jan. 24, 1819, Diary 1810–1819, box 84-B, Carey Papers.

81. Mar. 5 and 6, 1821, Diary 1791, 1796, 1820–1821, p. 186, box 84-B, Carey Papers.

82. Solomon Mordecai to Ellen Mordecai, Apr. 9, 1824, subser. 1.3, folder 33; Mordecai Papers, UNC; Solomon Mordecai to Samuel Mordecai, Mar. 29, 1824, box 1822–1824, folder Jan.–June 1824, Mordecai Papers, Duke. On Solomon's rejection by the Tennent family, see Berman, *Richmond's Jewry,* pp. 116–17.

83. Rachel Mordecai to Ellen Mordecai, [May 20, 1824], subser. 1.3, folder 34,

Mordecai Papers, UNC. Often the Protestant families into which religious minorities married were not intact, and this lessened the social distance between insiders and outsiders. For example, Benjamin Gratz and Moses Mordecai took Protestant wives from fatherless families (Rebecca Gratz to Maria Fenno Hoffman, Oct. 31, 1819, box 4, Gratz Papers; [Ellen Mordecai] to Caroline Mordecai Plunkett, Jan. 10, 1824, box 1822–1824, folder Jan.–June, Mordecai Papers, Duke). Similarly, among Protestant men at a social disadvantage were Isaac Lea, expelled by the Quakers for bearing arms during the War of 1812, and Achilles Plunkett, a refugee from slave violence in Santo Domingo (Bradley, *Henry Lea*, pp. 15–16; MacDonald, ed., *Education of the Heart*, p. 331).

84. On American Romanticism, see Ahlstrom, *Religious History of the American People*, chs. 37–38, and Anne C. Rose, *Victorian America and the Civil War* (Cambridge, Eng.: Cambridge University Press, 1992), esp. "Introduction." The best general interpretation of Romanticism remains M. H. Abrams, *Natural Supernaturalism: Tradition and Revolution in Romantic Literature* (New York: Norton, 1971).

85. On James Blaine's visit to Ohio, see Thomas Ewing, Jr., to Ellen Ewing, July 2, 1841, box 152, pt. 1 (1838–Oct. 15, 1851), Thomas Ewing Family Papers, LC. For Philemon's visit to Brownsville, see Maria Ewing to Ellen Ewing, [1840–1841], box 152, pt. 1, Ewing Family Papers. One biographer of Blaine states that the visit occurred during the summer of 1840; perhaps this was an error or else James visited his Ewing relatives in successive years. See David Saville Muzzey, *James G. Blaine: A Political Idol of Other Days* (1934; rpt. Port Washington, N.Y.: Kennikat Press, 1963), p. 14.

86. Maria Ewing to Ellen Ewing, June 10, 1840, box 152, pt. 1, Ewing Family Papers. Representative Catholic news may be found in Maria to Ellen, Nov. 1839 (on the construction of a church), June 10, 1840 (children's study for first communion), and Jan. 7, 1842 (baptisms, first communions, and a festival), box 152, pt. 1, Ewing Family Papers.

87. Rt. Rev. Jos. Selinger, *A Catechism on Pledges: Required for Dispensation for a Mixed Marriage* (St. Louis: Central Bureau, Catholic Central Verein of America, 1930), p. 19, PGEN (General Pamphlets Collection), no. 3771, Notre Dame. On the religious division of the children in the Blaine family, see Muzzey, *Blaine*, pp. 5–6.

88. Maria Ewing to Ellen Ewing, Nov. 1841, box 152, pt. 1, Ewing Family Papers. Discussion of the possible conversions to Catholicism of family members and friends was a staple of Maria's letters to her daughter Ellen. See, e.g., Sept. 10 and Oct. 28, 1841, Aug. 15, 1845, May 27, 1847, box 152, pt. 1, Ewing Family Papers.

89. Thomas Ewing, Jr., to James G. Blaine, Aug. 23, 1884, quoted in Muzzey, *Blaine*, p. 309. Ellen gave voice to her Irish pride in a letter to Maria Ewing, Oct. 29, 1854, Ellen Sherman Papers.

90. "Manuscript Sermon of Carroll," no pagination, box 1, folder 8, CABA, Notre Dame.

91. Henry Joseph Richter, *Pastoral Letter of the Rt. Rev. Henry Joseph Richter, Bishop of Grand Rapids, on Mixed Marriages* (n.p.: reprinted 1904–1916), p. 10, box 3, folder 20, PCLW (Clergy Writings, Printed), Notre Dame. Explanation of the danger of "grave scandals" appears in William A. O'Mara, *Canonical Causes for Matrimonial Dispensations: A Historical Synopsis and Commentary*, The Catholic University of America Canon Law Studies, no. 96 (Washington, D.C.: Catholic University of America, 1935), p. 34. On "perils of perversion," see Joseph Machebeuef [Bishop of Denver], *Mixed Marriages* (New York: The Vatican Library, 1889), p. 6, box 1, folder 1, item 39, PDRP (Drop File, Printed), Notre Dame.

92. Carlos Blanchard, *The Canonical Causes for Matrimonial Dispensations*, Regional Meeting, Canon Law Society of America, Denver, Colorado, Sept. 25–26, 1951 (n.p., n.d.), p. 2. *Disparitatis cultus* with regard to marriage appears, for example, on Aug. 14, 1845, and *disparitatis fidei* on Oct. 19, 1847, in "Liber Dispensationum ab Matrimonium Spectantium, 1844–57, Notre Dame du Lac Ecclesiae," Baptismal, Burial, Marriage, and Dispensation Records, Sacred Heart Church, Notre Dame, microfilm roll 1, MSHC, Notre Dame.

93. Hamilton, *Blaine*, p. 55.

94. Eleanor Ewing, typescript "Maria Boyle Ewing," unpaginated, Ellen Sherman Papers.

95. Thomas Ewing, *The Autobiography of Thomas Ewing*, ed. Clement L. Martzolff (Columbus: F. J. Herr, 1912), p. 31, offprint, Ellen Sherman Papers.

96. I infer that Ewing was raised Presbyterian because his mother's brother was a Presbyterian minister, as he noted in his *Autobiography*, pp. 7–14, Ellen Sherman Papers. Helpful biographical information may also be found in the "Biographical Note," Ewing Family Papers.

97. Thomas Ewing to Maria Ewing, Dec. 9, 1831, box 16, folder 14, Sherman Family Papers.

98. Maria Ewing to Ellen Ewing Sherman, Feb. 25, 1854, box 152, pt. 2, Ewing Family Papers. On Tom's education at Brown, see "Biographical Note," Ewing Family Papers.

99. One biographer argues that this slogan was attached to Blaine during the presidential campaign of 1884 by admirers among the Protestant clergy; see Muzzey, *Blaine*, p. 317. Blaine soon defended himself against anti-Catholicism in a speech in New Haven on Nov. 1: "I should esteem myself of all men the most degraded if, under any pressure or under any temptation, I could, in any presence, make a disrespectful allusion to that ancient faith in which my mother lived and died" (James G. Blaine, *Political Discussions: Legislative, Diplomatic, and Popular, 1856–1886* [Norwich, Conn.: Henry Bill, 1887], p. 462).

100. Mar. 6, 1821, Diary 1791, 1796, 1820–1821, p. 187, box 84-B, Carey Papers.

101. Hurley dined with the Careys, for example, on Nov. 14, 1813, Diary 1810–

1819, box 84-B, Carey Papers. Since the diary called him "Mr. Hurley," it is possible that the guest was Michael's father Thomas, who died in 1817. Either way, the Hurleys were friends of the Carey family. According to Dale Light, Michael Hurley was "an almost stereotypical Irish immigrant of the lower classes," crude and heavy-drinking; his willingness to marry Frances and Isaac may have been influenced by the fact that his stepmother was a Protestant. See *Rome and the New Republic: Conflict and Community in Philadelphia Catholicism between the Revolution and the Civil War* (Notre Dame: University of Notre Dame Press, 1996), p. 89.

102. May 10, 1821, Diary 1791, 1796, 1820–1821, p. 225, box 84-B, Carey Papers.

103. Henry Lea to Isaac and Frances Lea, June 30, [1837], Correspondence Box, folder "Letters to Isaac and Frances Anne," Henry Charles Lea Papers, Rare Book and Manuscript Library, Van Pelt-Dietrich Library, University of Pennsylvania, Philadelphia, Pennsylvania.

104. Isaac Lea to Mathew Carey, Mar. 13, 1821, box 91, no. 572, Carey Papers. Among Carey's business interests in Pittsburgh was buying paper for his publishing company.

105. Isaac Lea to Mathew Carey, Apr. 3, 1821, box 91, no. 571, Carey Papers. On Thomas Gibson, see manuscripts titled "Isaac Lea (1792–1886)" and "Elizabeth Gibson (1762–1833)," folder "Notes of Isaac Lea," Isaac Lea Papers. On the partnerships that bound Lea to the Careys, see Bradley, *Lea*, p. 29.

106. "La Promenade," notebook "Journal, Mar. 21, 1834," n.p. (pagination ends at p. 25), box 1 (Juvenile Notebooks, 1830-Jan. 1840), Henry Lea Papers.

107. Notebook "Bible Studies, Feb. 21, 1838," box 1, Henry Lea Papers.

108. On Isaac Lea's interests, see Bradley, *Lea*, pp. 17–19. Henry's various notebooks are found in boxes 1–4, covering the years 1830–1845, Henry Lea Papers.

109. In light of Lea's later work as a historian of the Middle Ages, it seems strange that Latin was not one of his childhood languages. But there is no Latin notebook among his childhood journals, boxes 1–4, Henry Lea Papers.

110. Manuscript titled "A Pencilled Memorandum in the Hand of and Signed by Isaac Lea (1792–1886)," July 12, 1849, p. 3, folder "Notes of Lea," Isaac Lea Papers.

111. Only Eliza, among the children, attended Mass regularly enough for Carey to mention it in his diary. She accompanied her mother on Sept. 3, 1820, her father on Sept. 17, 1820, and went alone May 27, 1821, Diary 1791, 1796, 1820–1821, pp. 85, 96, 234, box 84-B, Carey Papers. George Washington Doane, controversial High Church Episcopal Bishop of New Jersey, 1832–1859, was rector of St. Mary's. See Nelson R. Burr, *The Anglican Church in New Jersey* (Philadelphia: The Church Historical Society, 1954), pp. 457–

58,463–65, 493–98. On Henry and Patty's involvement in St. Mary's, see Green, *Carey*, pp. 45–48.

112. Henry C. Baird to [Charles or Arthur Lea], Apr. 28, 1910, Correspondence Box, folder "Henry Carey Baird," Henry Lea Papers.

113. Rachel Mordecai to Moses Mordecai, Oct. 4, 1817, subser. 1.2, folder 13, Mordecai Papers, UNC.

114. Samuel Mordecai to Ellen Mordecai, Sept. 14, 1824, box 1822–1824, folder July-Dec. 1824, Mordecai Papers, Duke. Rachel's words are found in a letter to Samuel, Sept. 19, 1824, in the same location.

115. Rachel Mordecai Lazarus to Ellen Mordecai, Oct. 17, 1824, box 1822–1824, folder July-Dec. 1824, Mordecai Papers, Duke.

116. George Mordecai to Samuel Mordecai, Oct. 22, 1824, box 1822–1824, folder July–Dec. 1824, Mordecai Papers, Duke.

117. The children of Moses and Margaret did attend Caroline's school in Warrenton around 1828 (she ran the school from 1827 to 1830). Caroline moved to Raleigh to supervise their education in 1830, but left to live in Wilmington, North Carolina, in 1831. All this suggests uncertainty and perhaps conflict about the children's upbringing; but it is clear that the Mordecais and Lanes made joint decisions about the orphans. See the memoir of Moses' daughter Ellen Mordecai, *Gleanings from Long Ago* (1933; rpt. Raleigh Historic Properties Commission and Mordecai Square Historical Society, 1974), esp. ch. 15, and Nuermberger, "Notes on the Mordecai Family," pp. 369–70.

118. Solomon Mordecai to Jacob Mordecai, July 15, 1824, box 1822–1824, folder July–Dec. 1824, Mordecai Papers, Duke. In 1817, Moses Mordecai had waited until the last minute to tell his father about his marriage plans. Benjamin Gratz also gave his sister Rebecca little warning about his wedding, which took place on Nov. 24, 1819. Although Rebecca had been acquainted for some months with Benjamin's fiancée Maria Gist, both personally and by mail, it seems that the wedding plans only became known in late October. See Rebecca Gratz to Maria Fenno Hoffman, Oct. 31, 1819, box 4, Gratz Papers.

119. See accounts in Berman, *Richmond's Jewry*, p. 100, and Ellen Mordecai to Caroline Mordecai Plunkett, Mar. 30 and Apr. 22, 1821, subser. 1.3, folder 19, Mordecai Papers, UNC.

120. On the controversy surrounding Jacob's mother and on Jacob's role in the 1838 marriage, see Berman, *Richmond's Jewry*, pp. 6, 100–01. There has been much scholarship in recent years on the democratic, often anticlerical, and frequently contentious religious life of the early republic. This temperament seems to have crossed religious boundaries and favored exceptions to general proscriptions of intermarriage. See esp. Hatch, *Democratization of American Christianity;* Carey, *People, Priests, and Prelates;* and Marcus, *United States Jewry,* 1: ch. 7.

121. Sarah Jane Picken Cohen describes her conversion to Judaism in Philadel-

phia in 1806 in order to marry Abraham Cohen, in *Henry Luria; or, the Little Jewish Convert: Being Contained in the Memoir of Mrs. S. J. Cohen, Relict of the Reverend Doctor A. H. Cohen, Late Rabbi of the Synagogue in Richmond, Va.* (New York: John F. Trow, 1860), pp. 56–64.

122. Rachel described Caroline's depression prior to her baptism, an event not named explicitly but possible to infer: "Her friends [in Warrenton] perceived her melancholy & attributing it to her wavering state of mind on religious subjects, used every argument to induce her to employ the means which had brought comfort to themselves." Now Rachel feared that "the weight of a father's anger is more than she [Caroline] can bear." See Rachel to Ellen Mordecai, Apr. 14, 1834, box 1833–1855, folder 1833–1836, Mordecai Papers, Duke. On Solomon's baptism, see Berman, *Richmond's Jewry,* p. 119.

123. Ellen Mordecai to Ellen Mordecai (Moses' daughter), Mar. 7, 1859, subser. 1.6, folder 86, Mordecai Papers, UNC. The children were Elizabeth Hasted Broun and Waller Mordecai Broun, the daughter and son of Solomon's daughter Ellen (b. 1830). On Solomon's children, see Nuermberger, "Notes on the Mordecai Family," p. 369.

124. Ellen Mordecai to Ellen Mordecai, Mar. 7, 1859, subser. 1.6, folder 86, Mordecai Papers, UNC. Suny was probably Solomon's daughter Susan (b. 1837).

125. Solomon Mordecai to Ellen Mordecai, Sept. 24, 1820, subser. 1.3, folder 18, Mordecai Papers, UNC. On Jewish self-hatred, see Sander L. Gilman, *Jewish Self-Hatred: Anti-Semitism and the Hidden Language of the Jews* (Baltimore: Johns Hopkins University Press, 1986).

126. Rachel Mordecai Lazarus to Ellen Mordecai, Apr. 14, 1834, box 1833–1855, folder 1833–1836, Mordecai Papers, Duke. Caroline wrote to her sister Ellen that she moved to Tennessee because she believed "you would be best pleased that I should be at a distance from you" (July 5, 1835, box 1833–1855, folder 1833–1836, Mordecai Papers, Duke). Ellen and Rachel tried to help Caroline, however, financially and emotionally. She spent most of her life after 1836 in Mobile (MacDonald, ed., *Education of the Heart,* p. 371).

127. Ellen Mordecai to Ellen Mordecai, Mar. 7, 1859, subser. 1.6, folder 86, Mordecai Papers, UNC.

128. Ellen Mordecai to Ellen Mordecai, Feb. 6, 1859, subser. 1.6, folder 86, Mordecai Papers, UNC.

129. *Richmond in By-Gone Days, Being Some Reminiscences of An Old Citizen* (Richmond: George M. West, 1856), p. 122.

130. For example, Samuel delivered a eulogy for victims of a local fire in 1811 at Beth Shalome; see Berman, *Richmond's Jewry,* p. 93. An Episcopal minister conducted his funeral; see Alexander Wilbourne Weddell, "Samuel Mordecai: Chronicler of Richmond, 1786–1865," *The Virginia Magazine of History and Biography* 53 (1945): 279.

131. Berman, *Richmond's Jewry,* p. 166.
132. "Foreword" to Caroline Myers Cohen, *Records of the Myers, Hays, and Mordecai Families from 1707 to 1913* (Washington, D.C.: privately printed, n.d.), quoted in Berman, *Richmond's Jewry,* pp. 119–120.
133. Bradley, *Lea,* p. 20.
134. The quote from the editors of *Lippincott's* to Lea appears in Bradley, *Lea,* p. 173. Bradley described Catholic criticisms of Lea's scholarship as "voluminous," p. 260.
135. "The Religious Reform Movement in Italy," *North American Review* 107 (1868): 54.
136. "Infallible church" appears in "Religious Reform Movement," p. 72. The remaining phrases appear in his review of *The Roman Church and Free Thought: A Controversy between Archbishop Purcell of Cincinnati and Thomas Vickers, Minister of the First Congregational Church of the Same City, North American Review* 106 (1868): 724–25. For similar views, see also his "Temporal Power of the Church," *North American Review* 92 (1861): 415–65.
137. *Address to Bishop Conwell,* p. 4.
138. These and other measures to strengthen papal authority, undertaken in large part in reaction to challenges to the Catholic Church during the prolonged "age of revolution," did not proceed without internal conflict. For a good account of the controversy surrounding the decree of papal infallibility, see Philip Hughes, *The Church in Crisis: A History of the General Councils, 325–1870* (Garden City, N.Y.: Hanover House, 1971), ch. 20. Indications of American Catholic reactions to these developments appear in Gerald P. Fogarty, *The Vatican and the American Hierarchy: From 1870 to 1965* (Wilmington, Del.: Michael Glazier, 1985), esp. pp. 1–9.
139. Bradley, *Lea,* ch. 5. On his marriage to his cousin and his partnership with another cousin, Christian Febiger, beginning in 1880, see ibid., p. 79, 52. His older brother, Mathew Carey Lea, married the sister of Henry's wife, ibid., p. 79. Lea's correspondence with the Furness family is found in folders marked "William Henry Furness" and "Horace Henry Furness," Correspondence Box, Henry Lea Papers. Despite Lea's Unitarian loyalties, the weddings of his two sons (the only two of his four children to marry) were held in Episcopal churches: Charles's at St. Mary's in Burlington, N.J., in 1895, and Arthur's at St. Paul's in Philadelphia in 1897. See, respectively, wedding notices in the *Philadelphia Inquirer,* Dec. 4, 1895, p. 11, and Mar. 3, 1897, p. 3. Charles was a widower, and his first wedding had been held in St. James Church, Philadelphia, probably also Episcopal (*Inquirer,* Oct. 29, 1880).
140. Henry Carey Baird to Henry Charles Lea, Apr. 30, 1901, June 17, 1907, Correspondence Box, folder titled "Henry Carey Baird," Henry Lea Papers.
141. Hamilton, *Blaine,* p. 119. Blaine met Harriet Stanwood when they were both teaching in Kentucky. Stanwood was a descendant of Puritan fore-

bears who arrived in Goucester, Mass., in 1654. See Muzzey, *Blaine,* pp. 20–21.

142. Blaine to Maria Gillespie Blaine, Dec. 19, 1857, quoted in Hamilton, *Blaine,* p. 124.

143. Hamilton, *Blaine,* p. 119.

144. This information appears in Harriet Blaine to Margaret Blaine, July 3, 1881, in *Letters of Mrs. James G. Blaine,* ed. Harriet S. Blaine Beale (New York: Duffield, 1908), 1: 210. On Alice's schooling, see James Blaine to Walker Blaine, Apr. 27, 1869, quoted in Hamilton, *Blaine,* p. 238; and Father Murphy's gift, Harriet Blaine to Margaret Blaine, Feb. 8, 1883, in *Letters of Mrs. Blaine,* ed. Beale, 2: 86.

145. Harriet Blaine to Margaret Blaine, Jan. 1, 1883, in *Letters of Mrs. Blaine,* ed. Beale, 2: 73. Alice may have met Coppinger when she visited Fort Leavenworth, Kansas, in March, 1882; she lived at the fort immediately after her marriage. See Harriet Blaine to Margaret Blaine, Mar. 1, 1882, in ibid., 1: 315.

146. Margaret Blaine to Harriet Blaine, Feb. 11, 1883, reel 4, containers 5–6, folder "Family Correspondence, Jan.-Mar. 1883," James G. Blaine Papers, LC.

147. Harriet Blaine described the wedding ceremony to Margaret Blaine, Feb. 8, 1883, in *Letters of Mrs. Blaine,* ed. Beale, 2: 85. She spoke of Coppinger in approving terms in an undated letter, ibid., 2: 79.

148. Margaret Blaine to James G. Blaine, [Jan. 28–Feb. 5,1883], reel 4, containers 5–6, folder "Family Correspondence Jan.–Mar. 1883," Blaine Papers.

149. Margaret Blaine to Harriet Blaine, Jan. 28, 1883, reel 4, containers 5–6, folder "Family Correspondence, Jan.–Mar. 1883," Blaine Papers. She commented on her uniform in a letter to Harriet, Nov. 22, 1882, reel 3, container 4–5, folder "Family Correspondence," and on being observed, to Harriet, Dec. 3, 1882, reel 3, container 4–5, folder "Family Correspondence Dec. 1882," Blaine Papers.

150. Oct. 28, 1882, Diary 1881–1882, reel 1, containers 1–2, section headed "Margaret Blaine Damrosch Diaries, 1881–1882," Blaine Papers. The entry was labelled "Augusta"; but since she wrote home from Paris on Nov. 1, the notation was probably incorrect. When she decided to attend the convent school, Mrs. Morton, the person in Paris who came later to take her away at her father's command, expressed fear that Margaret might convert. Margaret wrote to her mother on Nov. 1, 1882: Mrs. Morton "seems to think there might be great danger of my becoming a Catholic, and that she certainly would take no responsibility on that score. I had seen so little possibility of that, that I had not even thought of your making objection for that reason" (reel 3, containers 4–5, folder "Family Correspondence," Blaine Papers). After she was taken away from the convent, she told her father that she wished to return: "I am anxious to go back to the con-

vent. I frankly had no idea how much I liked it until I was so 'preemptorily' taken away" ([1883], reel 4, containers 5–6, folder "Family Correspondence, Jan.–Mar. 1883," Blaine Papers).

151. Oct. 24, [18]88, reel 1, containers 1–2, section "Diaries 1881–1882." The entry was dated by a different hand than Margaret's and followed entries for 1882. Even if what Margaret labeled "Dorothea's Creed" did belong to a later year, the quote still gave evidence of a commonplace ennui among educated and especially religious women who had little chance for a vocation except marriage. Jane Addams described this kind of identity crisis in young, educated women, in "The Subjective Necessity of Social Settlements" (1892), excerpted in Charles Capper and David Hollinger, eds., *The American Intellectual Tradition*, 2d ed. (New York: Oxford University Press, 1993), 2: 160–64.

152. Margaret Blaine to James G. Blaine, Feb. 5, 1883, reel 4, containers 5–6, folder "Family Correspondence, Jan.–Mar. 1883," Blaine Papers.

153. Harriet Blaine to Margaret Blaine, Jan. 28, 1883, in *Letters of Mrs. Blaine*, ed. Beale, p. 80.

154. Margaret Blaine to James G. Blaine, [1883], reel 4, containers 5–6, folder "Family Correspondence Jan.–Mar. 1883," Blaine Papers.

155. On the funeral and Margaret's marriage, see Muzzey, *Blaine*, pp. 490, 461.

156. Harriet Blaine to Walker Blaine, Mar. 18, 1887, in *Letters of Mrs. Blaine*, ed. Beale, p. 148. Mother Angela felt warmly enough about her cousin James to send a letter of encouragement to "my dearest cousin" from her convent at Notre Dame, Indiana, during the presidential campaign of 1884. See Sept. 1, [18]84, reel 4, containers 5–6, folder "Family Correspondence, 1884 and 1886," Blaine Papers. The common grandparents of Mother Angela and Blaine were Neal Gillespie, Jr., and his wife Tamar Purcell. Sherman's thoughts about the presidential nomination appear in a letter to Blaine cited in Muzzey, *Blaine*, pp. 274–75.

157. Letter to Anthony Gerard Van Schaick (Ellen's great-grandson), June 29, 1912, in *Gleanings of Long Ago*, pp. 105–06.

158. Aunts Laura, Eliza, and Emma were mentioned in ibid., pp. 46, 48. One reason they did not become "second mothers" to Ellen is that they were not too much older than she was. Ellen was born in 1820; Eliza was born in 1809, Emma in 1812, and Laura in 1818. Ellen mentioned the two-year visit to Spring Farm in ibid., p. 43.

159. Ibid., p. 47.

160. Ibid., p. 48.

161. On her marriage, see Nuermberger, "Notes on the Mordecai Family," pp. 366, 369.

162. *Some Modern Teachings: A Layman's Protest, Address Delivered at the St. James Protestant Episcopal Church, Richmond, Va., May 13, 1923*, 2d ed. (n.p.: "printed by request," n.d.), p. 4.

163. Ibid., pp. 3, 4. John Mordecai helped Ruth Nuermberger with early schol-arship in the 1940s on the Mordecai family. See her "Some Notes on the Mordecai Family," p. 364, n.1.
164. Ibid., pp. 13, 3.
165. Jacob Mordecai, "Remarks on Harby's Discourse," p. 3.

2. Conversations about Interfaith Marriage

1. *Arthur Mervyn; or, Memoirs of the Year 1793* (Philadelphia: David McKay, 1887), 1: 20. The two volumes are paginated separately. The novel's plot is complex, and although Brown told the reader that Welbeck gets a woman pregnant (1: 88–89), Clemenza is not identified specifically. This, however, is the logical inference.
2. Ibid., 2: 179, 197, 216.
3. Ibid., 2: 230. Stevens, Arthur's friend, describes Ascha as bewitching (2: 218) and had compared her to a hag (see n. 2). Brown presented Ascha as Jewish, although she had converted to Anglicanism in order to marry her first husband. Arthur remarks that "those eyes of yours have told me a se-cret'"; "'they said that you were—*a Jew.*' At this sound, her features were instantly veiled with the deepest sorrow and confusion." Collecting herself, she confesses: "'Your surmise was just and natural, and could not always have escaped you'" (2: 198). Donald A. Ringe explains that Brown initially planned to have Mervyn marry Eliza, in *Charles Brockden Brown,* rev. ed. (Boston: Twayne Publishers, 1991), p. 56; but Arthur tells Ascha that he would not marry Eliza because she lacks "'maturity of intelligence'" (2: 187). See also Louise A. Mayo, *The Ambivalent Image: Nineteenth-Cen-tury America's Perception of the Jew* (Rutherford: Fairleigh Dickinson University Press, 1988), p. 48, and for broader discussions of gender and ethnicity in fiction, Mary V. Dearborn, *Pocahontas's Daughters: Gender and Ethnicity in American Culture* (New York: Oxford University Press, 1986), and Riv-Ellen Prell, *Fighting to Become Americans: Jews, Gender, and the Anxiety of Assimilation* (Boston: Beacon Press, 1999).
4. *Arthur Mervyn*, 2: 179.
5. Studies that are helpful in identifying the way nineteenth-century religious communities perceived one another include Mayo, *Ambivalent Image;* Egal Feldman, *Dual Destinies: The Jewish Encounter with Protestant America* (Urbana: University of Illinois Press, 1990), esp. chs. 7–12; and Jenny Franchot, *Roads to Rome: The Antebellum Protestant Encounter with Ca-tholicism* (Berkeley: University of California Press, 1994).
6. The rise of religious pluralism between the 1840s and the turn of the cen-tury may be traced in Sydney E. Ahlstrom, *A Religious History of the Amer-ican People* (New Haven: Yale University Press, 1972), esp. pts. 5 and 7; Jay P. Dolan, *The American Catholic Experience: A History from Colonial Times to the Present* (Notre Dame: University of Notre Dame Press, 1992),

chs. 5–12; Jacob Rader Marcus, *United States Jewry, 1776–1985* (Detroit: Wayne State University Press, 1989–1993), vols. 2–3; and Hasia R. Diner, *A Time of Gathering: The Second Migration, 1820–1880* (Baltimore: Johns Hopkins University Press, 1992). These works also explain ethnic differences and tensions within religious communities. For this period, I assume these ethnicities were culturally dominant: Irish and, increasingly, German Catholics; German-born Jews; and Protestants of Anglo-Saxon ancestry.

7. Editor's [Isaac Mayer Wise's] commentary on Rev. Dr. [Solomon] Sonneschien, "Should a Rabbi Perform the Ceremonies at the Intermarriage between Jew and Gentile?," *Israelite* 52 (May 7, 1880): 4. The earlier Jewish estimates appeared in Simeon Abrahams, "Intermarrying with Gentiles," *Occident* 2 (Mar. 1845): 586, and [Isaac Leeser], "Intermarriage," *Occident* 23 (Mar. 1866): 549.

8. Joseph Prosetus Machebeuef, *Mixed Marriages* (New York: Vatican Library, 1889), pp. 3, 1, 6, box 1, folder 1, item 39, PDRP (Drop File, Printed), Notre Dame.

9. Stanislaus Woywod, "Should Dispensations for Mixed Marriages Be Absolutely Abolished?" *The Homiletic and Pastoral Review* 28 (1928): 703.

10. Anon., "How to Discourage Runaway Marriages," *Ladies' Home Journal* 1 (July 1884): 2, and anon., "Offhand Marriages," *Ladies' Home Journal* 6 (July 1889): 10. The phrase "unsuitable matches" appeared in "Runaway Marriages," p. 2. Similar warnings about inappropriate marriages were found in Rev. William M. Baker, "Married on the Rebound," *Independent* 32 (Apr. 1, 1880): 27, and Baker, "Wicked Weddings," *Independent* 32 (Sept. 2, 1880): 26. Each issue of both of these magazines was paginated separately.

11. The absence of reliable institutional records on intermarried couples and local variations in rates of mixed marriage have left scholars, no less than clergy, with widely varying estimates of their frequency. Jacob Rader Marcus speculates that before 1840, between ten and fifty percent of American Jews living in cities (where most Jews resided) intermarried; but in the large community of Eastern European immigrants in New York City at the turn of the twentieth century (1895–1904), he estimates that the rate was less than one percent (*United States Jewry*, 1: 608, 3: 400). In some Catholic neighborhoods, Jay Dolan is probably correct to say that intermarriage was "not common during the nineteenth century" (*American Catholic Experience*, p. 228). Leslie Tentler shows, in contrast, that nearly one-third of the families in several Detroit parishes around 1880 involved mixed couples, in *Seasons of Grace: A History of the Catholic Archdiocese of Detroit* (Detroit: Wayne State University Press, 1990), p. 100. Simple demographics, such as the size of the marriage pool, accounts for some of the variety; differing attitudes equally shaped the statistical outcome. In light of so much variation, I believe guesses about overall rates of interfaith marriage for the three religious communities would be misleading.

12. Ambrose Marechal, ms. fragment on families (untitled, undated, and un-paginated), box 4, folder 21, CABA (Diocese of Baltimore Collection), No-tre Dame.

13. [John Purcell], *The Pastoral of the Most Rev. Archbishop of Cincinnati, on Marriage, and Family Duties in General* (Cincinnati: John P. Walsh, 1853), p. 8, box 1, folder 1, item 38, PDRP, Notre Dame.

14. Ibid., pp. 8, 9.

15. Ibid., p. 7.

16. *Acta et Decreta*, Third Plenary Council (1884), quoted in Peter Guilday, *A History of the Councils of Baltimore, 1791–1884* (1932; rpt. New York: Arno Press and the New York *Times*, 1969), p. 238. The Catholic hierarchy had stressed the importance of parochial schooling for many decades, but the year 1884 was the turning point for the implementation of a national system of Catholic schools.

17. *Pastoral Letter of the Right Reverend Michael Joseph O'Farrell, Bishop of Trenton, on Christian Marriage, 1882* (New York: Benziger Brothers, 1883), pp. 5, 5–6, box 2, folder 107, PCLW (Clerical Writings, Printed), Notre Dame.

18. Ibid., p. 11. Section 3 on "Mixed Marriages" took up pages 12–17 of a nineteen-page text.

19. *Pastoral of the Archbishop of Cincinnati*, p. 11.

20. Machebeuf, *Mixed Marriages*, pp. 6, 7.

21. Ibid., pp. 11, 12.

22. Machebeuf, for example, used sexual language in 1889 to describe inter-marriage as "so pregnant to the ruin of souls," posing an "extreme peril of perversion as well to the Christian party as to the children," ibid., pp. 1, 5–6. In canon law, a number of the impediments to marriage, such as incest, concerned sexual taboos. It was a small step to apply the language of illicit sexuality to conditions fostering spiritual corruption. For a summary of im-pediments and grounds for dispensations, see P. J. Lydon, *Ready Answers in Canon Law: A Practical Summary of the Code for the Parish Clergy*, rev. ed. (New York: Benziger Brothers, 1948), pp. 374–402.

23. The sixteen canonical reasons for dispensations, issued May 9, 1877, may be found in Carlos Blanchard, *The Canonical Causes for Matrimonial Dis-pensations*, Regional Meeting, Canon Law Society of America, Denver, Colorado, Sept. 25–26, 1951 (n.p., n.d.), pp. 2–5. The 1877 instruction was the most important in a series of nineteenth-century Vatican pronounce-ments on mixed marriage. Others included papal and Propaganda Office instructions, respectively, in 1858 and 1868 (O'Farrell, *Pastoral Letter*, pp. 13–14) and a papal encyclical in 1888 (Machebeuf, *Mixed Marriages*, p. 1). The 1917 Code of Canon Law systematized these policies, ratifying more than changing nineteenth-century practices. Canons 1060–1063 for-bade intermarriage, unless there was "danger of perversion" to the Catholic and the couple promised to raise the children in the church. The Catholic

"must work prudently for the conversion of the non-Catholic." See Paul H. Besanceney, *Interfaith Marriages: Who and Why* (New Haven: College and University Publishers, 1970), pp. 117–18.

24. O'Farrell, *Pastoral Letter,* pp. 13–14.

25. Dispensation forms, for example, for the Diocese of Vincennes, Ind., dated Aug. 21, 187[4?] and Feb. 11, 1888, may be found in box 2, folder 13, CAUD (Ernest Audran Papers), Notre Dame. Even earlier, the handwritten parish records of Notre Dame du Lac church, Notre Dame, Ind., include a separate section for dispensations beginning in 1844, which suggests that the practice was already accepted. See "Liber Dispensationum ab Matrimonium Spectantium, 1844–57, Notre Dame du Lac Ecclesiae," Baptismal, Burial, Marriage, and Dispensation Records, Sacred Heart Church, microfilm roll 1, MSHC, Notre Dame.

26. *Laws Concerning the Solemnization, Record and Returns of Marriages, in Massachusetts: Designed for Clergymen and Other Persons Authorized by Law to Solemnize Marriages* (Boston: Wright and Potter, State Printers, 1873), pp. 4, 7, PGEN (General Pamphlets Collection, Printed), no. 2943, Notre Dame.

27. Purcell, *Pastoral of the Archbishop of Cincinnati,* p. 2. Purcell drew on standard arguments of Christian triumphalism, as explained for the early centuries of the Common Era by Edward H. Flannery, *The Anguish of the Jews: Twenty-Three Centuries of Antisemitism,* rev. ed. (New York: Paulist Press, 1985), esp. pp. 38–42, and in a modern context by Leon Klenicki, "Jacques Maritain's Vision of Judaism and Anti-Semitism," in Robert Royal, ed., *Jacques Maritain and the Jews* (Notre Dame: American Maritain Association, 1994), pp. 72–88.

28. Purcell, *Pastoral of the Archbishop of Cincinnati,* p. 2.

29. O'Farrell, *Pastoral Letter,* p. 19.

30. Purcell, *Pastoral of the Archbishop of Cincinnati,* p. 11.

31. *The Correct Thing for Catholics,* 12th ed. (New York: Benziger Brothers, 1891), pp. 49, 46.

32. Ibid., pp. 39, 40. The phrase "grave reasons" appeared on p. 40, discussion of excommunication on p. 174. Similar advice books include Alban Stolz, *Mixed Marriage: The Forbidden Fruit for Catholics,* trans. Msgr. H. Cluever, 4th ed. (New York: Fr. Pustet, 1883), and Francis X. Lasance, *The Catholic Girl's Guide: Counsels and Devotions for Girls in the Ordinary Walks of Life and in Particular for the Children of Mary* (New York: Benziger Brothers, 1906), esp. chs. 71–73.

33. O'Farrell, *Pastoral Letter,* p. 12.

34. *Pastoral Letter of the Rt. Rev. Henry Joseph Richter, Bishop of Grand Rapids, on Mixed Marriages,* rev. and rpt. (n.p., 1904–1916), p. 10, box 3, folder 20, PCLW, Notre Dame.

35. Selinger, *Catechism on Pledges,* pp. 16, 27.

36. "Intermarrying with Gentiles," pp. 586, 588, 587–88. 588. Leeser ex-

plained that Abrahams' piece was a response to an earlier article, unsigned but presumably by Leeser, "The Dangers of Our Position," *Occident* 2 (Jan. 1845): 458–66. On the *Occident*, see Lance J. Sussman, *Isaac Leeser and the Making of American Judaism* (Detroit: Wayne State University Press, 1995), pp. 138–43. Jacob Marcus identifies Abrahams as a "Dr." and lecturer to the Hebrew Literary and Religious Association of Congregation Shearith Israel in New York, *United States Jewry*, 1: 372.

37. Untitled article on Congregation Anshe Mayriv, Chicago, *The Asmonean, A Family Journal of Commerce, Politics, Religion, and Literature, Devoted to the Interests of the American Israelites* 12 (May 4, 1855): 20. For biographical information on Lyon and his position in the New York Jewish community, see anon., "Death of Mr. Robert Lyon" and "Funeral of Robert Lyon, Esq.," *Asmonean* 17 (Mar. 12 and 19, 1858): 172, 180.

38. [Robert Lyon], "The Cemeteries," *Asmonean* 14 (June 6, 1856): 60.

39. "Intermarrying with Gentiles," p. 586.

40. "Who is a Jew?," *Israelite* 36 (June 19, 1890): 5. Felsenthal's thoughts stand in revealing contrast to a layman's address to the Hebrew Literary Association of New Orleans, Lewis Florance, Jr., "What Constitutes a Jew?," *Occident* 13 (Jan. 1856): 485–89. To Florance, a Jew was simply a person who was observant: "There are too many among us who are Jews nominally speaking, as they have entered into the covenant; but they have not enough of Jewish practice to merit the appellation of Jew" (p. 489). On classic methods of analyzing the Talmud, see Adin Steinsaltz, *The Essential Talmud*, trans. Chaya Galai (New York: Basic Books, 1976), esp. chs. 27–28, 31, and Louis Jacobs, *The Talmudic Argument: A Study in Talmudic Reasoning and Methodology* (Cambridge, Eng.: Cambridge University Press, 1984), esp. ch. 1.

41. "Rabbi [Isaac] Moses," Proceedings of the Convention held in New York City, Nov. 9–16, 1909, Julian Morgenstern, David Lefkowitz, and David Philipson, eds., *CCAR Yearbook, 1909* (CCAR, 1910), 19: 329.

42. Moses' escape was described in Rev. Dr. [Solomon] Sonneschien, "Should a Rabbi Perform the Ceremonies at the Intermarriage between Jew and Gentile?," p. 4. An account of the marriage, taken from the Milwaukee *Sentinel*, appeared as "A Clandestine Marriage," *Israelite* 52 (Mar. 19, 1880): 4. The editor censored Moses' action.

43. On these developments, see Alan Silverstein, *Alternatives to Assimilation: The Response of Reform Judaism to American Culture, 1840–1930* (Hanover, N.H.: University Press of New England, 1994), ch. 4.

44. Dr. Mayer, letter to the editor, June 15, *Israelite* 8 (June 20, 1862): 405.

45. Untitled editorial, *Israelite* 52 (Apr. 2, 1880): 4. A similar judgment, set in italics, appeared the previous year: "Once more, be it said, we will answer no more letters on this topic: *The child of a Jewish mother, or certainly of a Jewish father, if it be begotten of a lawful marriage, is considered a Jewish child by the rabbis of the Talmud, and must be treated as such in all religious or ceremonial questions by all who conform to the laws of the ancient*

rabbis" (Israelite 33 [Aug. 1, 1879]: 4). A change in the method of numbering volumes accounts for the discontinuous series.

46. Untitled editorial, *Israelite* 45 (Apr. 13, 1899): 4.

47. [Isaac Mayer Wise], "A Presbyterian Lady Embraces the Jewish Faith," *Israelite* 6 (Jan. 6, 1860): 210.

48. [Isaac Leeser], "Interesting Jewish Ceremony: Reception of a Christian Female Proselyte," *Occident* 17 (Jan. 26, 1860): 262.

49. "Presbyterian Lady," p. 210. A similarly untraditional conversion occurred at Shearith Israel, San Francisco, reported in an untitled article, copied from the *Alta California,* in the *Israelite* 6 (Oct. 28, 1859): 134.

50. "Some Remarks on Milah," *Israelite* 37 (Oct. 2, 1890): 4. Henry Berkowitz, one of the rabbis who accepted an uncircumcised convert, had written to the *Israelite* on July 23 in defense of waiving circumcision, in "An Important Inquiry to Learned Rabbis," *Israelite* 37 (July 31, 1890): 4.

51. Editorial comment on Abrahams, "Intermarrying with Gentiles," p. 589.

52. "Shall We Seek Converts?," *Israelite* 36 (Nov. 15, 1889): 4. Reform Jews, who believed Judaism had an ethical message for gentiles, were more favorable to proselytism than their conservative contemporaries. Despite his reservations, Philipson approved the distribution of informational tracts. But Christian proselytizing of Jews was never far from mind. See, e.g., anon., "Conversion of the Jews," *Israelite* 7 (July 13, 1860): 12. In fact, Philipson's blanket denial of Jewish interest in conversion obscures Jewish openness to proselytes during the rabbinic period of the first centuries of the Common Era; see Joseph R. Rosenbloom, *Conversion to Judaism: From the Biblical Period to the Present* (Cincinnati: Hebrew Union College Press, 1978), pt. 2.

53. Sonneschien, "May the Rabbi Perform the Ceremonies at the Intermarriage between Jew and Gentile?," p. 4.

54. Ibid., p. 4.

55. Quotations from the proposed and final resolutions appear in Michael Cook, "The Debates of the Central Conference of American Rabbis on the Problems of Mixed Marriage: 1907–1968," typescript, 1969, pp. 9, 10, AJA.

56. By 1909, the *Israelite* used equivocal language to estimate that "not a few" rabbis performed intermarriages, "Rabbis Officiating at Intermarriages," 56 (Sept. 30, 1909): 4. But before the turn of the century, the majority opinion seemed to follow Wise's assertion that rabbis should not marry mixed couples, in "Jew and Gentile: Why They Should Not Intermarry," Friday evening lecture, Mar. 7, 1879, *Israelite* 32 (Mar. 14, 1879): 4.

57. On *responsa* literature, see Solomon B. Freehof, *The Responsa Literature* (Philadelphia: Jewish Publication Society of America, 1955), and Edward Fram, "Responsa," in R. J. Zwi Werblowsky and Geoffrey Wigoder, eds., *The Oxford Dictionary of the Jewish Religion* (New York: Oxford University Press, 1997), pp. 581–83.

58. Abrahams, "Intermarrying with Gentiles," p. 586.

59. On the nineteenth-century disputes, see M[oses]. Mielziner, *The Jewish Law of Marriage and Divorce in Ancient and Modern Times, and Its Relation to the Law of the State*, 2d rev. ed. (New York: Bloch, 1901), pp. 47–49, and Mendel Silber, "Intermarriage," in Julian Morgenstern, David Lefkowitz, and David Philipson, eds., *CCAR Yearbook, 1908* (CCAR, 1909), 18: 271–73. On methods of resolution in the Talmud, see Steinsaltz, *Essential Talmud*, esp. ch. 31.

60. Goldwin Smith's letter to the *Nation*, dated Feb. 25, was reprinted in "Prof. Goldwin Smith and the Jewish Question," *Israelite* 27 (Mar. 18, 1881): 300. All the quotations appear on p. 300. Smith repeated this argument in "New Light on the Jewish Question," *North American Review* 153 (Aug. 1891): 129–42.

61. Editor's comment on Smith's letter, "Goldwin Smith and the Jewish Question," p. 300.

62. "Jew and Gentile," p. 4.

63. I infer local autonomy not only from Judaism's basic commitment to freedom of thought, but from the variety of local situations described in Jewish periodicals. Questions about the conduct of weddings, conversions, and circumcisions indicate that these events were not governed by clear rules in Reform circles during the nineteenth century.

64. Anon., "The Anti-Shemitic Crusade in America," *Independent* 32 (June 3, 1880): 14. Each issue of the *Independent* was paginated separately. All the articles cited are anonymous unless otherwise noted.

65. Ibid., p. 14. This incident was a variation on the infamous refusal of lodging to the banker Joseph Seligman at Saratoga, New York, in 1877 because he was Jewish. The case reported in the *Independent* was different, however, because the woman was not Jewish, but intermarried. Discrimination against her reveals the gray area inhabited by interfaith families who wished to be accepted in Christian society. On this kind of discrimination, see Marcus, *United States Jewry*, 3: 156–59.

66. In addition to the sources cited below, I surveyed the Methodist *Ladies Repository* (1841–1876) and the Baptist *Christian Union* (1870–1893), which later become the *Outlook* (1893–1928). Secondary sources on mainstream Protestant denominations rarely address the subject of mixed marriage, probably reflecting the perspectives of the churches themselves. Strict sects, particularly in their early years when they rigorously protected purity, did try to enforce endogamy. See Christine Heyrman, *Southern Cross: The Beginnings of the Bible Belt* (Chapel Hill: University of North Carolina Press, 1997), pp. 139–42, and Carl F. Bowman, *Brethren Society: The Cultural Transformation of a "Peculiar People"* (Baltimore: Johns Hopkins University Press, 1995), pp. 66–71.

67. The idea that intermarriage was the route to harmony also appeared in the comments of prominent Protestants interviewed for "Prejudice Against the Jew: Its Nature, Causes and Remedies. A Consensus of Opinions by Non-

Jews," *American Hebrew,* Apr. 4, 1890, reprinted as Philip Cowen, ed., *Prejudice Against the Jew* (New York: Philip Cowen, 1928), pp. 87–88, 105, 142.

68. "The Universal Renaissance," *Independent* 32 (Nov. 4, 1880): 16. The title of the periodical will not be repeated in the notes when it is clear from the text. On missions to the Jews, see, e.g., "Conversion Amongst the Jews," 12 (Feb. 23, 1860): 3, and "Jewish Mission Notes," 42 (Mar. 13, 1890): 18. The *Independent* was established by Leonard Bacon and other Congregational ministers; Henry Ward Beecher edited it briefly in the 1860s. During the antebellum decades, it supported antislavery.

69. Hale, "Insincerity in the Pulpit," 32 (Nov. 11, 1880): 1; Thwing, "The Passing of Religion?," 52 (Nov. 29, 1900): 2856–57.

70. "The Jews Banished from Morocco," 12 (Jan. 12, 1860): 1; "The Jews of Germany," 32 (Feb. 19, 1880): 14; "School and College," 32 (Aug. 12, 1880): 16; "School and College," 32 (Nov. 4, 1880): 10.

71. "Pope Leo XIII as a Reformer," 32 (Aug. 12, 1880): 16; "Rapid Increase of the Celtic Race," 12 (Mar. 1, 1860): 3; "Religious Notes," 42 (June 19, 1890): 15.

72. Deshon, "Catholic Evangelism Conducted by the Paulist Fathers," 42 (June 5, 1890): 2–4; Mendes, "The Judaic Sabbath," 42 (July 10, 1890): 10–11.

73. "The Modest Naturalized Citizen," 42 (July 3, 1890): 11.

74. "The Roman Catholic Schools and the Public Schools," 42 (Apr. 10, 1890): 2–3; R. Wheatly, "Talmud Torah Schools," 42 (Oct. 23, 1890): 2–3.

75. "Prejudice Against the Jews," 42 (Apr. 10, 1890): 11.

76. Ibid., p. 11.

77. Eben E. Rexford, "Talks about Flowers: Christmas Decorations," *Ladies' Home Journal* 6 (Dec. 1888): 14. Each issue was paginated separately. The name of the magazine will not be repeated in the notes when it is clear from the text. Articles were anonymous unless otherwise noted. On the goals of the magazine, see Salme Harju Steinberg, *Reformer in the Marketplace: Edward W. Bok and The Ladies' Home Journal* (Baton Rouge: Louisiana State University Press, 1979).

78. "How to Discourage Runaway Marriages," 1 (July 1884): 2; "Offhand Marriages," 6 (July 1889): 10; M. K. D., "How Girls Deceive their Parents," 1 (Nov. 1884): 3. Additional warnings appeared in Mrs. M. P. Handy, "Early Marriages: What Young Lovers Should Look at Before Going to the Altar," 1 (Oct. 1884): 2.

79. The classic analysis of Americans' fear of deceitful appearances is Karen Halttunen, *Confidence Men and Painted Women: A Study of Middle-Class Culture in America, 1830–1870* (New Haven: Yale University Press, 1982).

80. Zebulon Vance to Florence Martin, Mar. 3 [1880], PC 15.21, folder "Correspondence Mar. 1–15, 1880," Zebulon Baird Vance Papers, NC State Archives.

81. Ibid.

82. Among sources on Yulee, only the entry on "David Levy Yulee" by R. S. C., in Dumas Malone, ed., *Dictionary of American Biography* (New York: Scribner's, 1936), 20: 638, mentions his Presbyterian affiliation or the fact that the minister of the church conducted his funeral. This is not a reason to doubt the truth of the information, although his association with the church may have been more social than spiritual and the funeral at the request of his family. A letter to Yulee from his wife Nannie, dated Dec. 4, 1874, demonstrates that he had not been baptized by then, because she urges him to do so. I am grateful to Chris Monaco for a copy of this letter. Jewish sources downplay his Christian connections; see the anonymous entry on Yulee in Isaac Landman, ed., *The Universal Jewish Encyclopedia* (New York: Universal Jewish Encyclopedia, Inc., 1942), 10: 621, and Leon Huhner, "David L. Yulee, Florida's First Senator," *Publications of the American Jewish Historical Society*, no. 25 (1917): 1–29.

83. "The Scattered Nation," in Thomas B. Reed, ed., *Modern Eloquence* (Philadelphia: John D. Morris, 1900), 6: 1122, 1129.

84. Ibid., pp. 1115, 1118, 1132.

85. Glenn Tucker argues that "The Scattered Nation" grew out of Vance's interest in the Bible and his friendship with a Jewish immigrant from Poland, Samuel Wittkowsky, in *Zeb Vance: Champion of Personal Freedom* (Indianapolis: Bobbs-Merrill, 1965), p. 470. As a man of forty-eight, Vance had a conversion experience after his first wife's death in 1878 and joined a Presbyterian church. He may well have been reading the Bible with unusual attention during the years he developed the speech.

86. These were not the only works of fiction about interfaith marriage of the middle and late nineteenth century. My choice of pieces by Sadlier and Davis can be justified by each one's prestige in her religious community. Wolf was less well known, but she is a useful example because few Jewish women wrote on the controversial topic of mixed marriage. Secondary literature that discusses interfaith marriage in fiction includes Mayo, *Ambivalent Image*, Dearborn, *Pocahontas's Daughters,* and Diane Lichtenstein, *Writing Their Nations: The Tradition of Nineteenth-Century American Jewish Women Writers* (Bloomington: Indiana University Press, 1992).

87. *The Blakes and Flanagans: A Tale, Ilustrative of Irish Life in the United States* (New York: D. and J. Sadlier, 1855), p. vi. Paul R. Messbarger explains that the Catholic clergy was suspicious of fiction, in part because it was an American form of writing that might be expected to convey Protestant messages, in *Fiction with a Parochial Purpose: Social Uses of American Catholic Literature, 1884–1900* (Boston: Boston University Press, 1971), p. 27. Gradually, though, the American church began to recruit fiction as a didactic tool (p. 20). On early American Catholic literature, see also Anne C. Rose, *Voices of the Marketplace: American Thought and Culture, 1830–1860* (New York: Twayne Publishers, 1995), pp. 141–45.

88. For biographical information, see *A Round Table of Representative American Catholic Novelists, at Which Is Served a Feast of Excellent Stories by Eleanor C. Donnelly and Ten Others* (New York: Benziger Brothers, 1896), pp. 239–40, and Thomas N. Brown, "Mary Anne Sadlier," in Edward T. James, Janet Wilson James, and Paul S. Boyer, eds., *Notable American Women* (Cambridge, Mass.: Harvard University Press, 1971), 3: 219–20. Sadlier lived in Montreal from 1846 to 1860, the years of some of her most popular writing about Irish life in the United States. Her novels first appeared serially in Canadian and American Catholic periodicals.

89. *Blakes and Flanagans,* pp. 378, 255, 232, 280. The speaker is identified either in my text or in the notes in cases where this information might make a difference in how the phrase is understood.

90. Ibid., p. 202.

91. Ibid., p. 378.

92. The struggle between ambition and loyalty to Catholicism was also the subject of Sadlier's bestselling novel, *Willy Burke; or, The Irish Orphan in America* (Boston: Patrick Donahoe, [1850]).

93. *Blakes and Flanagans,* p. 286.

94. Ibid., pp. 383, 384.

95. Ibid., p. 384, 387. Sadlier described the stepmother of Eliza's children as both a Unitarian and an "evangelical" (p. 389). Although she must have realized the difference, perhaps she wished to underscore the heresies of Protestantism.

96. Stolz, *Mixed Marriage,* p. 9. Stolz's other predictions appeared on pp. 26, 19, 6. Many of the prelates' pastoral letters blended fire-and-brimstone imagery with sentimental pictures of domestic unhappiness, so much that it is difficult to know how these rhetorical styles influenced one another. Bishop Joseph Machebeuef, for example, concluded his *Mixed Marriages* (1889) with a literary flourish: "And St. Augustine adds that they vow their bodies to each other whilst they rend the body of Christ, and become a scandal, a triumph to the devil and the ruin of souls" (p. 14).

97. The foregoing quotations may all be found in *Blakes and Flanagans,* p. 12.

98. Ibid., p. 11.

99. Ibid., p. 232. Chs. 5 and 12, respectively, describe St. Peter's School and the ordination of the Flanagans' sons.

100. For Dr. Powers's role, see ibid., pp. 204–06.

101. [Rosa Sonneschien], "Editor's Desk," *American Jewess* 1 (June 1895): 153. Exclusion of married women from membership remained the norm despite a resolution of the Central Conference of American Rabbis in 1892 to grant women "equality" in the synagogue (Marcus, *United States Jewry,* 3: 469). By the late 1880s, widows in some Reform congregations could retain their husbands' seats and membership rights; soon the unmarried adult daughters of members began to exercise similar privileges (Silverstein, *Alternative to Assimilation,* p. 91). These arrangements should be seen in light

of the fact that Jewish women attended services far more frequently than men after midcentury, a trend consistent with other religious groups of the era. See Karla Goldman, *Beyond the Synagogue Gallery: Finding a Place for Women in American Judaism* (Cambridge, Mass.: Harvard University Press, 2000).

102. "Intermarriage," p. 548.

103. Editorial comment on Abrahams, "Intermarrying with Gentiles," p. 590.

104. *Other Things Being Equal* (Chicago: A. C. McClurg, 1892), pp. 152, 155.

105. Marcus, *United States Jewry*, 3: 469.

106. On Wolf, see Lichtenstein, *Writing Their Nations*, pp. 78–85. Lichtenstein explains that much nineteenth-century writing by Jewish women focused on the conservative image of the "mother in Israel," ch. 2. Eliot J. Baskin reaches a similar conclusion after studying the Jewish periodical for children, the *Sabbath Visitor;* see his "The Image of Women in the *Sabbath Visitor,*" typescript, 1983, Small Collections 763, AJA.

107. *Other Things Being Equal,* p. 181.

108. Ibid., p. 163.

109. Ibid., pp. 11, 181, 184. In light of Ruth's professed respect for Christian values, it is hard to know how to interpret the book's headnote from 1 Corinthians 13.13: "And now abideth faith, hope, love, these three; but the greatest of these is love." On the one hand, love is clearly the problem in the novel, which would force an ironic reading of the biblical verse, especially from a Jewish writer. But on the other, Wolf seemed genuinely attracted by the idea that love conquers all.

110. Ibid., p. 22. Similarly, Kemp unthinkingly observes that the "'Jewish appetite is known to dote on the fat of the land.'" Ruth replies, "'We always make the reservation that the fat be clean.'" The exchange ended: "'Miss Levice,' he exclaims contritely, 'I completely forgot—I hope I was not rude.' 'Why, certainly not,' she answered half merrily, half earnestly" (p. 54).

111. Ibid., pp. 176, 179.

112. Ibid., pp. 9, 10.

113. Ibid., p. 128. An observant Jew lights a *yahrzeit* candle on the yearly anniversary of a relative's death.

114. Ibid., pp. 104, 105.

115. For an excellent comparative discussion of Christian and Jewish women's benevolent work, see Goldman, *Beyond the Synagogue Gallery,* pp. 137–50. On Christian women's efforts, see Lori D. Ginzberg, *Women and the Work of Benevolence: Morality, Politics, and Class in the Nineteenth-Century United States* (New Haven: Yale University Press, 1990), and on the National Council of Jewish Women, Marcus, *United States Jewry,* 3: 471–74.

116. *Other Things Being Equal,* p. 258.

117. Ibid., p. 273.

118. *Heirs of Yesterday* (Chicago: A. C. McClurg, 1900), pp. 165, 283.

119. Ibid., pp. 238, 285. The phrase "what our religion has made us" is a statement by Jean's uncle Daniel Willard. This time Wolf chose a headnote by a Jewish writer, Israel Zangwill, in contrast to her selection for *Other Things Being Equal* (see n. 109): "For something larger had come into his life, a sense of a vaster universe without, and its spaciousness and strangeness filled his soul with a nameless trouble and a vague unrest. He was no longer a child of the Ghetto." This quotation expressed the key issue posed by the novel—the hazards of assimilation—and lacked the complicated undertone of the headnote to *Other Things*.

120. I have used the text of "How the Widow Crossed the Lines" in Kathleen Diffley, *Where My Heart Is Turning Ever: Civil War Stories and Constitutional Reform, 1861–1876* (Athens: University of Georgia Press, 1992), pp. 150–67. The quotation appears on p. 167. The story was published originally in *Lippincott's Monthly Magazine,* Dec. 1876.

121. "How the Widow Crossed the Lines," p. 158.

122. Ibid., p. 158. Although I use "West Virginia" to designate Davis's childhood residence and the setting of the story, it is good to remember that this area was part of Virginia until Virginia joined the Confederacy in 1861.

123. Ibid., pp. 154, 155.

124. Ibid., p. 154.

125. Ibid., p. 155.

126. On Davis's parents, upbringing, and her son's marriages, see Gerald Langford, *The Richard Harding Davis Years: A Biography of a Mother and Son* (New York: Holt, Rinehart and Winston, 1961), ch. 1, 17–18, and Sharon M. Harris, *Rebecca Harding Davis and American Realism* (Philadelphia: University of Pennsylvania Press, 1991), pp. 20–24. "Aunt Blaine" was Rebecca Wilson Blaine, the sister of Rebecca Harding Davis's mother, who married James Blaine of Washington, Pennsylvania. This means that Davis was related by marriage to the Presbyterian side of the Blaine family; Ephraim Blaine, a Presbyterian, perhaps the brother of James Blaine, and the father of James G. Blaine, had married Maria Gillespie, a Catholic (see Chapter 1, above).

127. "How the Widow Crossed the Lines," p. 154.

128. *Hope Leslie; or, Early Times in Massachusetts,* ed. Mary Kelley (New Brunswick: Rutgers University Press, 1987), p. 189. An Indian woman named Magawisca uses the words "she bows to the crucifix"; the other phrases are Hope's.

129. Ibid., p. 188.

130. *Lady Alice; or, The New Una,* 2 vols. (New York: D. Appleton, 1849). On Huntington, see R. J. P., "Jedediah Vincent Huntington," in Malone, ed., *DAB,* 9: 417–18. Jenny Franchot highlights the symbolic importance of the encounter of Protestantism and Catholicism to the Protestant imagination, in *Roads to Rome.* She argues that Protestants were both repelled by and at-

tracted to Catholicism as Protestantism's perceived opposite, a conclusion illustrated by the differing views of Catholicism in *Hope Leslie* and *Lady Alice.*

131. *Daniel Deronda,* ed. Graham Handley (Oxford, Eng.: Oxford University Press, 1984). Eliot was much influenced by Judaism, as William Baker explains, in *George Eliot and Judaism* (Salzburg: Institut für Englische Sprache und Literatur, Universität Salzburg, 1975). Even then, she did not have the romantic attraction between Daniel and Gwendolyn result in their marriage. After Daniel discovers and embraces his Jewish roots, he marries the story's Jewish heroine, Mirah Cohen. An interfaith marriage, portrayed in positive terms on the whole, does occur between Catherine Arrowpoint and the musician Klesmer. Contemporary European readers, as well as later literary critics, were perplexed by the blending of Jewish and gentile themes and characters, as explained by Shmuel Werses, "The Jewish Reception of *Daniel Deronda,*" in Alice Shalvi, ed., *Daniel Deronda: A Centenary Symposium* (Jerusalem: Jerusalem Academic Press, 1976), pp. 11–43. It is likely that readers were disconcerted because Eliot deviated from stereotyped characters in interfaith relationships.

132. "How the Widow Crossed the Lines," p. 166.

133. Ibid., pp. 166, 167.

134. Ibid., p. 167.

135. Ibid., pp. 167, 159.

136. Anon., "Cupid Conquers," *Enquirer,* May 30, 1878, Small Collections 13082, AJA. All subsequent quotations appear on a single page, without page number on the archive's copy. Over the years, the *Israelite* took varying views of high-society interfaith weddings, sometimes condemning them as lamentable, but alternatively casting them as evidence of Jewish success. Isaac Mayer Wise wrote in 1873 that Hannah Rothschild's marriage to Lord Roseberry was not noteworthy: the "very rich Barons Rothchild" were not "wiser or better" because of their wealth (untitled editorial, 20 [Apr. 4, 1873]: 4). But when Marie Heine, "a princess of Hebrew birth," married the Prince of Monaco in 1889, the *Israelite* reprinted without comment a piece from the New York *Jewish Chronicle* that claimed the wedding brought "dignity" to Jewry "unprecedented in Hebrew annals": "This is the most splendid matrimonial connection which has yet been achieved by any of the wealthy Jewish families of Europe, who have given their daughters in marriage to Gentile nobles" (untitled, 36 [Oct. 10, 1889]: 4). The non-Jewish press continued to report mixed marriages involving gentry as fairytale fantasies. See, e.g., newspaper accounts of the marriage of the New York socialite and philanthropist Graham Stokes to Rose Pastor, the Jewish cigarmaker and socialist, in 1905, in Arthur and Pearl Zipser, *Fire and Grace: The Life of Rose Pastor Stokes* (Athens: University of Georgia Press, 1989), pp. 36–41.

137. Love-above-all was one conclusion to be drawn from the embrace of romance by the nineteenth-century middle class, analyzed by Karen Lystra, in

Searching the Heart: Women, Men, and Romantic Love in Nineteenth-Century America (New York: Oxford University Press, 1989).

3. Piety and Politics

1. Virginia Clay-Clopton, *A Belle of the Fifties: Memoirs of Mrs. Clay of Alabama, Covering Social and Political Life in Washington and the South, 1853–66,* ed. Ada Sterling (New York: Doubleday, Page, 1905), p. 43. Clay hyphenated her name after her second marriage, but was best known as Virginia Clay. Rose Brown, daughter of the landlady of Brown's Hotel where the southern delegates dined, married Richard Wallach, at one time mayor of the city (p. 43). Jacob Rader Marcus describes Wallach as "a Unitarian, son of a Roumanian father who, it is not too audacious to venture the guess, was born a Jew," in *United States Jewry, 1776–1985* (Detroit: Wayne State University Press, 1989–1993), 2: 80.

2. Clay-Clopton, *Belle of the Fifties,* pp. 33, 39, 72.

3. Ibid., p. 54.

4. Ibid., p. 277.

5. The seminal argument on the feminization of American religion remains Ann Douglas, *The Feminization of American Culture* (New York: Knopf, 1977). Jenny Franchot explains that Protestants perceived Catholicism as "feminine," in *Roads to Rome: The Antebellum Protestant Encounter with Catholicism* (Berkeley: University of California Press, 1994), esp. pp. xxi, xxiii–xxv. On Catholic households, see Colleen McDannell, *The Christian Home in Victorian America, 1840–1900* (Bloomington: Indiana University Press, 1986). Among the extensive literature on the development of a political culture based on party competition, see Richard Hofstadter, *The Idea of a Party System: The Rise of Legitimate Opposition in the United States, 1780–1840* (Berkeley: University of California Press, 1969). I discuss the relationship of religious and political mind-sets during this era in *Victorian America and the Civil War* (Cambridge, Eng.: Cambridge University Press, 1992), chs. 1, 5. The inclination of mid-nineteenth-century Americans to engage in institutional life has been widely noted; see, e.g., Daniel Walker Howe, "Victorian Culture in America," in Howe, ed., *Victorian America* (Philadelphia: University of Pennsylvania Press, 1976), pp. 3–28.

6. *American Notes for General Circulation,* quoted in Constance McLaughlin Green, *Washington: Village and Capital, 1800–1878* (Princeton: Princeton University Press, 1962), p. 172.

7. Working from contemporary periodicals, Green reports that 19 of 52 senators and 72 of 221 representatives had their families with them during the winter of 1845 (*Washington,* p. 155). On the city's urban problems, see ibid., p. 274, and on slavery, see John Davis, "Eastman Johnson's *Negro Life at the South* and Urban Slavery in Washington, D.C.," *Art Bulletin* 80 (1998): 1–26.

8. Robert W. Johannsen, *Stephen A. Douglas* (New York: Oxford University

Press, 1973), p. 541; Marie Perpetua Hayes, "Adele Cutts, Second Wife of Stephen A. Douglas," *Catholic Historical Review* 31 (1945): 185. I rely on the account of Douglas's death in Johannsen, *Douglas,* p. 872. Some contemporary reports claimed Douglas became a Catholic on his deathbed, although Gilbert J. Garraghan concludes that the rumors were unfounded, in "Chicago's Catholic Century of Progress," *Catholic World* 137 (1933): 459–60.

9. *Funeral Obsequies of the Late Hon. S. A. Douglas and Oration of Rt. Rev. Jas Duggan, D. D., Bishop of Chicago, June 6, 1861* (Chicago: J. J. Kearney, 1861), box 2, folder 11, Stephen A. Douglas Papers, 1993 Acquisition, Chicago (hereafter Douglas Papers, 1993). On the controversy surrounding the funeral, see Hayes, "Adele Cutts," p. 189, and Johannsen, *Douglas,* p. 873.

10. The *Evening Post* ran the story the day after the Douglases' wedding, which took place on Nov. 20, 1856; see Hayes, "Adele Cutts," p. 182.

11. Clay-Clopton, *Belle of the Fifties,* pp. 36, 35.

12. "O'Neale" appears in an untitled genealogical manuscript, p. 3, folder "Miscellany, Writings of James Madison Cutts II," Cutts Family Papers, LC. "Neale" is used by both Hayes, "Adele Cutts," p. 181, and Johannsen, *Douglas,* p. 541. James Madison Cutts II identified the O'Neales as "one of the most distinguished Catholic families" of Maryland (p. 3); Johannsen repeated that they were "a prominent Roman Catholic family" (p. 541). But how much Cutts's original assessment was self-promotion is unclear. James Madison Cutts, Adele's father, is identified as Second Comptroller of the Treasury in an undated condolence note from his coworkers, folder "Miscellany, Resolutions on Deaths of J. Madison Cutts, Sr. and Mrs. J. Madison Cutts, Sr.," Cutts Family Papers. One sign of the prestige the Cutts family gained by caring for Dolley Madison in her old age was the condolence note of James Buchanan to James Madison Cutts, July 15, 1849, folder "Correspondence, 1843–1849," Cutts Family Papers.

13. Millard Fillmore to "Miss [Martha] Cutts," Dec. 31 and 27, 1850, folder "Correspondence, 1850–1859," Cutts Family Papers. Fillmore was then president.

14. Receipt for tuition and lessons at the Academy of the Visitation, May 9, 1853, series 2, box 41, folder 11, Stephen A. Douglas Papers (hereafter Douglas Papers). All subsequent quotations from the Douglas Papers come from "series 2." The dates of Adele's attendance at the academy are unclear, but she was certainly a student there in 1843 and 1848 (Hayes, "Adele Cutts," pp. 181–82).

15. Adelaide Granger to [Stephen A. Douglas], Sept. 18, 1850, box 41, folder 11, Douglas Papers.

16. Clay-Clopton, *Belle of the Fifties,* p. 133. Contemporaries noted the improvement Adele worked in Douglas's appearance and manners, as explained by Johannsen, *Douglas,* p. 542.

17. Mrs. Henry W. Miller to Adele Cutts Douglas, Aug. 19, 1860, box 41, folder 5, Douglas Papers. Similarly, F[rancis]. A. Gibbons urged Adele, following Douglas's death, to visit his hotel in Pennsylvania's Allegheny Mountains: "My house is one mile from the church and mission, which you are well aware was established by the good and sincere man, Prince Gallitizin, about fifty years ago" (July 8, 1861, box 41, folder 6, Douglas Papers).

18. "Copy of Will [of Stephen A. Douglas]," July 21, 1884, box 41, folder 30, Douglas Papers. The original will was dated Sept. 4, 1857, with a codicil added July 16, 1861. Priests called on the Douglases in 1859 to urge them to send Douglas's sons to Catholic schools; see Hayes, "Adele Cutts," p. 185. On the couple's charitable contributions, see A. de Magallon to Mrs. [Stephen A.] Douglas, no date, box 41, folder 10, Douglas Papers, and Hayes, "Adele Cutts," p. 185.

19. Hayes, "Adele Cutts," p. 187.

20. "The Congress Closes," Baltimore *Mirror,* ca. Sept. 13, 1893, clipping, box 42, folder 12, Douglas Papers.

21. Clipping on Martin Francis Douglas and Robert Martin Douglas, Greensboro [N.C.] *Record,* undated, box 43, folder 5, Douglas Papers. The letter from James Cardinal Gibbons to Robert Douglas, Oct. 28, 1913, is located in box 42, folder 8, Douglas Papers. Robert Douglas recorded his attendance at Mass, Feb. 21, 1869, in his diary for 1869, box 42, folder 10, Douglas Papers.

22. Hayes, "Adele Cutts," pp. 182–83, 186; Johannsen, *Douglas,* pp. 605, 713, 767.

23. St. Aloysius Parish diary, Jan. 11, 1859, quoted in Hayes, "Adele Cutts," p. 185.

24. Col. J. Madison Cutts, *Dolly [sic] Madison: A Paper Read Before the Columbia Historical Society, May 2, 1898* (Washington: Columbia Historical Society, 1900), folder "Miscellany, Writings of James Madison Cutts II," Cutts Family Papers. His genealogical manuscript, with notes on his New England ancestry (pp. 1–2), is found in the same folder.

25. Genealogical manuscript, p. 4, folder "Miscellany, Writings of James Madison Cutts II," Cutts Family Papers. James Madison Cutts II wrote frequently to "my dear brother," Stephen Douglas. See Cutts's letters to him in the late 1850s in box 41, folder 2, Douglas Papers.

26. Genealogical manuscript, p. 3, folder "Miscellany, Writings of James Madison Cutts II"; copy of Marriage Certificate of Mary Elizabeth Cutts and Benjamin Ogloe Taylor, Sept. 1, 1904, folder "Certificates," Cutts Family Papers. I infer that Mary Cutts was his granddaughter because of the year of her marriage.

27. Florence Martin to Zebulon Vance, Apr. 15, 1880, box 15.22, folder Apr. 1–15, 1880, Zebulon Baird Vance Papers, NC State Archives. All the correspondence cited between the Vances is found in this collection. Florence

mentioned the circumstances of their first meeting in the same letter, but erroneously dated it just after Christmas, 1880.

28. Vance to Martin, [Feb.] 19, [1880], box 15.21, folder Jan.–Mar., 1880.

29. Vance to Martin, Mar. 15, [1880], and Mar. 26, 1880, box 15.21, folders Mar. 1–15, 1880, and Mar. 16–31, 1880, respectively.

30. Vance to Martin, [mid-March 1880], box 15.21, folder Mar. 16–31, 1880. On Vance and his second marriage, see Glenn Tucker, *Zeb Vance: Champion of Personal Freedom* (Indianapolis: Bobbs-Merrill, 1965), pp. 463–64, and Rose, *Victorian America and the Civil War*, pp. 29, 39–40, 150.

31. Martin to Vance, Apr. 15, 19, 1880, box 15.22, folder Apr. 1–15, 1880.

32. Vance to Martin, Feb. 24, 1880, box 15.21, folder Jan.–Mar., 1880. Vance referred to Florence's consent to marry him in a letter dated Feb. 11, 1880, in the same folder.

33. Vance to Martin, May 20, 1880, box 15.22, folder May 1880. This is the second letter in a sequence of two that are both dated May 20.

34. Vance to Martin, Mar. 4, 1880, box 15.21, folder Mar. 1–15, 1880. Subsequent quotations in this paragraph are found in the same letter.

35. A. J. Witherspoon to Vance, Jan. 2, 1879, box 15.10, folder July 1877–Nov. 1880.

36. Vance to Martin, Feb. 23, [1880], box 15.21, folder Jan.–Mar., 1880.

37. Vance to Martin, Apr. 18, [1880], box 15.21, folder Apr. 16–30, 1880.

38. Vance to Martin, Mar. 15, [1880], box 15.21, folder Mar. 1–15, 1880.

39. Vance to Martin, Mar. 26, 1880, box 15.21, folder Mar. 16–30, 1880.

40. Martin to Vance, May 23, 1880, box 15.22, folder May 1880. Vance's friends' skeptical reactions to her Catholicism elicited Florence's testy response. Trying to smooth the way for her welcome in North Carolina, Zebulon had "written and spoken to dozens in confidence" about her faith (Vance to Martin, May 20, 1880, box 15.22, folder May 1880 [first letter of two dated May 20]). But on May 23 she wrote how insulted she was that his old friend Cornelia Spencer had offered "you *sympathy* and *pity*" for marrying a Catholic. She sensed the good intentions behind Vance's campaign, but also took offense at the assumption that her Catholicism was a flaw.

41. Vance to Martin, Mar. 4, 1880, box 15.21, folder Mar. 1–15, 1880.

42. Vance to Martin, Mar. 10, 1880, box 15.21, folder Mar. 1–15, 1880. Bertram Wyatt-Brown demonstrates that southern men were much concerned with personal honor, in *Southern Honor: Ethics and Behavior in the Old South* (New York: Oxford University Press, 1982).

43. Vance to Martin, June 1, 1880, box 15.23, folder June–Sept. 1880.

44. James Gibbons was a liberal prelate who sympathized with the "Americanists" in the turn-of-the-century controversy over how much the Catholic Church should accommodate American values. Named archbishop of Baltimore in 1877, he became the first American cardinal in 1886. See Arlene Boucher and John Tehan, *Prince of Democracy: James Cardinal*

Gibbons (Garden City, N.Y.: Doubleday, 1962). Among the interfaith families studied here, there is no evidence that priests who were less liberal overall than Gibbons were less hospitable to mixed-faith couples.

45. Florence Martin Vance to Zebulon Vance, Sept. 19, 1880, box 15.23, folder June–Sept., 1880. Zebulon used the phrase "tribe of poor kin" in a letter to Florence, [ca. Mar. 16, 1880], box 15.21, folder Mar. 16–30, 1880. There are few surviving letters about Harry's upbringing, but Florence did encourage him to practice his religion. Writing to "my little darling" from Richmond in 1882, she reported that she planned to hear the bishop preach and asked her son to "go to church and pray for Mama" ([ca. May 6], box 15.25, folder May–Sept. 1882).

46. Zebulon wrote almost daily to Florence when she vacationed at the Atlantic Hotel in Morehead City during the summer of 1890; see box 15.36, folder 1890. Vance was reelected to the Senate in 1884 and 1890; he had an eye removed in 1889 (Tucker, *Vance*, p. 465, 468, 471, 477). On his regular attendance at a Baptist Church, see ibid., p. 475.

47. Vance to Martin, Mar. 17, [1880], box 15.21, folder Mar. 16–31, 1880.

48. John Quincy Adams, diary, May 16 and 25, 1842, June 21, 1841, quoted in Leon Huhner, "David L. Yulee, Florida's First Senator," *Publications of the American Jewish Historical Society*, no. 25 (1917): 13, 13, 12.

49. On Yulee's acquisition, see "List of Slaves Purchased At Public Sale at St. Augustine, November 11, 1845 for $7180.00," Moses Elias Levy Diary, Correspondence, and Miscellaneous, 1830–52, microfilm 932, AJA. The collection will be cited hereafter as Levy Papers; the original manuscripts are located at the University of Florida, Gainesville, Fla. The purchaser of the slaves is not named on the receipt, and the owner was possibly Yulee's father, Moses Elias Levy, who was not only an abolitionist but also a slaveholder; see Chris Monaco, "Moses E. Levy of Florida: A Jewish Abolitionist Abroad," *American Jewish History* 86 (1998): 377–96. Some of Yulee's own papers appear in the Levy Papers, however, and this list has been catalogued alongside letters to Yulee. A receipt with Yulee's name on it for five slaves valued at $3,250, dated Feb. 24, 1854, appears in the Levy Papers, indicating his continuing participation in the domestic slave trade. T. [?] O. Bro. Jorgensen, Keeper of the Danish Records Office, estimated that the Levy family in St. Thomas owned between three and six slaves, 1805–1824, in his letter to a Yulee descendant, Mary MacRae, Jan. 15, [19]50, Levy Papers. When Levy divorced his wife in St. Thomas, he agreed to leave her the slaves in her possession, as specified in the deed of divorce, May 12, 1815, cited in Jorgensen to MacRae. C. Wickliffe Yulee noted that many of the slaves included in Nannie's dowry were literate, in "Senator Yulee of Florida: A Biographical Sketch," offprint, *Florida Magazine of History*, [ca. 1931], p. 28, David Levy Yulee Papers, Small Collections 13329, AJA.

50. Huhner argues that David Levy added "Yulee" to his name in December 1845 at his fiancée's insistence, in "David L. Yulee," pp. 18–19. Countering

claims that "Yulee" simply transposes the letters of "Levy," Huhner asserts that Yulee is a traditional Sephardic Jewish name (p. 19). C. Wickliffe Yulee believed that Yulee had been the surname of David's grandfather in Morocco, later dropped by David's father, then reclaimed by David with his father's consent, in "Senator Yulee," p. 5, Yulee Papers. However the name Yulee figured in David's heritage, its adoption must have reflected his growing sense of accomplishment and desire for respectability.

51. Mrs. [Nannie] Yulee to Virginia Clay, undated, quoted in Clay-Clopton, *Belle of the Fifties*, p. 202. So little is known about Yulee's wife that her name is often cited in vague or erroneous ways. Almost all secondary sources simply call her "Miss Wickliffe" or "daughter of Charles A. Wickliffe"; see, e.g., R.S.C., "David Levy Yulee," in Dumas Malone, ed., *Dictionary of American Biography* (New York: Scribner's, 1936), 20: 638. Writing to Walter Hart Blumenthal, editor of the *Standard Jewish Encyclopedia*, June 25, 1931, Rabbi Joseph Rauch of Louisville referred to her as "Nancy," Yulee Papers. David, however, called her "Nannie" in a letter to his father-in-law, Charles A. Wickliffe, May 15, 1847, Levy Papers.

52. Clay-Clopton, *Belle of the Fifties*, p. 55.

53. David Yulee to Nannie Yulee, May 14, 1848, Yulee Papers.

54. David discussed the Christian books he acquired in letters to his wife, May 14 and July 4, 1848, Yulee Papers. His family belonged to the New York Avenue Presbyterian Church in Washington at the time of his death (R.S.C., "Yulee," p. 638), although as late as Dec. 4, 1872, Nannie urged him in a letter to be baptized. Similarly, in a letter to an unidentified daughter, Dec. 4, 1874, Nannie tried to persuade the daughter to become a Christian as an example for her father and brother. I am grateful to Chris Monaco for copies of these letters. Despite his apparent equivocation, Yulee left other evidence of Christian interests. When he compiled a letterbook in the 1860s of his father's correspondence, he paraphrased a letter from Levy to his son Elias, Apr. 1834, in this way: "This letter shows conclusively that although Mr. Levy knew of his sons having adopted a different faith it did not prevent his affection as a father—it was not till 1836 that the climax of his hallucinations of mind took place that he commenced to repudiate his sons Elias & David." See "Diary of Moses Levy," p. 22, Levy Papers.

55. David Yulee to Nannie Yulee, July 4, 1848, Yulee Papers.

56. Yulee to Douglas, Jan. 28, 1853, Yulee Papers. When the Whig Party collapsed in the 1850s, Yulee allied with the Democrats. See Yulee to Stephen A. Douglas, Jan. 28, 1853, and to Franklin Pierce, Feb. 5, 1853, Yulee Papers.

57. "A Letter Book & Account Book in Which Are Intermixed Many Memoranda of His State of Mind," pp. 66, 48, Levy Papers. This manuscript volume is bound together with "Diary of Moses Levy," though each one is paginated separately. Distinguishing Levy's own words from Yulee's paraphrases of Levy's ideas is often difficult. Not all of the entries are dated, but

they range from 1838 to 1850. The volumes appear in the Levy Papers along with Yulee's "Narrative of My Administration of My Father's Estate: Relations with My Father's Family," compiled around 1868. I assume Yulee edited his father's papers at about the same time. On Levy, see Monaco, "Moses E. Levy," and Joseph Gary Adler, "Moses Elias Levy and Attempts to Colonize Florida," in Samuel Proctor, Louis Schmier, and Malcolm Stern, eds., *Jews of the South: Selected Essays from the Southern Jewish Historical Society* (Macon, Ga.: Mercer University Press, 1984), pp. 17–29.

58. "Letter Book & Account Book," p. 81, Levy Papers.

59. R[amah]. M. DaCosta to Moses Levy, Sept. 17, 1854, Levy Papers. Levy had died Sept. 7.

60. "Letter Book & Account Book," p. 44, Levy Papers. Letters included in the "Diary of Moses Levy" suggest the breadth of his intellectual interests and contacts. He wrote several times to Rebecca Gratz, including undated, July 6 and Apr. 7, 1851, pp. 5–9; once in 1848 to Michael Boas [*sic*] Israel, a Quaker convert to Judaism born Warder Cresson, pp. 10–11; and George Bush, a Swedenborgian minister, Nov. 4, 1852, p. 13, Levy Papers.

61. Levy to N[annie]. C. Yulee, Jan. 6, 1847, in "Narrative of My Administration of My Father's Estate," Levy Papers. Yulee noted his father's feeling for Nannie in the same unpaginated "Narrative."

62. Yulee to Levy, May 21, 1849, Yulee Papers.

63. Yulee's paraphrase of Moses Levy to Elias Levy, Apr. 1834; P. S. Smith to Levy, 1841, "Diary of Moses Levy," pp. 22, 21. Apparently Levy commented on his differences with David on Smith's letter to Levy.

64. Yulee discussed the details of his ongoing dispute with his father in "Narrative of My Administration of My Father's Estate," Levy Papers. On Yulee's business relations with Levy, see also Yulee to Levy, June 13, 1850, Yulee Papers. The will, drafted in 1838, remained long in dispute. See details in Yulee's "Narrative," as well as a copy of the will filed in County Judge's Court, Lake County, Florida, July 19, 1916, Yulee Papers.

65. David Yulee to Nannie Yulee, July 4, 1848, Yulee Papers.

66. "Narrative of My Administration of My Father's Estate," Levy Papers. On the burning of his estate and his imprisonment, see Clay-Clopton, *Belle of the Fifties,* p. 54, and Huhner, "David L. Yulee," pp. 27–29.

67. I discuss the differing consequences for families of the conversion of the husband or wife in "Some Private Roads to Rome: The Role of Families in American Victorian Conversions to Catholicism," *Catholic Historical Review* 85 (1999): 35–57. Husbands exercised enough domestic authority to bring their entire families into the church; wives controlled their own religious choices and often those of their children, but could not dictate religiously to husbands. Conversions to Catholicism during this period may be seen as consequences of awakened piety, but they were also expressions of liturgical and sometimes social conservatism. They were consistent with a broader Victorian taste for institutional life, though in the minds of Protes-

tants, entering the Catholic Church was an extreme step. Jenny Franchot offers a reasonable estimate when she says there were about 350,000 conversions during the nineteenth century, 57,400 during the period 1831–1860 alone, in *Roads to Rome,* p. 281. Patrick Allitt provides an overview of converts of the nineteenth and twentieth centuries, in *Catholic Converts: British and American Intellectuals Turn to Rome* (Ithaca: Cornell University Press, 1997).

68. Georgianna Bruce was reported to have said this to Margaret Fuller, as Katherine Burton relates in *Paradise Planters: The Story of Brook Farm* (New York: Longmans, Green, 1939), p. 140.

69. Ibid., p. 303. Among the many commentators on Brook Farm, Burton took special note of the community's Catholic interests because she herself was a convert to Catholicism in 1930; see her *The Next Thing: Autobiography and Reminiscences* (New York: Longmans, Green, 1949). Background on the philosophy of Brook Farm and other Catholic conversions among the Transcendentalists may be found in Anne C. Rose, *Transcendentalism as a Social Movement, 1830–1850* (New Haven: Yale University Press, 1981), pp. 130–61, 210–12.

70. There is much good scholarship on Hecker, founder in 1858 of the Missionary Society of St. Paul the Apostle (Paulist Fathers); for this period, see esp. Isaac T. Hecker, *The Diary: Romantic Religion in Ante-Bellum America,* ed. John Farina (New York: Paulist Press, 1988).

71. George Ripley to Isaac Hecker, Sept. 18, 1843, quoted in Walter Elliott, *The Life of Father Hecker,* 2d ed. (New York: Columbus Press, 1894), p. 91.

72. Sophia Ripley to Ruth Charlotte Dana, [Mar. 1848], box 10, Dana Family Papers, Massachusetts Historical Society, Boston, Massachusetts. "Ruth" was Charlotte Dana's first name, but she was called Charlotte or, often by Sophia, "Lotty."

73. Ibid.

74. George Ripley to Charlotte Dana, Feb. 8, 1862, box 16, Dana Family Papers.

75. Sophia Ripley to Charlotte Dana, July 18, [1848], box 10, Dana Family Papers. Brownson, who experienced a number of religious transformations between the Presbyterianism of his childhood and Transcendentalism of the early 1840s, became a leading American Catholic polemicist following his conversion in 1844. See Henry F. Brownson, *Orestes A. Brownson's Early Life, Middle Life, and Latter Life,* 3 vols. (Detroit: H. F. Brownson, 1898–1900).

76. George Ripley to John Sullivan Dwight, Nov. 22, [18]47, John Sullivan Dwight Papers, Rare Books and Manuscripts Department, Boston Public Library, Boston, Massachusetts. On this phase of Fourier activity, see Carl J. Guarneri, *The Utopian Alternative: Fourierism in Nineteenth-Century America* (Ithaca: Cornell University Press, 1991), sect. 4.

77. Sophia Ripley to Charlotte Dana, Apr. 1, 1848, box 10, Dana Family Papers.
78. Sophia Ripley to Charlotte Dana, Dec. 6, [18]57, box 15, Dana Family Papers.
79. George Ripley to Marianne Ripley, Apr. 9, 1865, George Ripley Letters Microfilm (1824, 1852–82), Division of Archives and Manuscripts, State Historical Society of Wisconsin, Madison, Wisconsin.
80. Burton, *Paradise Planters,* p. 309.
81. David Baldwin, "Puritan Aristocrat in the Age of Emerson: A Study of Samuel Gray Ward," Ph.D. diss., University of Pennsylvania, 1961, pp. 289–90.
82. Ibid., p. 290.
83. Anna Barker Ward to Thomas Wren Ward (1786–1858), Oct. 18, 1851, Nov. 9, 1852, Samuel Gray Ward and Anna Hazard Barker Ward Papers, bMS Am 1465, Houghton Library, Harvard. All of the Ward family manuscripts cited are located in this collection. I include Thomas Wren Ward's dates of birth and death because this was also the name of Anna's son (1844–1940); no letters to her son are cited here. On the Wards' close relations with the Transcendentalists, see Charles Capper, *Margaret Fuller: An American Romantic Life* (New York: Oxford University Press, 1992).
84. Anna Barker Ward to Thomas Wren Ward, Aug. 1, 1855. I infer Mary's death from repeated references to her ill health in Anna Barker Ward to her mother-in-law, Lydia Ward, July 1 and Aug. 15, 1853. David Baldwin states that the Wards had three children ("Puritan Aristocrat," p. 290); but at one time there seem to have been five: Mary, Annie, Bessie, Lily, and Thomas (Anna to Lydia Ward, Aug. 15, 1853). Family correspondence suggests that Bessie, Lily, and Thomas lived to adulthood.
85. Jenny Lind Goldschmidt to Anna Barker Ward, Oct. 29, 1857.
86. An example of this salutation and closing to her father-in-law may be found in Anna Barker Ward to Thomas Wren Ward, Dec. 29, 1850. Richard D. Birdsall dates her conversion March 1858, in "Emerson and the Church of Rome," *American Literature* 31 (1959): 273. Manuscript sources do not provide the exact date.
87. Birdsall discusses these textual changes in Emerson's letter to Anna, in ibid., p. 279.
88. Jacob Barker to Anna Barker Ward, June 24, 1863. "Thy fond father" appears, e.g., in his letter to Anna of Dec. 19, 1848; "my much loved daughter" in his of July 7, 1868.
89. Jenny Lind Goldschmidt to Anna Barker Ward, Feb. 9, 1858 and [1858]. Jenny Lind, the period's preeminent singer, was married in the Wards' home. Lind wrote sentimentally on Feb. 5, 1872: "*Today 20* years ago I was married at *your* house in Boston, dear Mrs. Ward." This was the last letter in their warm, two-decade correspondence. Lind addressed her letter of Feb. 9, 1858, to "Dear Darling"; one on Mar. 13, 1863, to "My Beloved

Mrs. Ward." Their friendship was like the many intimate relationships between women of the era, classically described by Carroll Smith Rosenberg, "The Female World of Love and Ritual: Relations between Women in Nineteenth-Century America," in her *Disorderly Conduct: Visions of Gender in Victorian America* (New York: Knopf, 1985), pp. 53–73.

90. Charles Eliot Norton to Samuel Gray Ward, Oct. 30, 1900.

91. Anne Easby-Smith, *William Russell Smith of Alabama: His Life and Works* (Philadelphia: Dolphin Press, 1931), p. 238.

92. Ibid., pp. 139, 238, 212.

93. Ibid., p. 138. Details about the family's dispersion and Wilhelmine's conversion appear on pp. 136–39. Wilhelmine became William's third wife in 1854, and her conversion must have been complicated by the fact that she was the stepmother of children from his first two marriages. Because she was the only child of William Easby, a shipyard owner and Commissioner of Public Buildings in Washington, Easby insisted on a prenuptial agreement that Wilhelmine and her children would use the hyphenated name "Easby-Smith" (p. 71).

94. On Wilhelmine's education and Episcopal activities, see ibid., pp. 68, 138. The Oxford Movement in the British and American Episcopal communities was characterized by heightened concern for historical authority in the Christian church, leading to insistence on apostolic succession and a taste for liturgical traditionalism. A number of participants in the Oxford Movement became Roman Catholics. On the precedents of the American movement, see Robert Bruce Mullin, *Episcopal Vision/American Reality: High Church Theology and Social Thought in Evangelical America* (New Haven: Yale University Press, 1986), and on the movement itself, Sydney E. Ahlstrom, *A Religious History of the American People* (New Haven: Yale University Press, 1972), pp. 621–29.

95. William Russell Smith to Chief of Staff, Madras (?), Miss., Aug. 18, 1864; Tom Ball, Office of the Provost Marshall, to William Russell Smith, Aug. 16, 1864, folder "Easby-Smith Family, 1863–1864," Easby-Smith Family Papers, LC.

96. Easby-Smith, *William Russell Smith*, p. 139.

97. Ibid., p. 139. Information on Smith's Know-Nothing activities may be found in ibid., pp. 72–86, and "Outstanding Events in the Life of William Russell Smith of Alabama," typescript, William Russell Smith Papers, Collection 1873, UNC.

98. William Russell Smith to Mamie (Mary) Easby-Smith, Sept. 18, 1862, Smith Papers.

99. Agnes A. M. Easby to William Russell Smith, May 13, 1862, Smith Papers.

100. The seven Catholic couples are: Judah Benjamin and Natalie St. Martin (married 1833), George Ripley and Sophia Dana Ripley (Sophia's conversion 1847 or 1848, married 1827), William Tecumseh Sherman and Ellen Ewing (1850), Stephen A. Douglas and Adele Cutts (1856), Samuel Gray

Ward and Anna Barker Ward (Anna's conversion 1858, married 1840), William Russell Smith and Wilhelmine Easby-Smith (Wilhelmine's conversion 1862, married 1854), and Joel Chandler Harris and Esther La Rose (1873). I have not included Zebulon Vance and Florence Martin (1880), because each spouse practiced his or her own religion; they were not drawn into the sphere of the Catholic Church. Two additional interfaith couples, married between 1830 and 1880 but not including a Catholic, were David Levy Yulee and Nannie Wickliffe (1846) and James Molony and Helen Wise (1878).

101. Easby-Smith, *William Russell Smith*, pp. 194, 199, 200. A similar memoir was written by Evelyn Harris about Esther La Rose Harris, "A Little Story About My Mother," 1949, typescript, ser. 5, box 34, folders 1–2, microfilm 25, Joel Chandler Harris Papers, Emory.

102. Baldwin notes Anna Barker's convent schooling near New Orleans, in "Puritan Aristocrat," p. 289. Wilhelmine Easby-Smith did not mention her education at the Academy of the Visitation as a source of her attraction to Catholicism, but did connect her early Catholic associations in Washington with her conversion when she recalled: "It is likely that in the visits to Georgetown College the first impressions were made upon my mind which, after a score of years and long research, brought me into the Catholic Church" (*Personal Recollections of Early Washington and a Sketch of the Life of Captain William Easby: A Paper Read Before the Association of the Oldest Inhabitants of the District of Columbia, June 4, 1913* [Washington: The Association, 1913]). On Ellen Sherman's upbringing, see Chapter 1, above.

103. William Tecumseh Sherman to Ellen Ewing, May 13, 1837, box 1, folder 100, William Tecumseh Sherman Family Papers, Notre Dame.

104. Essie [Esther] La Rose, "Farewell to My Convent Home," [1868?], unpaginated manuscript, ser. 1, subser. 4, box 7, folder 6, Joel Chandler Harris Papers.

105. Samples may be found in ser. 1, subser. 4, box 7, folder 5, Joel Chandler Harris Papers. A drawing of a chalice situated near a heart in a small boat, surrounded by flower chains, was accompanied by a poem about giving her soul to Jesus: "Mon âme Ah! que rendre au Seigneur / Prends son ineffable calice / Bois à l'exemple du Sauveur / A la coupe du sacrifice / Mais en faisant de la douceur / Un tribut de reconnaissance / Dis encore sans son empoissance / Mon âme Ah! que rendre au Seigneur."

106. Sophia Ripley to Charlotte Dana, Oct. 26, [1852], box 12; [1855?], box 14, Dana Family Papers. Just prior to George's remarriage to a Protestant in 1865, he told his sister that he identified with "the liberal Unitarians of the school of Mr. [Octavius Brooks] Frothingham." See George Ripley to Marianne Ripley, Apr. 9, 1865, George Ripley Letters Microfilm. It was only after Sophia's death in 1861 that George openly reasserted his Protestant beliefs.

107. W. T. Sherman to Ellen Ewing, Nov. 28, 1842, box 1, folder 103, Sherman Family Papers.

108. Ellen Sherman to W. T. Sherman, postscript dated July 30 to July 21, 1855, and Sept. 13, 1855, box 2, folders 63, 65, Sherman Family Papers. Ellen told her mother Maria Ewing that Cump accompanied her to church in St. Louis, Jan. 11, 1852, as well as to a lecture by the convert Orestes Brownson, Jan. 28, 1852. She reported the gift of a crucifix in a letter to Maria, Feb. 28, 1852. The correspondence is located in the Ellen Boyle Ewing Sherman Papers, Huntington. Perhaps Ellen was also giving unusual thought to salvation following a shipwreck on her trip to California in the spring of 1855, described in Michael Fellman, *Citizen Sherman: A Life of William Tecumseh Sherman* (New York: Random House, 1995), pp. 42–43.

109. Easby-Smith, *William Russell Smith,* ch. 8; Julia Collier Harris, *The Life and Letters of Joel Chandler Harris* (Boston: Houghton Mifflin, 1918), ch. 30; Katherine Burton, *Three Generations: Maria Boyle Ewing (1801–1864), Ellen Ewing Sherman (1824–1888), Minnie Sherman Fitch (1851–1913)* (New York: Longmans, Green, 1947), pp. 191–93.

110. Ellen Sherman to W. T. Sherman, June 1, 1859, Apr. 9, 1864, typescripts of letters destroyed by Philemon Tecumseh Sherman, box 2, folders 75, 113, Sherman Family Papers.

111. Sophia Ripley to Charlotte Dana, July 18, [1848], Dec. 6, [18]57, boxes 10, 15, Dana Family Papers.

112. Isaac Hecker to Anna Barker Ward, July 24, [1861], Ward Papers.

113. Easby-Smith, *William Russell Smith,* p. 221. The calling card reads "Le P. Theod. Ratisbonne, Missre. Apostolique Sup. de la Cong. de N. D. de Sion," item 1445, Ward Papers. Theodore's brother P[ère?]. Marie de Ratisbonne wrote to Anna as "bonne et charitable madame" to thank her for her contribution to their mission to the Jews of "Terre Sainte," the Holy Land, Mar. 18, 1874, item 981, Ward Papers. I infer that the call by Theodore occurred in the 1870s because the brothers were in touch with Anna at that time about missions. Both priests were Jewish converts to Catholicism. The conversion narrative of M. Alphonse Ratisbonne (Marie?) is included in William James, *The Varieties of Religious Experience: A Study in Human Nature* (1902, rpt. New York: Macmillan, 1961), pp. 184–87.

114. The wish for her father's conversion came from Mamie, expressed in an undated letter to a family member cited in Easby-Smith, *William Russell Smith,* p. 139. His courtesy was remembered by Easby-Smith, p. 212.

115. Joel Chandler Harris to Lillian Harris, Apr. 25, 1896, quoted in Julia Harris, *Life and Letters of Harris,* p. 351.

116. Ellen asked her husband twice to call on Henry Cardinal Manning, Apr. 15 and May 28, 1872, box 2, folder 132, Sherman Family Papers. Sherman's reply that summer is quoted in Fellman, *Citizen Sherman,* p. 343.

117. The couple's visit to Bishop John Hughes of New York was recorded in El-

len Sherman to Maria Ewing, May 8, 1850; on the call of the Archbishop of San Francisco, see Ellen to Maria, Jan. 3, 1854, Ellen Sherman Papers.

118. William Russell Smith to Mamie Easby-Smith, Jan. 8, 1866, Smith Papers.

119. "The Honey-Moon," manuscript, Smith Papers. Despite her conversion, Wilhemine "retained his [William's] chivalric worship to the very end," their daughter, Anne, recalled. It was his habit to write an annual sonnet for her birthday, as well as poems for other family occasions. See Easby-Smith, *William Russell Smith*, pp. 147, 69.

120. Joel Chandler Harris to Lillian Harris, Oct. 25, [1896], quoted in Julia Harris, *Life and Letters of Harris*, p. 357.

121. Julian La Rose Harris, "Autobiography: Early Years—Duplicate Pages," p. 2, unpublished manuscript, 1940s, box 30, folder 14, Julian La Rose Harris Papers, Emory.

122. "About Books & Washington—by Weems," undated typescript, Smith Papers.

123. "To Meester Abraham Linhern," manuscript, [1861], box 11, folder 6, microfilm reel 17, Joel Chandler Harris Papers.

124. Fellman explains Sherman's repeated refusal of overtures that he run for president, in *Citizen Sherman*, pp. 310–15. Although Sherman did not respect politicians or like politics, he managed his postwar public career with instinctive skill, maintaining his good name and keeping up his visibility precisely by skirting electioneering. Ripley mainly wrote literary criticism for the *Tribune*, but Horace Greeley's paper was known for its advocacy of social reforms. See Charles Crowe, *George Ripley: Transcendentalist and Utopian Socialist* (Athens: University of Georgia Press, 1967), ch. 10. On Ward's involvement with the *Nation*, see Baldwin, "Puritan Aristocrat," pp. 272–75, and letters from Charles Eliot Norton to Ward, May 21 and 28, 1866, Ward Papers. On Harris and the *Constitution*, see Julia Harris, *Life and Letters of Harris*, ch. 9.

125. The phrase "your church" appears in W. T. Sherman to Ellen Ewing, Feb. 8, 1844, box 1, folder 104, Sherman Family Papers.

126. Thomas Ewing, Sherman's foster father, described his inspection of Georgetown College in a letter to his wife, Maria, Mar. 5, 1831, box 16, folder 14, Sherman Family Papers; she told Ellen that he accompanied her to the consecration of the Cincinnati cathedral in letters dated Oct. 14, 1844 and Nov. 2, [18]45, Ellen Sherman Papers. On Sherman's baptism, see Ellie Ewing Brown, with editorial additions by Eleanor Sherman Fitch, "Notes on Boyhood of Philemon Beecher Ewing and William Tecumseh Sherman," unpaginated typescript, ca. 1932, box 7, folder 7, Sherman Family Papers.

127. Easby-Smith, *William Russell Smith*, p. 193. Similarly, the daughter-in-law of Joel Chandler Harris recalled that he was comfortable in the midst of the family's Catholic activities. The "annual Catholic festival that took place on the lawn surrounding the house was a matter of lively interest to him, and

when the church members and friends and neighbors gathered on these occasions, he mingled freely with them, his soft hat on the back of his head and his hands in his pockets" (Julia Harris, *Life and Letters of Harris,* pp. 238–39).

128. William Russell Smith to [Mamie Easby-Smith], Dec. 10, 1868, Smith Papers.

129. Clipping on Martin Francis Douglas and Robert Martin Douglas, Greensboro *Record,* undated, box 43, folder 5, Douglas Papers; on Tom Sherman, Joseph T. Durkin, *General Sherman's Son* (New York: Farrar, Straus and Cudahy, 1959), pp. 22–26; Julia Harris, *Life and Letters of Harris,* p. 270.

130. William Russell Smith to [Mamie Easby-Smith], Oct. 22, 1867, Smith Papers.

131. Joel Chandler Harris to Julian Harris, July 6, 1890, OP box 1, folder 2, microfilm reel 1, Joel Chandler Harris Papers; Esther La Rose Harris to Julian Harris, Nov. 20, 1890, box 25, folder 4, Julian Harris Papers.

132. Sidney Smith was the only child of William Russell Smith's first wife of three. He was away with the Confederate army as a musician at the time of his stepmother's conversion (Easby-Smith, *William Russell Smith,* pp. 128, 190–91). I infer that he did not become a Catholic because he was not listed among the Smith children baptized, p. 139, and he seems to have married an Episcopalian, p. 190. Thomas Wren Ward grew up to marry a Catholic, but did not enter the Catholic Church until shortly before his death in 1940, as explained in Margaret Snyder, "'The Other Side of the River' (Thomas Wren Ward, 1844–1940)," *New England Quarterly* 14 (1941): 423–36.

133. Joel Chandler Harris to Julian Harris, Sept. 1, [1890], quoted in Julia Harris, *Life and Letters of Harris,* p. 271. Hugh T. Keenan confirms that Joel was more demanding of Julian than of the younger sons and, again, harder on his sons than daughters, in *Dearest Chums and Partners: Joel Chandler Harris's Letters to His Children, A Domestic Biography,* ed. Keenan (Athens: University of Georgia Press, 1993), pp. xxi–xxviii. With all the family discussion of Julian's proposed study at the Marist school, it is not clear that he finally attended (ibid., ch. 16). At home in Georgia, he had been a student at the Gordon Military School.

134. Easby-Smith, *William Russell Smith,* pp. 232–33; Durkin, *General Sherman's Son,* ch. 4; Fellman, *Citizen Sherman,* p. 372; Evelyn Harris, "Little Story about My Mother," p. 55, Joel Chandler Harris Papers.

135. Quotations from unidentified sources, 1935, ca. 1939–1940, in Snyder, "'Other Side of the River,'" pp. 434, 435.

136. Easby-Smith, *William Russell Smith.*

137. Journal, 1863, quoted in Birdsall, "Emerson and the Church of Rome," p. 276.

138. Julia Harris, *Life and Letters of Harris,* p. 580.

139. Pierce Butler, *Judah P. Benjamin* (Philadelphia: George W. Jacobs, 1906), p. 35; Robert Douthat Meade, *Judah P. Benjamin: Confederate Statesman*

(New York: Oxford University Press, 1943), p. 58; Eli N. Evans, *Judah P. Benjamin: The Jewish Confederate* (New York: Free Press, 1988), p. 33. Because all of these biographies have the same title, I will cite them by author only, without short title.

140. Benjamin to Eugenia Kruttschnitt, May 8, 1880, quoted in Evans, p. 392.

141. Francis Lawley paraphrase of Benjamin, 1883–1884, quoted in ibid., p. 398. Evans reports that Benjamin's obscurantism about his life was deliberate: he burned his papers just prior to his death as well as in 1865, p. xii.

142. Butler, p. 173.

143. Benjamin to Lawley, Sept. 12, 1882, quoted in Evans, p. 398. Natalie's English may never have been strong. She was sixteen when her parents hired Benjamin to teach her English in 1832; leaving for France in 1845, she would only have used the language for a few years, assuming the family spoke English at home at all. The absence of personal papers belonging to Natalie might also be explained by her illiteracy. I am indebted to Philip Jenkins for this suggestion.

144. Max J. Kohler, "Judah P. Benjamin: Statesman and Jurist," *Publications of the American Jewish Historical Society,* no. 12 (1904): 83.

145. Details about Natalie's background and dowry may be found in Butler, p. 35, and Meade, p. 34.

146. Evans, p. 25; Meade, p. 34.

147. Meade, p. 344.

148. Evans, p. 402.

149. Meade, p. 76. Evans explains that Judah and Natalie lived with or next door to the St. Martins for the first ten years of their marriage, p. 26. They even moved with the St. Martins during that time from one residence to another.

150. On Judah's relations with the Benjamin family, see Evans, p. 3–14, 36, 47, and Meade, pp. 368–69. On his close ties with Jules St. Martin, see Evans, pp. 26, 118–19.

151. The Benjamins also traveled in social circles in which interfaith marriage was more the norm than the exception, and this might have lent support to their relationship. In New Orleans, Judah had business and political ties with John and Thomas Slidell, originally Episcopalians from New York. John married Mathilde Deslonde, a Catholic and sister-in-law of P. G. T. Beauregard, and although Evans argues that they lived as Episcopalians, a historian of the Stephen Douglas family cites parish records showing that a priest called on Mrs. Slidell in Washington in 1859 (Louis Martin Sears, *John Slidell* [Durham: Duke University Press, 1925], pp. 13–14; Evans, p. 46; Hayes, "Adele Cutts," p. 185). One of their daughters married a Catholic, becoming Comtesse de St. Roman; another married Emile Erlanger, a baptized French Jew who arranged a loan to the Confederacy (Sears, p. 12; Evans, p. 195). Jane, the Slidells' sister in New York, had wed Commodore Matthew C. Perry in 1814; their daughter Caroline was the

wife of August Belmont, a nonpracticing Jew. This religiously complex social network indicates that the Benjamins were not isolated by their interfaith marriage.

152. Evans, pp. 5, 26, 399.

153. Meade, p. 36.

154. Evans, p. 31.

155. Clay-Clopton, *Belle of the Fifties,* p. 54. The earlier phrases appear on p. 53. Natalie left for Paris before the second house at Bellechasse was constructed; Judah, however, had already ordered the plans and went ahead (Meade, p. 59; Evans, p. 35). All of Benjamin's biographers accept contemporary rumors of Natalie's infidelities. Although the reports probably had foundation because they were persistent, no firm evidence has been offered of her liaisons. Evans alludes to diaries and cites one reminiscence to establish her faithlessness, pp. 31, 41.

156. Meade, p. 364.

157. The possibility that Yulee's grandfather was adviser to the sultan appears in Adler, "Levy," pp. 18–19; Yulee's grandson, C. Wickliffe Yulee, suggested that his ancestor might have been a Muslim, in "Senator Yulee of Florida," p. 5, Yulee Papers.

158. Thomas R. R. Cobb of Georgia, a political opponent, used the word "eunich" in a letter to his wife, Jan. 15, 1862, quoted in Evans, p. 145. Francis Bacon charged Benjamin with theft at Yale in the New York *Independent,* an antislavery periodical, Jan. 31, 1861, in ibid., pp. 18–19.

159. Benjamin to [John Finney], Mar. 12, 1878, typescript, Judah P. Benjamin Papers, Small Collections 889, AJA. Despite Benjamin's frustration with erroneous reports, he and other intermarried people contributed to myths about themselves. Often upwardly mobile and, in part through their marriages, intent on self-creation, they either devised fictions about their pasts or at least suppressed mundane realities.

160. Kohler, "Benjamin," pp. 68, 83; Butler, p. 35; Meade, p. 35.

161. Evans, p. 14; Meade, p. 22.

162. Evans, p. 207. Wise's recollection, appearing in his memoir published in 1900, is quoted in Kohler, "Benjamin," p. 82.

163. Evans, p. 47. Evans elaborates on this statement: "He could stand apart from his Jewishness in public, but he could not run very far from it psychologically" (pp. xvi–xvii).

164. "Cupid Conquers," *Enquirer,* May 30, 1878, clipping, Small Collections 13082, AJA. See discussion of the story in Chapter 2, above.

165. Iphigene Molony Bettman questionnaire, May 9, 1964, unpaginated, AJA. All quotations not otherwise identified in this discussion of the Wise, Molony, and Bettman families are found in this typescript.

166. Certificate of Marriage of Gilbert Bettman and Iphigene Molony, 1916, 5676 [the Jewish year], signed by David Philipson, Nearprint Box, Alfred Bettman Papers, AJA. The certificate acknowledged the marriage "accord-

ing to the laws of the State of Ohio and the religion of Israel." It was not a traditional marriage contract *(ketubah)*. The collection also contains the couple's civil marriage license, June 28, 1916. In the 1964 questionnaire, Iphigene erroneously dated her wedding 1915.

167. "True Love Falters Not," *The American Jews' Annual for 5646 A.M.* (Cincinnati: Bloch, 1885–86), pp. 1–27. Letters from Harry Wise to Helen Wise Molony include Dec. 3, 1884, and Jan. 21, 1885, Small Collections 13071, AJA. The file also contains letters from her brother Isidore.

168. Molony's occupation is identified in "Cupid Conquers."

4. The Uncertain Limits of Liberalism

1. For the hero's declaration, see *The Melting-Pot: Drama in Four Acts* (New York: Macmillan, 1911), p. 37. The dedication to Roosevelt appeared in the first edition of 1909 as well as later ones, including 1910, 1911, 1914, and 1917. Citations may be found in the 1911 edition unless otherwise noted.

2. Ibid., p. 197. The exchange between David and his uncle is found on pp. 100–01.

3. Ibid., p. 81. Vera refers to Jews as a "race" on pp. 77, 97. David similarly uses "race" on p. 101. An "Afterword" to the 1914 edition about racial amalgamation in America, with specific references to Mendelian genetics, indicates that Zangwill's choice of language was not accidental. See *The Melting-Pot* (New York: Macmillan, 1914), pp. 194–214. George W. Stocking explains that the genetic laws of Gregor Mendel (1822–1884) were rediscovered in 1900. During the following decade, Mendel's conclusions edged aside the reigning principles of Jean-Baptiste Lamarck (1744–1829), making this a period of sharp debate in genetics. See Stocking, *Race, Culture and Evolution: Essays in the History of Anthropology* (New York: Free Press, 1968), ch. 10. On Charles Davenport, see Stocking, p. 289, and Elazar Barkan, *The Retreat of Scientific Racism: Changing Concepts of Race in Britain and the United States between the World Wars* (Cambridge, Eng.: Cambridge University Press, 1992), pp. 70–74. On the writing and reception of *The Melting-Pot*, see Joseph H. Udelson, *Dreamer of the Ghetto: The Life and Works of Israel Zangwill* (Tuscaloosa: University of Alabama Press, 1990), ch. 9.

4. The phrase appears in the 1914 "Afterword," p. 203.

5. The section heading comes from Jeremiah 13.23 (Revised Standard Version). Among variant translations, the *Tanakh: The Holy Scriptures* (Philadelphia: Jewish Publication Society, 1985) substitutes "Cushite" for "Ethiopian," perhaps to emphasize the linguistic (Cushitic) rather than racial identity of this East African people.

6. Barkan, *Retreat of Scientific Racism*, p. 77. On European and American racial theories, see also Stocking, *Race, Culture and Evolution;* William Stanton, *The Leopard's Spots: Scientific Attitudes Toward Race in America,*

1815–59 (Chicago: University of Chicago Press, 1960); Reginald Horsman, *Race and Manifest Destiny: The Origins of Racial Anglo-Saxonism* (Cambridge, Mass.: Harvard University Press, 1981); Carl N. Degler, *In Search of Human Nature: The Decline and Revival of Darwinism in American Social Thought* (New York: Oxford University Press, 1991); John M. Efron, *Defenders of the Race: Jewish Doctors and Race Science in Fin-de-Siècle Europe* (New Haven: Yale University Press, 1994); Eric L. Goldstein, "'Different Blood Flows in Our Veins': Race and Jewish Self-Definition in Late Nineteenth Century America," *American Jewish History* 85 (1997): 29–55; and Matthew Frye Jacobson, *Whiteness of a Different Color: European Immigrants and the Alchemy of Race* (Cambridge, Mass.: Harvard University Press, 1998). Yosef Hayim Yerushalmi adds a historical perspective to these studies by identifying racial language used in connection with the persecution of Jews in the Iberian peninsula beginning in 1391, in *Assimilation and Racial Anti-Semitism: The Iberian and German Models* (New York: Leo Baeck Institute, 1982).

7. Philip Cowen, ed., *Prejudice against the Jew: Its Nature, Its Causes and Remedies; A Symposium by Foremost Christians and Published in "The American Hebrew," Apr. 4, 1890* (New York: Philip Cowen, 1928), p. 31. Cowen was editor of the *American Hebrew* in 1890 and reissued the results of the periodical's poll in 1928.

8. John Boyle O'Reilly, editor of *The Pilot*, in ibid., p. 123.

9. The phrase "race antipathy" was used by J. M. Taylor, president of Vassar College, and "general education and enlightenment" by Col. John Hay, in ibid., pp. 103, 121. John Burroughs's metaphors and judgments were among the harshest (p. 116).

10. Horsman, *Race and Manifest Destiny*, p. 301. Stocking notes that Americans at this time nearly equated "race" with "culture" and "civilization," in *Race, Culture and Evolution*, pp. 253, 259. This was the traditional view of Jean-Baptiste Lamarck, in contrast to the new theory of Gregor Mendel, who believed that genetics, unaffected by environment, followed its own laws.

11. *Prejudice against the Jew*, p. 71. The president of Tufts was E. N. Capen; his comments are found on p. 105.

12. Dr. Oscar Levy of Geneva made this comment in the 1915 introduction to Arthur de Gobineau, *The Inequality of Human Races*, trans. Adrian Collins (New York: Howard Fertig, 1967), p. ix.

13. Ibid., p. 67.

14. Stanton, *Leopard's Spots*, p. 75.

15. *The Passing of the Great Race; or, The Racial Basis of European History* (New York: Scribner's, 1916), pp. 44–45. Grant's criticism of theologians appears on p. 4.

16. Francis J. Gilligan, *The Morality of the Color Line* (1928), quoted in John T. McGreevy, *Parish Boundaries: The Catholic Encounter with Race in*

the *Twentieth-Century Urban North* (Chicago: University of Chicago Press, 1996), p. 33. The language of many races coexisted at the turn of the century with broader racial categories, usually white, black, and yellow. Matthew Jacobson explains these overlapping usages and argues that after 1924 color-based categories gained dominance, in *Whiteness of a Different Color*, esp. chs. 2–3. For an instance of a Jewish leader, Isaac Mayer Wise, who identified Jews as "white," see "Why They Should Not Intermarry," *Israelite* 32 (Mar. 14, 1879): 4. In America, the distinction between white and black—the equivalent of free and slave, person and chattel—had long been fundamental, and these discussions about race must be set against a background of extensive miscegenation laws. It was not until 1967 that the Supreme Court struck down state laws making interracial marriage illegal. See Peter Wallenstein, "Race, Marriage, and the Law of Freedom: Alabama and Virginia, 1860s–1960s," *Chicago-Kent Law Review* 70 (1995): 371–436, and Eleanor Rose, "Fighting for Interracial Marriage: *Loving v. Virginia*, 1967," National History Day paper, 1996. On Jim Crow legislation more generally, see C. Vann Woodward, *The Strange Career of Jim Crow*, 3d rev. ed. (New York: Oxford University Press, 1974), esp. ch. 3.

17. J. C. Nott and Geo. R. Gliddon, *Types of Mankind; or, Ethnological Researches, Based upon the Ancient Monuments, Paintings, Sculptures, and Crania of Races, and upon Their Natural, Geographical, Philological, and Biblical History* (Philadelphia: Lippincott, Grambo, 1854), pp. 114–15.

18. *The Jews: A Study of Race and Environment* (London: Walter Scott Publishing Company, 1911), pp. v–vi, 194. With varying motives, other race theorists in addition to Fishberg identified Jews as the quintessential impure or mongrel race, as Sander Gilman points out in *The Jew's Body* (New York: Routledge, 1991), pp. 174–75. These included the British anti-Semite Houston Stewart Chamberlain. Although wildly differing conclusions seem almost a function of the hysterical quality of the racial literature, American writers tended to stress Jewish racial purity.

19. Fishberg, *The Jews*, pp. 214, 221, 525. The other opinions cited may be found in Gobineau, *Inequality of Human Races*, p. 29; Grant, *Passing of the Great Race*, p. 19; Josiah Nott's opinions published in *De Bow's Review* (1851) summarized by Horsman, *Race and Manifest Destiny*, p. 155; and Ignatz Zollschan, *Jewish Questions: Three Lectures* (New York: Bloch, 1914), p. 36.

20. Zollschan, *Jewish Questions*, pp. 41, 35, 42. For biographical information on Zollschan, see Efron, *Defenders of the Race*, pp. 153–166.

21. *Intermarriage* (New York: Jewish Welfare Board, United States Army and Navy, 1918), pp. 3, 6.

22. Ibid., pp. 5, 15, 14, 16. Pool (1885–1970) had just finished a term (1916–1917) as president of the New York Board of Rabbis when the pamphlet appeared, and perhaps he saw its production as part of his responsibility as a community leader. On Pool, see his autobiographical account in Louis

Finkelstein, ed., *Thirteen Americans: Their Spiritual Autobiographies* (New York: Institute for Religious and Social Studies/Harper and Brothers, 1953), pp. 201–29.

23. "Magic Circle of Race Integrity," *Israelite* 55 (Mar. 4, 1909): 3; "Jews a 'Recessive' Race Type: A Discussion of Mendel's Theory," *American Hebrew* 88 (Nov. 18, 1910): 71.

24. Joseph Silverman, "The Religious Training of Children," *American Hebrew* 87 (Oct. 21, 1910): 636. The other article cited is Rev. Dr. Rudolph Grossman, "The Duties of Mothers to the Religious School," *American Hebrew* 66 (Mar. 9, 1900): 545–47. Mrs. Eli Strouse offered similar views, in "Duties of Parents to Religious Schools," *American Hebrew* 66 (Apr. 6, 1900): 677–80.

25. "National Constitution," quoted in *Hadassah News Letter,* no. 23, July–Aug. 1916. There were no volume or page numbers in the early issues; some issues from the 1910s are missing from the microfilm edition produced by the American Jewish Periodical Center, Hebrew Union College-Jewish Institute of Religion, Cincinnati, Ohio. Volume numbers on extant copies begin with v. 3, no. 10, Aug. 1917. See representative articles on nursing in Palestine, no. 5, Dec. 1914; American sewing circles producing clothing for Palestinian Jews, no. 33, June 1917; and efforts to establish Young Judaea in America as well as to promote study in Palestine for American children, no. 12, July 1915, and 4 (May 1924): 3. European Zionists were more favorable to racial language, as explained by Klaus Hödl, "The Language of the Zionists in the Context of Eugenics," conference paper, "Multilingualism in Western Ashkenazic Jewry: Ideology, Intertextuality, and Transmission," Middelburg, Holland, October, 1999.

26. "Prejudice against the Jews," *Independent* 42 (Apr. 10, 1890): 11.

27. "A White Woman Who Married a Chinaman" and "Her Chinese Husband," *Independent* 68 (Mar. 10, 1910): 518–28, and 69 (Aug. 18, 1910): 358–61.

28. "Marrying of Black Folk," *Independent* 69 (Oct. 13, 1910): 812–13.

29. Pastoral Letter of 1919, in Peter Guilday, ed., *The National Pastorals of the American Hierarchy (1792–1919)* (Washington, D.C.: National Catholic Welfare Council, 1923), p. 274. On the Catholic struggle over theological modernism in the American setting, see R. Scott Appleby, *"Church and Age Unite!": The Modernist Impulse in American Catholicism* (Notre Dame: University of Notre Dame Press, 1992).

30. Guilday, ed., *National Pastorals,* p. 286.

31. Ibid., pp. 293, 313. See also McGreevy's excellent discussion of race relations and racial language in the Catholic Church at this time, in *Parish Boundaries,* ch. 2.

32. In *Popular Science Monthly,* see C[harles]. B. Davenport, "Euthenics and Eugenics," 78 (Jan. 1911): 16; T. D. A. Cockerell, "The Future of the Human Race," 77 (July 1910): 19; and Charles A. Briggs, "Is the Christian Religion Declining?" 56 (Feb. 1900): 423.

33. Henry Pratt Fairchild, *The Melting-Pot Mistake* (Boston: Little, Brown, 1926), p. 22.

34. "Central Conference of American Rabbis," *Israelite* 56 (Nov. 18, 1909): 1. All quotations that report conference proceedings may be found in this article. Rabbi Mendel Silber, who gave a paper on "Intermarriage" at the CCAR conference of 1908, denounced pro-intermarriage views voiced by Edwin J. Kuh in the *Atlantic Monthly* in April 1908. See Julian Morgenstern, David Lefkowitz, and David Philipson, eds., *CCAR Yearbook, 1908* (CCAR, 1909), 18: 273. Similar critiques of the advocacy of intermarriage may be found in the *Israelite:* Emanuel A. Hirsch, "'The Melting Pot': Will the Jews Become Merged in It and Disappear?" 55 (May 4, 1909): 1; David Lefkowitz, "Are Jews Disintegrating?" 56 (Oct. 28, 1909): 1; and Stephen S. Wise, "Zangwill and His Critics," 56 (Oct. 28, 1909): 1. Two other commissioned papers by Reform rabbis on the subject of intermarriage, delivered at the 1909 convention, are Ephraim Feldman, "Intermarriage Historically Considered," and S. Schulman, "Mixed Marriages in Their Relation to the Jewish Religion," in Morgenstern, Lefkowitz, and Philipson, eds., *CCAR Yearbook, 1909* (CCAR, 1910), 19: 271–335. On these discussions, see Steven Lebow, "An Early Intermarriage Debate in the Pages of the C.C.A.R. Year Book," typescript, 1980, Small Collections 6717, AJA. Less liberal Jews observed the Reform debate about interfaith marriage with disapproval and did not raise the issue in their own circles, most likely because there was no possibility of alternative positions. The Union of Orthodox Congregations publicly censured the CCAR's intermarriage resolution, as reported by David Philipson, "The Central Conference and Its Critics," *Israelite* 56 (Dec. 16, 1909): 4. Aaron Rothkoff portrays Orthodoxy as less organized than the Americanized Reform movement and perhaps less equipped to produce a systematic marriage policy even if it wished, in *Bernard Revel: Builder of American Jewish Orthodxy* (Philadelphia: Jewish Publication Society of America, 1972), ch. 1. Conservative Jews did not create a national organization until 1913.

35. The choice of Isaac Moses to preside is an intriguing one, because he had been run out of Milwaukee in 1880 for performing a mixed marriage against the wishes of his congregation. He was still willing to voice fairly liberal views on the subject in 1909, recorded in part in Morgenstern, Lefkowitz, and Philipson, eds., *CCAR Yearbook, 1909*, 19: 328–35. By now he was rabbi of Ahawath Chesed Shaar Hashomayim Congregation in New York, however, and had become more circumspect with age. When he returned to Milwaukee for the silver anniversary of his old congregation (Emanu-El), he acknowledged that his reminiscences "might not be wholly appropriate at this occasion to rehearse." He proceeded to defend the authority of religion against science and to propose a plan to limit the voice of converts in congregations, in "The Ideal Religion: Words Spoken at the Silver-Jubilee of Emanu-El Congregation, Milwaukee, Wis., by I. S. Moses," undated ms., box 1, folder 8, Isaac Moses Papers, AJA.

36. For discussion of the texts of the several resolutions, see Michael Cook, "The Debates in the Central Conference of American Rabbis on the Problem of Mixed Marriage, 1907–1968," typescript, 1969, pp. 9–10, AJA.

37. July 21, 1905, Jan. 10, 1906, Diary titled "Journal, July 19, 1905–Feb. 22, 1906" (hereafter cited as Diary), ser. C, box 3, David Philipson Papers, AJA.

38. Jan. 10, 1906, Diary, Philipson Papers.

39. July 21, 1905, Jan. 4, 1906, Diary, Philipson Papers.

40. This is the way Philipson described Bernhard Felsenthal (1822–1908), rabbi of Sinai Congregation in Chicago, Jan. 10, 1906, Diary, Philipson Papers. Philipson's response to Orthodox criticism appeared as "The Central Conference and Its Critics."

41. Edith Zangwill to David Philipson, Jan. 17, [1904], box 2, folder 6, Philipson Papers. Philipson's gift must have seemed natural in the context of his friendship with Zangwill, shown by several letters from Zangwill to Philipson from Oct. 13, [18]98 to June 17, [19]02, box 2, folder 6, Philipson Papers. Many of Zangwill's Jewish friends behaved similarly to Philipson. Although there was private comment on Zangwill's marriage to a gentile, Jewish friends made no public fuss (Udelson, *Dreamer of the Ghetto*, p. 151). Those who were dubious about his choice might have been gratified to know that Zangwill's descendants were Roman Catholics. See Floyd S. Fierman, "Israel Zangwill's Family: A Note," typescript, [1964], Israel Zangwill Papers, AJA.

42. Anon., "Intermarriage Difficulties: London Has New and Vexed Question," *Israelite* 55 (Feb. 11, 1909): 1.

43. Zollschan, *Jewish Questions,* p. 28; Fishberg, *Jews,* p. 205.

44. "Intermarrying with Gentiles," *Occident* 2 (Mar. 1845): 588–90. Despite his opinion, such conversions did occur at the time; see Chapter 1, n. 121.

45. Blank handwritten conversion document for a woman on congregational letterhead, dated Mar. 22, 1906, box 1, folder 4, Isaac Moses Papers.

46. *Minister's Hand Book* (New York: CCAR/Bloch, 1917), p. 33, box 9, Philipson Papers.

47. Pledges, including signatures of the couples, come from Congregation Beth El, Detroit, Nov. 5, 1914, Jan. 3, 1916, and Dec. 22, 1918, Small Collections 5402, AJA.

48. Zepin to Sol A. Herzog, Nov. 3, 1916, box 2, folder 18, Philipson Papers. Zepin was the Director of the Department of Synagog and School Extension, Union of American Hebrew Congregations (UAHC).

49. Harry Sigmond to George Zepin, Oct. 30, 1916, box 2, folder 18, Philipson Papers. The rabbi who sent a critique of the Confirmation manual to Zepin was Abram Simon, Dec. 20, 1916.

50. The results of the survey were summarized in "Union of Hebrew Congregations and Temple Sisterhoods Meet at Buffalo," *Israelite* 67 (June 2, 1929): 1. Michael A. Meyer confirms these reported difficulties when he writes that

Jews shared the prevailing mood of the 1920s, "lassitude with regard to observance and education, the conception of religion as an ornament of bourgeois culture," in *Response to Modernity: A History of the Reform Movement in Judaism* (Detroit: Wayne State University Press, 1995), p. 296. Reform rabbis "often complained that the synagogue failed to attract many of the unaffiliated," although membership in raw numbers climbed until the beginning of the Depression (pp. 307, 306).

51. Joseph Leister, in a professed effort to reclaim scholarliness from emotionalism, spoke against the widespread practice of allowing women to officiate at religious services, in "Shall Women Enter the Jewish Ministry?" *Israelite* 67 (July 29, 1920): 4. The shortage of rabbis was the subject of "More Rabbis Needed," 67 (May 5, 1921): 4. Representative reports of other public issues appeared as "Jew Baiting in Fiction," 67 (Aug. 26, 1920): 4; "Is Anti-Semitism Growing in America?" 67 (Sept. 30, 1920): 1; and "The Synagog No Place for Radicals," 67 (Feb. 24, 1921): 4.

52. "The Melting Pot" was an ongoing column; see, e.g., *American Hebrew* 106 (Jan. 16, 1920): 291.

53. Canon 1061, quoted in Paul H. Besanceney, *Interfaith Marriages: Who and Why* (New Haven: College and University Press, 1970), p. 117. Besanceney included the texts of the canons on mixed marriage (numbers 1060–63) in his discussion, pp. 117–18. For explanations of the canons on marriage (numbers 1012–1141), see P. J. Lydon, *Ready Answers in Canon Law: A Practical Summary of the Code for the Parish Clergy,* 3d rev. ed. (New York: Benziger Brothers, 1948), pp. 374–402.

54. T. Lincoln Bouscaren and Adam C. Ellis, *Canon Law: A Text and Commentary* (Milwaukee: Bruce, 1946), p. 7. Although the 1917 Code may have seemed systematic in comparison to earlier forms of church law, the next revision of the Code, completed in 1983, further reduced the number of canons from 2,414 to 1,752. See John A. Alesandro, "General Introduction," in James A. Coriden, Thomas J. Green, and Donald E. Heintschel, eds., *The Code of Canon Law: A Text and Commentary* (New York: Paulist Press, 1985), pp. 4–8.

55. On the process of revision, see Alesandro, "Introduction," in Coriden, Green, and Heintschel, eds., *Code of Canon Law,* p. 4, and Walter H. Peters, *The Life of Benedict XV* (Milwaukee: Bruce, 1959), pp. 202–12. Biographical information on Gasparri may be found in Peters, *Life of Benedict XV,* pp. 91–92, and W. H. Peters, "Pietro Gasparri," *New Catholic Encyclopedia* (New York: McGraw-Hill, 1967), 6: 296–97. Ironically, Gasparri's success as a reformer owed more to intuitive insight than bureaucratic skill. Peters notes that when Gasparri served as the Vatican's secretary of state, "his methods of maintaining a secretariat of state were most unsystematic," at the same time that he possessed "acuteness of mind and faculty for arriving at the heart of a problem" (*Life of Benedict XV,* p. 92).

56. Jos. Selinger, *A Catechism on Pledges: Required for Dispensation for a*

Mixed Marriage (St. Louis: Central Bureau, Catholic Central Verein of America, 1930), p. 28, PGEN (General Pamphlet Collection [Printed]) 3771, Notre Dame. Selinger discussed the canonical reasons on p. 13.

57. Lydon, *Ready Answers in Canon Law,* pp. 380–81.

58. John A. O'Brien, *The Church and Marriage* (Fort Wayne: Courtney, 1934), p. 126.

59. Pastoral Letter of 1919, in Guilday, ed., *National Pastorals,* pp. 272–73.

60. Ibid., pp. 312–17. Outwardly, there was much to suggest Catholic success, ecclesiastical and social, during this period; see, e.g., Paula M. Kane, *Separatism and Subculture: Boston Catholicism, 1900–1920* (Chapel Hill: University of North Carolina Press, 1994). But the decline of Victorian culture in early twentieth-century America also brought an erosion of traditional morals. This makes the diagnosis of the Pastoral Letter more credible. Catholic fiction seconded clerical worry about family problems. See, e.g., Frank H. Spearman's novel about interfaith marriage, irreligion, and divorce, *Robert Kimberly* (New York: Grosset and Dunlap, 1911).

61. Claudia Carlen, ed., *The Papal Encyclicals, 1903–1939* (n.p.: The Pierian Press, 1990), p. 404. Comments on failure to respect marriage's sanctity appear on p. 398.

62. *Church and Marriage,* p. 120. Texts of the pledges appear on p. 121. O'Brien was a chaplain at the University of Illinois. Pope Pius VI first specified in 1782 that the Catholic partner in a mixed marriage must pledge before two witnesses to remain loyal, raise his or her children as Catholics, and try to convert the spouse. See the text of his letter in Besanceney, *Interfaith Marriages,* p. 117.

63. Carlen, ed., *Papal Encyclicals, 1903–1939,* p. 404.

64. On Gasparri's reaction to American racial problems, see McGreevy, *Parish Boundaries,* p. 7; on his diplomatic career, see Peters, "Gasparri," p. 297.

65. Jim McClaren, quoted in Rosette Barron Haim, "Christian Clergy's Attitudes toward Mixed Marriages," typescript, 1988, p. 12, Miscellaneous File, Small Collections 4471, AJA. Overall, Haim stresses that the lack of centralized authority in Protestantism left much to the individual conscience and resulted in wide variation even among the clergy in awareness and practices (pp. 9–10).

66. The Episcopal resolution, adopted by the General Convention of the Protestant Episcopal Church in 1948, was "one of the first" such resolutions, according to Besancency, *Interfaith Marriages,* p. 118. Besancency includes the text on p. 118. Other Protestant resolutions were passed between 1950 and 1953 (ibid., p. 119). Haim cites one earlier denominational resolution—passed by the Presbyterian General Assembly—in 1946, in "Christian Clergy's Attitudes toward Mixed Marriages," p. 12.

67. Sydney E. Ahlstrom, *A Religious History of the American People* (New Haven: Yale University Press, 1972), p. 899.

68. Unidentified speaker, quoted in O'Brien, *Church and Marriage,* pp. 126–27.

69. *The Promised Land,* 2d ed. (Boston: Houghton Mifflin, 1969), p. xix.

70. Oscar Handlin reported publication information on *The Promised Land* in his foreword, p. v. Lewisohn's *Up Stream: An American Chronicle* (New York: Modern Library, 1926) was in its second edition by 1926. Although the popularity of *I Am a Woman—and a Jew* is less clear, Stern's earlier reminiscence, *My Mother and I* (New York: Macmillan, 1917), included a foreword by Theodore Roosevelt, who "cordially commended" it as "a profoundly touching story—of the Americanization of a young girl" (n.p.). Stern was not an unknown author. Similarly, Yezierska's *All I Could Never Be* was not as popular as her earlier books, including *Hungry Hearts* (1920) and *Bread Givers* (1925); but it was the work of a respected writer. See Mary V. Dearborn, *Love in the Promised Land: The Story of Anzia Yezierska and John Dewey* (New York: Free Press, 1988), p. 156. On Lewisohn as a professional, see Susanne Klingenstein, *Jews in the American Academy, 1900–1940: The Dynamics of Intellectual Assimilation* (New Haven: Yale University Press, 1991), ch. 4. All these books occupy a middle ground between fact and fiction. The authors often changed real names of individuals or locations and sometimes created fictional characters to enact actual stories. I approach the works as autobiographical narratives that have been crafted by writers in ways that reflect their values. More generally, Riv-Ellen Prell explores the relationship of love and Americanization among Jewish women, in *Fighting to Become Americans: Jews, Gender, and the Anxiety of Assimilation* (Boston: Beacon Press, 1999), esp. pp. 61–87, and Todd M. Endelman discusses contemporaneous British writing about Jewish assimilation, in *Radical Assimilation in English Jewish History, 1656–1945* (Bloomington: Indiana University Press, 1990), ch. 4, 6.

71. *I Am a Woman—and a Jew* (1926; rpt. New York: Arno Press and the New York Times, 1969), p. 1. Stern published the book under the pseudonym Leah Morton.

72. *Promised Land,* pp. 203, 243, 205.

73. *All I Could Never Be* (New York: Brewer, Warren and Putnam, 1932), p. 35.

74. Ibid., pp. 45, 61.

75. *I Am a Woman—and a Jew,* pp. 141, 201.

76. Ibid., pp. 362, 234.

77. *Up Stream,* pp. 45, 53, 53–54.

78. Ibid., pp. 239, 288, 284.

79. Ibid., p. 154.

80. *I Am a Woman—and a Jew,* pp. 329, 330.

81. Ibid., p. 103. When Stern first mentioned the note in the book, she said it read "new gods" (p. 67). For a discussion of biblical prohibitions linking intermarriage with idolatry, see my introduction.

82. Ibid., p. 102.

83. The views of both Stern and her husband are found in ibid., p. 189.

84. Ibid., p. 181.

85. On Lewisohn's stormy relations with his successive lovers and wives, see Ralph Melnick's masterly biography, *The Life and Work of Ludwig Lewisohn,* 2 vols. (Detroit: Wayne State University Press, 1998). Lewisohn's motives for suppressing these difficulties transcended delicacy. When he wrote a novel in 1909 documenting the problems of his first marriage, the government censor Anthony Comstock destroyed the plates before the book was published. Lewisohn attacked Mary openly in the revised edition of *Up Stream* in 1926; when she threatened to sue, the publisher destroyed all but a few copies. See Melnick, 1: 136, 417–21, 431–32. Given Lewisohn's inclination to tell all about his love life, it is noteworthy that he conformed so closely to the more disciplined norms of immigrant autobiography.

86. *All I Could Never Be,* pp. 54, 38.

87. Ibid., p. 185.

88. Ibid., pp. 65, 66. Dearborn confirms the basic accuracy of Yezierska's fictional account, in *Love in the Promised Land,* ch. 6.

89. See the fascinating story of how manuscript poems written by Dewey during the love affair and retrieved in 1939 from his wastebasket at Columbia University help to establish his link with Yezierska, in Jo Ann Boydston, "Introduction," to Boydston, ed., *The Poems of John Dewey* (Carbondale: Southern Illinois University Press, 1977), pp. ix–xvii. Boydston was responsible for solving the puzzle.

90. *I Am a Woman—and a Jew,* p. 240.

91. Ibid., p. 240.

92. Scholars generally agree that the family was a central institution of American Victorian culture and that Victorianism persisted into the early twentieth century, although increasingly in competition with other value systems. See Henry May, *The End of American Innocence: A Study of the First Years of Our Own Time, 1912–1917* (New York: Knopf, 1959); Stanley Coben, *Rebellion against Victorianism: The Impetus for Cultural Change in 1920s America* (New York: Oxford University Press, 1991); and Anne C. Rose, *Victorian America and the Civil War* (Cambridge, Eng.: Cambridge University Press, 1992).

93. Kathleen Norris, *Little Ships* (Garden City: Doubleday, Page, 1925), p. 427. On Norris, see Arnold Sparr, *To Promote, Defend, and Redeem: The Catholic Literary Revival and the Cultural Transformation of American Catholicism, 1920–1960* (New York: Greenwood Press, 1990), pp. 86–87, as well as her autobiographies, *Noon: An Autobiographical Sketch* (Garden City: Doubleday, Page, 1925), and *Family Gathering* (Garden City: Doubleday, 1959).

94. *Little Ships,* p. 343.

95. Ibid., pp. 366, 416.

96. Ibid., pp. 385, 25, 388.

97. Ibid., p. 303.
98. Ibid., p. 427.
99. Ibid., p. 125. On *The Blakes and Flanagans,* see Chapter 2, above. Thematic continuities in Irish Catholic fiction may not necessarily carry over into Catholic literature written by members of other ethnic groups. Garibaldi M. Lapolla's *The Fire in the Flesh* (1931; rpt. New York: Arno Press, 1975), for example, an Italian-American novel contemporaneous with *Little Ships,* centers on the sexual weakness of priests rather than the risks of interfaith romance. The prominence of interfaith marriage in Catholic fiction may be associated with Irish dominance in Catholic circles, a situation increasingly challenged in the twentieth century.
100. *Little Ships,* p. 135.
101. Ibid., p. 245.

5. Fitting Religion into Complicated Lives

1. Ralph Barton Perry to Rachel Berenson, Apr. 6, 1905, HUG 4683.70, box 3, Ralph Barton Perry Papers, Harvard University Archives, Nathan Marsh Pusey Library, Harvard. All manuscripts of the Perry and Berenson families cited in this chapter are located in this collection. Ralph expressed apprehension that his father would not attend the wedding in a letter to Rachel, Apr. 30, 1905, in the same box.
2. Rachel Berenson to Ralph Barton Perry, [July 27, 1905], HUG 4683.70, box 3.
3. Rachel Berenson to Ralph Barton Perry, June 16 and June 11, 1905, HUG 4683.70, box 3. Through Bernard, Rachel had contact with a European social circle composed of expatriate American and British intellectuals who considered marriage an open-ended arrangement. Bertrand Russell, in 1905 the husband of Bernard's sister-in-law Alys, held especially radical views. See Ray Monk, *Bertrand Russell: The Spirit of Solitude* (London: Jonathan Cape, 1996), chs. 5–6. Bernard and his wife, Mary (Alys's sister), lived openly together before the death of Mary's husband and her marriage to Bernard in 1900. See Ernest Samuels, *Bernard Berenson: The Making of a Connoisseur* (Cambridge, Mass.: Harvard University Press, 1979), esp. chs. 9, 25. Rachel, an innocent by comparison, made her wedding plans in this context. Writing to Ralph from Constantinople, May 12, 1905, she proposed a ceremony at the English home of Mary Berenson's mother to coincide with Bernard's regular summer visit. From Athens four days later, she said instead that they might marry at Bernard's villa in Florence (HUG 4683.70, box 3). In the end Mary Berenson, but not Bernard, witnessed the Perrys' wedding in London. See the marriage certificate, HUG 4683.70, box 5, folder "Wedding Presents."
4. Rachel Berenson to Ralph Barton Perry, May 12, 1905, HUG 4683.70, box 3.

5. Rachel Berenson to Ralph Barton Perry, July 10 and June 16, 1905, HUG 4683.70, box 3.

6. George Perry to Ralph Barton Perry, Sept. 13, 1905; George Perry to Rachel Berenson Perry, Sept. 13, 1905, HUG 4683.70, box 1. A handwritten obituary of Ralph Barton Perry, dated Jan. 23, 1957, identified his parents as George Adelbert and Susannah Chase Perry, who lived in Vermont when their son was born in 1876 (HUG 4683.7). George, a Civil War veteran, recalled his service in a letter to Ralph, Apr. 10, 1913, HUG 4683.70, box 1. He may have been an Episcopalian in 1912, because he told Ralph on Jan. 25 that he asked his "Rector" to pray for his son's safe passage to Italy (HUG 4683.70, box 1).

7. The "privatization" of religion has gained most attention from sociologists who identify it as a recent development. See Robert Bellah et al., *Habits of the Heart: Individualism and Commitment in American Life,* rev. ed. (Berkeley: University of California Press, 1996), ch. 9, and Robert Wuthnow, *The Restructuring of American Religion: Society and Faith Since World War II* (Princeton: Princeton University Press, 1988), esp. chs. 4–6. Slightly differently, Alexis de Tocqueville observed how much individualism shaped American religion, in *Democracy in America* (1835–1840), ed. J. P. Mayer (Garden City: Doubleday, 1969), esp. pp. 528–30. Some scholars note that women's religious commitment declined during the nineteenth century, including Lori D. Ginzburg, *Women and the Work of Benevolence: Morality, Politics, and Class in the Nineteenth-Century United States* (New Haven: Yale University Press, 1990). Yet none specifically connects this trend with the gradual disengagement of families from churches and synagogues, one expression of privatization.

8. On the Gibson girl as a popular type, see Steven Warshaw, ed., *The Gibson Girl: Drawings of Charles Dana Gibson* (Berkeley: Diablo Press, n.d.).

9. Ralph Barton Perry to Rachel Berenson, [Feb. 5, 1903], HUG 4683.70, box 3.

10. Rachel Berenson to Bernard Berenson, Dec. 8, 1901, HUG 4683.70, box 3. Albert, the father of Rachel and Bernard, was never financially successful in America; Bernard contributed to the family's support and paid for Rachel's education (Samuels, *Berenson,* p. 430). This helps explain why she so seriously discussed her plans with a brother, for he was in effect the head of the family. Bernard also promised to contribute $1,500 to cover the cost of Rachel's wedding (Rachel to Ralph, May 28, 1905, HUG 4683.70, box 3).

11. "Wife and Family," section of unpaginated autobiographical typescript, HUG 4683.70, box 6.

12. Rachel Berenson to Ralph Barton Perry, May 16, 1905, HUG 4683.70, box 3.

13. Journal, May 31, 1944, in Bernard Berenson, *Rumour and Reflection, 1941–1944* (London: Constable, 1952), p. 284. The volume consists of a journal Berenson kept during the fascist era in Italy.

14. Journal, Feb. 27, 1905, Rachel Berenson Diary, [1904–1905], HUG 4683.71, box 3; Ralph Barton Perry to Rachel Berenson, Apr. 23, 1905, HUG 4683.70, box 3. The entries in Rachel's diary are literally layered: she began entries when she arrived in Europe in June 1904, and when she reached the spring of 1905 simply wrote beneath the entries of the previous year.

15. Bessie [Elizabeth] Berenson to Ralph Barton Perry, Aug. 14, [1953], HUG 4683.8, box "Letters from the Berenson Family," folder "Mary Berenson." On the details of religious practice in the Berenson family, see Samuels, *Berenson*, pp. 15–16.

16. Bessie Berenson to Ralph Barton Perry, [June 28, 1905], HUG 4683.70, box 3, folder "Rachel to Ralph, May–Dec. 1905."

17. Journal, Jan. 20, 1943, in Berenson, *Rumour and Reflection*, p. 120.

18. Bernhard Berenson, "Contemporary Jewish Fiction," *The Andover Review: A Religious and Theological Monthly* 10 (1888): 602. There was an "h" is Bernard's name when he arrived in the United States in 1875 at age eleven; he retained the spelling until World War I.

19. Journal, Oct. 23, Nov. 17, 1943, in Berenson, *Rumour and Reflection*, pp. 128, 149. Berenson lived in Florence from 1889 until his death. He lived openly until the German occupation of Italy, then went into hiding on Sept. 10, 1943.

20. Journal, May 31, 1944, Jan. 1, 1941, in Berenson, *Rumour and Reflection*, pp. 280, 15.

21. Journal, Jan. 15, [1905], Rachel Berenson Diary, HUG 4683.71, box 3. The previous phrase appears in Journal, Jan. 20, 1943, in Berenson, *Rumour and Reflection*, p. 120. Daily chapel and Sunday worship were required at Smith during Rachel's years as an undergraduate. See Helen Lefkowitz Horowitz, *Alma Mater: Design and Experience in Women's Colleges from Their Nineteenth-Century Beginnings to the 1930s* (New York: Knopf, 1984), pp. 77, 217. It seems likely that the American School of Classical Archeology, where Rachel studied in Athens, also required Protestant worship.

22. Rachel Berenson to Ralph Barton Perry, May 12, 1905, HUG 4683.70, box 3.

23. "Anti-Semitism," unpaginated typescript, [1940s?], HUG 4683.7.

24. *The Moral Economy* (New York: Scribner's, 1909), pp. 229, 240. On Perry as a philosopher, see Bruce Kuklick, *The Rise of American Philosophy: Cambridge, Massachusetts, 1860–1930* (New Haven: Yale University Press, 1977), esp. pp. 254–55, 338–50.

25. Ralph Barton Perry, "Realism in Retrospect," in George P. Adams and Wm. Pepperell Montague, eds., *Contemporary American Philosophy: Personal Statements* (New York: Macmillan, 1930), 3: 187.

26. Bessie Berenson to Ralph Barton Perry, [June 28, 1905], HUG 4683.70, box 3, folder "Rachel to Ralph, May–Dec. 1905." Ralph reported to Rachel

that he had attended the Monet exhibition with Bessie and the girls' mother, Judith, Apr. 9, [1905], HUG 4683.70, box 3.

27. Mary Berenson to Rachel Berenson Perry, Nov. 29, 1905, Apr. 7, 1906, Dec. 30, 1910; Mary Berenson to Ralph Barton Perry, Dec. 3, 1911, HUG 4683.8, box "Letters from the Berenson Family," folder "Bernard Berenson." "Scappatura" means "a quick visit."

28. Soon after Ralph boarded the S. S. Sant' Anna on Jan. 27, 1912, bound for Marseilles, he noted that a Rev. Mr. Dickinson of Rochester conducted services (Feb., Ralph Barton Perry Diary 1912, HUG 4683.71, box 3).

29. Berenson wrote to his friend Henry Coster on Sept. 10, 1953, that Ralph had spent the month of August at Villa I Tatti, in *The Selected Letters of Bernard Berenson,* ed. A. K. McComb (Boston: Houghton Mifflin, 1964), p. 277. Ralph received a detailed account of the Berensons' childhood religious practice from Bessie, postmarked Aug. 14 (HUG 4683.8, box "Letters from the Berenson Family," folder "Mary Berenson"). I infer that questions concerning religion came up during Ralph's stay with Bernard.

30. Rachel Berenson Perry to Ralph Barton Perry, Jan. 12, 1933, HUG 4683.70, box 5.

31. "Introduction" to unfinished autobiography, unpaginated typescript, 1938, box 26, folder 38, Julian La Rose Harris Papers, Emory. See also Julia Harris, "About My Mother," typescript, July 16, 1949, box 26, folder 20, Julian Harris Papers.

32. Julia Harris, "Introduction," Julian Harris Papers. See also William F. Mugleston, "Julia Florida Collier Harris," Kenneth Coleman and Charles Stephen Gurr, eds., *Dictionary of Georgia Biography* (Athens: University of Georgia Press, 1983), 1: 402–03.

33. Julia Collier to Julian Harris, June 3, 1897, box 24, folder 3, Julian Harris Papers.

34. On the education of Julia's brothers John and Charles at Sacred Heart Seminary, see John Collier to Julia Collier, Oct. 14, 1897, box 34, folder 5, Julian Harris Papers. Julia and Julian's wedding was reported in the Atlanta *Constitution,* Oct. 27, 1897; the minister was Dr. I. A. Hopkins, identified as a Methodist by Julian in a letter to Edwin Mims, Nov. 14, 1925, p. 8, box 14, folder 24, Julian Harris Papers (hereafter "Harris to Mims"). The *Constitution* reported the weddings of Julian's siblings on the dates noted as follows: Lucien, Dec. 12, 1895, by Father Kennedy; Evelyn, Oct. 28, 1903, by Rev. J. E. Gunn according to the Catholic rite; Lillian, Jan. 16, 1908, by Father Jackson of St. Anthony's; and Mildred, October 28, 1909, by Father O. N. Jackson. Joel Chandler Harris, Jr., married twice in 1911 and 1922, neither time in Atlanta. Evelyn noted that none of the children married Catholics in "A Little Story About My Mother," typescript, 1949, p. 55, Joel Chandler Harris Papers, Emory. On Julia's prayer with Charles, see the entry for "The First Prayer," Feb. 1902, *Baby's Record,* box 37, folder 3; on Pierre's Catholic baptism, see the entry for "Rites and Ceremonies,"

The Baby's Biography, box 37, folder 11, Julian Harris Papers. "Dr. A. S. Bradley" and "Dr. H. S. Bradley" of Trinity Methodist Church were the names connected with the funerals of Charles and Pierre, respectively, in "Charles Collier Harris Dies at Early Hour To[day?]" [torn], [Dec. 1903], clipping, box 37, folder 10, and "Funeral of Pierre Harris," [Feb. 1904], clipping, box 37, folder 15, Julian Harris Papers.

35. Harris to Mims, p. 8.
36. "Introduction," 1938, Julian Harris Papers.
37. Julia Harris to Esther Harris, Feb. 10, 1920, box 25, folder 9, Julian Harris Papers.
38. Untitled manuscript on Pierre's illness, p. 1, box 37, folder 13, Julian Harris Papers; "About My Mother," pp. 1, 2.
39. "Introduction," 1938, Julian Harris Papers; untitled manuscript on Pierre's illness, Julian Harris Papers; Joel Chandler Harris to "Dear Folks Alive," Feb. 15, 1906, and to "Dear Folks," 1906, Clearwater, Florida, OP box 1, folder 1, Joel Chandler Harris Papers; and "Introduction." At least in the early years of the century, Julia's problems were not primarily psychosomatic. She had gynecological surgery, for example, after Pierre's birth (untitled manuscript on Pierre's illness). She did not associate physical symptoms with her rest cures after about 1930.
40. Julia Harris to Esther Harris, Feb. 10, 1920, box 25, folder 9, Julian Harris Papers.
41. Joel Chandler Harris to Julian La Rose Harris, Sept. 1, [1890], in Julia Collier Harris, *The Life and Letters of Joel Chandler Harris* (Boston: Houghton Mifflin, 1918), p. 272.
42. Harris to Mims; Julian to Joel and Esther Harris, Sept. 28, 1890, box 25, folder 2, Julian Harris Papers.
43. F. L. S., "Just From Georgia (In Memorium—Charles Collier Harris)," xerox of clipping from Atlanta *Constitution,* [Dec. 30, 1903], box 24, folder 7, Julian Harris Papers.
44. Thomas Boyd, "Defying the Klan," *Forum* 76 (1926): 53, 49, offprint, box 14, folder 30, Julian Harris Papers.
45. Tom Loyless, quoted in William G. Shepherd, "Fighting the K.K.K. on Its Home Grounds," *Leslie's Illustrated Weekly* 133 (1921): 511, offprint, box 13, folder 19, Julian Harris Papers. "Famous *exposé*" is Loyless's phrase in the same article, p. 511. On the Leo Frank case, see Jacob Rader Marcus, *United States Jewry, 1776–1985* (Detroit: Wayne State University Press, 1989–1993), 3: 154–56.
46. Julian used the phrase "hurled convincing arguments" in his letter to Mims, p. 6. Bradley Chester described Julia's resistance to anti-evolution teaching, in "Julian Harris' Fight for Principles Wins Honor for His Paper," [*Enquirer-Sun*, 1926], clipping, box 14, folder 30, Julian Harris Papers.
47. Harris to Mims, p. 6; an account of threats and acts of violence against the newspaper office and the Harrises personally may be found in the same let-

ter, as well as Boyd, "Defying the Klan," pp. 50–51. Information on the finances of the *Enquirer-Sun* appears in Harris to Mims, p. 8, and an untitled autobiographical typescript by Julia on "Mrs. Julian La Rose Harris" letterhead (final draft), [early 1950s], box 26, folder 20, Julian Harris Papers.

48. "Columbus Paper Awarded Prize," *Constitution,* May 4, 1926, clipping, box 14, folder 30, Julian Harris Papers.

49. Julia used the word "crusades" in her autobiographical typescript; "awakening" appears in "Mr. Julian Harris of Georgia," Pittsburgh *Courier,* undated clipping, box 13, folder 31. "Valiant service" was the phrase used by Evelyn Harris to describe the church's view in his letter to Julian, Aug. 11, 1954, box 26, folder 5. The documents are in the Julian Harris Papers.

50. "Justice to Negro Pays in Georgia," *Bee,* May 22, 1926, p. 10, clipping, box 13, folder 31, Julian Harris Papers.

51. Quoted in Arthur Zipser and Pearl Zipser, *Fire and Grace: The Life of Rose Pastor Stokes* (Athens: University of Georgia Press, 1989), p. 40. The previous quotations are found on p. 36.

52. Quoted in Zipser and Zipser, *Fire and Grace,* p. 36. Graham's letter to his mother, dated May 22, 1905, is quoted on p. 41.

53. Graham's aunts' estimate appears in Rose Pastor Stokes, *"I Belong to the Working Class": The Unfinished Autobiography of Rose Pastor Stokes,* ed. Herbert Shapiro and David L. Sterling (Athens: University of Georgia Press, 1992), p. 100. Her letter to Graham as a "saint," Apr. 26, 1905, is quoted in Zipser and Zipser, *Fire and Grace,* p. 41.

54. Rose Pastor Stokes to Graham Stokes, Mar. 6, 1925, box 4, folder 139, Rose Pastor Stokes Papers microfilm, AJA. The original documents are located in the Yale University Library. All manuscripts connected with Rose Pastor Stokes cited here may be found in the microfilm collection.

55. Graham used this phrase in an interview with the New York *Press,* Jan. 20, 1907, quoted in Zipser and Zipser, *Fire and Grace,* p. 63.

56. Rose's siblings were Maurice, Cecil, Bernard, Robert Emmanuel, Lillian, and Florence (Zipser and Zipser, *Fire and Grace,* p. 98). She wrote to them as "Dear Children," Jan. 5, 1905, on the eve of her wedding, box 3, folder 95A. Letters from them explaining their continuing hardships, all in box 4, include Bernard to Rose, May 19, 1915, folder 125; Lillian to Rose, Aug. 29, 1932, folder 123; and Maurice to Rose, no date, folder 126. Rose asked Graham to continue a stipend to her mother, Feb. 10, 1926, box 4, folder 139. E. P. Behringer, apparently at Graham's request, sent Anna Pastor thirty-five dollars as the first of a series of payments on Mar. 31, 1926, box 4, folder 124.

57. Interview, *Jewish Daily News,* July 19, 1903, in Zipser and Zipser, *Fire and Grace,* p. 10. Rose used "Comrade-lover" in a letter to Anna Walling, Jan. 21, 1911, quoted on p. 92.

58. This was the opinion expressed by Graham's brother, Anson Phelps Stokes,

an Episcopalian rector, to the Philadelphia *Evening Transcript,* 1905, quoted in Zipser and Zipser, *Fire and Grace,* p. 37. On the Stokes family, see ibid., pp. 27–30, 76, 176–77, and Roy Lubove, "Olivia Egleston Phelps Stokes and Caroline Phelps Stokes," Edward T. James, Janet Wilson James, and Paul S. Boyer, eds., *Notable American Women* (Cambridge, Mass.: Harvard University Press, 1971), 3: 382–84.

59. Rose Pastor Stokes to Anson Phelps Stokes, June 6, 1916, quoted in Zipser and Zipser, *Fire and Grace,* p. 140.

60. *"I Belong to the Working Class,"* ed. Shapiro and Sterling, p. 4.

61. On these developments, see Zipser and Zipser, *Fire and Grace,* pp. 24, 49–51, 70, as well as her report in a letter to Graham of funds from the Council of Jewish Women, Mar. 21, [19]15, box 4, folder 139, and Phil Russ of the Jewish Educational Alliance to Rose Pastor Stokes, Feb. 18, 1917, box 4.

62. Rose Pastor Stokes diary, Jan. 7, 1913, quoted in Zipser and Zipser, *Fire and Grace,* p. 94; Graham Stokes to Rose Pastor Stokes, [1925], box 4, folder 136.

63. Rose Pastor Stokes to Graham Stokes, Feb. 10, 1926, box 4, folder 139.

64. Rose Pastor Stokes to Graham Stokes, Mar. 6, 1925, box 4, folder 139; Graham Stokes to Rose Pastor Stokes, [1925], box 4, folder 136.

65. Rose Pastor Stokes to Jerome Isaac Romaine, Mar. 30, 1932, box 4, folder 129. The friend who wrote about Russia was Olive Tilford Dargan, Feb. 13, [19]33, box 1, folder 25.

66. The couples married between 1883 (Charles Sanders Peirce and Juliette Pourtalai) and 1912 (Richard Harding Davis and Bessie McCoy). I have included the Peirces in this group because they resembled interfaith families of the late nineteenth century more than those of the middle decades. Scholars understand that Americans have increasingly devised their own religious answers; this is part of the "privatization" described in n. 7. Because of the nature of individualized religion, any list of choices seems a hodge-podge. The best general discussions of the unusual beliefs and practices found among these families are Sydney E. Ahlstrom, *A Religious History of the American People* (New Haven: Yale University Press, 1972), chs. 60–61, and Catherine L. Albanese, *America: Religion and Religions,* 2d ed. (Belmont, Ca.: Wadsworth Publishing Company, 1992), ch. 8.

67. Unpaginated numerological studies of Julian and Julia Harris, [1938?], box 26, folder 19, Julian Harris Papers. The same folder contains a character reading of Julian or Julia, [1919?], and "Chirological Chart: Mr. Julian La Rose Harris," Apr. 1930.

68. Julia Harris to Julian Harris, no date, box 24, folder 20, Julian Harris Papers. The book Julia edited was written by Petre Ispirescu, *The Foundling Prince and Other Tales,* trans. by Julia Collier Harris and Rea Ipcar (Boston: Houghton Mifflin, 1917).

69. On Peirce's affair with Juliette, family suspicions about his physical abuse of both wives, and his difficulties at Johns Hopkins, see Joseph Brent, *Charles*

Sanders Peirce: A Life (Bloomington: Indiana University Press, 1993), esp. pp. 99, 141–43, 147–48, 156. Juliette disguised her past so effectively that it is not clear whether her maiden name was Pourtalai or Froissy (p. 141). Following Brent, I call her Juliette Pourtalai.

70. Sarah Mills Peirce to Juliette Peirce, Sept. 19, [1884], Jan. 1, 1884, L341, folder 2; James Mills Peirce to Juliette Peirce, Feb. 11, 1891, Jan. 30, 1902, L551, Charles Sanders Peirce Papers, Houghton Library, Harvard. All manuscripts connected with the Peirce family cited here are located in this collection.

71. Review of Henry James, Sr., *The Secret of Swedenborg* (1869), in *North American Review* 110 (1870): 465; "A Neglected Argument for the Reality of God," *Charles S. Peirce: Selected Writings,* ed. Philip P. Wiener (New York: Dover, 1958), p. 366.

72. Milford *Dispatch,* July 18, 1918, quoted in Brent, *Peirce,* p. 320. Joseph Jastrow offered the characterization of Juliette, in "The Widow of Charles S. Peirce," *Science* 80 (1934): 440–41. Interest in communion with spirits was quite widespread in America; on spiritualism in American culture, see Ann Braude, *Radical Spirits: Spiritualism and Women's Rights in Nineteenth-Century America* (Boston: Beacon Press, 1989).

73. Ellen Hopkins to Juliette Peirce, July 4, [1894?], L532.

74. Helen Peirce Ellis to Juliette Peirce, [Apr. 23, 1914], L514. She sent the telegram to Juliette on Apr. 21.

75. Brent, *Peirce,* p. 319.

76. "Vera, the Medium," in Richard Harding Davis, *The Scarlet Car* (New York: Scribner's, 1919), p. 265.

77. Ibid., pp. 256, 312.

78. Ibid., p. 193. Jenny Franchot analyzes anti-Catholic stereotypes, in *Roads to Rome: The Antebellum Protestant Encounter with Catholicism* (Berkeley: University of California Press, 1994). Arthur Lubow explains the development of "Vera, the Medium" as a story and places it in relation to Davis's life, in *The Reporter Who Would Be King: A Biography of Richard Harding Davis* (New York: Scribner's, 1992), pp. 264–66. Davis did not find clairvoyance problematic when the seer was a man. Philip Endicott's temporary ability to read thoughts is the basis for comedy in "The Mind Reader," in Davis, *The Red Cross Girl* (New York: Scribner's, 1912), pp. 203–44. Perhaps the difference was that a medium's power to penetrate secrets ran counter to traditional images of women's passivity and reserve.

79. This particular character, named Faust, was a crooked art dealer, in "The Mind Reader," pp. 227–29. A similarly suspicious Jew appears in "The Scarlet Car," in *The Scarlet Car.*

80. Lubow, *Reporter Who Would Be King,* pp. 277–79; Gerald Langford, *The Richard Harding Davis Years: A Biography of a Mother and Son* (New York: Holt, Rinehart and Winston, 1961), pp. 278–80. Langford explains that it was painful for Bessie to forego a Catholic wedding. Her mother and sister did not attend the ceremony, conducted by a justice of the peace.

81. Richard Harding Davis to Bessie McCoy Davis, Nov. 20, 1915, in Charles Belmont Davis, ed., *Adventures and Letters of Richard Harding Davis* (New York: Scribner's, 1918), pp. 392–93. In letters to Bessie from London and Rome, respectively, Sept. 7, 1914, and Dec. 24, 1915, Richard noted that he lit votive candles; he said he wore her St. Rita's medal and a cross, Aug. 31, 1914, and a scapular, Nov. 20, 1915, pp. 375, 401, 373, 392.

82. Richard Harding Davis to Bessie McCoy Davis, Apr. 30, 1914, in ibid., p. 356.

83. H. A. L. Fisher, *Our New Religion* (London: Watts, 1933), pp. 133, 128, 136, 69. The tone of criticism in the pamphlet is sharp. Scholarly writing on Christian Science does not stress how controversial Christian Science was; e.g., Stephen Gottschalk, *The Emergence of Christian Science in American Religious Life* (Berkeley: University of California Press, 1973), pp. 196–215.

84. Bessie McCoy Davis, "Appreciation of the Late Richard Harding Davis," New York *Tribune*, Nov. 23, 1919, p. 8.

85. "The Grave Defying Romance of Richard Harding Davis and His Dancer Wife," *Examiner*, Oct. 14, 1917; "Does Richard Harding Davis Guide the Daily Career of Little Hope?," *Herald*, Mar. 19, 1922, cited in Lubow, *Reporter Who Would Be King*, pp. 414, 426.

86. "Appreciation of Richard Harding Davis," p. 8.

87. Olive Dargan to Rose Pastor Stokes, Oct. 16, 1923, box 1, folder 25. On Gibran (1883–1931), see Jean Gibran and Kahlil Gibran, *Kahlil Gibran: His Life and World* (Boston: New York Graphic Society, 1974).

88. Olive Dargan to Rose Pastor Stokes, Feb. 1920, box 1, folder 25; Rose Pastor Stokes to Olive Dargan, Sept. 14, 1923, box 3, folder 95A; Olive Dargan to Rose Pastor Stokes, [Feb. 1920], box 1, folder 25. Similarly, Olive expressed her hope to Rose that "Faith is softly pushing open a door to your heart," Mar. 29, 1920, box 1, folder 25.

89. Olive Dargan to Rose Pastor Stokes, Jan. 9, 1919, box 1, folder 24, and Mar. 29, 1920, box 1, folder 25.

90. Olive Dargan to Rose Pastor Stokes, Jan. 1, [1924], box 1, folder 25.

91. Rose Pastor Stokes to Jerome Romaine, May 2, 1931, box 4, folder 136. The previous quotations may be found in Rose Pastor Stokes to Olive Dargan, Sept. 14, 1923, Oct. 12, 1926, and Oct. 10, 1923, box 3, folder 95A.

92. *Israel* (New York: Horace Liveright, 1925), p. 280.

93. Lewisohn to Joel Elias Spingarn, Sept. 16, 1927, quoted in Ralph Melnick, *The Life and Work of Ludwig Lewisohn* (Detroit: Wayne State University Press, 1998), 1: 443. On Lewisohn's return to Judaism and marriage to Thelma, see ibid., 1: 316, 375, 384–99. Thelma's book, published under her maiden name, appeared as *First Fruits* (Paris: Edward W. Titus at the Sign of the Black Maniken, 1927).

94. "The Return to Jerusalem," *Nation* 119 (1924): 725. Michael A. Meyer explain the bitter conflicts over Zionism among Reform rabbis between the wars, in *Response to Modernity: A History of the Reform Movement in Ju-*

daism (Detroit: Wayne State University Press, 1995), pp. 326–34. Jews outside the Reform sphere were more favorable to Zionism; but there was no consensus among American Jews, and Lewisohn became valuable to Zionist leaders as a bold, if unconventional, advocate of the restoration of a homeland in Palestine. James Waterman Wise edited Lewisohn's Zionist writings as *A Jew Speaks: An Anthology from Ludwig Lewisohn* (New York: Harper and Brothers, 1931).

95. *Israel*, pp. 157, 218, 223, 224.

96. Ludwig Lewisohn to Philip Bernstein, Oct. 14, 1938, box 1, folder 3, Ludwig Lewisohn Papers, AJA. All manuscripts pertaining to Lewisohn cited here are found in this collection. A "zaddik" is a righteous man, usually a charismatic religious leader.

97. Stephen Wise to Philip Bernstein, Nov. 20, 1939, box 1, folder 3. On the chaos preceding Ludwig's marriage to Edna, see Melnick, *Lewisohn*, 2: chs. 35 and 36.

98. The children were Hope Davis and James Lewisohn.

99. Zina Fay Peirce, "The Externals of Washington," *Atlantic Monthly* 32 (1973): 701.

100. Quoted in Brent, *Peirce*, p. 95. The source of the quotation is not identified. Brent discusses Zina's preference that marriage be platonic on p. 64.

101. Quoted in Lubow, *Reporter Who Would Be King*, p. 202. Zina's words appeared in the Cleveland *Leader*, May 7, 1916; not until after Richard's death did this personal detail come to light. Eager reports of Zina's distaste for sex may be interpreted as an oblique expression of Americans' growing public interest in sexuality.

102. Lubow, *Reporter Who Would Be King*, p. 277.

103. Richard's near idolatry of his mother appeared in a letter to his infant daughter Hope, Oct. 19, 1915, where he said, "except my mother there never was a mother like yours," in "The Love Letters of Richard Harding Davis to Bessie McCoy," ed. Gouverneur Morris, *Metropolitan*, Nov. 1917, p. 14.

104. Brent, *Peirce*, p. 99.

105. Quoted in Lubow, *Reporter Who Would Be King*, p. 268.

106. "Appreciation of Richard Harding Davis," p. 8.

107. Sarah, Charles's mother, admitted changing her mind for the better about Juliette, and Cornelia Pinchot, wife of the environmentalist Gifford Pinchot, thought highly of her; see Brent, *Peirce*, pp. 145–46, 143.

108. Simon Newcomb to his wife, quoted in ibid., p. 151. Brent argues that it was Peirce's willingness to marry his mistress that damaged his reputation, p. 151.

109. Mimille, "Praise Your Wife," *Ladies' Home Journal* 1 (Mar. 1884): 5; "Editorial Notices," *Independent* 42 (Jan. 2, 1890): 12.

110. Daniel Coit Gilman crossed out this phrase before sending the letter to Peirce on Apr. 12, 1884; quoted in Brent, *Peirce*, p. 159.

111. Brent, *Peirce,* pp. 169–70. The Washington *Post* headline is quoted on p. 169.

112. Quoted in Lubow, *Reporter Who Would Be King,* p. 270.

113. "Farrar Scandal Only Whispered in London," New York *World,* Nov. 24, 1911, p. 18, quoted in ibid., p. 276.

114. Lubow, *Reporter Who Would Be King,* p. 276.

115. "Farrar Scandal Only Whispered in London," cited in ibid., p. 276.

116. "Love Letters of Richard Harding Davis to Bessie McCoy," p. 14. Lubow explains the inflation of fifty to five hundred mothers, in *Reporter Who Would Be King,* pp. 280, 416 (n. 52).

117. *All I Could Never Be* (New York: Brewer, Warren, and Putnam, 1932), pp. 48, 51, 51, 51, 54, 100, 101, 117. This was not the only work of fiction by Yezierska about the relationship. See, e.g., "Wild Winter Love," *Century Magazine* 113 (1927): 485–91. Here, the Jewish woman commits suicide after the affair ends. On the relationship, see Mary V. Dearborn, *Love in the Promised Land: The Story of Anzia Yezierska and John Dewey* (New York: Free Press, 1988).

118. "Two Weeks," *The Poems of John Dewey,* ed. Jo Ann Boydston (Carbondale: Southern Illinois University Press, 1977), p. 15.

119. Ibid., p. 14.

120. On the discovery of the poems, see Boydston's introduction to *Poems of John Dewey,* pp. ix–xi. On the disposition of their letters, see Dearborn, *Love in the Promised Land,* pp. 122, 136. 164. Dearborn has to rely to an extent on what Yezierska reported in her novel. Yezierska said that although Dewey asked her to return his letters to her, she refused to do so for ten years after the affair. She burned her letters to him (*All I Could Never Be,* pp. 186–90).

121. Both the narrator and Henry Scott himself refer to Scott as a "Yankee Puritan," *All I Could Never Be,* pp. 203, 63. The poem by Dewey she included was "Generations of Stifled Words," p. 43.

122. Ibid., p. 28.

123. Ibid., p. 43.

124. Ibid., p. 65.

125. Quoted in Melnick, *Lewisohn,* 2: 194. On these details of his life, see ibid., 1: 641, and 2: 194, 231, 269, 273.

126. "Love Letters of Richard Harding Davis," ed., Morris, p. 16.

127. Lubow, *Reporter Who Would Be King,* p. 335.

128. Ibid., p. 335.

129. Ellen Mordecai, *Gleanings from Long Ago* (1933; reprint ed., [Raleigh]: Raleigh Historic Properties Commission and Mordecai Square Historical Society, 1974); Caroline Myers Cohen, *Records of the Myers, Hays, and Mordecai Families from 1707 to 1913* (Washington, D.C.: privately printed, n.d.); Anne Easby-Smith, *William Russell Smith of Alabama: His Life and Works* (Philadelphia: Dolphin Press, 1931); C. Wickliffe Yulee,

"Senator Yulee of Florida: A Biographical Sketch," reprinted from *Florida Magazine of History,* [ca. 1931], David Levy Yulee Papers, Small Collections 13329, AJA; Henrietta Clay, "Bits of Family History: Paper Read Before the John Bradford Club, Lexington, Kentucky, December 8, 1932," AJA. Ellen Mordecai wrote *Gleanings* in 1912.

130. "Reminiscences of Early Days," typescript, 1940, pp. 1, 48–49, William Tecumseh Sherman Family Papers (CSHR), box 7, folder 1, Notre Dame.

131. Atlanta Council No. 660, Knights of Columbus, to Evelyn and Lucien Harris, July 19, 1908, ser. I, subser. 4, box 7, folder 3, Joel Chandler Harris Papers; Evelyn Harris to Julian Harris, Aug. 9, 1954, box 26, folder 5, Julian Harris Papers.

132. Joel Chandler Harris, Jr., to Esther Harris, Nov. 28, 1918, ser. I, subser. 4, box 7, folder 10, Joel Chandler Harris Papers. The letter on Knights of Columbus stationery was dated Nov. 18, 1918; he used YMCA stationery on Nov. 3 and Nov. 22, 1918. All the correspondence is in the same folder.

133. Esther Harris to Julian Harris, Nov. 9, 1924, box 25, folder 7, Julian Harris Papers.

134. Mildred Harris to Julian Harris, [Aug. 19, 1954], box 25, folder 13; Lillian Harris to Julian Harris, May 11, [19]26, Box 26, folder 13, Julian Harris Papers.

135. Similarly, Julia wrote to Esther Harris as "Dear Mother," Mar. 28 and May 17, 1920, box 25, folder 9, Julian Harris Papers.

136. Elliott B. Macrae to Julian Harris, Mar. 7, 1946, box 30, folder 10, Julian Harris Papers. The contract dated Apr. 2, 1946 specified "A full-length Autobiography," box 30, folder 10.

137. Julian La Rose Harris, "Joel Chandler Harris, as His Eldest Son Remembers Him," Atlanta *Journal Magazine,* clipping, box 30, folder 9, Julian Harris Papers.

138. Autobiography typescript, ch. 1, p. 24, box 30, folder 15; ch. 6, p. 38, box 30, folder 25; ch. 1, p. 14, box 30, folder 15, Julian Harris Papers. The page numbers refer to handwritten numbers.

139. Julian Harris to Nicholas Wreden, Oct. 28, 1946, June 19, [19]48, box 30, folder 11, box 30, folder 11, Julian Harris Papers.

140. "Little Story About My Mother," pp. 13, 18, 37–38, 28. Julian wrote that Esther called her husband "Cephas" in a typescript of ch. 1, p. 22, box 30, folder 18; that they had Jewish neighbors, "Notes Chaper 1," box 30, folder 13; and that she had met few blacks before moving to Georgia, "Important Notes—Early Days," box 30, folder 13, Julian Harris Papers.

141. Julian repeated his conversation with Evelyn in a letter to Lucien, Aug. 10, 1939, box 26, folder 7, Julian Harris Papers. On the 1954 argument, see Evelyn Harris to Julian Harris, Aug. 9, 1954, box 26, folder 5.

142. Lillian Harris to Julian Harris, May 21, [1946], box 26, folder 13, Julian Harris Papers.

143. "Little Story About My Mother," pp. 3, 37, 38, 38.

144. Bernard Berenson to Axel Boethius, Mar. 3, 1957, in *Letters of Berenson,* ed. McComb, p. 293. In 1954, for example, Perry published *Realms of Value: A Critique of Human Civilization.*

145. Bessie Berenson to Ralph Barton Perry, Feb. 16, [1954], HUG 4683.8, box "Letters from the Berenson Family," folder "Mary Berenson."

146. Mary Berenson to Rachel Berenson Perry, Dec. 30, 1909, HUG 4683.8, box "Letters from the Berenson Family," folder "Bernard Berenson."

147. Bessie Berenson to Ralph Barton Perry, Feb. 15, [1954], HUG 4683.8, box "Letters from the Berenson Family," folder "Mary Berenson." Bessie spent time in Italy with Bernard and Mary and with Senda and her husband, as noted in Mary Berenson to Ralph Barton Perry, Jan. 8, 1910, and Mary Berenson to Rachel Berenson Perry, July 31, 1911, in the same folder.

148. Bernard Berenson to Ralph Barton Perry, Feb. 25, [19]54, HUG 4683.8, box "Letters from the Berenson Family," folder "Bernard Berenson." Nicky Mariano described Ralph's illness to Lawrence Berenson, [Nov.–Dec. 1944], *Letters of Berenson,* ed. McComb, p. 199.

149. Bernard Berenson to Ralph Barton Perry, Aug. 26, 1905, HUG 4683.8, box "Letters from the Berenson Family," folder "Bernard Berenson." See Bernard's similarly polite comments on *The Moral Economy,* Dec. 17, [19]09, in the same folder. Berenson said more directly that he did not care for philosophy in a letter to T. S. Perry, June 2, 1926, *Letters of Berenson,* ed. McComb, p. 99.

150. Bernard Berenson to Henry Coster, Sept. 6, 1928, *Letters of Berenson,* ed. McComb, p. 103. Mary called Bernard "Mr. Crazy" in a letter to Rachel, Jan. 10, 1929, HUG 4683.8, box "Letters from the Berenson Family," folder "Bernard Berenson."

151. Bernard Berenson to Learned Hand, May 16, 1937, Sept. 26, 1934, *Letters of Berenson,* ed. McComb, pp. 139, 125, 127.

152. Bernard Berenson to Ralph Barton Perry, Mar. 11, 1936, Mar. 17, [19]54, HUG 4683.8, box "Letters from the Berenson Family," folder "Bernard Berenson."

153. Mary Berenson to Ralph Barton Perry, June 6, 1929; Mary Berenson to Rachel Berenson Perry, Jan. 10, 1929, HUG 4683.8, box "Letters from the Berenson Family," folder "Bernard Berenson."

154. Bernard Berenson to Ralph Barton Perry, Nov. 7, 1934, HUG 4683.8, box "Letters from the Berenson Family," folder "Bernard Berenson."

155. The clipping, marked in handwriting to be from "Bernard," is in HUG 4683.8, box "Letters from the Berenson Family," folder "Bernard Berenson."

156. Ralph Barton Perry to Bernard Berenson, Feb. 19, 1945, HUG 4683.8, box "Letters from the Berenson Family," folder "Bernard Berenson."

157. Journal, Aug. 4, 1944, in Berenson, *Rumour and Reflection,* p. 335; Bernard Berenson to Learned Hand, Jan. 5, 1944 [really 1945], in *Letters of Berenson,* ed. McComb, p. 205.

158. Bernard Berenson to Henry Coster, Sept. 10, 1953, in *Letters of Berenson,* ed. McComb, p. 277.

159. Bernard Berenson to Lawrence Berenson, June 3, 1951, in ibid., pp. 267–68. Lawrence was Bernard's attorney for thirty-five years (p. 147).

Epilogue

1. James A. Pike, *If You Marry Outside Your Faith: Counsel on Mixed Marriages* (New York: Harper and Brothers, 1954), p. 15.

2. James H. S. Bossard and Eleanor Stoker Boll, *One Marriage, Two Faiths: Guidance on Interfaith Marriage* (New York: Ronald Press, 1957), p. 54.

3. *An Apostolic Letter Issued "Motu Proprio" Determining Norms for Mixed Marriages, March 31, 1970 (Matrimonia Mixta)* (Washington: National Conference of Catholic Bishops, 1970), p. 1, CGUM (Papers of Bishop Thomas J. Gumbleton), box 27, folder 4, Notre Dame. The pope's guidelines reflected discussions initiated by Vatican II (pp. 3–4).

4. Albert I. Gordon, *Intermarriage: Interfaith, Interracial, Interethnic* (Boston: Beacon Press, 1964). Additional books on interracial and international relationships include Ernest Porterfield, *Black and White Mixed Marriages* (Chicago: Nelson-Hall, 1978), and Dugan Romano, *Intercultural Marriage: Promises and Pitfalls,* 2d ed. (Yarmouth, Me.: Intercultural Press, 1997).

5. These themes appear in Bossard and Boll, *One Marriage, Two Faiths,* pp. 61–64; Pike, *If You Marry Outside Your Faith,* p. 16; and Pope Paul VI, *Apostolic Letter,* p. 1. Abraham J. Klausner pointed to an emerging ethic of universal kinship, in *Weddings: A Complete Guide to All Religious and Interfaith Marriage Services* (Columbus: Alpha, 1986), p. 1. As the authority of social science and the popularity of psychological counseling increased, clergy often classified themselves as social scientists and counselors, blurring the line between inquiry and guidance. Rabbis who said they were social scientists include Samuel Glasner, "Counseling Parents on Problems of Intermarriage," in Sidney L. Regner, ed., *CCAR Yearbook, 1962* (New York: CCAR, 1963), 72: 166, and Gordon, *Intermarriage,* p. ix. On the adoption of psychology by Protestant clergy, see E. Brooks Holifield, *A History of Pastoral Care in America: From Salvation to Self-Realization* (Nashville: Abington Press, 1983), esp. chs. 7–8.

6. Carle C. Zimmerman and Lucius F. Cervantes, *Successful American Families* (New York: Pageant Press, 1960), p. 37, quoted in Gordon, *Intermarriage,* p. 95. Value judgments similarly colored the research of Reuben B. Resnick, who argued that people inclined to intermarry were "promiscuous," "demoralized," and "rebellious," or, somewhat more positively, "emancipated," "adventurous," and "acculturated," in "Some Sociological Aspects of Intermarriage of Jews and Non-Jews," *Social Forces* 12 (1933): 94–102, quoted in Gordon, *Intermarriage,* p. 59.

7. Man Keung Ho, *Intermarried Couples in Therapy* (Springfield, Ill.: Charles

C. Thomas, 1990). Written primarily for therapists, this book acknowledges the problems of intercultural marriages without intimating that every such relationship is troubled, which was the tone of nearly all writing before the mid-1960s.

8. The position statement of the Rabbinical Assembly of America for 1958 may be found in Gordon, *Intermarriage,* pp. 184–85; a supplemental statement in 1959 appears in "Committee on Jewish Law and Standards," Alex J. Goldman and Jules Harlow, eds., *Proceedings of the Rabbinical Assembly of America, 1959* (Rabbinical Assembly of America, 1960), 23: 115–16. The Orthodox have discussed interfaith marriages even less than Conservatives, although there have been several Orthodox *responsa* on the subject, cited in "Reform Judaism and Mixed Marriage," Elliot L. Stevens, ed., *CCAR Yearbook, 1980* (New York: CCAR, 1981), 90: 101.

9. Klausner, *Weddings.*

10. *Protestant—Catholic—Jew: An Essay in Religious Sociology,* rev. ed. (Garden City, N.Y.: Doubleday, 1960), p. 234.

11. Texts of these and other denominational resolutions may be found in Gordon, *Intermarriage,* pp. 131, 128. Official Protestant statements were cited widely in commentary on interfaith marriage; see, e.g., two books by Catholic authors, Bossard and Boll, *One Marriage, Two Faiths,* p. 79–85, and Paul H. Besanceney, *Interfaith Marriages: Who and Why* (New Haven: College and University Press, 1970), pp. 118–19. Generally, however, the issue of interfaith marriage kept nearly as low a profile among Protestants as it had historically. Essays on family and gender in the *Drew Gateway,* a Methodist journal, for example, do not mention interfaith marriage; see Hazen G. Werner, "The Changing Family in a Changing Society," 24 (1954): 143–50, and Joanna B. Gillespie, "Rebellion in the Marriage Mart: Inquiry into a Changing Norm," 46 (1975–1976): 65–77.

12. Rev. Myron W. Fowell, Secretary of the Massachusetts Congregational Christian Conference, to Albert Gordon, Nov. 22, 1961, in Gordon, *Intermarriage,* p. 123.

13. Leland Foster Wood, *If I Marry a Roman Catholic* (New York: The Commission on Marriage and the Home of the Federal Council of Churches in Christ in America, 1945), p. 10.

14. Pike, *If You Marry Outside Your Faith,* pp. 86, 74, 80, 85, 108, 104.

15. Father John L. Thomas offered these statistics in *The American Catholic Family* (Englewood Cliffs: Prentice-Hall, 1956); they are cited in Bossard and Boll, *One Marriage, Two Faiths,* p. 55.

16. "Culture," in John H. Miller, ed., *Vatican II: An Interfaith Appraisal* (Notre Dame: University of Notre Dame Press, 1966), pp. 456, 463, 474. Although the Council's attention to relationships of Catholics with non-Catholic partners brought renewed focus to intermarriage, birth control overshadowed other family issues. See Bernard Haring, "Marriage and the Family," in ibid., pp. 439–66.

17. "Mixed Marriages and Canon Law after Vatican II," undated typescript,

pp. 9, 23, box 7, folder 11, Synod of Bishops 1967, CDRD (Cardinal John Francis Dearden Papers), Notre Dame.

18. *Statement of the National Conference of Catholic Bishops on the Implementation of the Apostolic Letter on Mixed Marriages* (n.p.: National Conference of Catholic Bishops, 1971), p. 2, CGUM (Papers of Bishop Thomas J. Gumbleton), box 27, folder 4, Notre Dame.

19. H. A. Ayrinhac, *Marriage Legislation in the Code of Canon Law,* rev. ed. (New York: Benziger Brothers, 1935). Although the Catholic Church issued an occasional manual on mixed marriage for laypeople before Vatican II, most writing consisted of commentary for priests on canon law. See, e.g., William A. O'Mara, *Canonical Causes for Matrimonial Dispensations: An Historical Synposis and Commentary* (Washington: Catholic University of America, 1935), and P. J. Lydon, *Ready Answers in Canon Law: A Practical Summary of the Code for the Parish Clergy,* 3d ed. (New York: Benziger Brothers, 1948).

20. "Mixed Marriages and Canon Law after Vatican II," p. 4.

21. *Statement on the Implementation of the Apostolic Letter on Mixed Marriages,* pp. 1, 8.

22. Fishbein offered a minority report as part of the "Report of the *Ad Hoc* Committee on Mixed Marriage," Joseph B. Glasner and Elliot L. Stevens, eds., *CCAR Yearbook, 1973* (New York: CCAR, 1974), 83: 64.

23. The "Report of the Special Committee on Mixed Marriages" cited the data collected by Rabbi Leo J. Stillpass in 1943, in Regner, ed., *CCAR Yearbook, 1962,* 72: 89. Stillpass said that outside the northeast the ratio of rabbis who did and did not perform intermarriages was about fifty-fifty. Roland Gittelson quoted the higher statistic in 1973, in Glasner and Stevens, eds., *CCAR Yearbook, 1973,* 83: 80–81. But as early as 1962 Nathan A. Perilman argued that fifty percent of Reform rabbis performed mixed marriages (Regner, ed., *CCAR Yearbook, 1962,* 72: 100). This was such a highly charged issue among Reform rabbis that it was clearly difficult to collect reliable information.

24. Regner, ed., *CCAR Yearbook, 1962,* 72: 101, 97.

25. Ibid., p. 105.

26. Glasner and Stevens, eds., *CCAR Yearbook, 1973,* 83: 97. There was no single vote on the resolution because it was considered in sections; but the average margin of the several votes was three-to-two. See the extended debate and votes in ibid., pp. 59–97. At earlier postwar conferences in 1947 and 1962, the CCAR declined to change the wording of the 1909 resolution against mixed marriage (see Chapter 4 above). See Isaac E. Marcuson, ed., *CCAR Yearbook, 1947* (CCAR, 1948), 57: 158–84, and Regner, ed., *CCAR Yearbook, 1962,* 72: 86–105. The controversial addition to the 1973 resolution was the statement of opposition to rabbinic participation in interfaith weddings.

27. Glasner and Stevens, eds., *CCAR Yearbook, 1973,* 83: 78, 68, 69, 70.

28. Ibid., p. 65.
29. Nelson Glueck, "Authority and Freedom," Sidney Regner, ed., *CCAR Yearbook, 1960* (CCAR, 1961), 70: 167. Glueck, president of Hebrew Union College, included advice on how to maintain a rabbi's control of his congregation in this sermon at the 1960 CCAR meeting. His image of Moses in the wilderness, a powerful one for his audience, was a sign that the mood of tension between rabbis and people transcended the issue of intermarriage.
30. "Report on Mixed Marriage and Intermarriage," Marcuson, ed., *CCAR Yearbook, 1947*, 57: 171. Although the acceptance of these children in Reform religious schools and the use of confirmation as a proxy for conversion became formal Reform policy in 1947, it is likely that these practices were already commonplace. In a *responsum* titled "Children of Mixed Marriages" (1919), Kaufman Kohler said that "when raised as a Jew, the child could afterwards, through Confirmation, be adopted into the Jewish fold like any proselyte," in Walter Jacob, ed., *American Reform Responsa: Collected Responsa of the Central Conference of American Rabbis, 1889–1983* (New York: CCAR, 1983), pp. 194–95.
31. The "Conversion Committee" wished to make Jewish status dependent on education, and the "Committee on Responsa" objected that this would undercut the birthright foundation of Judaism, in "Report of the Committee on Responsa," Stevens, ed., *CCAR Yearbook, 1980*, 90: 81. These were perhaps self-selected committees in terms of ideological orientation: those reviewing conversion policies might be more practical-minded, while those who wrote *responsa* might be inclined to protect *halakhic* (legal) traditions.
32. Elliot L. Stevens, ed., *CCAR Yearbook, 1983* (New York: CCAR, 1984), 93: 160. These resolutions have not brought an end to discussion of interfaith marriage as a controverted subject among Reform rabbis. Although the organization's "Statement of Principles for Reform Judaism," passed in Pittsburgh in 1999, welcomed "all individuals and families, including the intermarried, who strive to create a Jewish home," the wording provoked opposition from some rabbis who felt that the statement endorsed interfaith marriage (forthcoming in Elliot L. Stevens, ed., *CCAR Yearbook, 1999–2000* [New York: CCAR, 2001]; currently available on the internet at ccarnet.org).
33. Glasner and Stevens, eds., *CCAR Yearbook, 1973*, 83: 97.

Index